Libgdx Cross-platform Game Development Cookbook

Over 75 practical recipes to help you master cross-platform 2D game development using the powerful Libgdx framework

David Saltares Márquez

Alberto Cejas Sánchez

[PACKT] PUBLISHING

open source *
community experience distilled

BIRMINGHAM - MUMBAI

Libgdx Cross-platform Game Development Cookbook

First published: October 2014

Production reference: 1221014

Published by Packt Publishing Ltd.
Livery Place
35 Livery Street
Birmingham B3 2PB, UK.

ISBN 978-1-78328-729-1

www.packtpub.com

Cover image by Pratyush Mohanta (tysoncinematics@gmail.com)

Credits

About the Authors

David Saltares Márquez is a C++ software developer at a top-tier financial data company. He was an Artificial Intelligence programmer at Crytek, UK, for two years, where he developed emergent systems for *Homefront: The Revolution*. He then moved to Sony Computer Entertainment Europe to work on multimedia applications for PlayStation 4. He is part of the Libgdx core team, works on small indie games in his spare time, loves game jams, and often delivers presentations at universities. Find out more about his work on his personal blog at `http://siondream.com`.

To Anda, who stood by me during good and bad times, and my parents, who unconditionally encouraged me from afar.

Alberto Cejas Sánchez is an indie game programming enthusiast who graduated with an MSc in Computer Science and whose work revolves around games and simulations across 2D/3D technologies with different target platforms. He has also worked on automatic game code generation tools.

To those responsible for making me feel proud as a son.

About the Reviewers

[name unclear] (PhD) is currently a senior engineer at Sony Computer Entertainment Europe with a career spanning over a decade. He holds a PhD in Computer Science from the University of Sussex where his research focused on distributed systems, ad hoc social networks, Q & A, security, and privacy. He has taken part in game jams including #OneGameAMonth and is currently working on several games using Libgdx.

Joost van Ham (Xoppa) founded the Xoppa company in 2001 and graduated in Computer Science in the Netherlands in 2004. Since then, he has served a wide variety of companies with their business automation. He's been working on Libgdx since 2012, where his main focus is on the 3D API, linear algebra, and 3D physics wrapper. He's also the author of a series of comprehensive tutorials covering 3D game development with libGDX, which can be found at `http://blog.xoppa.com`.

Manuel Palomo-Duarte is currently a Lecturer and Degree Coordinator for Computer Science at the University of Cadiz (Spain), where he received his PhD in 2011. He has been working for several years as a Director to the Free Software and Open Knowledge office at the same university and is a board member of Wikimedia Spain. His teaching focuses on subjects related to open data and video game development using open source software. His main research interests are learning technologies, serious games, and collaborative development. In these fields, he has published different contributions in peer-reviewed journals and research conferences.

André Schmode is a 40-year-old German developer with a passion for video games. He lives in Berlin and holds a degree in Business Computer Science. He started developing with Commodore C16, C64, and Amiga, turned over to Visual Basic, and finally fell in love with Java. He started development with Libgdx in 2012 and released the game *bubblr – dummy in trouble* for Android devices and OUYA consoles. Game development is just a hobby for him. He loves to be creative and bring his fantasies to life. The only limit when developing a video game is his imagination! (and minor technical difficulties).

www.PacktPub.com

Support files, eBooks, discount offers, and more

You might want to visit www.PacktPub.com for support files and downloads related to your book.

Did you know that Packt offers eBook versions of every book published, with PDF and ePub files available? You can upgrade to the eBook version at www.PacktPub.com and as a print book customer, you are entitled to a discount on the eBook copy. Get in touch with us at service@packtpub.com for more details.

At www.PacktPub.com, you can also read a collection of free technical articles, sign up for a range of free newsletters and receive exclusive discounts and offers on Packt books and eBooks.

PACKTLiB™

http://PacktLib.PacktPub.com

Do you need instant solutions to your IT questions? PacktLib is Packt's online digital book library. Here, you can access, read and search across Packt's entire library of books.

Why Subscribe?

- ▸ Fully searchable across every book published by Packt
- ▸ Copy and paste, print and bookmark content
- ▸ On demand and accessible via web browser

Free Access for Packt account holders

If you have an account with Packt at www.PacktPub.com, you can use this to access PacktLib today and view nine entirely free books. Simply use your login credentials for immediate access.

Table of Contents

Table of Contents

Preface

Libgdx is a powerful Java-based open source cross-platform game framework. It allows developers to target Windows, Mac, Linux, Android, iOS, and HTML5 with a single codebase, sparing them the hassle of dealing with low-level, platform-specific details.

libGDX

For more information, please refer to http://libgdx.badlogicgames.com/.

Through a clean and simple API, Libgdx offers a vast set of features, which are as follows:

- Low-level OpenGL access: This includes vertex arrays, meshes, framebuffers, shaders, and immediate mode renderer
- 2D graphics: This includes bitmaps, texture atlases, particles, scene graph, user interface, and maps
- 3D graphics: This includes model loading, lighting, decal batching, particles, and so on
- Audio: This includes streaming music, sound effects (MP3, WAV, and OGG), pitch control, and direct access to recording devices
- Input: This includes keyboard, mouse, touch, accelerometer, compass, and controller events as well as gesture detection
- Math and physics: This includes matrices, vectors, shapes, interpolators, frustum, intersection utilities, and full Box2D and Bullet physics JNI wrappers
- File I/O: This includes cross-platform file access, preferences storage, XML, and JSON parsing
- Utilities: This includes fast custom collections and easy multiresolution handling
- Tools: This includes project creation, particle editor, bitmap font generator, and texture packer

Libgdx is incredibly fast, thanks to the use of JNI wrappers and heavy emphasis on avoiding garbage collection. This becomes crucial when deploying on mobile devices and browsers. Its framework nature allows you to choose which components to use as it does not enforce a single way of working like most engines do.

The community behind the framework is large, welcoming, and always willing to provide support. The GitHub repository shows how active the project is, with many commits every day, constant releases, and rich documentation. For more information, refer to `https://github.com/libgdx/libgdx`.

Thanks to its permissive Apache 2.0 license, Libgdx can be used for both commercial and noncommercial projects without having to necessarily disclose the source. According to AppBrain, 1.44 percent of all the Android applications (both games and nongames) are built on top of it, which reinforces its flexibility and ease of use. For more information, refer to `http://appbrain.com/stats/libraries/details/libgdx/libgdx`.

This book provides excellent coverage of the aforementioned systems focusing on 2D game development. Each chapter covers a set of related features through a series of recipes. A recipe explains with simple steps how to carry out a particular task with Libgdx such as rendering a texture on the screen. The practical approach will give you a very good insight on how things actually work, preparing you to use this technology on real-life projects.

After reading through the recipes in this book, you will have a solid understanding of how all the systems in Libgdx work and how to better leverage them in order to implement your games. The good practices exposed here will give you an edge to produce clean and efficient code.

What this book covers

Chapter 1, Diving into Libgdx, introduces the reader to the Libgdx development environment so as to get ready for the rest of the book. It also presents the basic architecture of the framework, how to run applications across devices, and how to put a project under source control.

Chapter 2, Working with 2D Graphics, covers the most important aspects of the Libgdx 2D API. The readers will learn how to render and animate textures, work with cameras, and deal with different resolutions.

Chapter 3, Advanced 2D Graphics, shows the reader how to achieve juicy effects with particles, shaders, and image composition.

Chapter 4, Detecting User Input, explains how to make your applications interactive across different devices. Keyboard, mouse, touch, and controller-based inputs are all found in this chapter.

Chapter 5, Audio and File I/O, shows readers how to play background music and sound effects to give that extra sparkle to the project. It also covers how to use the file's API and read popular formats such as JSON and XML.

Chapter 6, Font Rendering, details the different approaches to render text through Libgdx. Moreover, it also teaches how to overcome common pitfalls such as special characters and font scaling.

Chapter 7, Asset Management, provides information on how to control your assets' life cycle so as to accommodate low memory devices and make the most out of the hardware. It also gives insight into how to achieve asynchronous loading, so apps stay responsive while they stream content.

Chapter 8, User Interfaces with Scene2D, covers the powerful Libgdx scene hierarchy API focusing on how to build UI layouts. Moreover, it goes as far as skinning and custom widget creation. The reader will learn how to create great menus and in-game HUDs.

Chapter 9, The 2D Maps API, explains the simple Libgdx mechanisms to load and render levels created with tools such as Tiled as well as to query their metadata. The maps 2D API also allows users to provide loaders and renderers for additional formats.

Chapter 10, *Rigid Body Physics with Box2D,* shows the reader how to use the many features of the popular physics library that comes with Libgdx. Bodies, shapes, joints, sensors, collision handling, level geometry, raycasting, and fixed timestep are all covered in this chapter.

Chapter 11, Third-party Libraries and Extras, goes through the most popular Libgdx extensions, so the reader can make use of their enhancements. It covers a wide range of topics such as lighting, skeletal animation, localization, and entity systems.

Chapter 12, Performance and Optimizations, provides the readers with advice to achieve their performance targets. This becomes crucial when targeting mobile devices and browsers.

Chapter 13, Giving Back, lays out the process of publishing a finished application as well as contributing to the main Libgdx repository.

What you need for this book

As a minimum, you need a computer running Windows, Mac, or a Linux distribution that also supports hardware acceleration. No need to worry; currently, even the most considerably old machines support this. Additionally, to target Android devices, a phone or a tablet running Android 2.2 or higher is required. In order to target iOS, a Mac with XCode is needed, and when testing on a real device, an Apple developer subscription becomes a must.

All software dependencies are free to use even for commercial purposes. However, the Apple developer license is subject to yearly payments.

Installation instructions for additional software will be provided when needed.

Who this book is for

This book is aimed at developers who are already familiar with object-oriented programming principles, know the basics of game development, and want to use the power of Libgdx to make awesome cross-platform games without the hassle of having to deal with platform-specific nonsense.

Although Libgdx is based on Java, having experience with the language is only recommended and not a must. It can easily be learned as you go, even more so when coming from C++ or C#.

Conventions

In this book, you will find a number of styles of text that distinguish between different kinds of information. Here are some examples of these styles, and an explanation of their meaning.

Code words in text, database table names, folder names, filenames, file extensions, pathnames, dummy URLs, user input, and Twitter handles are shown as follows: "The action takes place within the overridden processEntity() method responsible for the logic"

A block of code is set as follows:

```
public class DesktopResolver implements PlatformResolver {
    @Override
    public void rateGame() {
        System.out.println("Desktop");
        Gdx.net.openURI("https://facebook.com");
    }
}
```

When we wish to draw your attention to a particular part of a code block, the relevant lines or items are set in bold:

```
public String getCurrentLanguage() {
return currentLanguage;
}
public void setCurrentLanguage(String name) {
if(languages.containsKey(name.toLowerCase()))
currentLanguage = name;
}
```

Any command-line input or output is written as follows:

```
tar -xzvf android-sdk.r22.2.1-linux.tgz
```

New terms and **important words** are shown in bold. Words that you see on the screen, in menus or dialog boxes for example, appear in the text like this: "Install the **Gradle IDE** entry and restart Eclipse for the last time."

[Warnings or important notes appear in a box like this.]

[Tips and tricks appear like this.]

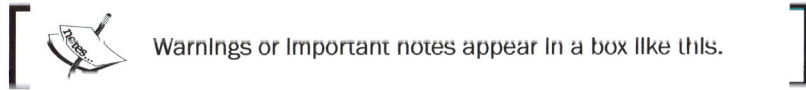

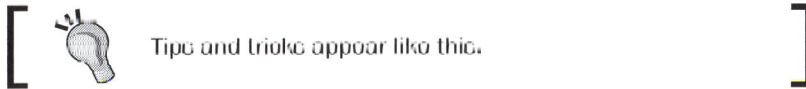

Reader feedback

Feedback from our readers is always welcome. Let us know what you think about this book—what you liked or may have disliked. Reader feedback is important for us to develop titles that you really get the most out of.

To send us general feedback, simply send an e-mail to feedback@packtpub.com, and mention the book title via the subject of your message.

If there is a topic that you have expertise in and you are interested in either writing or contributing to a book, see our author guide on www.packtpub.com/authors.

Customer support

Now that you are the proud owner of a Packt book, we have a number of things to help you to get the most from your purchase.

Downloading the example code

You can download the example code files for all Packt books you have purchased from your account at http://www.packtpub.com. If you purchased this book elsewhere, you can visit http://www.packtpub.com/support and register to have the files e-mailed directly to you. This book is full of rich working examples you can experiment with. Access the following link to download the most up-to-date version: https://github.com/siondream/libgdx-cookbook.

Downloading the color images of this book

We also provide you a PDF file that has color images of the screenshots/diagrams used in this book. The color images will help you better understand the changes in the output. You can download this file from: https://www.packtpub.com/sites/default/files/downloads/7291OS_coloredimages.pdf.

Errata

Although we have taken every care to ensure the accuracy of our content, mistakes do happen. If you find a mistake in one of our books—maybe a mistake in the text or the code—we would be grateful if you would report this to us. By doing so, you can save other readers from frustration and help us improve subsequent versions of this book. If you find any errata, please report them by visiting http://www.packtpub.com/submit-errata, selecting your book, clicking on the **errata submission form** link, and entering the details of your errata. Once your errata are verified, your submission will be accepted and the errata will be uploaded on our website, or added to any list of existing errata, under the Errata section of that title. Any existing errata can be viewed by selecting your title from http://www.packtpub.com/support.

Piracy

Piracy of copyright material on the Internet is an ongoing problem across all media. At Packt, we take the protection of our copyright and licenses very seriously. If you come across any illegal copies of our works, in any form, on the Internet, please provide us with the location address or website name immediately so that we can pursue a remedy.

Please contact us at copyright@packtpub.com with a link to the suspected pirated material.

We appreciate your help in protecting our authors, and our ability to bring you valuable content.

Questions

You can contact us at questions@packtpub.com if you are having a problem with any aspect of the book, and we will do our best to address it.

1
Diving into Libgdx

In this chapter, we will cover the following recipes:

- ▶ Setting up a cross-platform development environment
- ▶ Creating a cross-platform project
- ▶ Understanding the project structure and application life cycle
- ▶ Updating and managing project dependencies
- ▶ Using source control on a Libgdx project with Git
- ▶ Importing and running the Libgdx official demos

Introduction

Before thinking about how to render an animated character onscreen, it is very important that you prepare all the required tools to create cross-platform applications with Libgdx and understand its basic principles. This is, precisely, the purpose of this initial chapter.

First, we will cover how to install everything that is required for the three major operating systems, Windows, Mac, and GNU/Linux. Though we all know you want to go straight to the fun bit, a stable and productive working environment is vital in order to avoid future headaches. After we make sure that all is in order by testing a sample project, it will be time to take a closer look at how all Libgdx projects are structured.

Often, a developer wants to use a newer version of Libgdx or some third-party library because it includes an incredible feature or solves a problem they were losing sleep over. For these reasons, it will prove very useful to know how to properly update a project so as to enjoy some fresh goodies.

Finally, as you are probably very much aware, using source control for every single one of your endeavors is surely a life saver. Not only does it give us a backup system straightaway, but it also empowers us to share and keep track of the changes in the repository. This is extremely useful when you want to blame someone else for something that went wrong! In this chapter, we will show how to efficiently use source control with a Libgdx project using Git as an example.

Setting up a cross-platform development environment

Once you go through this recipe, you will be able to enjoy Libgdx in all its glory and start developing games for all the supported platforms.

Let's begin with a short disclaimer. For the most part, Libgdx relies on open source software that is widely available at no cost. This means that anyone can target desktops, Android, and browsers using a Windows, Mac, or GNU/Linux distribution. The only restriction applies to iOS, for which you will specifically need a Mac. Moreover, if you wish to test your work on a real device, an Apple developer account is essential and further costs apply.

Getting ready

You need to be aware of the operating system version you will use to pick the right versions of the software packages we will install. The main explanation thread will focus on Windows 8 64-bit, but further comments will be provided whenever there are differences across systems.

> Keep in mind that software versions might change after the release of this book, so think of this recipe as more of a guideline than a sacred text. The names of the downloaded packages will typically include the version number, and they will change over time.

How to do it...

Here is our little software shopping list:

- Java Development Kit
- Eclipse IDE
- The Gradle plugin for Eclipse
- Android SDK, only for those who want to target Android devices
- The RoboVM plugin for Eclipse, only if you want to target iOS
- XCode, only for Mac users that want to target iOS

Java Development Kit

Libgdx is based on Java, and therefore, **Java Development Kit** is a requirement. The installation step is as follows:

Go to Oracle's download site, `http://www.oracle.com/technetwork/java/javase/downloads`, and click on the latest release of Java SE Development Kit that corresponds to your operating system. Note that you need to differentiate between the x86 and x64 builds.

> Be careful; Java 7 is the minimum JDK required, Java 6 will just not work.

Windows and Mac users

Perform the following installation steps:

1. Run the installer and follow the provided instructions. The process is quite straightforward, but when using Windows, you will have to remember the destination folder you picked; the default folder is `C:\Program Files\Java\jdk_version`.

2. You need to tell the system where the JDK is located.

3. If you are under Windows, right-click on **My Computer**, click on **System Properties**, access the **Advanced** section, and click on **Environment Variables**. Select **New**, and enter `JAVA_HOME` as the name and your installation path as a value. In my case, the value is `C:\Program Files\Java\jdk1.7.0_45`.

4. Mac users will have to edit their `~/.bash_profile` file and add the following:

   ```
   export JAVA_HOME=`/usr/libexec/java_home -v 1.7`
   ```

GNU/Linux users

Perform the following installation steps:

1. Move the downloaded package to the desired installation folder and decompress it. You can do this from a desktop environment or the much more classic console. We will assume the file is `jdk-7u45-linux-x64.gz`; it's in the `~/Downloads` directory, and the installation folder is `~/dev/jdk1.7.0_45`:

   ```
   mkdir -p ~/dev/jdk
   cd ~/Downloads
   tar -xzvf jdk-17u45-linux-x64.gz
   mv jdk1.7.0_45 ~/dev
   rm jdk-7u45-linux-x64.gz
   ```

> **Downloading the example code**
>
> You can download the example code files for all Packt books you have purchased from your account at `http://www.packtpub.com`. If you purchased this book elsewhere, you can visit `http://www.packtpub.com/support` and register to have the files e-mailed directly to you. This book is full of rich working examples you can experiment with. Access the following link to download the most up-to-date version: `https://github.com/siondream/libgdx-cookbook`.

2. In GNU/Linux, the system also needs to know where the JDK is. In order to do so, open the `~/.bashrc` file with your text editor of choice and add the following at the bottom:

```
export JAVA_HOME=$HOME/dev/jdk1.7.0_45
export PATH=$PATH:$JAVA_HOME/bin
```

3. Close the file, and run the following command to reload the user configuration:

```
source ~/.bashrc
```

> Alternatively, you can install **OpenJDK**, the open source implementation of the Java platform.

Eclipse

Eclipse is the most popular IDE for Libgdx game development, and it is thus the one we will focus in this book. If it is not of your liking, you can use IntelliJ IDEA, Netbeans, or any editor along the command line. Perform the following installation steps:

1. Go to the Eclipse downloads section at `http://www.eclipse.org/downloads` and select **Eclipse Standard**. The Eclipse 4 codename, Juno, is the minimum version needed to use the required plugins.

2. Simply pick the right version for your operating system and wait for it to download; be wary that it is also 32/64-bit sensitive.

3. Once this is complete, extract the compressed file where you want to use Eclipse from and you will be done.

4. From a GNU/Linux system, you can do the following:

```
cd ~/Downloads
tar -xzvf eclipse-standard-kepler-SR1-linux-gtk-x86_64.tar.gz
mv eclipse ~/dev
rm eclipse-standard-kepler-SR1-linux-gtk-x86_64.tar.gz
```

Android SDK

Follow these instructions to install Android Development Kit, which is essential to target Android devices:

1. Access the download page at `http://developer.android.com/sdk`.

2. Scroll down and unfold the **View all downloads and sizes** section and, again, choose your operating system from the **SDK Tools Only** section. Google has an easy-to-use installer for Windows users, so if you want to be spared part of the hassle, use the installer.

3. The installer is really simple. Limit yourself to follow the instructions, and if JDK is properly added to the environment variables, everything should be completely smooth. The installation folder does not really matter.

Mac users

Unzip the package wherever you want, as long as you tell the system where it is. Again, this is done by editing the `~/.bash_profile` file and adding something similar to this:

```
export PATH=$PATH:/dev/android-sdk-mac_x86_64/tools
export PATH=$PATH:/dev/android-sdk-mac_x86_64/platform-tools
```

GNU/Linux users

Perform the following installation steps:

1. Unzip the package, move it to the desired installation folder, and add the export location to the PATH environment variable. The commands needed will be something similar to this:

```
cd ~/Downloads
tar -xzvf android-sdk.r22.2.1-linux.tgz
mv android-sdk-linux ~/dev
rm xzvf android-sdk.r22.2.1-linux.tgz
```

2. Just like with JDK, edit the `~/.bashrc` file and add the following lines at the end:

```
export PATH=$PATH:~/dev/android-sdk-linux/tools
export PATH=$PATH:~/dev/android-sdk-linux/platform-tools
```

3. Again, close the file and reload the `~/.bashrc` file:

```
source ~/.bashrc
```

4. After this, go to to the Android SDK folder and run SDK Manager, which will help us install specific packages. On GNU/Linux, you first need to give execution permissions to the user on the SDK folder:

```
cd ~/dev/android-sdk-linux
chmod -R 744 *
```

All users

Perform the following steps:

1. Create an ANDROID_HOME environment variable pointing to the root of Android SDK. This is done the same way as we did with the JAVA_HOME variable in the previous section.

2. Run SDK Manager found in the tools folder. GNU/Linux users need to run an Android executable.

3. Several Android SDK tools will appear selected by default; leave them selected. The Google USB driver is not compatible with GNU/Linux, but you should select it if you can.

4. The SDK tool corresponding to the latest Android version available will be ticked as well. Feel free to choose whichever SDK you prefer, but keep in mind that Libgdx requires Android 2.2 or later.

> If you use Android-specific code somewhere in your project, it is advisable to keep SDK for the oldest Android version you want to target. This way, you can ensure compatibility at all times.

5. Regardless of the Android version you pick, it is always advisable to consider backwards compatibility so as to reach as wide an audience as possible. As a developer, you will want to be thorough when it comes to testing on multiple devices.

6. Having said this, select **Install packages** and accept the licenses.

Eclipse plugins

Getting tired? Worry no more, we are getting close to the finish line! We are about to install several plugins that will allow us to manage our build process and target iOS devices:

► Gradle (mandatory)

► The Google plugin for Eclipse (mandatory)

► Developer tools for Android (only to target Android)

► Google Web Toolkit SDK (only to target browsers)

► RoboVM for iOS (only to target iOS)

A course on how to use an IDE is out of the scope of this book. However, pertinent explanations will be provided when having to deal with Eclipse-specific issues. The installation steps are as follows:

1. Run Eclipse and create a new workspace to import your recipe's code into. Just so we are all on the same page, let's name it `libgdx-cookbook`.

   Once you see the welcome panel, close it and select **Help | Install New Software**. The Android Developer Tools and the Google Web Toolkit plugins can be found at `http://dl.google.com/eclipse/plugin/4.3`.

> Be aware that this will only work with Eclipse 4.3 Kepler. If you use a different Eclipse release, use the matching version number. Google has this URL available on its developers help guide for Eclipse at `https://developers.google.com/eclipse/docs/getting_started`.

2. Select **Developer Tools**, **Google Plugin for Eclipse**, and **Google Web Toolkit SDK**, and proceed with the installation. A modal dialog will warn you about installing unsigned content because there is always an inherent risk when installing plugins. Rest assured Google's tools are safe. Upon completion, Eclipse will need to restart, and you will be prompted to enter the Android SDK location.

3. Now, follow the same process for the **RoboVM** plugin, you will find it at `http://download.robovm.org/eclipse`.

4. There is only one option within the repository, so select it, carry on with the installation, and restart Eclipse once again.

Gradle is an open source build automation system. It will gracefully handle all the dependencies of our projects, doing most of the cumbersome heavy lifting. Perform the following steps:

1. Once again, go to the **Install new software** option in Eclipse and introduce the URL `http://dist.springsource.com/release/TOOLS/gradle`.

2. Install the **Gradle IDE** entry and restart Eclipse for the last time.

Great! One more task can be crossed out from our shopping list.

XCode

XCode is the Apple IDE required to develop for their platforms. Mac users who want to target iOS can get hold of XCode free of charge from Apple Store.

Fixing character encoding and line endings

Eclipse has the impolite practice of not using UTF-8 encoding and Unix line endings if you are under a Microsoft operating system. While this will not affect you initially, it will prove to be a huge pain when it comes to using other peers' code as many conflicts will appear to ruin the party. Perform the following steps:

1. Character encoding is applied on a per-workspace basis, and to fix it, you need to access the `libgdx-cookbook` workspace you just created.

2. Click on **Window**, select **Preferences | General**, then select **Workspace**, and make sure **UTF-8 encoding** and **Unix line endings** are your choices.

> Remember to always be aware of how you encode your project files because encoding derived issues is the worst and you do not want to deal with them!

Making sure everything is in order

The time of truth has come as we are about to import a Libgdx project to our workspace for the first time and see whether we have made any mistakes along the way. This is the most basic Libgdx project you can possibly make if you want to target all platforms. Use the source code provided with this book. Perform the following steps:

1. Once you have Eclipse open in front of you, right-click on **Package Explorer**, select **Import**, and choose **Gradle project** inside the **Gradle** node.

2. Select the `[cookbook]/environment` folder, and click on **Build Model**.

3. Make sure you select all listed projects, and click on **Finish** to start importing the projects. Gradle will now download all the dependencies, which may take a while.

4. As long as everything goes according to plan, the only error you might see on the **Problems** pane will be in the Android project. This is because it is set to use an Android SDK different from the one you installed. In such a case, right-click on `environment-test-android`, go to **Properties**, and tick your installed Android SDK under the **Android** tab. You can also install the missing SDK if you prefer to do so.

5. All the assets are located inside the `environment-test-android` project and will be shared across all platforms.

6. We now need to tell the desktop project where the assets are located. Right-click on the desktop project (`environment-test-desktop`), select **Properties | Run/Debug Settings**, select **DesktopLauncher**, and click on **Edit**.

7. Open the **Arguments** tab and select **Other** as the working directory.

8. Now enter this in the input box:

   ```
   ${workspace_loc:environment-test-android/assets}
   ```

As long as you followed this recipe correctly, there should be no errors hanging around; so, it is time to run the project on every platform as a final test.

First, let's try the desktop project, which is the easiest of all.

Right-click on it, select **Run As** followed by **Java application**, and then choose the entry point (`DesktopLauncher`). You will see the following window:

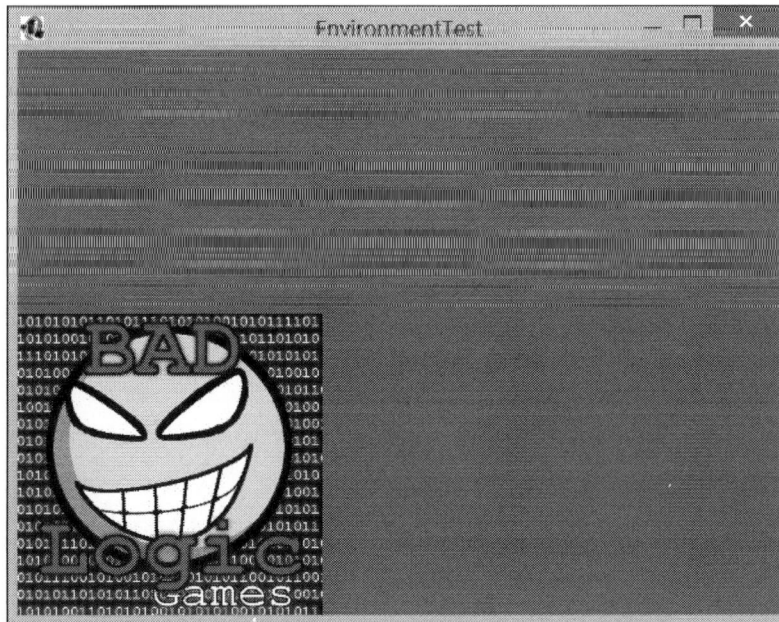

Android is next in the queue.

> I strongly advise you against testing a Libgdx game on the emulator because of its extremely poor performance. A device is so much better, and you will run your project through the desktop version most of the time anyway. This rapid iteration cycle is the main point in Libgdx's philosophy.

To pair your Android device, be it a phone or tablet, you need to enable **USB debugging** on your Android device, which can be a little obscure in later versions. Perform the following steps:

1. On the device, go to **Settings**, enter **About Phone**, and tap the **Build Number** block seven times to enable developer options. Yes, do not ask why.

2. Once you get a message saying you just became a developer, you can go to **Settings | Developer options** and enable **USB debugging**.

3. Now, you can run the environment test on your device by right-clicking on the Android project, entering the **Run As** menu, and selecting **Android Application**. Finally, choose your device from the list.

> Note that the device drivers have to be installed in your development machine. We cannot possibly cover all drivers due to their huge variety.

Let's try the HTML project now. Perform the following steps:

1. Right-click on the `environment-test-gwt` project and select **Run As Gradle build...**.

2. On the next window, type *Ctrl* + Space, and scroll down and double-click on the **gwtSuperDev** task. Click on **Apply** followed by **Run**.

3. The first time you do this, it will take quite a while. Under the hood, the build process will launch a Jetty web server on your computer.

4. After a while, you will be able to access it through the following URL:

   `http://localhost:8080/gwt`

5. A background code server will accept build requests from the browser, so no manual full compilation is needed once you kick it off. You will notice a particular message in the compiler output:

   ```
   The code server is ready.
   Next, visit http://localhost:9876/
   ```

6. Access the URL and drag the **Dev Mode On** bookmarklet onto the browser's bar. You will never need to do this again.

7. Back on your running environment test tab, click on the newly added bookmarklet, and select **compile**. Any change to the game code will be recompiled and reinjected in the web server.

8. After a short time, the page will refresh and you can run the most recent version of your code.

Additionally, Mac users can run the iOS project by right-clicking on `environment-test-ios` and going to the **Run As** menu. Inside, you will find three options of interest:

- ▸ **iOS Device App**: This requires you to have an actual connected device and an Apple developer subscription
- ▸ **iOS Simulator App (iPad)**
- ▸ **iOS Simulator App (iPhone)**

Pretty much like the HTML5 project, the first build will take a long time; it should be fine after this.

Congratulations! Now, you can run your Libgdx projects on all targetable platforms.

How it works...

The Libgdx development environment installation process is pretty much self-explanatory. However, it is worth mentioning a few details of how it is designed to facilitate cross-platform development and what technologies it relies on. You will at least know why you just installed so many things!

Libgdx has a multiplatform API that allows users to write platform-agnostic Java code once and deploy it on all the supported platforms, while achieving the same behavior. Every platform has a backend that implements low-level subsystems: Application, Graphics, Audio, Input, Files, and Network.

This way, we can happily request to draw a sprite onscreen, play some background music, or read a text file through the common graphics, audio, and file interfaces, respectively, and it will run everywhere. Magic!

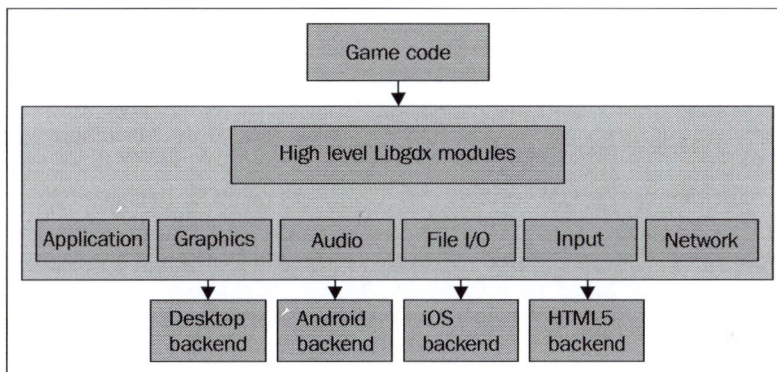

Deployment on platforms such as Android, iOS, or HTML5 might not be the fastest process ever, but this is usually mitigated by the ability of the desktop backend to serve as a debugging platform. Remember that this will become increasingly important as you and Libgdx become friends.

The desktop backend mostly relies on **LWJGL** (**Light Weight Java Game Library**). At the same time, LWJGL is built on top of the magnanimous **OpenGL** (**Open Graphics Library**). A fun fact is that *Minecraft* was created using LWJGL.

For Android development, Libgdx finds its resources on the official **Android SDK** as well as the embedded system-specific version of OpenGL, which is called **OpenGL ES**.

This gets a lot trickier when it comes to HTML5 support because the technologies are quite different. HTML5 can display incredibly visually rich applications through WebGL and JavaScript, but unfortunately, this has little to do with the Libgdx toolchain. Compatibility with browsers is achieved through **Google Web Toolkit** (**GWT**), which compiles Java code into optimized JavaScript code, thanks to, what I like to call, black magic.

Last but not least, we have iOS support that relies on RoboVM. This magnificent piece of open source software eats Java code for breakfast and spits out native ARM or x86 code. It also provides full access to Cocoa Touch API, allowing us to deploy on iOS devices, as long as we have a Mac.

There are quite a few more technologies involved to make this happen, but this serves as a broad overview of what goes on under the hood.

There's more...

You can use Android SDK Manager to gain access to more Android APIs such as Google Play Game services, advertisement platforms, or **Intel Hardware Accelerated Execution Manager** (**HAXM**). HAXM is an alternative Android emulator, much faster than the default one. Feel free to explore!

See also

▶   In the next recipe, you will learn how to create brand new Libgdx-based cross-platform projects. Let the fun begin!

▶   For instructions on how to deploy your Libgdx applications, go to the first four recipes in *Chapter 13, Giving Back*.

Creating a cross-platform project

In this recipe, we will lay out a series of very simple steps for you to set up Libgdx cross-platform projects really quickly. With very little hassle, you will have a functional barebones application ready to take your brilliant game logic in.

Getting ready

Make sure you have all Libgdx dependencies installed in your development machine. If you didn't follow all the steps in the *Setting up a cross-platform development environment* recipe, proceed to do so before carrying on.

How to do it...

Libgdx makes use of Gradle to handle the build process. Gradle is an open source build automation tool, very similar to Apache Ant and Apache Maven. It handles your project's dependencies and downloads external libraries when necessary; you only have to declare that you want to include them in your project.

Luckily enough, you do not need to learn a lot about Gradle to start working on Libgdx projects because our framework bundles a tool that creates a skeleton application with all the basics for you to use.

The **gdx-setup** tool offers a very straightforward user interface as well as a command-line option. Feel free to use whichever you are most comfortable with; we will explain both here. Perform the following steps:

1. First, download the latest version of the tool from http://libgdx
   badlogicgames.com ... ...

2. Running the .jar file with no additional arguments opens up the user interface straightaway. Filling the form in does not entail any mystery at all.

3. Simply enter the project folder name, Java package name, name of the game logic entry point class, folder where the projects will be created, and location of your Android SDK. Once you are ready, click on the **Generate** button, as shown in the following screenshot:

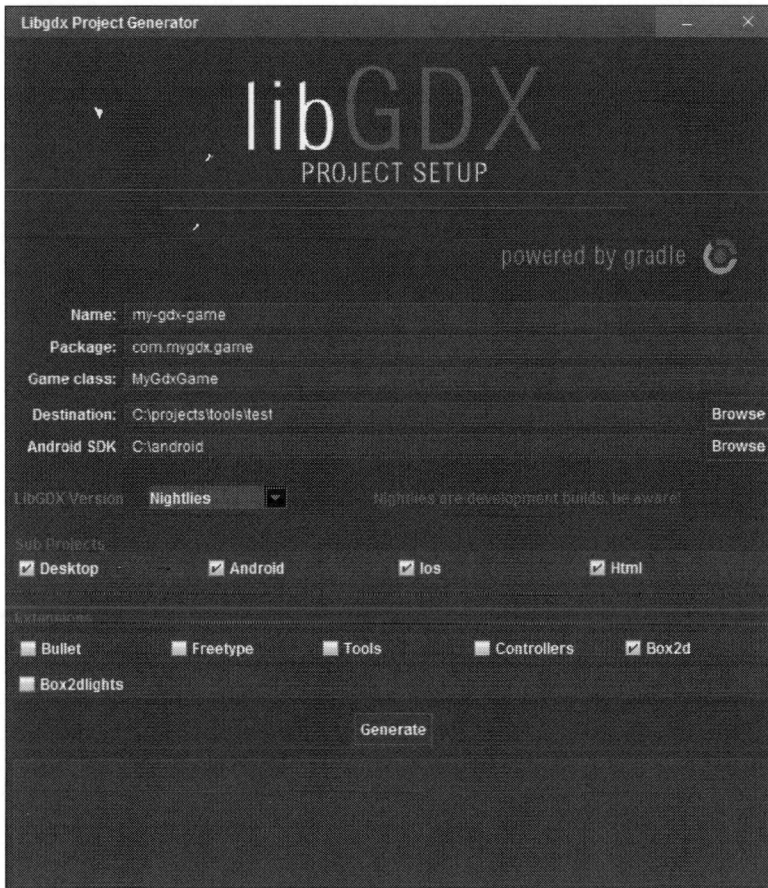

For those who fancy the command-line version of the tool, here is its usage:

```
java --jar gdx-setup.jar --dir <dir-name> --name <app-name>
--package <package_name> --mainClass <main_class> --sdkLocation
<sdk_location>
```

- ❏ `--dir`: This is the destination folder of the projects
- ❏ `--name`: This is the name of the application, which will determine the project folders' names
- ❏ `--package`: This is the name of the Java package where the code will live
- ❏ `--mainClass`: This is the class name for the game code entry point
- ❏ `--sdkLocation`: This is the path to your Android SDK

For example, to call the tool from the command line with the settings shown in the previous screenshot, you will have to enter:

```
java –jar gdx-setup.jar –dir E:\projects\tools\test –name my-gdx-
game –package com.mygdx.game –mainClass MyGdxGame –sdkLocation C:\
android
```

Done! Just like we did with `environment-test` in the previous recipe, now it is time to import the project in Eclipse.

4. Right-click on **Package Explorer**, select **Import**, and choose the **Gradle** project inside the **Gradle** tab.

   Select your destination folder and click on **Build Model**.

   > Remember that you need to set the working directory for the desktop project so that it can find the assets that are located within the Android project.

5. Right-click on the desktop project. Go to **Properties | Run/Debug Settings**, select **DesktopLauncher**, and click on **Edit**.

6. Open the **Arguments** tab and select **Other** as the working directory.

7. Now, enter this in the input box:

   ```
   ${workspace_loc:my-gdx-game-android/assets}
   ```

8. You need to override the memory allowance for Gradle and specify the location of Android SDK so that Gradle can pick it up. Add the following lines to the `gradle.properties` file located under the `gradle` directory in your `user` folder:

   ```
   org.gradle.jvmargs=-Xms128m -Xmx512m
   sdk.dir=C:/android
   ```

> The Libgdx Gradle build system is also compatible with Intelij IDEA, Netbeans, and the command line. Feel free to explore and look for additional information on these lines.

Your newly created Libgdx project should be fully functional. Gradle will take care of the dependencies, download the necessary libraries, and handle the compilation process. Like we mentioned before, the first build can take quite a while, but it should be significantly smoother from then on.

Happy coding!

How it works...

At this point, you will notice how the Libgdx projects are structured. They are actually made of several projects, one per platform and another core project. The core project contains the actual logic of your game, while the platform-specific projects typically only have a launcher that calls the core entry point.

The resulting directory tree inside the `test` folder will look as follows:

```
|- settings.gradle      - project submodules
|- build.gradle         - main Gradle build config file
|- gradlew              - Build script for GNU/Linux
|- gradlew.bat          - Build script for Windows
|- local.properties     - Intellij IDEA only file
|
|- gradle/              - local Gradle
|
|- core
|   |- build.gradle     - Gradle build for core project, do not
modify
|   |- src/             - Game code
|
|- desktop
|   |- build.gradle     - Gradle build for desktop project
|   |- src/             - Desktop specific code
|
|- android
|   |- build.gradle        - Gradle build for Android project
|   |- AndroidManifest.xml - Android config
|   |- src/             - Android specific code
|   |- res/             - Android icons and other resources
|   |- assets/          - Shared assets
|
```

```
|- gwt
|    |- build.gradle      - Gradle build for GWT project
|    |- src/          - GWT specific code
|    |- webapp/         - War template
|
|- ios
|    |- build.gradle      - Gradle build for iOS project
|    |- src/            - iOS specific code
```

Gradle, our build system, is particularly good with multiproject solutions. It uses **domain-specific language** (**DSL**) rather than XML, like Ant and Maven do, to define targets as well as their dependencies. When we tell Gradle to build a project for us, it uses the build.gradle files to create a directed acyclic graph representing the dependencies. Then, it builds the dependencies in the right order.

The dependency graph for the Libgdx project skeleton will look as follows:

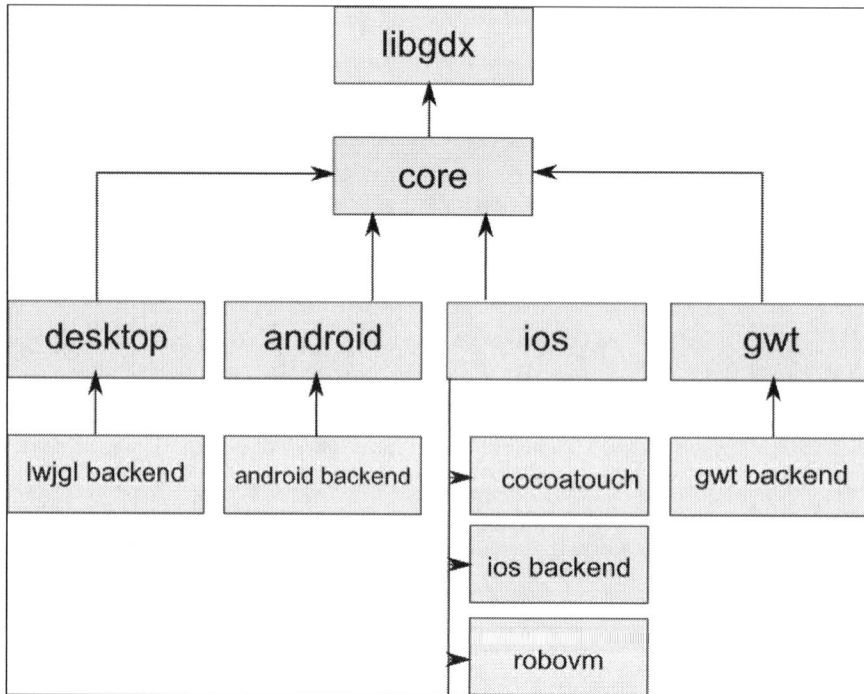

There's more...

Gradle is extremely configurable so as to accommodate the needs of a diverse set of developers and their environments. This is done through several `gradle.properties` files located at various specific places:

- The project build directory where the main `build.gradle` file is
- The user home, which will be `C:\Users\User\.gradle\gradle.properties` in Windows and `~/.gradle/gradle.properties` in UNIX/Linux
- The system properties

These settings are applied in descending order, which means that the lower settings can overwrite the higher settings.

Gradle downloads dependencies from repositories on demand. When your machine is behind a proxy, you need to specify this through one of the `gradle.properties` files by adding the following settings:

```
systemProp.http.proxyHost=www.somehost.org
systemProp.http.proxyPort=8080
systemProp.http.proxyUser=userid
systemProp.http.proxyPassword=password
```

For secure addresses, you only need to replace `http` with `https` in the previous properties.

As you surely understand, this is not a book on Gradle. If you wish to know more about it and how to tailor it for your needs, refer to the official user guide at `http://www.gradle.org/docs/current/userguide/userguide_single.html`.

See also

- For further details on the Gradle project and dependency management, read the *Updating and managing project dependencies* recipe of this chapter.

Understanding the project structure and application life cycle

Throughout this recipe, we will examine the typical project architecture of Libgdx and how it makes cross-platform development a much less cumbersome quest. We will also learn how to configure platform-specific launchers in order to tweak parameters such as resolution, colors, the OpenGL version, and so on. More importantly, we will go through the Libgdx application life cycle. This is the heart of any game you will ever make using our beloved framework, and therefore, one can imagine it is something worth getting acquainted with.

Getting ready

With the goal of illustrating the contents of this recipe, we will use the same environment test application we used in the *Setting up a cross-platform development environment* recipe to test that our Libgdx installation is working as expected. Fire up Eclipse and make sure you select your `libgdx-cookbook` workspace. Now, check you have the projects that compose the test application already available. If not, import the projects under `[cookbook]/environment` through Gradle, as shown in the previous recipe.

How to do it...

As we already mentioned before, Libgdx applications are typically split in several projects: core, desktop, Android, iOS, and HTML. The platform-specific projects serve as the application's entry points on each platform; their duty basically boils down to invoking the core project's main class and passing in the basic configuration parameters for the game to run.

> Imagine you were to target Android exclusively, you could probably get away with one single project containing both the platform-agnostic and Android-specific code. However, this is a bad practice and should be avoided. What happens if you decide to port your game to a different platform later on? No one would like to refactor the project structure to accommodate it to the new circumstances. Regardless of the platform and devices you work with, it is always preferable to keep the two categories as isolated as possible.

Using logging to get to know the application life cycle

Every Libgdx application has a very well-defined lifecycle controlling the states it can be in at a given time. These states are: creation, pausing, resuming, rendering, and disposing. The lifecycle is modeled by the `ApplicationListener` interface, which we are required to implement as it will serve as the entrance to our game logic. In our recipe's example, the `EnvironmentTest` class in the core project carries out such roles.

Meet the `ApplicationListener` interface:

```
public interface ApplicationListener {
    public void create ();
    public void resize (int width, int height);
    public void render ();
    public void pause ();
    public void resume ();
    public void dispose ();
}
```

Your `ApplicationListener` interface implementation can handle each one of these events in the way it deems convenient. Here are the typical usages:

- ▶ `create()`: This is used to initialize subsystems and load resources.
- ▶ `resize()`: This is used to handle setting a new screen size, which can be used to reposition UI elements or reconfigure camera objects
- ▶ `render()`: This is used to update and render the game elements. Note that there is no `update()` method as `render()` is supposed to carry out both tasks
- ▶ `pause()`: This is the save game state when it loses focus, which does not involve the actual gameplay being paused unless the developer wants it to.
- ▶ `resume()`: This is used to handle the game coming back from being paused and restores the game state.
- ▶ `dispose()`: This is used to free resources and clean up.

When do each of these methods get called? Well, that's a really good question! Before we start looking at cryptic diagrams, it is much better to investigate and find out for ourselves. Shall we? We will simply add some logging to know exactly how the flow works.

Take a look at the `EnvironmentTest.java` file:

```java
public class EnvironmentTest implements ApplicationListener {
    private Logger logger;
    private boolean renderInterrupted = true;

    @Override
    public void create() {
        logger = new Logger("Application lifecycle", Logger.INFO);
        logger.info("create");
    }

    @Override
    public void dispose() {
        logger.info("dispose");
    }

    @Override
    public void render() {
        if (renderInterrupted) {
            logger.info("render");
            renderInterrupted = false;
        }
    }
}
```

```
    @Override
    public void resize(int width, int height) {
        logger.info("resize");
        renderInterrupted = true;
    }

    @Override
    public void pause() {
        logger.info("pause");
        renderInterrupted = true;
    }

    @Override
    public void resume() {
        logger.info("resume");
        renderInterrupted = true;
    }
}
```

The `renderInterrupted` member variable avoids printing `render` for every game loop iteration.

> Whenever Eclipse complains about missing imports, hit *Ctrl + Shift + O* to automatically add the necessary modules.

The `Logger` class helps us show useful debug information and errors on the console. Not only does it work on desktops but also on external devices, as long as they are connected to Eclipse. Remember this little new friend as it will be truly useful for as long as you work with Libgdx. The constructor receives a string that will be useful to identify the messages in the log as well as on a logging level.

In order of increasing severity, these are the available logging levels: `Logger.INFO`, `Logger.DEBUG`, `Logger.ERROR`, and `Logger.NONE`. Several methods can be used to log messages:

- `info(String message)`
- `info(String message, Exception exception)`
- `debug(String message)`
- `debug(String message, Exception exception)`
- `error(String message)`
- `error(String message, Throwable exception)`

Logging levels can be retrieved and set with the `getLevel()` and `setLevel()` methods, respectively. Both the level and the method used to log a message will determine whether they will actually be printed on the console. For example, if the level is set to `Logger.INFO`, only messages sent through `info()` and `error()` will appear, and those sent through `debug()` will be ignored.

Now, run the application on all the platforms and pay attention to the console. Depending on how you play with the focus, the output will vary, but it should be similar to this:

```
Application lifecycle: create
Application lifecycle: resize
Application lifecycle: render
Application lifecycle: pause
Application lifecycle: render
Application lifecycle: resume
Application lifecycle: render
Application lifecycle: dispose
```

This should give you a pretty decent handle of how the application lifecycle works.

Placing breakpoints on each `ApplicationListener` overridden method is also a good way of discovering what is going on. Instruction breakpoints allow you to debug an application and stop the execution flow that reaches the said instruction. At this point, you can run the code instruction by instruction and examine the current state of the active variables. To set a breakpoint, double-click next to the corresponding line; a blue dot will confirm that the breakpoint is set. Once you are done, you can debug the application by right-clicking on the desired project and selecting the **Debug As** menu.

```java
@Override
public void render () {
    if (renderInterrupted) {
        logger.info("render");
        renderInterrupted = false;
    }

    Gdx.gl.glClearColor(1, 0, 0, 1);
    Gdx.gl.glClear(GL20.GL_COLOR_BUFFER_BIT);
    batch.begin();
    batch.draw(img, 0, 0);
    batch.end();
}
```

The Eclipse **Debug** view will then enter the stage with all its shiny panels. The **Debug** tab shows the current execution callstack, the **Variables** tab contains the current state of the variables within scope, and in the following screenshot, you can see the code with the current line highlighted. The arrow buttons in the upper toolbar can be used to step over the next instruction (*F6*) or move on to the next method (*F5*), where applicable, or out of the current method (*F7*), as shown in the following screenshot:

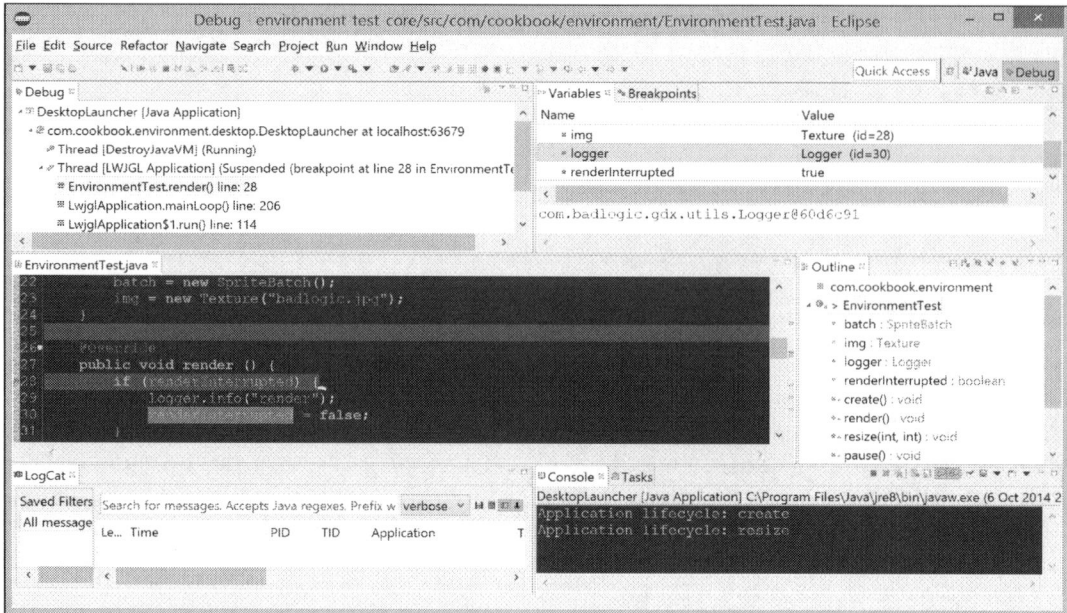

Starter classes and configuration

Every platform project consists of a starter class (or entry point). This class is responsible for constructing the platform-specific application backend. Each backend implements the `Application` interface. The starter class also passes a new instance of our `ApplicationListener` implementation to the application backend. This implementation typically lives in the core project and serves as an entry point to our cross-platform game code. Finally, it also submits a configuration object, and by doing so, it provides a mechanism to customize general parameters, as we will see later.

Desktop starter

The entry point of the desktop project is the `static main` method of the `DesktopLauncher` starter class:

```
public class DesktopLauncher {
    public static void main (String[] arg) {
        LwjglApplicationConfiguration config = new
LwjglApplicationConfiguration();
```

```
        new LwjglApplication(new EnvironmentTest(), config);
    }
}
```

As you can see, this creates `LwjglApplicationConfiguration`. Then, it instantiates a `LwjglApplication` object passing in a new `EnvironmentTest` instance along the recently created `config` object. Some of the most useful attributes of the configuration class are listed as follows:

- `r`, `g`, `b`, and `a`: This is the number of bits to be used per color channel, which are red, green, blue, and alpha, respectively.

- `disableAudio`: This is to set whether audio should be used. If it should, on operating the audio subsystem will return `null`.

- `width` and `height`: This is the size of the application window in pixels.

- `fullScreen`: This is to set whether the application should start in the full screen or windowed mode.

- `vSyncEnabled`: This is to set whether vertical synchronization should be enabled. This ensures that the render operations are in sync with the monitor refresh rate, avoiding potential partial frames.

- `title`: This is the string with the desired title of the window.

- `resizable`: This is to set whether the user should be able to resize the application window.

- `foregroundFPS` and `backgroundFPS`: This is the number of desired frames per second when the application is active and inactive, respectively.

Android starter

The Android starter can be found in `AndroidLauncher.java`:

```
public class AndroidLauncher extends AndroidApplication {
    @Override
    protected void onCreate (Bundle savedInstanceState) {
        super.onCreate(savedInstanceState);
        AndroidApplicationConfiguration config = new
AndroidApplicationConfiguration();
        initialize(new EnvironmentTest(), config);
    }
}
```

Android starters use the Android SDK Activity framework, which those who have developed for this platform before will be familiar with. In this case, an `AndroidApplicationConfiguration` instance is used. Some of the most useful attributes are listed as follows:

- r, g, b, and a: Just as with the desktop project, these refer to the number of bits used per color channel.

- ▶ `hideStatusBar`: This is to set whether the application should hide the typical Android status bar that shows up right at the top of the screen.

- ▶ `maxSimultaneousSounds`: This is the number of maximum sound instances that can play at a given time. As you can see in *Chapter 5, Audio and File I/O*, dedicated to audio, they only refer to short sound effects as opposed to long streams of audio.

- ▶ `useAccelerometer`: This is to set whether the application should care about the accelerometer; it defaults to true.

- ▶ `useCompass`: This is to set whether the Android application should update the compass values; it also defaults to true.

HTML starter

The HTML5 starter resides inside the `GwtLauncher.java` file and follows the pattern we already know:

```
public class GwtLauncher extends GwtApplication {
    @Override
    public GwtApplicationConfiguration getConfig () {
        GwtApplicationConfiguration cfg = new
GwtApplicationConfiguration(480, 320);
        return cfg;
    }

    @Override
    public ApplicationListener getApplicationListener () {
        return new EnvironmentTest();
    }
}
```

A `GwtApplicationConfiguration` object is used to configure the HTML5 backend. Its most important parameters are as follows:

- ▶ `antialiasing`: This is to set whether to enable antialiasing, which is computationally expensive, but helps to avoid rough edges when rendering.

- ▶ `canvasId`: This is the identifier for the HTML element to embed the game canvas in. When not specified, the system will create a canvas element inside the `<body>` element.

- ▶ `fps`: This is the target frames per second at which we desire to run the game.

- ▶ `width` and `height`: These are the dimensions of the drawing area in pixels.

iOS starter

Finally, the iOS starter is hosted by the `IOSLauncher.java` file:

```
public class IOSLauncher extends IOSApplication.Delegate {
    @Override
    protected IOSApplication createApplication() {
        IOSApplicationConfiguration config = new
IOSApplicationConfiguration();
        return new IOSApplication(new EnvironmentTest(), config);
    }

    public static void main(String[] argv) {
        NSAutoreleasePool pool = new NSAutoreleasePool();
        UIApplication.main(argv, null, IOSLauncher.class);
        pool.drain();
    }
}
```

The configuration object for this backend belongs to the `IOSApplicationConfiguration` class and here are its main parameters:

- `accelerometerUpdate`: This is the update interval to update the accelerometer values in seconds
- `orientationLandscape` and `orientationPortrait`: This is to set whether the application supports the landscape or portrait orientation, respectively
- `preferredFramesPerSecond`: This is the number of frames per second we try to reach while running the application
- `useAccelerometer`: Just as on Android, this sets whether to update the accelerometer values
- `useCompass`: This is to set whether to update the compass sensor values

How it works...

So far, you autonomously experienced how a Libgdx application is organized and the mechanism it uses to run across platforms. Also, you tested how the application lifecycle works and which events are triggered as a consequence of an event. Now, it is time to get a higher-level overview of all these systems and see how they fit together.

Here is an **UML** class diagram showing every piece of the puzzle that is involved in any way with game startups on specific platforms and in the application lifecycle. After a quick glance, we can observe how `EnvironmentTest`, our `ApplicationListener` implementation, is used by every launcher class along the various configuration classes:

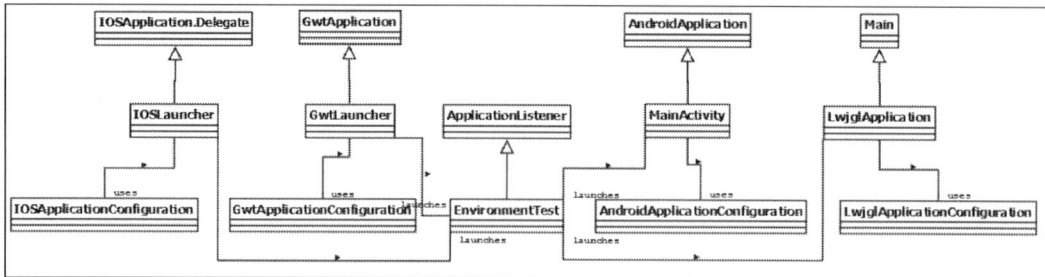

The next diagram depicts the mighty Libgdx application lifecycle. Every time the game starts, the `create()` method is called. Immediately after, there is a call to `resize()` so as to accommodate the current screen dimensions. Next, the application enters its main loop, where it calls `render()` continuously, while processing the input and other events, as required.

When the application loses focus (for example, the user receives a call on Android), `pause()` is invoked. Once the focus is recovered, `resume()` is called, and we enter the main loop again.

The `resize()` method is called every time the application surface dimensions change (for example, the user resizes the window).

Finally, it's called when the player gets bored of our game. Sorry, this will never happen! When the player runs out of time to play our game and exits, `pause()` will be called, followed by `dispose()`.

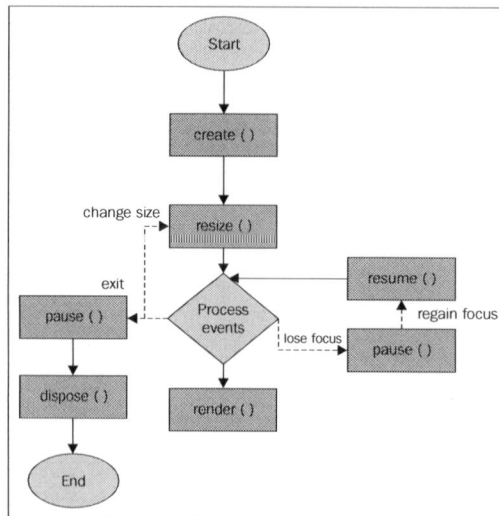

There's more...

After looking at the basic concepts behind a simple Libgdx project, let's move on to a couple of tricks to improve your quality of life.

Living comfortably with ApplicationAdapter

As you already know, every Libgdx game needs to have an `ApplicationListener` interface implementation in its core project for the launchers to use. We also saw how the developer is forced to implement the `create()`, `dispose()`, `render()`, `resize()`, `pause()`, and `resume()` methods of such an interface. However, those overridden methods might end up completely empty. What a waste of digital ink, and more importantly, our precious time!

Luckily enough, Libgdx provides a useful `ApplicationAdapter` class that already contains an empty implementation for each `ApplicationListener` interface method. This means that you can simply inherit from `ApplicationAdapter` and only override the methods you really need. This comes particularly in handy when writing small tests rather than big games. These small adapter classes are quite common within the API, and they are really comfortable to use as long as we do not need to inherit from anything else. Remember that Java does not support multiple inheritance.

The following will be perfectly valid if we want a completely empty application:

```
public class MyGame extends ApplicationAdapter {}
```

Managing a multiscreen application with Game

Most games are made out of several screens the player can navigate through. The main menu, level selection settings, or levels are some of the most common examples. Though this completely depends on the nature of each project, most of them definitely share the structure. Libgdx comes with an utterly minimalistic screen system built-in, which might just be enough for your requirements, so why not use it? Reinventing the wheel is rarely a good idea.

The two main components of this system are the `Game` abstract class and `Screen` interface. `Game` implements the well-known `ApplicationListener` interface, so you will only need your main class to inherit from `Game`.

The `Game` class holds a reference to the current `Screen` and provides the getter and setter methods for it. `Game` requires you to implement the `create()` method, but already provides implementations for the rest of the application lifecycle methods. Be aware that if you override any of the other methods, you will need to call the parent version so as to maintain screen behavior correctness. The helpful bit comes with the `render()` method, which will automatically update and render the active `Screen` reference, as long as it is not `null`.

What follows is an UML class diagram illustrating a sample game architecture based on the Game/Screen model. The user implemented MyGame as a Game derived class, and the SettingsScreen, GameScreen, LevelSelectionScreen, and MainMenuScreen classes were derived from Screen:

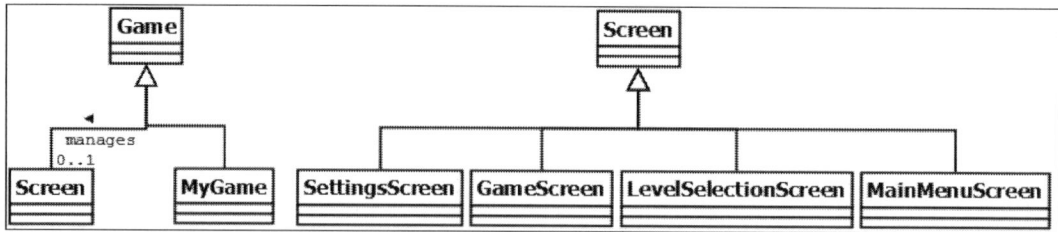

The Game public API looks like this. Note that method implementation has been omitted for space reasons:

```
public abstract class Game implements ApplicationListener {
    public void dispose ();
    public void pause ();
    public void resume ();
    public void render ();
    public void resize (int width, int height);
    public void setScreen (Screen screen);
    public Screen getScreen ();
}
```

The Screen interface is quite similar to the ApplicationListener interface, but its equivalent methods will only be called when it is the active screen. It also adds the hide() and show() methods that will be called when changed to and from a screen, respectively. In the following code, you will find an overview of the interface:

```
public interface Screen {
    public void render (float delta);
    public void resize (int width, int height);
    public void show ();
    public void hide ();
    public void pause ();
    public void resume ();
    public void dispose ();
}
```

> Just like we saw before with `ApplicationListener` and `ApplicationAdapter`, the `Screen` interface has a convenient implementation, unsurprisingly called `ScreenAdapter`. You can just inherit from it and override the methods that you need only.

See also

► Jump to *Chapter 2, Working with 2D Graphics*, to start rendering textures onscreen or carry on with the *Updating and managing project dependencies* recipe to learn more about Libgdx project configuration.

Updating and managing project dependencies

This recipe will show you how to leverage Gradle in order to maintain your project and its dependencies. By the end of the recipe, you will be able to upgrade to a newer version of Libgdx and add third-party extensions and arbitrary Java libraries.

Oftentimes, people tend to be reluctant to learn new technologies, especially build systems such as Gradle. However, they actually tremendously simplify the process, thus helping us make even more awesome games.

Getting ready

Let's start with the `environment-test` project we created in the *Setting up a cross-platform development environment* recipe. At this point, you should have the project up and running within Eclipse or the IDE of your choice.

How to do it...

Your application's dependencies are expressed in the `build.gradle` text file, which is pretty much the only file we will manipulate. Be advised against tinkering with the project-specific Gradle files as you stand a really good chance of making all hell break loose.

> This is not supposed to be a full Gradle manual; it's a mere introduction for you to get by and move on to making actual games.

Gradle build file primer

Throughout this primer, and for space reasons, we will only show small snippets from the build file.

Go ahead and open the `build.gradle` file from Eclipse. The first thing you will come across is the `buildscript` element, which defines the list of repositories and basic dependencies. Repositories act as a library-serving system. We can reference libraries by name, and Gradle will ask the list of repositories for a library that matches the name:

```
buildscript {
    repositories {
        maven {
            url 'https://github.com/steffenschaefer/gwt-gradle-plugin/
raw/maven-repo/'
        }
        . . .
    }

    dependencies {
        . . .
    }
}
```

The `allprojects` element contains a string with the application version. Additionally, it defines `appName` as well as the Libgdx and roboVM versions it should build against. It also provides a list of repositories to fetch from:

```
allprojects {
    apply plugin: "eclipse"
    apply plugin: "idea"

    version = "1.0"
    ext {
        appName = "environment-test"
        gdxVersion = "1.2.0"
        roboVMVersion = "0.0.13"
    }

    repositories {
        . . .
    }
}
```

Every project has a project element indicating its name. A skeleton application's core project will only depend on the previously defined Libgdx version:

```
project(":core") {
    apply plugin: "java"

    dependencies {
        compile "com.badlogicgames.gdx:gdx:$gdxVersion"
    }
}
```

Platform-specific projects, such as a desktop project, will depend on core as well as their corresponding backend and potentially native libraries:

```
project(":desktop") {
    apply plugin: "java"

    dependencies {
        compile project(":core")
        compile "com.badlogicgames.gdx:gdx-backend-lwjgl:$gdxVersion"
        compile "com.badlogicgames.gdx:gdx-
platform:$gdxVersion:natives-desktop"
    }
}
```

Do not panic if you do not fully understand everything that goes on inside the build script. However, you should at least have a very basic grasp on how the general structure holds itself together.

Now, let's get on to some useful business.

Updating existing dependencies

Dependencies that are pulled from repositories take the following typical Maven format:

```
compile '<groupId>:<artifactId>:<version>:<classifier>'
```

Intuitively, whenever you desire to change a dependency version, you just need to go and modify the version component of its declaration. Now, imagine the Libgdx team has released a new version and we are all very excited with the new features; it is time to try them out. Conveniently enough, throughout the script, the Libgdx version points to the gdxVersion variable. We only need to find the allprojects element and change the following:

```
gdxVersion = "1.1.0"
```

To the following, you are free to choose whichever version you like:

```
gdxVersion = "1.2.0"
```

To make Gradle fetch the new dependencies, select all the projects, right-click on **Gradle**, and then click on **Refresh All**.

> Libgdx has stable and nightly builds. Stable builds are well tested, planned builds that can be identified by their version number, 1.2.0, for instance. Nightly builds, in turn, are generated overnight from whatever the Git repository contains. To use nightly builds in your project, you need to set `1.2-SNAPSHOT` as the version identifier. Nightly builds are good to test and get the latest features as they are introduced; however, they are considerably riskier and prone to breaking. Use the stable builds if peace of mind is what you seek. Luckily enough, you can switch between them just by changing the `gdxVersion` variable.

Adding Libgdx extensions

Libgdx comes with several additional libraries that provide a ton of extra features. The reason they are not part of the core is because either not everyone is likely to need them or because they might not work on all backends. These extensions have been mavenized and can be fetched from the repositories.

> Linking against libraries you do not need will unnecessarily increase the size of your distributable package. Desktop downloads are not too big of a problem as we have AAA game downloads going up to 50 GB nowadays. However, mobile games need to be careful about this since some 3G connections have bandwidth limits.

Currently, the following are the Libgdx Gradle-ready extensions along with their required dependencies for each of the projects. The core dependency will add the interfaces for you to use within the game code, whilst the platform-specific dependencies will contain the implementation of such interfaces. You will need to add them inside the corresponding `dependencies` element.

Bullet

A bullet is a wrapper for the popular open source 3D physics library. Note that it is not compatible with the HTML5 backend as it needs to run native code.

Core

Here is the code for the core:

```
compile "com.badlogicgames.gdx:gdx-bullet:$gdxVersion"
```

Desktop

To use it with desktop, we use the following:

```
compile "com.badlogicgames.gdx:gdx-bullet-
platform:$gdxVersion:natives-desktop"
```

Android

Similarly, for Android, we use the following:

```
compile "com.badlogicgames.gdx:gdx-bullet:$gdxVersion"
natives "com.badlogicgames.gdx:gdx-bullet-
platform:$gdxVersion:natives-armeabi"
natives "com.badlogicgames.gdx:gdx-bullet-
platform:$gdxVersion:natives-armeabi-v7a"
```

iOS

Furthermore, we use the following code for iOS:

```
compile "com.badlogicgames.gdx:gdx-bullet:$gdxVersion"
natives "com.badlogicgames.gdx:gdx-bullet-
platform:$gdxVersion:natives-ios"
```

FreeTypeFont

The FreeTypeFont extension helps you generate bitmaps from TTF fonts on the fly. It is not compatible with the HTML5 backend.

Core

Here is the code for the core:

```
compile "com.badlogicgames.gdx:gdx-freetype:$gdxVersion"
```

Desktop

To use it with desktop, we use the following:

```
compile "com.badlogicgames.gdx:gdx-freetype-
platform:$gdxVersion:natives-desktop"
```

Android

For Android, this is what we use:

```
compile "com.badlogicgames.gdx:gdx-freetype:$gdxVersion"
natives "com.badlogicgames.gdx:gdx-freetype-
platform:$gdxVersion:natives-armeabi"
natives "com.badlogicgames.gdx:gdx-freetype-
platform:$gdxVersion:natives-armeabi-v7a"
```

iOS

Lastly, for iOS, we use the following:

```
compile "com.badlogicgames.gdx:gdx-freetype:$gdxVersion"
natives "com.badlogicgames.gdx:gdx-freetype-
platform:$gdxVersion:natives-ios"
```

Controllers

The Controllers extension provides an API to get events from the game controllers. It is not compatible with the iOS backend; although the project still compiles and runs, it will just not detect any controller or event. For more information on controllers, see *Chapter 4, Detecting User Input*.

Core

Here is the code for the core:

```
compile "com.badlogicgames.gdx:gdx-controllers:$gdxVersion"
```

Desktop

To use it with desktop, we use the following:

```
compile "com.badlogicgames.gdx:gdx-controllers-desktop:$gdxVersion"
compile "com.badlogicgames.gdx:gdx-controllers-
platform:$gdxVersion:natives-desktop"
```

Android

To use this extension with Android , we use the following:

```
compile "com.badlogicgames.gdx:gdx-controllers-android:$gdxVersion"
```

HTML5

For HTML5, the following code is used:

```
compile "com.badlogicgames.gdx:gdx-controllers:$gdxVersion:sources"
compile "com.badlogicgames.gdx:gdx-controllers-gwt:$gdxVersion"
compile "com.badlogicgames.gdx:gdx-controllers-
gwt:$gdxVersion:sources"
```

Box2D

The Box2D extension will provide you with a full-blown rigid body physics engine compatible with all backends. Read more about it in *Chapter 10, Rigid Body Physics with Box2D*.

Core

Here is the code for the core:

```
compile "com.badlogicgames.gdx:gdx-box2d:$gdxVersion"
```

Desktop

We run the following code to use it with desktop:

```
compile "com.badlogicgames.gdx:gdx-box2d-platform:$gdxVersion:natives-desktop"
```

Android

For Android, we use the following code:

```
compile "com.badlogicgames.gdx:gdx-box2d:$gdxVersion"
natives "com.badlogicgames.gdx:gdx-box2d-platform:$gdxVersion:natives-armeabi"
natives "com.badlogicgames.gdx:gdx-box2d-platform:$gdxVersion:natives-armeabi-v7a"
natives "com.badlogicgames.gdx:gdx-box2d-platform:$gdxVersion:natives-x86"
```

iOS

Likewise, for iOS, we will use the following code:

```
compile "com.badlogicgames.gdx:gdx-box2d:$gdxVersion"
natives "com.badlogicgames.gdx:gdx-box2d-platform:$gdxVersion:natives-ios"
```

HTML5

To use it with HTML5, we use the following code:

```
compile "com.badlogicgames.gdx:gdx-box2d-gwt:$gdxVersion:sources"
compile "com.badlogicgames.gdx:gdx-box2d:$gdxVersion:sources"
```

Tools

The Tools extension provides texture packing, font generation, and particle editor functionalities, only compatible with the desktop backend.

Core

```
compile "com.badlogicgames.gdx:gdx-tools:$gdxVersion"
```

Desktop

```
compile "com.badlogicgames.gdx:gdx-tools:$gdxVersion"
```

AI

Artificial Intelligence systems: steering behaviors, finite state machines, and behavior trees.

Core

Here is the code for the core:

```
compile "com.badlogicgames.gdx:gdx-ai:$gdxVersion"
```

Android

Similarly, for android, we use the following:

```
compile "com.badlogicgames.gdx:gdx-ai:$gdxVersion"
```

HTML

Lastly, for HTML, we use the following:

```
compile "com.badlogicgames.gdx:gdx-ai:$gdxVersion:sources"
```

Adding external repositories

It is possible to add extra repositories to Gradle to look for the files you need by adding them to the `allprojects` section. Gradle supports Maven- and Ivy-formatted repositories:

```
allprojects {
    ...

    repositories {
        ivy { url "https://some-ivy-repo.com/repo" }
        maven { url "https://some-maven-repo.com/repo" }
    }
}
```

Adding additional file dependencies

The library you want to use so desperately might not be in any Maven or Ivy repository. Is everything lost? Of course not! You can make projects depend on local files such as arbitrary JAR packages.

For instance, you can place the JAR files you need inside a `lib` folder in each project. Then, you will need to add the following entry to the `dependencies` section of the projects:

```
dependencies {
    compile fileTree(dir: 'libs', include: '*.jar')
}
```

Managing GWT dependencies

HTML5 projects will require extra attention when adding dependencies. The GWT compiler needs to know about the modules the application will use. This information needs to be specified in both the `GdxDefinition.gwt.xml` and `GdxDefinitionSuperdev.gwt.xml` files located in the class path. The following snippet shows a typical `gwt.xml` file highlighting the addition of the popular Universal Tween Engine dependency:

```
<module rename-to="html">
    <inherits name='com.badlogic.gdx.backends.gdx_backends_gwt' />
    <inherits name='com.cookbook.environment.EnvironmentTest' />
```

```
    <inherits name='aurelienribon.tweenengine'/>

        <entry-point class='com.cookbook.environment.client.GwtLauncher'
/>

        <set-configuration-property name="gdx.assetpath" value="../
android/assets" />
    </module>
```

The Box2D extension will require you to inherit from the following module.

```
    <inherits name='com.badlogic.gdx.physics.box2d.box2d-gwt' />
```

The Controllers extension will ask for the following module:

```
    <inherits name='com.badlogic.gdx.controllers.controllers-gwt' />
```

The AI extension will require the following:

```
    <inherits name='com.badlogic.gdx.ai' />
```

Managing GWT projects can be a bit fiddly, and we will cover this topic more thoroughly in the *Making libraries compatible with GWT* recipe of *Chapter 11, Third-party Libraries and Extras*.

Every time you add or update a dependency, it is advisable to rebuild the Gradle model so that everything is up to date and you can carry on working normally. Select **Gradle** and **Refresh All** from the project by right-clicking on the contextual menu.

There's more...

Telling Gradle to refresh a project's dependencies will automatically make the system download those that have changed when the dependency is a snapshot. For example, this is what happens with the Libgdx nightly builds:

```
    gdxVersion = "1.2.0"
```

However, you might want to force Gradle to redownload a specific dependency or even all of them. This can come in handy when a library changes, but the version number is still the same. Though rare, this can very well happen if someone makes a mistake.

Gradle downloads and puts dependencies in a .gradle directory inside the user's home folder. It is possible to delete either the whole folder or specific libraries to make Gradle download them again the next time it tries to build the project.

Digging a bit deeper, you can tell Gradle that a particular dependency is prone to change often. It will then check every 24 hours whether it has changed. If it has, it will redownload the dependency. This is achieved with the `changing` property:

```
dependencies {
    compile group: "group", name: "project", version: "1.1-SNAPSHOT",
changing: true
}
```

Once more, for further information on how to tune Gradle to your taste, refer to the official user guide.

See also

> ▶ If you want to know more about libraries and tools that work well with Libgdx and can help you in your game development adventure, do not forget to read *Chapter 11, Third-party Libraries and Extras*.

Using source control on a Libgdx project with Git

Writing software, in general, and making games, in particular, is a hard endeavor, which is why we should avoid unnecessary complications whenever we can using tools that will save us from despair. There are so many things that can go wrong during development; luckily for us, we can use source control as the first step to a better night's sleep.

What if your hard drive breaks, bursts in flames, or gets stolen? Yes, the right answer is continuous backups, tons of them, and then some more! Surely, online cloud storage services such as **Dropbox** or **Google Drive** provide this for you out of the box. They even let you share folders with others, which might lure you into thinking that it is a good way of working as a team, but it just stops cutting it the second things go a bit beyond trivial.

What if you come back home on a Saturday night after too many drinks and decide it is a great time to get some coding done? After all, you feel incredibly inspired! What follows is that you will wake up the next morning in sweat, tears and full of regret. Surely, Dropbox lets you revert changes on a per-file basis, but a lot of fiddling is required when the changes are spread across multiple systems, and you risk worsening things even more.

Finally, what if two members in your team make changes to the same file? Conflict solving in Dropbox is flaky at best; you will most likely enter the realms of hell in these cases. Manually merge two files every time this happens, and believe me, it will happen constantly, but this is not something you will enjoy.

Any good source control system gracefully solves each one of these little nightmares for you. A repository keeps track of every important file, and every time you make a set of changes, it is dead easy to create a new revision or snapshot of the whole project tree. These changes can be shared with your team members, and there is no problem in going back a few revisions whenever you realize a mistake has been made. Most source control systems also provide very intelligent mechanisms to merge files several people have modified.

After this little rant, it is time to proceed with the recipe. We will use Git to put only the essential files of our Libgdx project under source control, and in this way sleep a lot better at night. Keep in mind that the intent is neither to provide a detailed guide on how revision control works nor how to fully understand Git, but just the bare minimum to get you started.

> Why Git? Well, according to Linus Torvalds, if you do not use Git, you are ugly. For those who don't know him, Linus Torvalds is the father of both the Linux kernel and Git revision control system. He does not have a huge appreciation towards alternatives such as CVS or SVN. Check Linus' talk, as it is very interesting, at `http://www.youtube.com/watch?v=4XpnKHJAok8`.

Getting ready

First, you need to install the Git client on your computer, which was originally conceived as a command-line tool by Linus Torvalds. However, nowadays we have visual clients at our disposal, which make life much easier. On both Windows and Mac, I will personally recommend **SourceTree** because it is quite intuitive and has everything you are likely to need at hand. However, there are alternatives such as **Tortoise Git**. Both are free, and the latter is also completely open source. SourceTree's installer can be found on its official site at `http://sourcetreeapp.com`.

The package installation process varies across GNU/Linux distributions. In Debian-based distributions (most common ones), users can install the Git client using the command-line and `apt-get`:

```
sudo apt-get install git
```

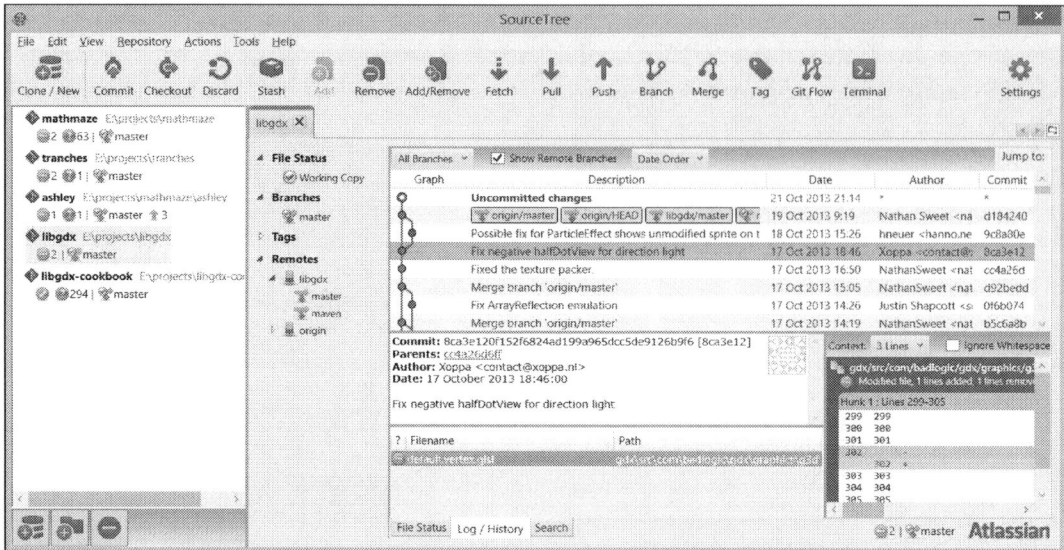

This is a program capture; the cropped text is not relevant

How to do it...

Every time you start a project, the first step should be to create a repository to keep track of everything that goes on with it. Services such as **GitHub**, **Gitorious**, and **Google Code** offer free repositories but require you to disclose the source. However, GitHub also allows you to create paid private repositories. **Bitbucket** is a competitive alternative if you seek a private repository at no cost. Last but not least, you can always host your own Git server at home, but then you will have to deal with problems such as backups, availability from the outside, and so on. Perform the following steps:

1. Choose your poison, and create an account and a repository to start with, such as:

   - GitHub, available at `http://github.com`
   - Gitorious, available at `http://gitorious.org`
   - Google Code, available at `http://code.google.com`
   - Bitbucket, available at `http://bitbucket.org`

2. The next step will be to clone your newly created repository so as to have a local copy to work with.

3. From SourceTree, click on **Clone/New**, select the **Clone Repository** tab, and enter the URL you received from the service of your choice.

4. After entering the destination path, you can simply click on **Clone**, and the empty repository will be available on the leftmost panel, as shown in the following screenshot:

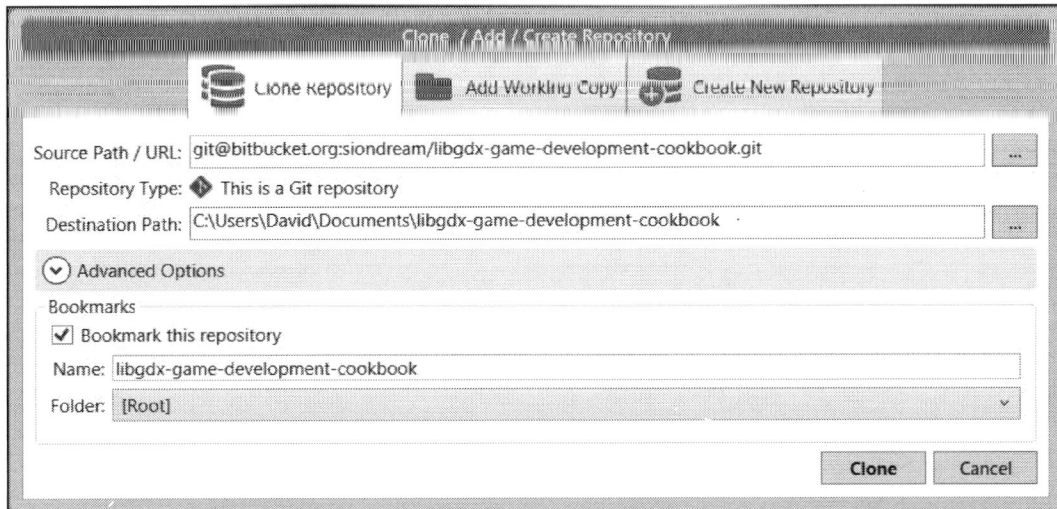

5. GNU/Linux users can get away with the following command:

    ```
    git clone <REPO-URL> <DESTINATION-FOLDER>
    ```

6. Have you already started working on your awesome game? Then, what you need to do is clone your brand new repository into an empty folder and pour all the project files there. Git requires an empty folder to either create or clone a repository.

7. With your repository selected on SourceTree, click on **Working Copy** and take a close look at the **Working Copy Changes** panel; there will be tons of files that are not under source control asking you to include them, as shown in the following screenshot:

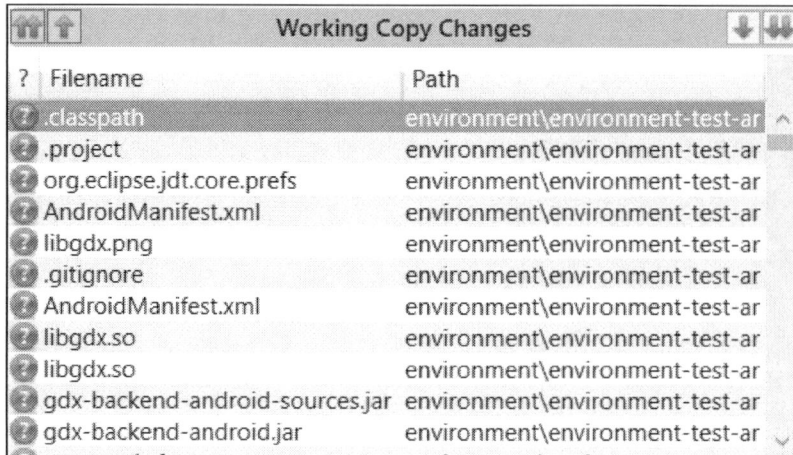

🏠🔼	Working Copy Changes	🔽🔽
?	Filename	Path
🔘	.classpath	environment\environment-test-ar
🔘	.project	environment\environment-test-ar
🔘	org.eclipse.jdt.core.prefs	environment\environment-test-ar
🔘	AndroidManifest.xml	environment\environment-test-ar
🔘	libgdx.png	environment\environment-test-ar
🔘	.gitignore	environment\environment-test-ar
🔘	AndroidManifest.xml	environment\environment-test-ar
🔘	libgdx.so	environment\environment-test-ar
🔘	libgdx.so	environment\environment-test-ar
🔘	gdx-backend-android-sources.jar	environment\environment-test-ar
🔘	gdx-backend-android.jar	environment\environment-test-ar

8. The list of candidates for addition, deletion, and modified files can also be queried from the following command line:

```
git status
```

We do not need all this nonsense! If you already compiled something, there will be tons of clutter that will certainly become a huge waste of cloud storage. Though this comes cheap these days, it will be painful to upload and download changes further down the line. Ideally, we only want to keep track of whatever is absolutely necessary for someone to download a snapshot from the other end of the world and be able to continue working normally.

Luckily enough, we can get rid of all the noise from `git status` and the **Working Copy Changes** panel by creating a `.gitignore` text file in the root folder of the repository with the following content:

```
bin/
target/
obj/
.gwt/
gwt-unitCache/
war/
gen/

*.class
```

It is time to add the `.gitignore` file to our repository. Perform the following steps:

1. From the **Working Copy Changes** panel, right click on the file and select **Add to Index**.

2. Then, click on **Commit**, add a meaningful message such as `Adds .gitignore file to make repository management easier.` and finish by clicking on the **Commit** button on the modal window, as shown in the following screenshot:

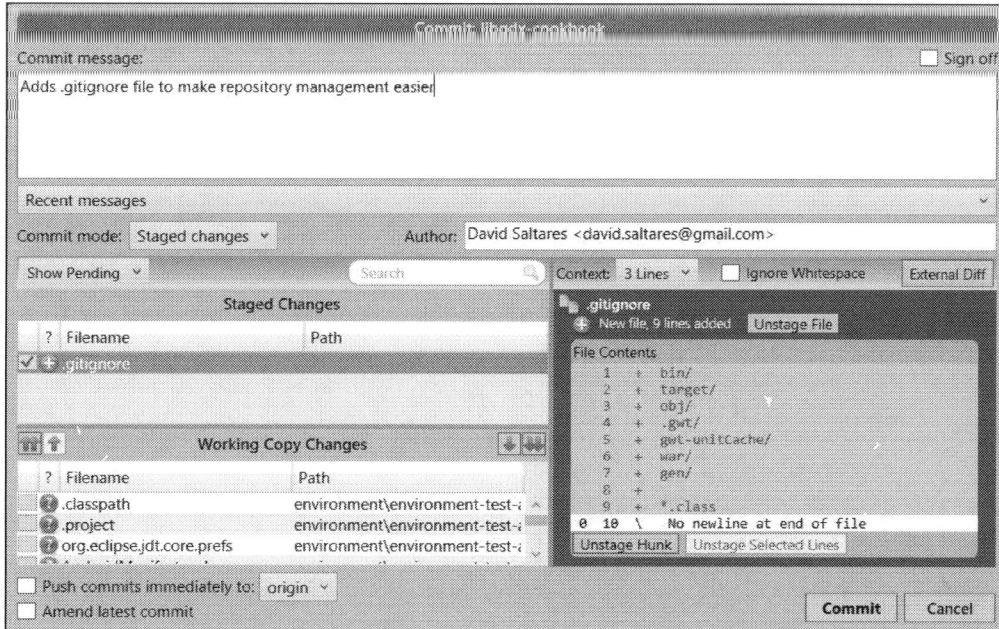

3. On the command line, it looks something like this:

```
git add .gitignore

git commit -m "Adds .gitignore file to make repository management
easier"
```

4. Now, you can safely proceed to add every remaining file and commit again. From GUI, follow the same process as with the `.gitignore` file. However, if you are a command-line lover, you can stage and commit all the files at once like this:

```
git add *

git commit -m "Adds project basic files"
```

Congratulations! Git is now keeping track of your project locally. Whenever you make changes, you simply need to add them again to the set of files about to be committed, and actually commit them. Obviously, you can achieve this with both the visual and command-line variants of the client.

> Writing meaningful commit messages might seem unimportant, but nothing is further away from the truth. Whenever you examine the history in search for the origin of a bug, you will want all the help you can get to understand what the person who made each commit was trying to do at that point in time.

It is time to push all the commits you have made from your local repository to the remote repository hosted by the provider of your choice. This is the way your teammates, and potentially the whole world in case the repository is public, will be granted access to the changes. Perform the following steps:

1. From SourceTree, click on **Push** and select the origin and destiny branches; typically, both will be named master. Once you are ready, click on **OK** and wait for the operation to finish, as shown in the following screenshot:

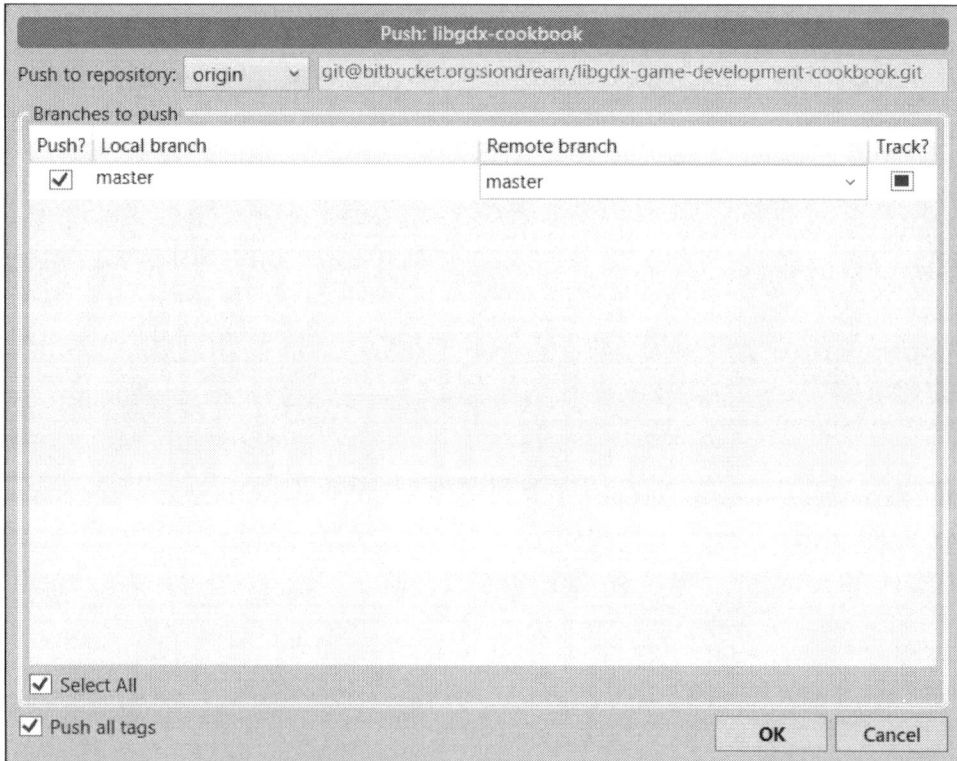

2. Here is the command-line version of the same song:

```
git push origin master
```

Let's imagine that our game developer buddies have been sweating blood to add new shiny features. Naturally, you are eager to check what they have been up to and help them out. Assuming they pushed their changes to origin, you now need to pull every new commit and merge them with your working branch. Fortunately, Git will magically and gracefully take care of most conflicts. Perform the following steps:

3. From *Repo Tree*, you can either click on the **Pull** button and select the remote repository and branch you are pulling from. For a simplistic approach, these will be **origin** and **master**. Once you are ready, click on the **OK** button, as shown in the following screenshot, and sit back and enjoy:

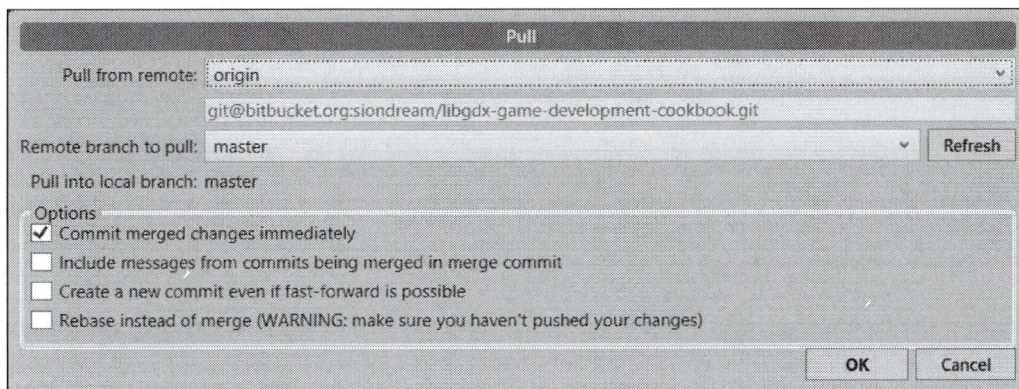

Pull		
Pull from remote:	origin	⌄
	git@bitbucket.org:siondream/libgdx-game-development-cookbook.git	
Remote branch to pull:	master ⌄	Refresh
Pull into local branch: master		

Options
- ✓ Commit merged changes immediately
- ☐ Include messages from commits being merged in merge commit
- ☐ Create a new commit even if fast-forward is possible
- ☐ Rebase instead of merge (WARNING: make sure you haven't pushed your changes)

OK Cancel

4. A pull operation can also be triggered from the command line:

```
git pull origin
```

> Sometimes, Eclipse will not be too happy after sudden external project modifications, and misbehave a little bit. If this happens, you just need to refresh the projects by selecting them, pressing *F5*, or restarting IDE.

How it works...

Git is a distributed revision control system. This means that, in principle, there is no central repository everyone commits to. Instead, developers have their own local repository containing the full history of the project.

The way Git keeps track of your files is quite special. A complete snapshot of all the files within the repository is kept per version. Every time you commit a change, Git takes a brand new picture and stores it. Thankfully, Git is smart enough to not store a file twice, unless it changes from one version to another. Rather, it simply links the versions together. You can observe this process in the following diagram:

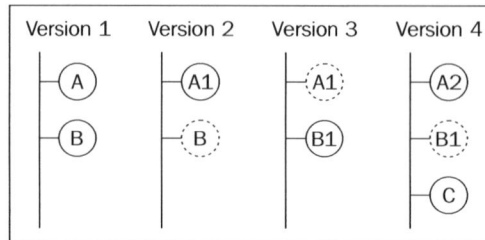

Version 1	Version 2	Version 3	Version 4
A	A1	A1	A2
B	B	B1	B1
			C

As per the previous diagram, Version 1 has two files, A and B. Then, a commit is made updating A, so Git stores the new file and creates a link to B because it has not changed. The next commit modifies B, so Version 3 stores this file and a link to the unchanged revision of A. Finally, Version 4 contains modifications to A, a link to B (unchanged), and the first revision of the newly created file C.

Basic operations

Most times you work with Git, you will operate locally because your repository contains everything that you need. It lets you check the full history, commit, and revert changes, among many others. This makes Git lightning fast and very versatile as it does not attach you to any Internet connection.

The typical usage of Git is as follows:

- Clone a remote repository and make it locally available with `git clone`
- Modify, add, or remove files
- Add files to the staging area for them to be committed to your local repository with `git add`
- Commit the files and create a new version within your local repository using `git commit`
- Receive changes from a remote repository with `git pull`
- Send your local changes to a remote repository with `git push`

Git branches

Though we didn't use them, the way to experience Git's true glory is through branching and merging. You can think of the history of your repository as a series of directory-tree snapshots linked together. A commit is a small object that points to the corresponding snapshot and contains information about its ancestors. The first commit will not have a parent and subsequent commits will have a parent, but when a commit is the result of merging several changes together, it will have several parents.

A branch is simply a movable pointer to one of these commits; you already know `master`, the default branch. The way we have been working, `master` will point to the last commit you made, as shown in the following diagram:

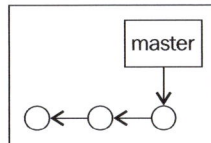

Branching in Git has a minimal overhead as the only thing it does is create a new pointer to a certain commit. In the following diagram, we create a new branch called `test`:

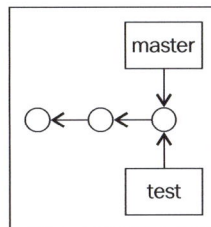

We can work on `test` for a while, go back to `master`, and then work on something different. Our repository will look something like this:

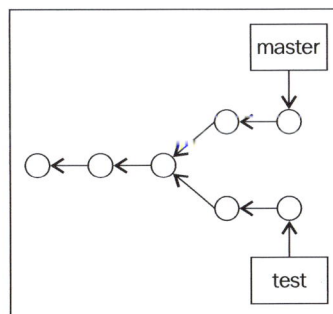

Someone in the team decides it is time to bring the awesome changes made on `test` over to `master`; it is now merging time! A new commit object is created, with the last commits from `master` and `test` as parents. Finally, the `master` branch pointer moves forward so that it points to the new commit. Easy as pie!

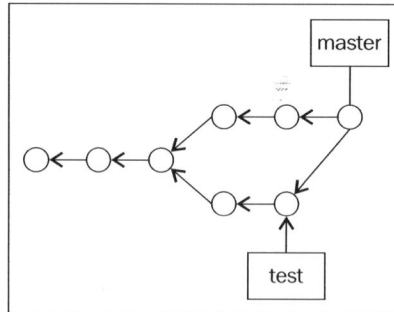

As we mentioned, this is not intended to be a comprehensive guide on Git but a mere introduction instead. If you are dying out of curiosity, I will wholeheartedly recommend Pro Git, which is freely available online under a Creative Commons license at `http://git-scm.com/book`.

Gitignore files

The `.gitignore` file we created earlier contains a list of rules that tell Git which files we are not interested in. Files under this branch of the directory tree that match the patterns and are not committed to the repository just yet, will not appear as candidates when running `git status` on the Source Tree **Working Copy Changes** panel.

Typically, you will want to ignore specific files, that is, every file with a specific extension or anything that is under a certain folder. The syntax for these, in the same order, is quite simple:

```
/game/doc/doc.pdf
*.jar
/game/game-core/bin
```

SourceTree lets us add files and paths to `.gitignore` very easily. Select the file you want to add to the ignore list from the **Working Copy Changes** panel, and right-click and select **Ignore**. A new modal window will appear giving you the options to ignore just this file, all the files with this extension, or everything placed under a certain folder from the file's path. Once you select the option you want, click on **OK**, as shown in the following screenshot:

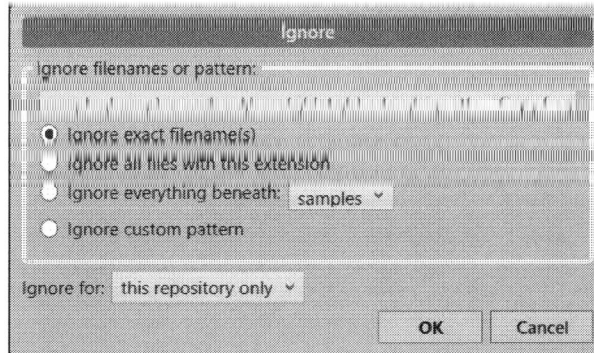

There's more...

This recipe was aimed at covering the very basics of the relationship between Libgdx and revision control systems. If you are interested in broadening your knowledge on the matter, read on.

Regardless of what Linus Torvalds might tell you, Git is not the only revision control system out in the wild, and it might not be the best fit in your case. The following are other alternatives:

- **Mercurial**: This is cross-platform, open source, and completely distributed, just like Git. It is available at `http://mercurial.selenic.com`.

- **Subversion**: This is also cross-platform and open source, but it's a centralized system. It is usually perceived as easier to learn than Git and works for most projects. However, it is much less flexible. It is available at `subversion.trigris.org`.

- **Perforce**: This is a proprietary centralized system, but free for up to 20 users. It is widely used in the games industry for its binary file management. It is available at `http://perforce.com`.

Pro Git is a freely available book on how to master the version control system. It is available at `http://git-scm.com/book`.

See also

The Libgdx community is built around Git and hosted on GitHub. The following recipes are highly related to this revision control system:

▶ The *Working from sources* recipe in *Chapter 13, Giving Back*

▶ The *Sending a pull request on GitHub* recipe in *Chapter 13, Giving Back*

Importing and running the Libgdx official demos

Libgdx comes with a few full games to serve as example projects. Developers are encouraged to check them out, try them, and read the source code. It is a fantastic way to learn how things are done the Libgdx way.

In this recipe, you will learn how to get and run the official demos.

Getting ready

You only need to make sure your development environment works. The process to get up and running is explained in the *Setting up a cross-platform development environment* at the beginning of this chapter.

How to do it...

There are eight official Libgdx demos. They are as follows:

▶ **Pax Britannica**: This is a one-button RTS available at `https://github.com/libgdx/libgdx-demo-pax-britannica`

▶ **Metagun**: This is a 2D platformer available at `https://github.com/libgdx/libgdx-demo-metagun`

▶ **Super Jumper:** This is a Doodle Jump clone available at `https://github.com/libgdx/libgdx-demo-superjumper`

▶ **Invaders:** This is a 2D Space Invaders clone available at `https://github.com/libgdx/libgdx-demo-invaders`

▶ **Vector Pinball**: This is a 2D pinball simulation using Box2D available at `https://github.com/libgdx/libgdx-demo-vector-pinball`

▶ **Cuboc**: This is a 2D platformer available at `https://github.com/libgdx/libgdx-demo-cuboc`

▶ **The Plane That Couldn't Fly Good**: This is a Flappy Bird clone available at
`https://github.com/badlogic/theplanethatcouldntflygood`

▶ **Very Angry Robots**: This is a 2D shooter platformer available at
`https://github.com/libgdx/libgdx-demo-cuboc`

We will work with Super Jumper, but the process is identical for any other project; just follow these steps:

1. Clone the repository using Git. The URL is available in the project page. Super Jumper's Git repository URL is `git://git.code.sf.net/p/libgdx/libgdx-demo-super-jumper.git`. If you do not know how to clone a Git repository, read the *Using source control on a Libgdx project with Git* recipe.

2. Import the project from its folder into Eclipse following the instructions in the *Setting up a cross-platform development environment* recipe.

3. Run each platform-specific project like any other Libgdx project.

Now, you can run Super Jumper, as shown in the following screenshot:

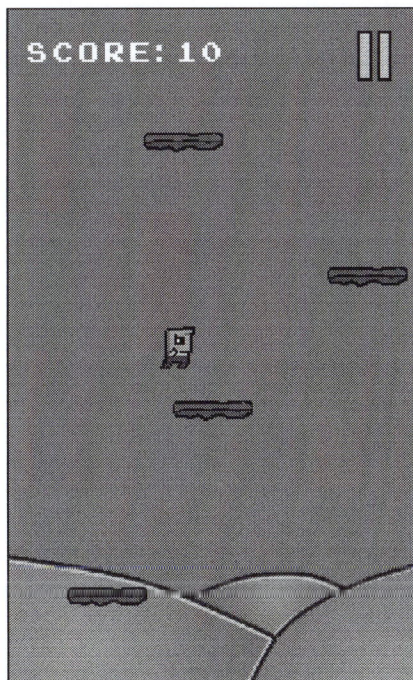

How it works...

All the Libgdx official demos use Gradle as a build system, so the process of importing them into an IDE, getting them to compile, and running them is exactly the same as we saw in the past.

As you progress through this book, it will be a great exercise to go back to the demos' source code and try to identify the concepts and techniques explained here.

There's more...

Luckily enough, the Libgdx community is big, active, and generous. This results in a great number of open source projects for people to study and learn from. Some of them can be found in the Libgdx gallery at `http://libgdx.badlogicgames.com/gallery.html`.

2
Working with
2D Graphics

In this chapter, we will cover the following recipes:

- ▶ Texture rendering with SpriteBatch
- ▶ More effective rendering with regions and atlases
- ▶ Taking advantage of Libgdx sprites
- ▶ Rendering sprite-sheet-based animations
- ▶ Understanding orthographic cameras
- ▶ Using ShapeRenderer for debug graphics
- ▶ Handling multiple screen sizes with viewports

Introduction

Games are interactive experiences that provide feedback to the player mainly through visual elements and audio cues. As a result, rendering becomes one of the most important pillars games are built upon. This chapter will take us on a journey through the basics of the Libgdx 2D graphics API.

You will learn how to efficiently render both static and animated sprites and handle the view with orthographic cameras. Moreover, we will present a series of solutions on how to deal with different screen sizes and resolutions, a very common problem when targeting tablets and phones.

Texture rendering with SpriteBatch

A texture is a bitmap image that gets applied to a surface through mapping. Rendering textures on the screen will be our first step in getting to know the Libgdx 2D graphics API. Once you learn a few simple operations with textures, you will be able to build relatively complex scenes for your games.

To illustrate the procedure, we are going to make use of a friendly caveman, who we will show at different positions, sizes, and orientations.

Getting ready

You need the `samples` projects to follow this recipe, so make sure you already have them in your Eclipse workspace. You will find the caveman texture in `data/caveman.png`, inside the `data` folder in the Android project.

How to do it...

The code for this recipe is hosted in the `SpriteBatchSample` class, which has the classic methods of an `ApplicationListener` interface implementation. Note that only the most relevant pieces of code are shown in this recipe as snippets; you can, however, study the full source. First of all, we are going to add a few static final fields to store configuration values for cleanliness:

```
private static final Color BACKGROUND_COLOR = new Color(0.39f, 0.58f,
0.92f, 1.0f);
private static final float WORLD_TO_SCREEN = 1.0f / 100.0f;
private static final float SCENE_WIDTH = 12.80f;
private static final float SCENE_HEIGHT = 7.20f;
```

The `BACKGROUND_COLOR` object is an object of the `Color` class, which is initialized with its RGBA components as float values ranging from 0.0 to 1.0. RGBA stands for red, green, blue, and alpha (transparency). In this case, we will be using light blue for the background. The `WORLD_TO_SCREEN` object will help us transform measures from world to screen and vice versa. The `SCENE_WIDTH` and `SCENE_HEIGHT` objects define the dimensions in world units of our scene. The scene dimensions refer to the space the camera will be able to focus on at one time.

Right after, we have some members that will actually do the scene composing and rendering jobs:

```
private OrthographicCamera camera;
private Viewport viewport;
private SpriteBatch batch;
private Texture cavemanTexture;
```

The `camera` member will help us define what portion of the world will be seen on the screen using an orthographic projection. As we will see later, the concept of a camera is pretty much parallel to that of the movies. For our resolution handling mechanism, we need a `Viewport` object. Render calls will be issued through `SpriteBatch`, which provides a simple mechanism to draw quads associated to textures with extreme efficiency. Finally, the crucial piece of this sample, we will use `cavemanTexture` to hold the image data of our little caveman.

Take a look at the `create()` method, where we construct a new `OrthographicCamera` object. Then, we proceed to create a new `Viewport` object with our scene dimensions, passing in the camera it will need to manage. We also instantiate a new `SpriteBatch` object. In the next step, we create a new `Texture` object using an internal handle pointing to the file data/caveman.png. Finally, we set the `Nearest` filter for our newly created texture, resulting in a pixelated effect when scaled. The code is as follows:

```
public void create() {
camera = new OrthographicCamera();
viewport = new FitViewport(SCENE_WIDTH, SCENE_HEIGHT, camera);
batch = new SpriteBatch();

cavemanTexture = new Texture(Gdx.files.internal("data/caveman.png"));
cavemanTexture.setFilter(TextureFilter.Nearest, TextureFilter.
Nearest);
}
```

> File handles will be covered in depth in *Chapter 5, Audio and File I/O*. We will take a look at texture filters later in this recipe.

The `Texture` and `SpriteBatch` objects allocate resources that need to be freed up so as to avoid nasty memory leaks. A very appropriate moment to do so is inside the `dispose()` method, because it is called right before the application instance is destroyed.

> More details on texture handling and other assets can be found in *Chapter 7, Asset Management*.

```
public void dispose() {
batch.dispose();
cavemanTexture.dispose();
}
```

> Imagine that every time we unload a level to go to the next one, we forget to dispose of the used resources. Our application will be continuously leaking non-negligible amounts of memory and could potentially crash due to an out of memory exception.

Now, let's take a look at the `render()` method, where the bulk of the action takes place:

```
public void render() { ... }
```

Every frame, we clear the screen with a background color and render our game scene from scratch. We can achieve that in two steps. First, we set the background color through the `glClearColor()` OpenGL function and then call the `glClear()` method to actually clear the render surface with the color we previously set:

```
Gdx.gl.glClearColor(BACKGROUND_COLOR.r, BACKGROUND_COLOR.g,
BACKGROUND_COLOR.b, BACKGROUND_COLOR.a);
Gdx.gl.glClear(GL20.GL_COLOR_BUFFER_BIT);
```

> In the good old days, computing power was extremely limited, and game developers could not afford to render the whole scene every frame. Those Spartan heroes would keep track of the elements that had moved from the previous frame. Then, they rendered the background on top of the element's old location and rendered it again where it was supposed to be.

Do not worry too much about camera operations just yet as they have their own recipe later in this chapter. Through the `setProjectionMatrix()` method, we tell the batch about the camera location, rotation, and zoom levels. This is done so it can properly transform the coordinates we pass during draw calls to actually draw elements according to what the camera is looking at:

```
batch.setProjectionMatrix(camera.combined);
```

The `SpriteBatch` class optimizes our render requests to achieve high performance even on mobile devices. In order for it to do its job, we are required to call its `begin()` method before any draw calls and its `end()` method once we are done. Please keep in mind that if we do not abide by this rule, a `java.lang.IllegalStateException` will be thrown:

```
batch.begin();
// draw scene
batch.end();
```

At last! we have now done all the necessary preparations to tell Libgdx to draw our friendly caveman on the screen. All drawing operations are done through one of the many versions of the `draw()` method in the `SpriteBatch` class. For educational purposes, we are going to use the most complete method.

For convenience, and to avoid repeating computations, we get the dimensions in pixels of the texture using the `getWidth()` and `getHeight()` methods. We also figure out the center of the texture counting from its bottom-left corner: this means the center would be at (`width / 2.0f`, `height / 2.0f`):

```
int width = cavemanTexture.getWidth();
int height = cavemanTexture.getHeight();
float originX = width * 0.5f;
float originY = height * 0.5f;
```

The first parameter we pass to `draw()` is the texture itself. Then, we pass in the world space coordinates where we want to draw. Considering the camera is centered at (0, 0) by default, we need to position our caveman at (`-originX`, `-originY`) starting from its center for it to appear right in the middle. The next parameters are the coordinates in pixels of our texture that we consider to be the origin starting from the bottom-left corner. As we said earlier, in our case, we want the origin to be the center of the texture. Then, we pass the dimensions of our texture and the scale along both axes (*x* and *y*).

A scale of `1.0f` indicates that we want to keep its size, `0.5f` would mean half the size, `2.0f` means double, and so on. However, we need to multiply our desired scale by `WORLD_TO_SCREEN` to transform our caveman from pixel units to world units. Next comes the rotation; note that the unit used is degrees and not radians. The parameters `srcX`, `srcY`, `srcWidth`, and `srcHeight` allow us to select a limited portion of the texture to be drawn; however, we want to show all of it. Finally, we can use two Booleans to flip the texture around its *x* or *y* axes:

```
// Render caveman centered on the screen
batch.draw(cavemanTexture,  // Texture
        -originX, -originY,  // x, y
         originX, originY,   // originX, originY
         width, height,  // width, height
         WORLD_TO_SCREEN, WORLD_TO_SCREEN,  // scaleX, scaleY
         0.0f,  // rot (degrees)
         0, 0,  // srcX, srcY
         width, height,  // srcWidth, srcHeight
         false, false);  // flipX, flipY
```

Inside `SpriteBatchSample`, we have four additional draw calls achieved with the same mechanism. However, these make modifications to our caveman by scaling him up/down, rotating him and flipping him around the *x* and *y* axes. Note that rotations are applied around the origin of the texture; in our case, it is the center, but it could very well be a corner or an arbitrary point.

The following screenshot shows the result of our demo:

Congratulations! Now you know how to use textures and manipulate them to build a scene.

How it works...

The Libgdx classes involved in rendering are pretty straightforward to use as you just saw. However, what happens under the hood is not quite as simple. We are now going to take a look at some of the basic concepts Libgdx uses, so you have a better understanding.

2D rendering using 3D techniques

Libgdx makes use of `OpenGL`, the well-known open source 3D graphics library. How come we use it for 2D applications too? Well, as a matter of fact, every Libgdx render operation takes place in 3D space. Three-dimensional vertices are sent to the graphics card regardless of whether we are working with 3D models or 2D textures. In our 2D context, `SpriteBatch` serves as an intermediary between our game logic and the rendering layer. It is responsible for sending quads with associated texture data to the graphics card. The vertices `SpriteBatch` sends to the GPU are laid on the same plane and rendered using an **orthographic projection**. This helps to make our scenes look bi-dimensional.

A **perspective projection** can also be used to render `SpriteBatch` objects, although the 2D effect would be lost.

The following figure illustrates how texture data is mapped to a tri-dimensional mesh that is rendered using an orthogonal projection:

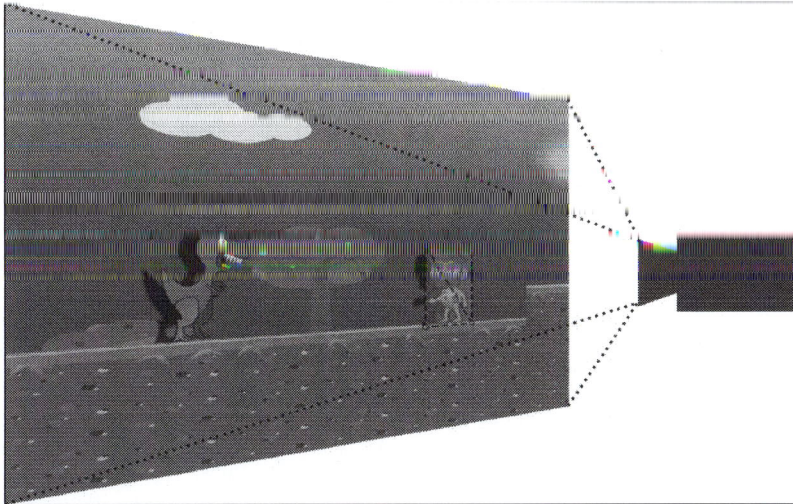

Coordinate system and camera setup

Knowing the coordinate system you are working with is paramount when modeling your game worlds. By default, Libgdx uses a **y-up** system. Looking at your screen, this means that positive *y* faces upwards and positive *x* grows to the right. When working with a batch, textures also have their origin at the bottom-left corner, with *y* facing upwards.

Interestingly enough, most 2D game libraries use a **y-down** approach, and you might feel a bit uncomfortable initially. Despite that, Libgdx lets you configure it to use a y-down approach; I would personally advise against this as it is the default in many subsystems. As much as you may be inclined to think otherwise, it is easier to adapt your brain to work with a y-up system; after all, it is how we all learned math.

When an `OrthographicCamera` is created, its origin, `(0, 0)`, is located at the center of the screen. The viewport in our example was `12.80` world units wide by `7.20` units high. This means that the four corners of the screen are located at `(6.40, 3.60)`, `(6.40, -3.60)`, `(-6.40, -3.60)`, and `(-6.40, 3.60)` if we enumerate them in clockwise order. Take a look at the following diagram for more clarity:

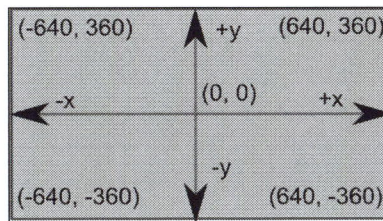

Assets location in Libgdx

Let's go back to the following line:

```
cavemanTexture = new Texture(Gdx.files.internal("data/caveman.png"));
```

The `Gdx.files.internal()` method returns a handle to a file that is expected to be found within the application bundle, as opposed to an arbitrary folder. Internal files need to be stored under the `assets` folder within the Android project. We already saw this in the previous chapter.

Draw order

Note that we do not send any depth values to `SpriteBatch` when rendering 2D images. There is no built-in depth sorting of sprites in Libgdx. Instead, elements are drawn on top of each other, according to the order they were asked to be drawn. This implies that if your gameplay needs to overlay entities according to their distance to the camera, you need to make sure you draw them first, so those that are closer stay on top.

You can easily achieve that by having some sort of rendering queue you push to from your game logic. Later on, the system sorts the queue using a z component you should have facilitated earlier and, ultimately, renders the images through `SpriteBatch`. The following diagram illustrates the process, assuming the bigger the entity z component is, the further away it is located:

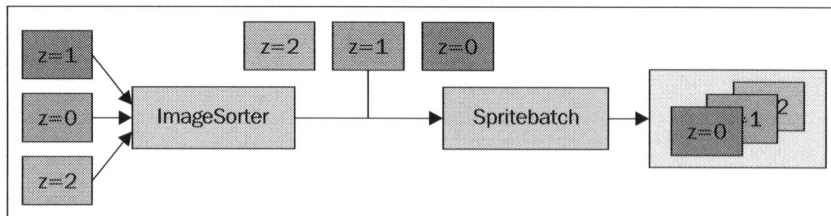

Texture filters

Right after we created our `cavemanTexture` object, we wrote the following line:

```
cavemanTexture.setFilter(TextureFilter.Nearest, TextureFilter.
Nearest);
```

Texture filters determine how image pixels are interpolated when scaled down or up. When a texture size is manipulated for rendering purposes, the system needs a way of reorganizing all its pixels, filling in the gaps when increasing size or erasing pixels when shrinking it. The `setFilter()` method precisely receives two parameters: upscale and downscale strategy respectively. The most common filters are as follows:

- ▸ `Nearest`: This chooses the closest pixel from the original image producing hard edges
- ▸ `Linear`: This interpolates the color of the surrounding pixels producing blurry images

The following cavemen portraits illustrate the differences between the `Nearest` and `Linear` filters, respectively. The first style usually works for 2D pixel art games while the latter is more common in textures for 3D games:

This image is purposely scaled up to show the difference between filters

There's more...

The `SpriteBatch` class also allows the user to set a tint color that will affect what the textures look like when rendered. This is done through the `setColor()` method and it affects all the following `draw()` operations. In the following example, we render our caveman with a cyan tone; but in order not to mess up our batch, we save its initial color with `getColor()` and restore it later when we are done:

```
oldColor.set(batch.getColor());
batch.setColor(Color.CYAN);
batch.draw(cavemanTexture, -200 - originX, -originY, originX, originY,
width, height, 1.0f, 1.0f, 0.0f, 0, 0, width, height, false, false);
batch.setColor(oldColor);
```

The result, while not spectacular, adds a little more variety to our scene. Color tints have multiple uses depending on your creativity. You could make a damage effect very easily by applying a red tint with variable alpha values over time on the character that is taking damage. Also, why not have enemies with different color tints to express different levels of power? Many games have done this in the past so as to avoid having to produce additional assets. Note that blending tints with images works better when the latter is grayscale. As you can see in the following figure, we added four new cavemen to `SpriteBatchSample`, tinted in cyan, red, green, and yellow:

[📝 Alpha equals transparency, which implies blending the two textures.]

You may have noticed in the previous snippet how we can use predefined color values. The `Color` class counts with multiple public final static fields to make life easier for us. Rather than defining a `Color` object and manually setting RGBA values, you can just type `Color.CYAN`. You can find the full list of predefined colors in the official API documentation at `http://libgdx.badlogicgames.com/nightlies/docs/api/com/badlogic/gdx/graphics/Color.html`.

The `SpriteBatch draw()` method has many versions we can use depending on our needs. Some of them are a lot simpler than the one we showed because they adopt default values for the missing parameters. The documentation can be found at `http://libgdx.badlogicgames.com/nightlies/docs/api/com/badlogic/gdx/graphics/g2d/SpriteBatch.html`.

See also

> ▸ In *Understanding orthographic cameras*, you will learn more about how to set up and manipulate cameras to visualize the 2D world

More effective rendering with regions and atlases

Creating `Texture` objects from different image files and rendering them with `SpriteBatch` is the most straightforward way of building scenes with Libgdx. However, it is far from being the most efficient one. Games are real-time, performance-critical applications, and writing efficient systems becomes even more important when dealing with resource-limited platforms such as tablets, phones, or browsers.

Surely drawing a handful of individual images is not going to make a massive impact when running the game on a high-end phone with a dedicated GPU. However, the landscape can rapidly change the second we add different backgrounds, dozens of different characters on screen, particle effects, and so on.

Luckily enough, it is fairly simple to set up our assets and rendering process so that it does the job amazingly fast. The key concept here is drawing thousands of little chunks from a massive texture is preferable than a few individual images. We will first pack all our game textures in a single big image so that we can then just draw portions of it.

Getting ready

The code for this recipe is in the `TextureAtlasSample.java` file within the
`[cookbook]/samples` folder. Make sure you have imported all the projects
contained within the aforementioned directory.

As part of the recipe, we are going to pack a collection of PNG images into a single one. The
individual images can be found in the `[cookbook]/samples/art/textureatlas` folder.
It contains a big background, our old friend the caveman, and a dangerous dinosaur.

How to do it...

Let's split the problem in two parts. First of all, we are going to pack our individual textures
into a single one. These uber textures are better known as atlases and come with a text file
to specify the rectangles that map to our old individual images. Secondly, we will show how
to use `SpriteBatch` to render sections of an atlas (`TextureRegion`) rather than complete
`Texture` objects.

Packing PNG files into an atlas

Fortunately, there are quite a few options when it comes to packing textures. The most
common ones are:

- **texturepacker-gui**: This option is written in Libgdx, which can be downloaded for free
  and is completely open source. It is available at `https://code.google.com/p/libgdx-texturepacker-gui/downloads/list`.

- **TexturePacker**: This option is commercially distributed but supports a wider variety
  of atlas file formats, so it can be used outside Libgdx. It is available at `http://www.codeandweb.com/texturepacker`.

However, for availability reasons, we are going to use the first of the two as it is more than enough for our purposes. They are both very similar anyway. The next screenshot shows the texturepacker-gui interface:

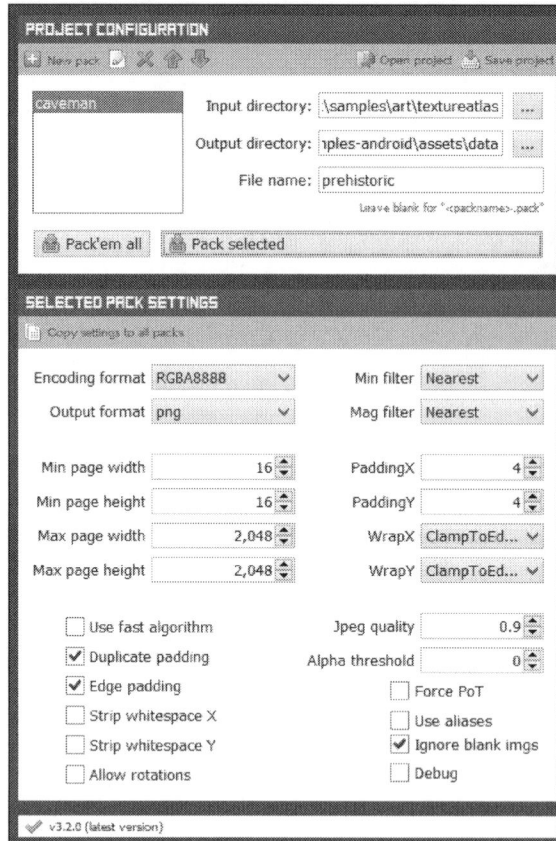

The following steps will help you pack your textures into an atlas:

1. Download the ZIP file, unpack it, and run the `gdx-texturepacker.jar` file.

2. Click on the **New pack** button and enter a name; for our example, we have used `caveman`.

3. Select the **Input directory** where all the images are located.

4. After that, proceed to select the **Output directory** where the uber texture and the atlas file will be saved. In our case, that is `[cookbook]/samples/samples-android/assets/data`. Remember that internal assets need to be located under the `assets` folder in the Android project.

5. Finally, select the **File name** value. This affects both the texture and the atlas file, which will adopt the `name.atlas` and `name.png` / `name.jpg` names, respectively.

    The lower panel helps us configure the packing process.

6. First of all, you can pick between PNG or JPG images with the **Output format** dropdown; although for 2D games, PNG compression offers better results most of the time.

7. On the right, you can use the **Min filter** and **Mag filter** dropdowns to determine what filter will be applied to the uber texture once it has been loaded in Libgdx.

8. Further down, you will find inputs to determine the allowed texture sizes. OpenGL 1 users need to tick the **Force PoT** checkbox. This is because, prior to OpenGL 2.0, every texture size needed to be a power of two (POT). Even though Libgdx now only runs on OpenGL 2.0 or later, it is still advisable to use POT textures, as some features require it.

    > POT textures have the advantage of being more efficient to render than those that do not have this property.

9. The **PaddingX** and **PaddingY** options establish the separation in pixels along the x and y axes between textures in the packed texture. When you also tick **Duplicate padding** and **Edge padding**, textures are extruded filling the separating space. This helps avoid rendering artifacts caused by interpolation issues.

10. The **Allow rotations** option becomes very useful when you are trying to pack too many textures, and the available space starts running short. Rest assured, they are automatically rotated back at load time.

11. Tick **Debug** if you want the software to render pink lines delimiting textures. This could be helpful to make sure the process has completed without any errors.

12. Once you are done tweaking the options, click on the **Pack'em all** button and both the new texture and the atlas text file will appear in the selected output folder.

You should have obtained something like the following screenshot:

Rendering regions of an atlas

We are going to examine the `TextureAtlasSample` code to discover how to render atlases so as to achieve a much better performance.

Our `TextureAtlasSample` needs several members to make the atlas magic happen. You are already acquainted with the camera, viewport, and batch trio. We now introduce the `TextureAtlas` class, which is used to hold the master texture data along with all its metadata to identify its portions. Each one of the members of type `TextureRegion` will help us cache our original images to treat them individually:

```
private OrthographicCamera camera;
private Viewport viewport;
private SpriteBatch batch;
private TextureAtlas atlas;
private TextureRegion backgroundRegion;
private TextureRegion cavemanRegion;
private TextureRegion dinosaurRegion;
```

The `create()` method is the place to load our texture atlas and fetch the references to the regions we are interested in. The `TextureAtlas` class constructor is identical to the `Texture` one, except that we now pass the `.atlas` file the packer software we created rather than the path to the image file. To initialize our regions, we call the `findRegion()` method of the `TextureAtlas` class passing in the name of the original image without its extension:

```
public void create() {
    ...

    // Load atlas and find regions
    atlas = new TextureAtlas(Gdx.files.internal("data/prehistoric.
atlas"));
    backgroundRegion = atlas.findRegion("background");
    cavemanRegion = atlas.findRegion("caveman");
    dinosaurRegion = atlas.findRegion("trex");
}
```

Atlases allocate memory to hold their associated texture data very much like `Texture` objects do. Therefore, it is polite to clean them up whenever we stop using them. Since we will render our images for as long as the example runs, we can only do this right before exiting, in the `dispose()` method:

```
public void dispose() {
    batch.dispose();
    atlas.dispose();
}
```

Finally, let's take a look at the pretty bit, the `render()` method. As in any classic Libgdx application, we clear the screen with a background color and set the camera combined matrix to `SpriteBatch` to appropriately transform our draw calls. To render the background centered on the screen, we first get its dimensions with the `getRegionWidth()` and `getRegionHeight()` methods. The camera is centered at (0, 0), so we need to render the background at negative half its width and negative half its height for it to also be centered.

The `SpriteBatch` class has quite a collection of overloaded `draw()` methods suitable for regions. In our case, we will go through the most complete one to illustrate all the possibilities. First of all, we pass in the region followed by its position in world units. Then, we indicate the local origin of the region starting from its bottom left corner. Now, we need to specify the dimensions of the region and the scale along both its axes (remember that you need to convert from world units to screen units here). Finally, we pass in the rotation in degrees:

```
public void render() {
    ...

    batch.begin();

    float width = backgroundRegion.getRegionWidth();
    float height = backgroundRegion.getRegionHeight();
    float originX = width * 0.5f;
    float originY = height * 0.5f;

    batch.draw(backgroundRegion,
            -originX, -originY,
            originX, originY,
            width, height,
            WORLD_TO_SCREEN, WORLD_TO_SCREEN,
            0.0f);

    // Render caveman and dinosaur at different positions
    ...

    batch.end();
}
```

The result, shown in the following screenshot, is a tricky situation for our caveman, since there is a dangerous-looking dinosaur staring right at him. As an exercise, you could render a crowded scene with both approaches, simple textures and atlases, measure the time it takes in each case, and see for yourself how much faster atlases are.

How it works...

Now that we have tackled how to make rendering more efficient, we are going to look at some of the mechanisms behind the principles we have built upon. First of all, we will learn how atlas files are structured, then we will see why atlases help with performance, and finally, we will comment on some of the limitations the approach presents.

Atlas file format

Take a look at this excerpt of the `prehistoric.atlas` file under the `[cookbook]/sample/samples-android/assets` folder:

```
prehistoric.png
format: RGBA8888
filter: Nearest,Nearest
repeat: none
caveman
  rotate: false
  xy: 1283, 320
  size: 83, 156
  orig: 83, 156
  offset: 0, 0
  index: -1
```

Nothing surprising, really; everything comes from what we established in the packer settings. The first line points to the master texture, which should be distributed along the atlas file. Then, the pixel format is specified; in this case, we tell Libgdx that the texture uses 8 bits per channel (red, green, blue, and alpha). Right after comes the filter to use when the image is downscaled and up-scaled respectively, and whether or not the texture should be repeated.

What follows is a list of the regions that compose the master texture. Every region starts with a name that is equal to that of the original texture minus the extension. Then, we can find parameters such as dimensions, position in the master texture, origin in the region local space, and offset. The two origin glyphs. Regions can be rotated to minimize space usage, which is also specified in the parameters.

How SpriteBatch works

The `SpriteBatch` class serves as an intermediary between your game code and the OpenGL API, which then communicates directly with the GPU. When you render a texture through a batch, the latter creates a quad and associates a set of texture coordinates to each one of the vertices that form the quad. As you keep rendering the same texture over and over again at different positions, the mesh of quads will grow. The moment you call the `SpriteBatch` `end()` method, the quads and their texture data are sent to OpenGL and, at last, rendered on the screen.

However, and here is the secret, every time you tell the batch to draw a different texture, it has to flush the previously built mesh to OpenGL and start from scratch. This is known as texture swapping and is a time-consuming operation. Now it becomes clearer how using a bigger texture and only drawing portions of it as we see fit can make such a great difference.

Imagine you have a background and 10 characters on screen. If each one of the entities has its own texture, the batch will need to swap textures nine times per frame and perform an additional flush operation after the call to `end()`. Nevertheless, if all those textures are packed, there will be exactly 0 texture swaps and only one draw call to OpenGL.

> We cannot forget that master textures take less disk space than individual images. While this may not be a huge deal on desktop, it becomes key for handheld devices. Bear in mind that phones tend to have less memory and download sizes are critical when not connected to a Wi-Fi network. Texture atlases are a win-win approach.

A note on texture size limitations

The biggest drawback of texture packing and atlases is that we cannot just sew all our game textures together regardless of the total size. The maximum supported texture size varies across devices and it can be queried using Gdx.gl20.GL_MAX_TEXTURE_SIZE:

```
int maxSize = Gdx.gl20.GL_MAX_TEXTURE_SIZE;
Gdx.app.log("TextureAtlasSample", "Max texture size: " + maxSize + "x"
+ maxSize);
```

There's more...

Remember how you can flip Texture objects when drawing through a SpriteBatch? You can also achieve the same effect with the TextureAtlas flip() method. It takes two Booleans, one per axis, horizontal and vertical respectively. Now add the following lines to our sample:

```
public void create() {
    ...

    // Flip caveman and dinosaur
    cavemanRegion.flip(true, false);
    dinosaurRegion.flip(true, false);
}
```

We would get the results shown in the following screenshot:

The SpriteBatch class also has several methods to draw TextureRegion objects; check the documentation at http://libgdx.badlogicgames.com/nightlies/docs/api/com/badlogic/gdx/graphics/g2d/SpriteBatch.html for the complete list.

Texture packing can be done programmatically with the `gdx-tools` extension. Every time we run our game, individual textures can be packed into atlases. This can streamline the content pipeline when developing a game, sparing us from having to manually generate the atlas. Read more about the `TexturePacker` class at the following URL:

https://github.com/libgdx/libgdx/wiki/Texture-packer

See also

> Continue to *Taking advantage of Libgdx sprites* to find out how to handle game characters more easily.

Taking advantage of Libgdx sprites

The `Texture` and `TextureRegion` objects have proven sufficient to render 2D game worlds, but Libgdx also offers the `Sprite` class to make our lives more enjoyable. The `Sprite` class is nothing less than a glorified `TextureRegion`, adding state properties such as color, position, scale, and rotation.

For this recipe's example, we have taken the jungle scene in `TextureAtlasSample` and added some modifications so we can play around with sprites. To begin with, Mr. Caveman will constantly follow the mouse. Whenever the user touches the screen or performs a left-click, the dinosaur will acquire a new color tint. Finally, the caveman will rotate upon scrolling and vary its size when scrolling while holding the right mouse button.

Getting ready

As always, import the sample projects into your Eclipse workspace.

How to do it...

As you will see in just a moment, sprites are extremely easy to use. Please focus your attention on `SpriteSample.java`. Besides the typical camera, viewport, and batch references, we have an atlas and, for each element in the scene, we have a `Sprite` member: `background`, `caveman`, and `dinosaur`. The `colors` array holds the list of tints to be applied to the dinosaur and `currentColor` keeps track of the color cycle:

```
private TextureAtlas atlas;
private Sprite background;
private Sprite dinosaur;
private Sprite caveman;
private Array<Color> colors;
private int currentColor;
```

Inside `create()`, our members are initialized. The `Sprite` class has many constructors, one of which only takes a `TextureRegion`; we pass the corresponding constructors to each one of the sprites. Later, we populate the `colors` array with a few values: white, black, red, green, and blue. The `setPosition()` method changes where the sprite's bottom-left corner is placed in the world space while the `setOrigin()` method establishes its center for rotation and scale operations. Finally, we tell Libgdx that we want `SpriteSample` to capture input events. The code is as follows:

```
public void create() {
    . . .

    atlas = new TextureAtlas(Gdx.files.internal("data/prehistoric.
atlas"));
    background = new Sprite(atlas.findRegion("background"));
    caveman = new Sprite(atlas.findRegion("caveman"));
    dinosaur = new Sprite(atlas.findRegion("trex"));

    background.setPosition(-background.getWidth() * 0.5f, -background.
getHeight() * 0.5f);
    caveman.setOrigin(caveman.getWidth() * 0.5f, caveman.getHeight() *
0.5f);
    dinosaur.setPosition(100.0f, -85.0f);

    currentColor = 0;
    colors = new Array<Color>();
    colors.add(new Color(Color.WHITE));

    . . .
}
```

We only need to worry about disposing `SpriteBatch` and `TextureAtlas` as sprites do not need any cleanup:

```
public void dispose(){
    batch.dispose();
    atlas.dispose();
}
```

In every game loop iteration, we transform the mouse/touch coordinates into the world space using `camera.unproject()` to place Mr. Caveman. We then proceed to render the game elements. Since `Sprite` holds state data, it knows how to draw itself, which is why we call its `draw()` method passing in the `SpriteBatch`:

```
public void render() {
    tmp.set(Gdx.input.getX(), Gdx.input.getY(), 0.0f);
    camera.unproject(tmp);
```

```
    caveman.setPosition(tmp.x - caveman.getWidth() * 0.5f, tmp.y -
caveman.getHeight() * 0.5f);

    ...

    batch.begin();
    background.draw(batch);
    caveman.draw(batch);
    dinosaur.draw(batch);
    batch.end();
}
```

When the user fires the `touchDown` event with `Buttons.LEFT`, we advance one position through the `colors` array and apply the tint to the dinosaur using `setColor()`:

```
public boolean touchDown (int screenX, int screenY, int pointer, int
button) {
    if (button == Buttons.LEFT) {
        currentColor = (currentColor + 1) % colors.size;
        dinosaur.setColor(colors.get(currentColor));
    }

    return true;
}
```

Upon mouse scrolling, we check whether or not the right mouse button is pressed, and if so, we scale the caveman using the `scale()` method; otherwise, we rotate him clockwise using the `rotate()` method:

```
public boolean scrolled (int amount) {
    if (Gdx.input.isButtonPressed(Buttons.RIGHT)) {
        caveman.scale(amount * 0.5f);
    }
    else {
        caveman.rotate(amount * 5.0f);
    }

    return true;
}
```

> Note that Libgdx angle-related operations work on degrees most of the time. If other systems within your game use radians, you can always convert values with `MathUtils.degreesToRadians` and `MathUtils.radiansToDegrees`.

After playing with the example for a bit, you can easily end up with a situation similar to the following screenshot:

How it works...

Essentially, the `Sprite` class makes it easier to manage visual entities in your game, rather than having to manage regions. To sum it up, it holds all the necessary data to model a texture quad that can be rotated, scaled, moved around, and tinted.

The `Sprite` class provides a ton of convenience methods to access and modify the state. The complete list is too vast to be pasted here. It is much more productive to check the official documentation at `http://libgdx.badlogicgames.com/nightlies/docs/api/com/badlogic/gdx/graphics/g2d/Sprite.html` to see what it can enable us to do.

There's more...

Let's dig into how we can use sprites to detect collisions between game objects and the design implications this approach entails.

Using bounds for collision detection

Many games need to perform some sort of collision detection. Even though you may not need all the fanciness provided by physics engines such as **Box2D**, you could still do with some simple polygon overlap tests. Luckily enough, we can check a sprite's bounding rectangle taking into account its full transform with `getBoundingRectangle()` and then call the `Rectangle overlaps()` method passing in another rectangle:

```
Rectangle cavemanRect = caveman.getBoundingRectangle();
Rectangle dinosaurRect = dinosaur.getBoundingRectangle();

if (cavemanRect.overlaps(dinosaurRect)) {
    // handleCollision();
}
```

Be aware that these are *axis-aligned bounding rectangles*, which means that if the objects are rotated, the bounding area could be a lot bigger than the sprite itself. This approach is extremely cheap but may not suit your needs. The following screenshot shows the potential inaccuracies of this approach:

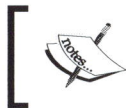

> The `Circle` class also has an `overlaps()` method to check for collisions. Moreover, the static `Intersector` class provides a huge variety of geometry tests that are worth checking.

See also

- ▶ More advanced collision detection is treated in *Chapter 10*, *Rigid Body Physics with Box2D*
- ▶ The *Component-based entity systems with Ashley* recipe in *Chapter 11*, *Third-party Libraries and Extras*, could give you more insight into how to manage your game entities

Rendering sprite-sheet-based animations

So far, we have seen how to render textures and regions of an atlas using Libgdx. Obviously, you can move textures around over time to produce a sense of motion. However, your characters will not come to life until they are properly animated. Not only should they go from one side of the screen to the other, but they should also seem like they are walking, running, or jumping according to their behavior.

Typically, we refer to characters physically moving in the game world as **external animation**, while we use the term **internal animation** to talk about their body movement (for example, lifting an arm).

In this recipe, we will see how to implement sprite-sheet-based animation using mechanisms provided by Libgdx. We will do so by populating our previous jungle scene with animated versions of the same characters. A sprite sheet is nothing more than a texture atlas containing all the frames that conform a character's animation capabilities. Think of it as having a notebook with drawings in a corner. If you go through the pages really fast, you will perceive the illusion of motion.

Behold our caveman's jumping skills! In the following screenshot, you can find an example of sprite-sheet-based animation, more specifically, a complete jump cycle:

Getting ready

You will also need the sample projects in your Eclipse workspace as well as `data/caveman.atlas` and `data/trex.atlas` along with their corresponding PNG textures.

How to do it...

First things first, the code for this recipe is located inside the `AnimatedSpriteSample.java` file, which uses the known `ApplicationListener` pattern. We are going to use two texture atlases created with texturepacker-gui that contain a walk cycle animation for our caveman and the merciless Tyrannosaurus Rex respectively. Feel free to catch up with atlases in the *More effective rendering with regions and atlases* recipe.

The caveman walk cycle can be found in the `caveman-sheet.png` and `caveman.atlas` files while the dinosaur is stored in the `trex-sheet.png` and `trex.atlas` files. As usual, everything is located under the `[cookbook]/samples/samples-android/assets/data` folder. Here is a simplified version of the dinosaur sprite sheet:

The `FRAME_DURATION` determines for how long (in seconds) we should show each frame of our sprite sheet before advancing to the next one. Since our animations were tailored to be displayed at `30` frames per second, we set it to `1.0f / 30.0f`:

```
private static final float FRAME_DURATION = 1.0f / 30.0f;
```

To achieve this demo's goal, we will need a camera, a sprite batch, and two atlases, one for the caveman and another one for the dinosaur walk cycles. We will also need a background texture if we do not want to show a dull black background:

```
private TextureAtlas cavemanAtlas;
private TextureAtlas dinosaurAtlas;
private Texture background;
```

Texture atlases simply provide a collection of texture regions we can retrieve by name. We need a way of specifying how our animations are going to be played. To that end, Libgdx provides us with the `Animation` class. Every distinct character animation should have its own `Animation` object to represent it. Therefore, we will use a `dinosaurWalk` instance and a `cavemanWalk` instance. Finally, we will control how our animations advance through the `animationTime` variable:

```
private Animation dinosaurWalk;
private Animation cavemanWalk;
private float animationTime;
```

Inside the `create()` method, we build the orthographic camera, rendering area, and batch. We also initialize our `animationTime` variable to `0.0f` to start counting from then onwards:

```
camera = new OrthographicCamera();
viewport = new FitViewport(SCENE_WIDTH, SCENE_HEIGHT, camera);
batch = new SpriteBatch();
animationTime = 0.0f;
```

The next step is to load the atlases for the caveman and the dinosaur as well as the background texture:

```
cavemanAtlas = new TextureAtlas(Gdx.files.internal("data/caveman.
atlas"));
dinosaurAtlas = new TextureAtlas(Gdx.files.internal("data/trex.
atlas"));
background = new Texture(Gdx.files.internal("data/jungle-level.png"));
```

Later, we retrieve the collection of regions of both our atlases using the `getRegions()` method and sort them alphabetically because that is how we have arranged the frames in our animation atlases.

```
Array<AtlasRegion> cavemanRegions = new
Array<AtlasRegion>(cavemanAtlas.getRegions());
cavemanRegions.sort(new RegionComparator());

Array<AtlasRegion> dinosaurRegions = new Array<AtlasRegion>(dinosaurAt
las.getRegions());
dinosaurRegions.sort(new RegionComparator());
```

> The `Array<T>` class is a Libgdx built-in container quite similar to the standard Java `ArrayList<T>`; the difference is that the former was written with performance in mind. Libgdx comes with more containers such as dictionaries, sets, binary arrays, heaps, and more. Using them rather than their standard counterparts is more than advisable, especially if you are targeting mobile devices.

The `RegionComparator` class is nothing more than a convenience inner class to sort our `AtlasRegion` arrays. `AtlasRegion` inherits from `TextureRegion` featuring additional data related to its packaging. In this case, we are interested in its name member so as to be able to sort the images alphabetically:

```
private static class RegionComparator implements
Comparator<AtlasRegion> {
    @Override
    public int compare(AtlasRegion region1, AtlasRegion region2) {
        return region1.name.compareTo(region2.name);
    }
}
```

It is now time to create the `Animation` instances. The constructor takes the frame duration, `Array<TextureRegion>`, representing all the frames that form the animation and the playback mode. Just like the name hints, `PlayMode.LOOP` makes an animation play over and over again. We will learn more about other play modes later on in this recipe. The code is as follows:

```
cavemanWalk = new Animation(FRAME_DURATION, cavemanRegions, PlayMode.
LOOP);
dinosaurWalk = new Animation(FRAME_DURATION, dinosaurRegions,
PlayMode.LOOP);
```

Finally, we position the camera to be at half its width and height so we can see the background properly, which will be rendered with its bottom-left corner at the origin:

```
camera.position.set(VIRTUAL_WIDTH * 0.5f, VIRTUAL_HEIGHT * 0.5f,
0.0f);
```

We do not want to be leaking memory all over the place. That would be disgusting and unacceptable! That is why we make sure to dispose of all the resources in the conveniently named `dispose()` method of our `ApplicationListener`:

```
@Override
public void dispose() {
    batch.dispose();
    cavemanAtlas.dispose();
    dinosaurAtlas.dispose();
    background.dispose();
}
```

Finally, we get to the key bit, the `render()` method. As usual, we first clear the screen with a black background color and set the viewport, that is, our rendering area in screen space. The next step is to increment our `animationTime` variable with the time that has passed since our last game loop iteration. We can get such information from `Gdx.graphics.getDeltaTime()`. To prepare the terrain for rendering, we update the camera matrices and frustum planes, set the sprite batch projection matrix, and then call `begin()`.

Which frame shall we draw? That is a good question. Luckily enough, as long as we provide `animationTime`, the `Animation` class has all the information it needs to figure it out: the list of frames, the frame time, and the playback mode. We can call `getKeyFrame()` passing in the time in seconds to obtain the frame to draw each frame and give it to the batch `draw()` method. That way, we can draw our two animated characters along the background texture. Easy as pie. The code is as follows:

```
public void render() {
    ...

    animationTime += Gdx.graphics.getDeltaTime();

    batch.begin();

...

    TextureRegion cavemanFrame = cavemanWalk.
getKeyFrame(animationTime);
    width = cavemanFrame.getRegionWidth();
    height = cavemanFrame.getRegionHeight();
    float originX = width * 0.5f;
    float originY = height * 0.5f;

    batch.draw(cavemanFrame,
            1.0f - originX, 3.70f - originY,
            originX, originY,
            width, height,
            WORLD_TO_SCREEN, WORLD_TO_SCREEN,
            0.0f);

    ...

    batch.end();
}
```

Now you can see our caveman and the dinosaur in motion!

> Animations can be flipped by calling `flip()` in the region
> returned by `getKeyFrame()`. This will toggle the flip state
> of the region, so avoid doing it for every frame or you will
> cause the sprite to flicker.

How it works...

The implementation of the `Animation` class is extremely simple, but it does a great job in helping us introduce animated characters in our games using sprite sheets. See for yourself by reading its implementation in the Libgdx GitHub repository. You will find that reading the Libgdx source at `https://github.com/libgdx/libgdx/blob/master/gdx/src/com/badlogic/gdx/graphics/g2d/Animation.java` is actually a great way of learning how it works internally; do not let it scare you away.

It holds a low-level Java array of `TextureRegion` references, the frame duration parameter, and caches the whole animation duration. The main part of the action takes place in the `getKeyFrameIndex()` method. It simply grabs the current frame index by dividing `stateTime` over `frameDuration`. Then, it accesses the region's array depending on the animation `PlayMode`. It makes sure not to pick an invalid frame and returns the appropriate index. Obviously, if you call the `getKeyFrame()` method directly, you will obtain the region straightaway.

There's more...

So far, we have seen the most basic operation you can do using the `Animation` class, simply retrieving the current frame on each iteration of the game loop for rendering purposes. However, if you want to use this system in slightly more complex situations, you will need further control. In this section, we will cover what different playback modes are at our disposal, how to check when a one-shot animation is done, and how to manage complex characters with tons of animations.

Using different play modes

`Animation` supports different ways of sequencing frames, which can be set and retrieved on a per instance basis through the `setPlayMode()` and `getPlayMode()` methods respectively. These take and return one of the `PlayMode` enumerated type values. Here is the complete list:

- `PlayMode.NORMAL`: This sequentially plays all the animation frames only once
- `PlayMode.REVERSED`: This plays all the animation frames once in reverse order
- `PlayMode.LOOP`: This continuously plays all the animation frames

▶ `PlayMode.LOOP_REVERSED`: This continuously plays all the frames in reverse order

▶ `PlayMode.LOOP_RANDOM`: This picks a random frame every time from the available ones

Checking when an animation has finished

Usually, we want to play certain animations in an infinite loop for as long as an action is being carried out, a character running for example. However, other animations should only be played once per trigger, such as a sword slash attack. It is very likely that we require to know which such animation has finished playing to allow the character to do something else. The `IsAnimationFinished()` method returns `true` when the given animation is finished provided it is played in `PlayMode.NORMAL` or `PlayMode.REVERSED` mode and with the looping flag set to `false`.

Handling a character with many animations

By now, you have probably figured out that having `Animation` objects hanging around is not very scalable when implementing a full game with dozens of characters. Also, manually providing the frames for every animation in code could become a truly gargantuan task. There is a need for some sort of abstraction and data-driven approach.

You could define your animated characters in XML or JSON providing all the necessary data to build a set of `Animation` objects. Here is a hypothetical example for our caveman:

```
<?xml version="1.0" encoding="UTF-8"?>
<animatedCharacter atlas="data/caveman.atlas"
          frameDuration="0.03333" >

    <animation name="idle" mode="loop" >
       <frame region="caveman0001" />
       <frame region="caveman0002" />
       <frame region="caveman0003" />
       ...
    </animation>

    <animation name="walk" mode="loop"> ... </animation>
    <animation name="jump" mode="normal">   ... </animation>
</animatedCharacter>
```

Naturally, you would need some code to manage all this in the game. Here is a skeleton of what could be an `AnimatedCharacter` class that reads the previous file format and loads the information into a dictionary of animation names to `Animation` objects. It also contains information of the current animation and the play time. The only thing it really does is provide a way of setting the current animation by name, controlling its play state, and retrieving the frame that should be shown at a given point in time.

Implementation details are left to you, but it should be pretty straightforward. The code is as follows:

```
public class AnimatedCharacter
{
    private ArrayMap<String, Animation> animations;
    private float time;
    private Animation currentAnimation;

    public AnimatedCharacter(FileHandle file);
    public void update(float deltaTime);
    public AtlasRegion getCurrentFrame();
    public String getAnimation();
    public void setAnimation(String name);
    public void setPlaybackScale(float scale);
    public void stop();
    public void pause();
    public void play();
}
```

See also

▶ To animate some game elements such as items and UI, you can also use interpolations. To know more, check out the *Smooth animations with Universal Tween Engine* recipe in *Chapter 11, Third-party Libraries and Extras*.

▶ Sprite sheet animations are often enough, but skeletal-based animations offer much cleaner results and a ton of other features worth considering. Go to the *Skeletal animations with Spine* recipe in *Chapter 11, Third-party Libraries and Extras*, to read more on the topic.

Understanding orthographic cameras

Very much like in films, Libgdx uses the concept of a camera as a tool to visualize the world. Throughout this recipe, we will learn how to wield the features of orthographic cameras, which make 2D scene rendering a much more enjoyable endeavor.

Among the topics shown, we can highlight camera sizes, movement, and zooming. This time around, in our example, we will load a massive texture and allow the user to move around, zooming in and out with both keyboard and touch controls. Naturally, in a real-life situation, you would have a level made out of chunks rather than a big texture.

Getting ready

Just make sure you already have the sample projects in your Eclipse workspace.

How to do it...

To start working with orthographic cameras, please open the `OrthographicCameraSample.java` file, which contains an implementation of our familiar friend, the `ApplicationListener` interface.

First of all, we define constants for the camera movement speed, area of the screen that will be touchable, zoom change speed, and zoom limits:

```
private static final float CAMERA_SPEED = 2.0f;
private static final float CAMERA_ZOOM_SPEED = 2.0f;
private static final float CAMERA_ZOOM_MAX = 1.0f;
private static final float CAMERA_ZOOM_MIN = 0.01f;
private static final float CAMERA_MOVE_EDGE = 0.2f;
```

For our example, we will use `OrthographicCamera` and `SpriteBatch` objects to render the 2D scene. The `levelTexture` object will reference our big texture data and, as in previous recipes, `viewport` will be used to define the drawable area of the screen. The `Vector3` object will represent the touch coordinates of the user interacting with the screen:

```
private OrthographicCamera camera;
private Viewport viewport;
private SpriteBatch batch;
private Texture levelTexture;
private Vector3 touch;
```

Within the `create()` method, we build new instances for our member variables. We use the default camera constructor since we are going to let `Viewport` handle its size. `Viewport` takes the camera dimensions in world units and the camera it will manage. In our case, a world unit equals 100 screen units, as indicated by the `WORLD_TO_SCREEN` constant. We also create objects for `Viewport` and `SpriteBatch`.

The next step is to load the `data/jungle-level.png` texture into a `Texture` object and apply the `Nearest` filter so it does not become blurry when zooming in. Note that this is just a matter of personal taste; you might want to use `Linear` if you prefer the results it offers.

Our image will be rendered at `(0.0f, 0.0f)` with its bottom-left corner as its local origin. For us to avoid showing black areas, we need to position the camera correctly. A camera's local origin is always its center, so we need to make it half its size. The code is as follows:

```
public void create() {
    camera = new OrthographicCamera();
```

```
    viewport = new FitViewport(SCENE_WIDTH, SCENE_HEIGHT, camera);
    batch = new SpriteBatch();
    touch = new Vector3();

    levelTexture = new Texture(Gdx.files.internal("data/jungle-level.
png"));
    levelTexture.setFilter(TextureFilter.Nearest, TextureFilter.
Nearest);

    camera.position.x = SCENE_WIDTH * 0.5f;
    camera.position.y = SCENE_HEIGHT * 0.5f;
}
```

Just before exiting, we need to get rid of the resources used by the sprite batch and the texture using their `dispose()` methods:

```
public void dispose() {
    batch.dispose();
    levelTexture.dispose();
}
```

Now, let's take a look at the `render()` method, where the bulk of the action takes place. The first step is to clear the background color. This time we select a solid black for the background; it is not going to be shown anyway. We are going to manipulate our camera over time using the Libgdx input system. To achieve a uniform effect, we need to consider the time between frames. The `Gdx.graphics.getDeltaTime()` method returns the time in seconds that has passed since the last frame:

```
float deltaTime = Gdx.graphics.getDeltaTime();
```

The following code detects whether the arrow keys are pressed and moves the camera along its *x* and *y* axis at `CAMERA_SPEED` pixels per second when appropriate. `Gdx.input.isKeyPressed()` receives a key value and returns a Boolean indicating the state of such a key:

```
if (Gdx.input.isKeyPressed(Keys.LEFT)) {
    camera.position.x -= CAMERA_SPEED * deltaTime;
}
else if (Gdx.input.isKeyPressed(Keys.RIGHT)) {
    camera.position.x += CAMERA_SPEED * deltaTime;
}

if (Gdx.input.isKeyPressed(Keys.UP)) {
    camera.position.y += CAMERA_SPEED * deltaTime;
}
else if (Gdx.input.isKeyPressed(Keys.DOWN)) {
    camera.position.y -= CAMERA_SPEED * deltaTime;
}
```

Neither phones nor tablets have keyboards, which means that if we are to support them, we need to consider touchscreens. The following fragment of code detects whether or not the user is touching the screen. If so, we get the touch point coordinates in screen pixel units with `Gdx.input.getX()` and `Gdx.input.getY()`. The `unproject()` method of the `OrthographicCamera` class takes touch coordinates and converts them to world coordinates using the camera transform. Touch coordinates are y-down, with the origin located at the top left of the screen. We will only move the camera in a certain direction when the user has touched the screen close to the edges:

```
if (Gdx.input.isTouched()) {
    touch.set(Gdx.input.getX(), Gdx.input.getY(), 0.0f);
    camera.unproject(touch);

    if (touch.x > VIRTUAL_WIDTH * (1.0f - CAMERA_MOVE_EDGE)) {
        camera.position.x += CAMERA_SPEED * deltaTime;
    }
    else if (touch.x < VIRTUAL_WIDTH * CAMERA_MOVE_EDGE) {
        camera.position.x -= CAMERA_SPEED * deltaTime;
    }

    if (touch.y > VIRTUAL_HEIGHT * (1.0f - CAMERA_MOVE_EDGE)) {
        camera.position.y += CAMERA_SPEED * deltaTime;
    }
    else if (touch.y < VIRTUAL_HEIGHT * CAMERA_MOVE_EDGE) {
        camera.position.y -= CAMERA_SPEED * deltaTime;
    }
}
```

Later, we check the state of the keys *Page Up* and *Page Down* and make the camera zoom in or out respectively:

```
if (Gdx.input.isKeyPressed(Keys.PAGE_UP)) {
    camera.zoom -= CAMERA_ZOOM_SPEED * deltaTime;
}
else if (Gdx.input.isKeyPressed(Keys.PAGE_DOWN)) {
    camera.zoom += CAMERA_ZOOM_SPEED * deltaTime;
}
```

We do not want the camera to move too far away so as to avoid running out of texture. This means we are forced to clamp its position:

```
MathUtils.clamp(value, min, max);
```

This utility function comes in very handy. We pass in a `value` and the bounds (`min`, `max`) we want to constraint said `value` to. The return `value` will be `min` or `max` if the original number was out of bounds or the `value` itself if it falls between `min` and `max`.

The maximum camera position will be the size of the texture in world units minus half the size of the camera. This works for both the *x* and *y* axes with its width and height, respectively. The minimum position will be half the camera size. Anything beyond those limits would show black areas. Note that we multiply by the zoom level as this affects how much we can see:

```
float halfWidth = VIRTUAL_WIDTH * 0.5f;
float halfHeight = VIRTUAL_HEIGHT * 0.5f;

camera.position.x = MathUtils.clamp(camera.position.x, halfWidth *
camera.zoom, levelTexture.getWidth() * WORLD_TO_SCREEN - halfWidth *
camera.zoom);
camera.position.y = MathUtils.clamp(camera.position.y, halfHeight *
camera.zoom, levelTexture.getHeight() * WORLD_TO_SCREEN - halfHeight *
camera.zoom);
```

> Note that we have been using multiplications by 0.5f to express divisions by 2. That is because multiplication is a lot faster than division.

The next step is to do the same thing with the zoom level. We want to limit it so we cannot zoom out too much that we can see black areas, nor zoom in too much that we invert the image:

```
camera.zoom = MathUtils.clamp(camera.zoom, CAMERA_ZOOM_MIN, CAMERA_
ZOOM_MAX);
```

Once we have finished manipulating the camera, we need to call its `update()` method. This triggers a recalculation of its projection and view matrices and the frustum planes. All those fancy terms basically mathematically define the state of the camera so the renderer knows how things would look through its eyes.

Then, we call `setProjectionMatrix()` on the batch passing the combined camera matrix. This makes the batch aware of the camera configuration, so it can transform the geometry we send accordingly:

```
camera.update();
batch.setProjectionMatrix(camera.combined);
```

Finally, we begin the sprite batch render process, draw the texture at the origin, and end the batch:

```
batch.begin();
batch.draw(levelTexture, 0.0f, 0.0f);
batch.end();
```

When running the sample, you should see something similar to the following screenshot:

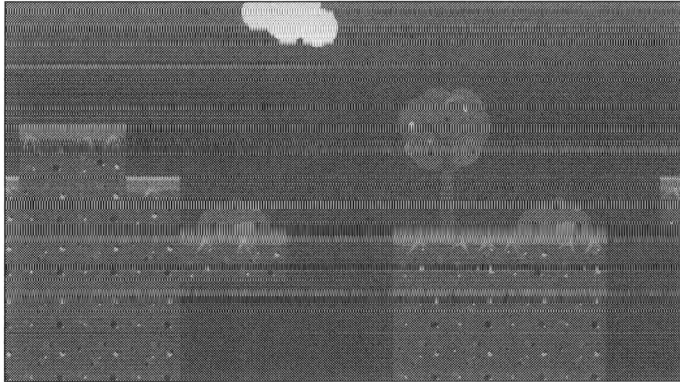

How it works...

The following diagram illustrates in a very straightforward manner the setup we put together in the previous example. The big arrows represent the world axis. You can observe the texture with its bottom-left corner at `(0, 0)`. The camera uses the scene dimensions `12.8 x 7.2` and we position it at half its width and height to avoid showing nontextured areas. Increasing the x component of the camera position moves it to the right, while doing the same with its y component moves it upwards. We have added coordinates for all the camera view plane corners in world units for clarity:

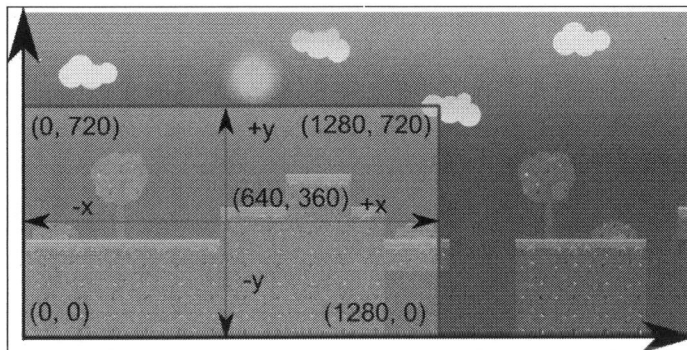

There's more...

We have seen how to create, move, and zoom cameras to control what can be seen in our scene. Cameras give us great power, which can be used to achieve a couple of tricks such as rendering UI on top of the game world or implementing split screen modes.

Rendering UI on top of the game world

Our camera moves around constantly, and so do other camera systems in most games. However, we often need to draw static elements on top of the game world that should stay where they are at all times. The HUD (heads up display) could be the most glaring example. Health bars, current score, or power meters should not be part of the world and hence should be left behind as we move.

A perfectly valid and simple solution is to have two `OrthographicCamera` objects. The first one could use world units and helps us render the scene and characters while the other one may use virtual pixel units and will serve us to render UI elements. Each camera would have a matching viewport.

The following code fragment illustrates the process of creation and usage of two cameras, one to render the game world and the other to do the same with the UI:

```
// create()
camera = new OrthographicCamera();
cameraHUD = new OrthographicCamera();

viewport = new FillViewport(SCENE_WIDTH, SCENE_HEIGHT, camera);
viewportHUD = new FillViewport(VIRTUAL_WIDTH, VIRTUAL_HEIGHT,
cameraHUD);

// render()

// Render game scene
camera.update();
batch.setProjectionMatrix(camera.combined);
batch.begin();
// ...
batch.end();

// Render UI elements
cameraHUD.update();
batch.setProjectionMatrix(cameraHUD.combined);
batch.begin();
// ...
batch.end();
```

> When modeling a game world, it is a lot easier to work in real units such as meters. Physics libraries, for instance, tend to work with the international metric system (although this can be adjusted). However, for UI-related work, we are much better off using pixels. We can also make the UI independent from asset sizes by scaling them to fit some given virtual dimensions.

Split screen

Many PC and console games split the screen to allow two or more players locally when the game characters are too far away to have just one camera. Shooters and racing games are genres that have made extensive use of this technique, especially before the online gaming boom.

The following diagram shows how two viewports are used to achieve split screen gameplay:

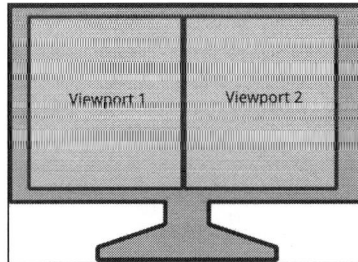

Split screen mode is achieved by having more than one viewport. That is, the available screen space is divided between the players and rectangles are created to model the dimensions and positions of each one of them. Several cameras are in place looking at different areas of the game world.

In a situation where we need to deal with two players, we would need two `Rectangle` objects, `viewport1` and `viewport2`, as well as `camera1` and `camera2` objects. We may also have a `camHUD` object. Every frame, if a camera has changed, we will update the cameras to show their associated player's perspective. In the `render()` method, we render the full scene twice.

When the application calls `resize()`, we need to make sure we update the viewport with half the width to leave room for both the viewports at the same time. We also need to position them correctly:

```
public void render() {
    // Player 1
    camera1.update();
    batch.setProjectionMatrix(camera1.combined);
    batch.begin();
    ...
    batch.end();

    // Player 2
    camera2.update();
    batch.setProjectionMatrix(camera2.combined);
    batch.begin();
    ...
    batch.end();
```

```
    // HUD
    cameraHUD.update();
    batch.setProjectionMatrix(cameraHUD.combined);
    batch.begin();
    ...
    batch.end();
}
```

Needless to say, this practice is computationally expensive since it renders the whole scene once per player. Some games are used to lower the rendering quality to allow multiple players in their local split screen modes.

See also

> ▸ Check the *Handling multiple screen sizes with viewports* recipe to know more about cameras and how to handle scene visualization with different screen resolutions across devices

Using ShapeRenderer for debug graphics

As your project grows in size and complexity, more bugs and glitches will appear. Regardless of how brilliant you are, this is inevitable. Traditional debugging techniques such as logging and stepping through code instructions are extremely helpful, but sometimes they are not the best when it comes to detecting issues in visually rich real-time applications, such as video games. This is especially true when you have many game objects on screen, which could lead to conditional breakpoints hell.

Sometimes it is a lot easier just to render some extra information on top of the game world. When you think your entities are not drawn at the right places, why not add a grid showing the world axis and units? Maybe adding circles at the agent's coordinates would help in narrowing the problem down. Imagine that the enemies in your top-down action game are moving in a strange way, why not draw their paths as line segments to find out whether the problem lies within the path finder or the path follower code?

Debug graphics can be a true life saver.

In this recipe, we will wield the tools Libgdx provides to add debug rendering in order to detect potential problems. The scope does not allow us to have a real-life game with debug graphics on. Instead, we will draw geometric shapes at arbitrary positions to illustrate how the system works. Later on, you can wire the procedure into your game to show useful information about your entities.

We will render the following:

> ▸ A grid showing the world axis
> ▸ Some circles, rectangles, and triangles

- ▸ The y = x2 function formed by line segments
- ▸ Arbitrary points

Obviously, you will not want to show all the available debug information at all times because it will clutter the screen rather quickly. In our example, the user will be able to toggle between several options to select what they want to display.

Getting ready

To follow this recipe, make sure the sample projects are already set in your Eclipse workspace.

How to do it...

For this recipe, you will find an example in the `ShapeRendererSample.java` file, which is nothing more than our classic `ApplicationListener` implementation.

First of all, we define some members that will help us with our debug graphics endeavor. We need `OrthographicCamera`, a viewport, and a `ShapeRenderer` object, which will actually do the heavy lifting:

```
private OrthographicCamera camera;
private Viewport viewport;
private ShapeRenderer shapeRenderer;
```

In order to enable rendering of different bits, we have a set of Booleans that will change the value on user key presses:

```
private boolean drawGrid = true;
private boolean drawFunction = true;
private boolean drawCircles = true;
private boolean drawRectangles = true;
private boolean drawPoints = true;
private boolean drawTriangles = true;
```

Finally, we have an array of floats that will contain the data for the y = x2 function. There is no need to allocate and calculate the array every time:

```
private float debugFunction[];
```

In the `create()` method, we instantiate our `camera`, `viewport`, and `shapeRenderer` objects.

We also create the array of floats and initialize its values. We are going to draw the function in the interval [-10, 10], and the required format asks for pairs of (x, y) values. That is why we need to allocate memory for 40 elements. The loop simply iterates the array inserting the function values.

Lastly, we set the camera position to be the origin, log the instructions to toggle the various options, and tell Libgdx we want `ShapeRendererSample` to capture input events through the `Gdx.input.setInputProcessor()` method:

```
public void create() {
    ...

    shapeRenderer = new ShapeRenderer();

    debugFunction = new float[40];

    for (int x = -10; x < 10; ++x) {
        int i = (x + 10) * 2;
        debugFunction[i] = x;
        debugFunction[i + 1] = x * x;
    }

    ...
}
```

The `ShapeRenderer` class implements the `Disposable` interface, and that hints that it requires us to do some cleanup when we stop needing it. In our case, we call its `dispose()` at the end of the application life cycle:

```
public void dispose() {
    shapeRenderer.dispose();
}
```

The actual debug rendering takes place in the `drawDebugGraphics()` function, which gets called from render. First, we inform our `shapeRenderer` about the camera projection matrix, so it knows how to transform the coordinates for the elements we pass in world space to screen space:

```
shapeRenderer.setProjectionMatrix(camera.combined);
```

The `ShapeRenderer` class works in a similar way to `SpriteBatch`, in that we need to enclose our render operations between calls to `begin()` and `end()`. However, now we also need to declare the `ShapeType` we are going to use when we begin the render process. It is possible to make `ShapeRenderer` use a specific color with the `setColor()` method.

Rendering lines

First of all, we render our grid as long as `drawGrid` is set to `True`, for which we call `begin()` passing in the `ShapeType.Line` mode. The axis will be drawn in red while the rest of the lines will be drawn in white. For every line, we call the `line()` method, which takes four floats representing the two points needed to define a segment: `x1`, `y1`, `x2` and `y2`. In the example source code, you will also find two for loops to render the horizontal and vertical lines of the grid:

```
if (drawGrid) {
    shapeRenderer.begin(ShapeType.Line);

    shapeRenderer.setColor(Color.RED);
    shapeRenderer.line(-SCENE_WIDTH, 0.0f, SCENE_WIDTH, 0.0f);
    shapeRenderer.line(0.0f, -SCENE_HEIGHT, 0.0f, SCENE_HEIGHT);

    ...

    shapeRenderer.end();
}
```

If `drawFunction` is `True`, we start a new draw operation with `ShapeType.Line`. We could have used the `line()` method in a loop again and manually sent the segments that conform the function. Luckily, we can just pass in an array of floats (with *x*, *y* pairs) to the `polyline()` method:

```
if (drawFunction) {
    shapeRenderer.begin(ShapeType.Line);
    shapeRenderer.setColor(Color.ORANGE);
    shapeRenderer.polyline(debugFunction);
    shapeRenderer.end();
}
```

Rendering circles

We continue by rendering a few circles at arbitrary places. This time, we use `ShapeType.Filled` in the `begin()` method to draw solid circles, not just the contours. Then, we call `circle()` passing the point (x, y), the radius, and the number of segments to approximate the circle shape:

```
if (drawCircles) {
    shapeRenderer.begin(ShapeType.Filled);
    shapeRenderer.setColor(Color.CYAN);
    shapeRenderer.circle(5.2f, 3.1f, 2.3f, 30);
    ...
    shapeRenderer.end();
}
```

Rendering rectangles

For the rectangles, we will also use `ShapeType.Filled`. The `rect()` method counts with several versions, but in our case, we pass the bottom-left corner of the rectangle (*x, y*), the dimensions (width, height), the origin in case we rotate it (*x, y*), and the rotation in degrees. The origin is relative to the bottom-left corner of the rectangle:

```
if (drawRectangles) {
    shapeRenderer.begin(ShapeType.Filled);
    shapeRenderer.setColor(Color.GREEN);
    shapeRenderer.rect(7.2f, 2.4f, 3.3f, 2.8f, 0.0f, 0.0f, 45.0f);
...
    shapeRenderer.end();
}
```

Rendering points

The `ShapeRenderer` class also helps us visualize points with more than single pixels; you can use `ShapeType.Line` and the `x()` method to draw two crossing-line segments at the specified coordinates (*x, y*) with the given radius:

```
if (drawPoints) {
    shapeRenderer.begin(ShapeType.Line);
    shapeRenderer.setColor(Color.MAGENTA);
    shapeRenderer.x(-5.0f, 0.0f, 0.25f);
...
    shapeRenderer.end();
}
```

Rendering triangles

Finally, we can also draw triangles. In this case, we only want the outline, so we use the `ShapeType.Line` mode. The `triangle()` function takes six arguments representing three points: x1, y1, x2, y2, x3, and y3:

```
if (drawTriangles) {
    shapeRenderer.begin(ShapeType.Line);
    shapeRenderer.setColor(Color.BLUE);
    shapeRenderer.triangle(-16.1f, -5.2f, -14.0f, -2.1f, -13.4f, 3.8f);
    shapeRenderer.end();
}
```

> Note that certain shapes such as circles, rectangles, and arbitrary polygons are compatible with both `ShapeType.Line` and `ShapeType.Filled`. Feel free to use either depending on whether you are only interested in the outline or a solid color shape.

The `keyDown()` method is called every time the user presses a key. Inside, we check whether keycode matches one of the keys we are interested in and change the value of the corresponding `boolean`:

```
public boolean keyDown (int keycode) {
    if (keycode == Keys.G) {
        drawGrid = !drawGrid;
    }
    else if (keycode == Keys.F) {
        drawFunction = !drawFunction;
    }
    else if (keycode == Keys.C) {
        drawCircles = !drawCircles;
    }
    else if (keycode == Keys.R) {
        drawRectangles = !drawRectangles;
    }
    else if (keycode == Keys.P) {
        drawPoints = !drawPoints;
    }
    else if (keycode == Keys.T) {
        drawTriangles = !drawTriangles;
    }

    return true;
}
```

The result is not pretty, but it will surely help you debug your games and live more comfortably:

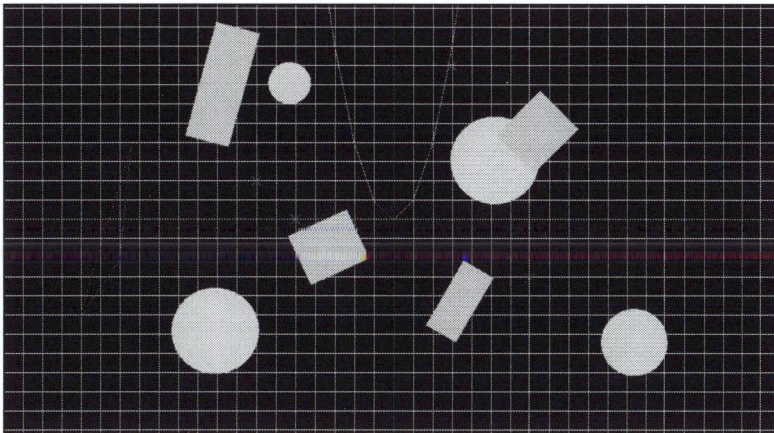

How it works...

The `ShapeRenderer` class draws shapes in batches to increase performance, very much like `SpriteBatch`. You can gather together all your shapes and send them all at once to the graphics card as long as you group them between the `begin()` and `end()` method invocations. Remember that it is significantly faster to send a lot of information to the GPU once rather than communicating many times with small sets of instructions.

In this case, it is not possible to bundle shapes using different draw methods: `ShapeType.Line`, `ShapeType.Point`, or `ShapeType.Filled`. This is because, internally, `ShapeRenderer` uses the OpenGL primitive draw methods, and these force you to send either points, segments, or triangle strips. The `ShapeRenderer` class is not extremely fast, but you should not worry because this is only intended to be used for debug graphics anyway. Ideally, debug graphics code should be disabled somehow or stripped away in release builds.

There's more...

Other shapes are available from `ShapeRenderer`; the complete collection adds arcs, cones, ellipses, and polygons with an arbitrary number of vertices:

```
void arc(float x, float y, float radius, float start, float angle);
void cone(float x, float y, float z, float radius, float height);
void ellipse(float x, float y, float width, float height);
void polygon(float[] vertices);
```

See also

- ▶ Logging and debugging an application in Eclipse are covered in the *Understanding the project structure and application life cycle* recipe in *Chapter 1, Diving into Libgdx*
- ▶ If you want to know more about what is going on under the hood, you may be interested in the *Profiling your application using Visual VM* recipe

Handling multiple screen sizes with viewports

The diversity of devices users play games on is vast and overwhelming, especially when targeting different platforms including phones, tablets, and browsers. This presents a lot of challenges for developers. Hundreds of different specs, processing power, screen sizes, APIs... It is a real mess. When it comes to games, it is not only the programmers who are affected, but designers, animators, and artists are also affected. The same level may not look the same on two devices and both level layout and assets need to cater for that.

Nowadays, it is not rare at all to find a situation like the one shown in the following figure:

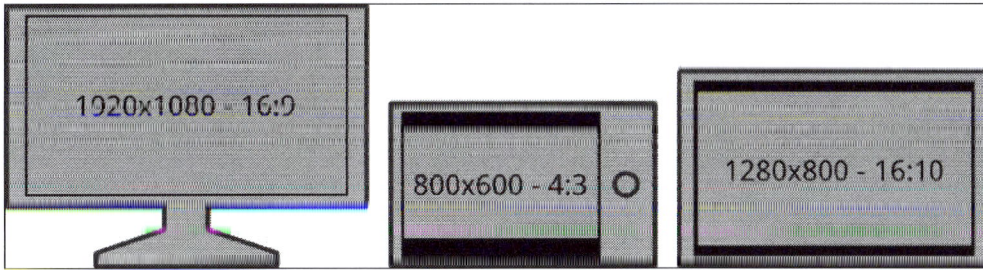

There is a range of strategies to tackle the varying screen resolution and different aspect ratios problem. Unsurprisingly, Libgdx has an out-of-the-box solution for this covering a subset of these strategies. Fortunately enough, its flexibility lets you implement your own in case your requirements are special.

These strategies involve adjusting the portion of the screen we render to as well as manipulating the resulting image to make it fit. Throughout this recipe, we will give you the tools to handle multiple aspect ratios, and it is up to you to decide which method suits you best, as each one of them has both perks and drawbacks.

The example for this recipe only consists of rendering a simple background texture that covers the entirety of our camera plane while offering Libgdx's strategies to handle multiple aspect ratios. The user can tap the screen or click the mouse to cycle through them and observe how the different approaches affect the end result.

Handling multiple screen sizes can be a pain, but you would be surprised how easy Libgdx makes the whole process.

Getting ready

The sample projects are required to follow this recipe. We will be working with the `ViewportSample.java` file.

How to do it...

Even though every recipe so far uses this approach to handle multiple screen sizes, we have not gone into a lot of detail about how it works until now. Feel free to dig into any of those `ApplicationListener` implementations; for simplicity, `SpriteBatchSample` might be a good choice.

You already know that game worlds are typically modeled using world units. When working with user interfaces and screen sizes, an option is to assume the screen to have a set of specific dimensions in virtual screen units. The aspect ratio strategy will then work out how to map the virtual-screen-sized image to the actual screen.

> When using world units, everything within game logic and assets will work on that basis. However, touch events come in actual screen pixel units, so be aware you need to unproject the touch coordinates from the screen to the world using your camera transform.

Let's start off with some static constants that define the screen dimensions we want to support:

```
private static final float MIN_SCENE_WIDTH = 800.0f;
private static final float MIN_SCENE_HEIGHT = 600.0f;
private static final float MAX_SCENE_WIDTH = 1280.0f;
private static final float MAX_SCENE_HEIGHT = 720.0f;
```

The `Viewport` class is the base class from which the different resolution handling strategies inherit. Since we want the user to cycle the basic ones, Let's add an `ArrayMap` of `String` and `Viewport` pairs, so we can associate each viewport with its name. We also need the current viewport index, a camera, a batch, and a texture object:

```
private ArrayMap<String, Viewport> viewports;
private int currentViewport;
```

The `create()` method contains no magic; we instantiate our camera, batch, and texture and call the `createViewport()` and `selectNextViewport()` methods. Remember to dispose of the batch and texture once you are done, in the `dispose()` method:

```
@Override
public void create() {

    ...

    createViewports();
    selectNextViewport();

    ...
}
```

The `createViewports()` method populates the associative array. Here you will find the list of built-in Libgdx Viewport implementations, which, like we said, are the ones responsible for handling multiple resolutions. Their constructors typically take scene dimensions in world units and the camera instance they are supposed to work with. Finally, we initialize our `currentViewport` Index to `-1`:

```
private void createViewports() {
    viewports = new ArrayMap<String, Viewport>();
    viewports.put("StretchViewport", new StretchViewport(MIN_SCENE_
WIDTH, MIN_SCENE_HEIGHT, camera));
    viewports.put("FitViewport", new FitViewport(MIN_SCENE_WIDTH, MIN_
SCENE_HEIGHT, camera));
    viewports.put("FillViewport", new FillViewport(MIN_SCENE_WIDTH,
MIN_SCENE_HEIGHT, camera));
    viewports.put("ScreenViewport", new ScreenViewport(camera));
    viewports.put("ExtendViewport (no max)", new ExtendViewport(MIN_
SCENE_WIDTH, MIN_SCENE_HEIGHT, camera));
    viewports.put("ExtendViewport (max)", new ExtendViewport(MIN_SCENE_
WIDTH, MIN_SCENE_HEIGHT, MAX_SCENE_HEIGHT, MAX_SCENE_WIDTH, camera));

    currentViewport = -1;
}
```

The `render()` method contains no secrets either. We simply render our texture centered on the screen as one would normally do:

```
@Override
public void render() {
    ...

    batch.setProjectionMatrix(camera.combined);
    batch.begin();
    batch.draw(background, -background.getWidth() * 0.5f, -background.
getHeight() * 0.5f);
    batch.end();
}
```

Every time the actual screen dimensions change, the `resize()` method is called with the new size in pixel units. The current viewport needs to be notified of such an event to recalculate its strategy. Remember that `resize()` also gets called right after `create()`:

```
@Override
public void resize(int width, int height) {
    viewports.getValueAt(currentViewport).update(width, height);
}
```

In order to cycle through our collection of viewports whenever the user taps the screen or clicks the mouse, we need to override the touchDown event and call the selectNextViewport() method:

```
@Override
public boolean touchDown (int screenX, int screenY, int pointer, int
button) {
    selectNextViewport();
    return true;
}
```

The selectNextViewport() function simply increments the currentViewport index, being careful not to escape the bounds of the viewport's ArrayMap. It needs to call an update on the newly selected viewport so as to let it adjust its strategy for the actual screen dimensions. Finally, it outputs the name of the viewport:

```
private void selectNextViewport() {
    currentViewport = (currentViewport + 1) % viewports.size;
viewports.getValueAt(currentViewport).update(Gdx.graphics.getWidth
(), Gdx.graphics.getHeight());
    Gdx.app.log(TAG, "selected " + viewports.
getKeyAt(currentViewport));
}
```

That is all! Feel free to launch the application on your desktop and resize the window with different viewports selected. This way, you will yourself experience how they behave. Nevertheless, we will cover them in great detail soon.

How it works...

Allow us to go through the list of built-in Viewport implementation describing their behavior.

The StretchViewport class takes a virtual screen's dimensions and always stretches them to fit the screen. The plus side is that you will not find any black bars, but if the virtual ratio significantly differs from the one on the screen, the image can potentially appear greatly distorted, as shown in the following screenshot:

The `FitViewport` class will scale the image to fit the screen while maintaining the virtual aspect ratio. Even though the image will not be distorted, black bars will appear if both aspect ratios do not match. Our rendered result will always be centered on the screen, as shown in the following screenshot:

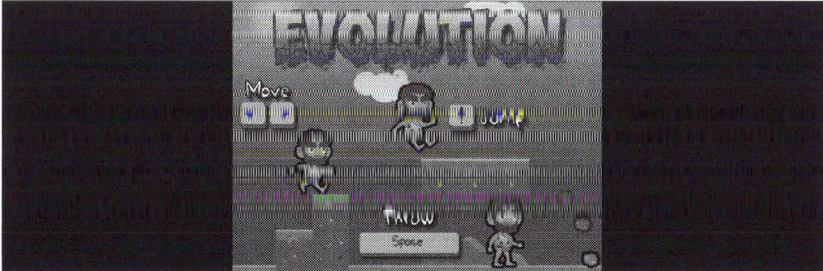

The `FillViewport` class keeps the aspect ratio, just like `FitViewport`. However, it does not introduce black bars, which means parts of the resulting image will end up being cut off, as shown in the following screenshot. Depending on the type of application you are working on, this may or may not be acceptable:

The `ScreenViewport` class will always match the actual screen dimensions, so no scaling is applied and you will not see any black bars at all, as shown in the following screenshot. Similar to `FillViewport`, this may affect gameplay since players with different screen sizes will see different portions of the world:

The `ExtendViewport` class is possibly the most complete and flexible solution. It keeps the provided aspect ratio without introducing black bars by extending the visible portion of the world in one direction. When a maximum set of dimensions is provided to the `ExtendViewport` dimensions, black bars will be added when the screen aspect ratio falls out of the supported range, as shown in the following screenshot:

Internally, the `Viewport` class calls `glViewport()` inside its `update()` method. This is a direct OpenGL call that defines the drawable area of the screen in screen pixel units.

There's more...

We have already seen how cool `Viewport` is, but there is more to it. Here we are going to take a look at some of the additional functionality you can get out of it.

Getting the most out of Viewport

Sometimes, a viewport can map the camera to the screen in such a way that black bars or *gutters* appear. We can get the view positioning information as well as the virtual sizes through the following methods:

```
int getViewportHeight()
int getViewportWidth()
int getViewportX()
int getViewportY()
float getWorldHeight()
float getWorldWidth()
```

The `Viewport` class provides access to the camera it manages with `getCamera()`. However, we can directly call some camera operations such as *projecting* a world point onto the screen and *unprojecting* a screen point to the world. These are extremely useful to work out the world coordinates that correspond to a tap event, so the user can interact with the world elements, for instance:

```
Vector2 project(Vector2 worldCoords)
Vector3 project(Vector3 worldCoords)
Vector2 unproject(Vector2 screenCoords)
Vector3 unproject(Vector3 screenCoords)
```

For further details on the `Viewport` API, please check the official documentation at `http://libgdx.badlogicgames.com/nightlies/docs/api/com/badlogic/gdx/utils/viewport/Viewport.html`.

Working with two cameras and viewports

Most games render a world through a dynamic camera that moves around and, on top of that, some static elements such as buttons, labels, and icons. These are typically known as the HUD (heads up display). The world camera works with world units while the HUD uses virtual screen units.

This is usually achieved through the use of a pair of two cameras and viewports, as we saw in the *Understanding orthographic cameras* recipe.

However, there is an important "gotcha". `Viewport` calls the OpenGL `glViewport()` function that establishes the area of the screen we render to, potentially leaving black bars. What happens when we have two viewports with different world units? Let's say meters for the simulation and pixels for the UI. Every time we update the second viewport on the resize method, it will stomp the previous setting, causing very ugly rendering problems.

To solve it, you have to update your viewports every frame in the `render()` method in the following way:

1. Update world viewport
2. Render world
3. Update UI viewport
4. Render UI

Floating elements

Strategies such as `ExtendViewport` are great because they look good across a bigger set of devices. However, you cannot predict which portion of the screen is going to be shown to the end user. We do not generally care about background elements, but we need to make sure the essential ones, such as buttons, are well positioned.

Imagine we need to add a Facebook icon to our background scene. If we place it in one of the texture corners, it may be hidden on 4:3 screens. We cannot put it closer to the center as it would look really odd on 16:9 devices. What we really want is to dynamically position certain elements depending on the viewport configuration and the actual screen size, just as shown in the following figure:

Assuming the UI camera has its bottom-left corner at (0, 0) and that it uses pixel units, the code to position the icon would be something like this:

```
icon.setPosition(viewport.getViewportWidth() - 20.0f, 20.0f);
```

Now, you can dynamically position floating elements to make your game look good everywhere without too much hassle.

> Hardcoding positioning for UI elements is always a bad practice. It is always advisable to define them in some sort of file, thus using a data-driven approach.

Build your own Viewport implementation

Libgdx offers a limited set of strategies to deal with multiple screen sizes and ratios. In the vast majority of cases, you will have more than enough with one of the previously mentioned viewport implementations. However, it may be possible that you want a different behavior. That is easy enough with Libgdx!

You need to create a new class that extends `Viewport` and override its `calculateViewport(width, height)` method. It takes the actual screen width and height in pixels and is responsible for updating its internal state.

Again, it is highly unlikely you will find yourself needing to do this. If you do and think someone else could benefit from it, contribute back to the community!

See also

- This recipe covers all the built-in strategies to handle multiple resolutions, and you should be fairly comfortable with them now. This means you can move on to more entertaining things like *Chapter 3, Advanced 2D Graphics*.

Advanced 2D Graphics

3

In this chapter, we will cover:

- ▶ Achieving juicy effects with particles
- ▶ Frame buffers and image composition
- ▶ Welcome to the world of shaders
- ▶ Passing parameters into shader programs
- ▶ 2D depth of field shader
- ▶ Embedding a Libgdx window into a Java desktop application

Introduction

Now that you know how to render sprites on the screen, it is time to move on to more exciting and brighter things. Games have to be attractive to the eyes so as to catch the players' attention, and in this chapter, we will show you how to achieve such an effect.

We will start off with particle effects and then continue with image composition. Later, we will learn about shaders and all the amazing things we can produce with a programmable graphics pipeline. Finally, we will teach you how to embed a Libgdx window into a Java Swing application, which is quite useful to develop auxiliary tools.

Some of the concepts explained here might be a bit complicated, but despair not! Take it easy and make sure you study and play around with the sample code.

Achieving juicy effects with particles

The devil is in the details, a fact that also applies to games. It is the little things, or a lack thereof, that your users will notice the most. This is why elements, small in appearance, such as particle or sound effects, are really important when it comes to achieving what we want to transmit with our product.

A **particle system** is nothing more than a bunch of small images in an orchestrated motion, following a set of rules specified upfront. The aim is to give the impression of a more complex effect. Through particles, we can add fire, explosions, smoke, or magical spells to our creations. Among Libgdx's wonders, you will find the fantastic particles subsystem, the power of which we will learn to harness throughout this recipe.

This recipe illustrates the process of effect creation through **Particle Editor** to render them later within a Libgdx app.

Getting ready

Before getting your hands dirty, you need to get the hang of Particle Editor, which is the official Libgdx tool to produce particle effects. As such, it is distributed along with the framework's main package. Simply access the list of stable releases at `http://libgdx.com/releases` and get the latest release. Once you have the package, unzip it in a folder of your choice.

As usual, you need to import the sample projects in your Eclipse workspace.

How to do it...

Particle systems are composed of a list of **emitters** that spawn and control particles. A particle is generally a texture along with a myriad of parameters, such as color, speed, direction, and so on, that define its behavior during its lifetime.

We will execute two steps here. First, we will give an overview of the helpful Particle Editor. Later, we will show you how to include fancy effects in your Libgdx applications.

The basics of Particle Editor

Follow these steps to create juicy effects with Particle Editor:

1. To run Particle Editor from Windows, open up a console, access the uncompressed libgdx release folder, and enter the following command:

```
java -cp gdx.jar;gdx-natives.jar;gdx-backend-lwjgl.jar;gdx-backend-lwjgl-natives.jar;extensions\gdx-tools\gdx-tools.jar com.badlogic.gdx.tools.particleeditor.ParticleEditor
```

Mac and GNU/Linux users must replace semicolons with colons and backslashes with forward slashes, as follows.

```
java -cp gdx.jar;gdx-natives.jar;gdx-backend-lwjgl.jar;gdx-backend-lwjgl-natives.jar:extensions/gdx-tools/gdx-tools.jar com.badlogic.gdx.tools.particleeditor.ParticleEditor
```

2. The top-left panel is the most important panel because it shows what your system will look like when rendered with Libgdx.

3. Below that panel, you have the **Effect Emitters** panel that contains the list of emitters. Every emitter has an editable name; you can add or remove them using the **New** and **Delete** buttons. The draw order is controlled with the **Up** and **Down** buttons.

4. Particle systems are saved as plain text files. You can save them by clicking on **Save**; click on **Open** to access them later.

> Particle systems use a plain text file format that does not require you to use a specific extension. However, it is good practice to keep your file naming conventions consistent. One way is to stick to the .particle extension or something similar.

5. To the right of the window, you will find the **Editor Properties** and **Emitter Properties** panels. Feel free to play around, and see the effects on the left. There is always a great deal of tweaking and experimentation when it comes to particle effects. Do not panic if you feel overwhelmed because we will go through all the details later in this chapter. For this recipe's purposes, we already have some premade particle systems, as shown in the following screenshot:

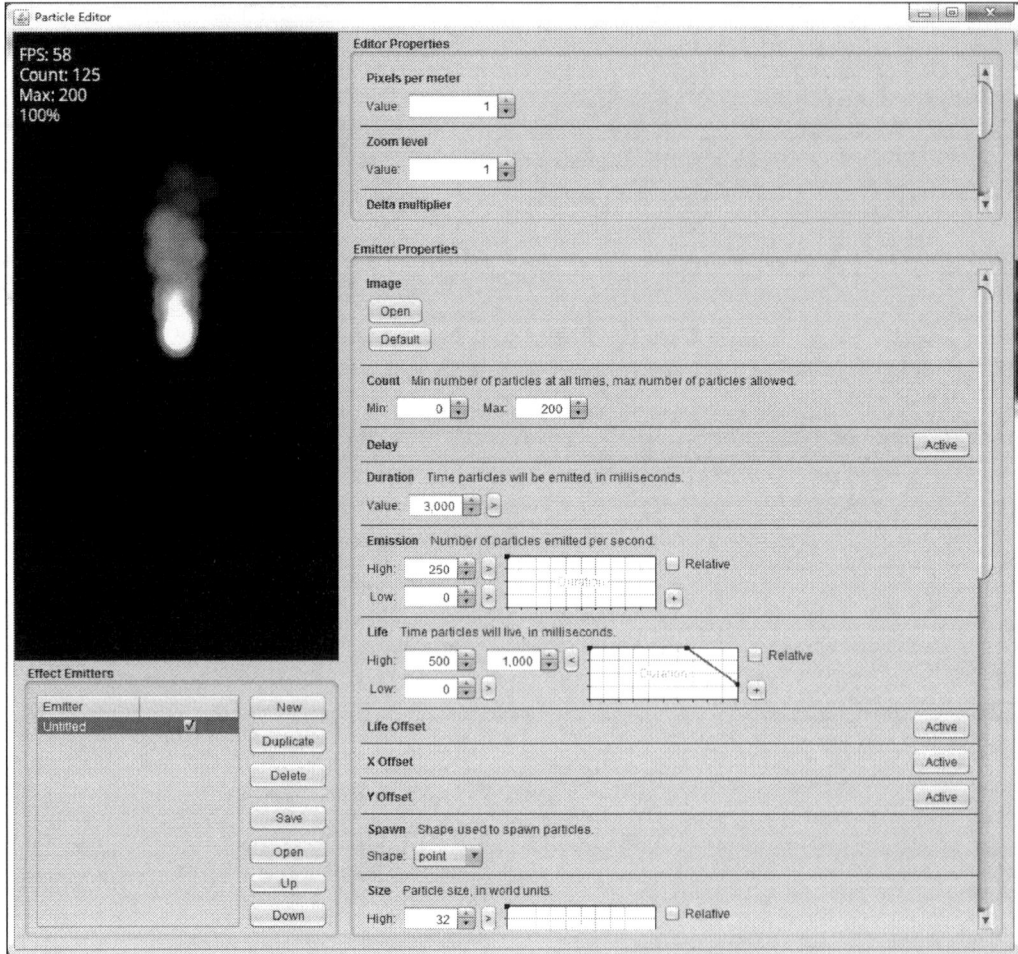

This is a program capture; the cropped text is not important

Rendering particle effects with Libgdx

The code for this recipe is located inside the `ParticleEffectsSample.java` file, while the necessary assets are found under the `assets` folder in the `android` project. We will proceed to load a collection of particle systems and render them, one at a time, at the mouse or touch coordinates. To iterate through the effects, the user can click or tap the screen.

Just like the past recipes, we first define a few static constants to handle stretching the render area to fit different-sized screens. Right after, we add a few member variables. We are already familiar with most of them: a camera to visualize the scene, a viewport to define the render area, and a batch to send our draw calls. Then, we have a classic Java array of `ParticleEffect` objects, which contains all the information and state of our particle systems. Finally, we add a `currentEffect` member that will serve as an index to access the array; we also add `touchPos` to cache the user's mouse/touch coordinates and translate them from the screen to the world space:

```
private ParticleEffect[] effects;
private int currentEffect;
private Vector3 touchPos;
```

In the `create()` method, we first construct the `camera`, `viewport`, `batch`, and `touchPos` objects. Then, we create the array of `ParticleEffect` objects and start populating it. For every effect, we instantiate an object of `ParticleEffect`, and then call its `load()` method, passing in the file handle for our locally stored particle system's text files. The `currentEffect` member variable starts pointing to the first element in the array. The `start()` method of `ParticleEffect` gets the party started by kicking off the effects simulation.

With the `Gdx.input.setInputProcessor()` method, we tell Libgdx that our `ParticleEffectsSample` instance will listen to input events. As will be demonstrated later, this will allow us to iterate through the effects when the user clicks or touches the screen. Consider the following code:

```
public void create() {
  ...

  effects = new ParticleEffect[3];
  currentEffect = 0;

  effects[0] = new ParticleEffect();
  effects[0].load(Gdx.files.internal("data/fire.particle"),
    Gdx.files.internal("data"));

  effects[1] = new ParticleEffect();
  effects[1].load(Gdx.files.internal("data/stars.particle"),
    Gdx.files.internal("data"));

  effects[2] = new ParticleEffect();
  effects[2].load(Gdx.files.internal("data/ice.particle"),
    Gdx.files.internal("data"));

  for (ParticleEffect effect : effects) {
    effect.start();
  }

  Gdx.input.setInputProcessor(this);
}
```

`ParticleEffect` implements the `Disposable` interface and, thus, should be disposed when appropriate. We proceed to do so in the `dispose()` method:

```
public void dispose() {
  batch.dispose();

  for (ParticleEffect effect : effects) {
    effect.dispose();
  }
}
```

The first step is to grab the current mouse/touch coordinates with the `Gdx.input.getX()` and `Gdx.input.getY()` methods. These come in the screen space, so we need to call the camera's `unproject()` method to convert them to the world space and be able to set the position of the effects correctly. In order to do this, we iterate over the effects array calling the `setPosition()` method, which just takes a set of 2D coordinates.

Particle effects have finite lifetimes, one-shot spells, explosions, and so on. However, for our demo, we want to make sure they play indefinitely. This is why we check whether they have finished with the `isComplete()` method and, if this is the case, kick them off again with the `reset()` method.

Finally, it is time to render the selected effect. We set the projection matrix of the batch and add a pair of `begin()` and `end()` calls. In between, we call the `draw()` method of the `effects` array element, pointed by the `currentEffect` position, passing in the batch and the time passed since the last game's loop iteration:

```
public void render() {
  ...

  touchPos.set(Gdx.input.getX(), Gdx.input.getY(), 0.0f);
  camera.unproject(touchPos);

  for (ParticleEffect effect : effects) {
    effect.setPosition(touchPos.x, touchPos.y);

    if (effect.isComplete()) {
      effect.reset();
    }
  }

  batch.setProjectionMatrix(camera.combined);
  batch.begin();
  effects[currentEffect].draw(batch, Gdx.graphics.getDeltaTime());
  batch.end();
}
```

The touchdown() method is declared by the InputListener interface and implemented by ParticleEffectsSample to react upon user clicks and screen tapping. Every time a user carries out this action, we increment the currentEffect member variable by 1 unit, while making sure we do not go past the bounds of the effects array. The module operation returns a number between 0 and array.length - 1, which makes the index go back to the start after the last effect.

```
public boolean touchDown (int screenX, int screenY, int pointer,
    int button) {
    currentEffect = (currentEffect + 1) % effects.length;
    return true;
}
```

The result is shown in the following screenshot. It is a great practice to play around with Particle Editor and modify the sample source to add your newly created particle systems.

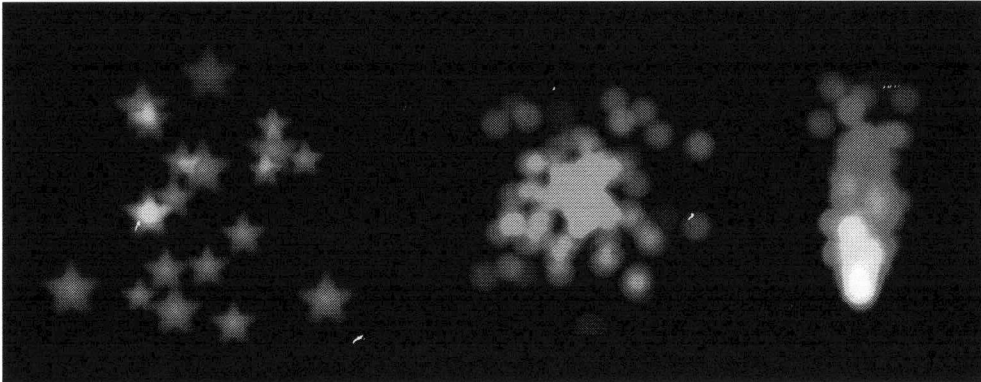

How it works...

Let's take a closer look at Particle Editor and the tools it offers us to control what our particle systems look like.

The **Editor Properties** panel simply provides a way of tweaking the particle previewer. The parameters in this panel are as follows:

- **Pixels per meter**: This constant is used to translate between pixel units to world space units.
- **Zoom level**: This controls the previewer camera zoom.
- **Delta multiplier**: This is the factor that scales the delta time passed in to the draw() method of ParticleEffect. It can be useful to preview the effect in slow motion and notice little details.

The **Emitter Properties** panel, as its name points out, actually contains the parameters that define the behavior of the particle systems:

▸ **Image**: This is the texture used as a base to render the particles. As it is shown in the example, it is usually better to use grayscale textures and tint them through the effect's properties. It is good to experiment with different shapes and preview the results.

▸ **Count**: This defines the minimum number of particles that will initially be spawned and the maximum number that will ever be active at once. Be wary of using big numbers here as it affects memory consumption, CPU performance, and rendering times.

▸ **Delay**: If **Active**, the effect will not start emitting any particle for the given amount of time in milliseconds.

▸ **Duration**: This is the time in milliseconds for which the effect will keep emitting particles.

▸ **Emission**: This is the number of particles emitted per second.

▸ **Life**: This is the time in milliseconds for which each one of the emitted particles will remain active.

▸ **Life Offset**: When enabled, this makes the effect start at the given value, in milliseconds, throughout its lifetime.

▸ **X Offset** and **Y Offset**: This is the distance along the x and y axes from the effect's position, in world units, where the particles will be emitted.

▸ **Spawn**: This is the shape used to spawn the particles; the available ones are point, line, square, and ellipse.

▸ **Size**: This is the particle size in world units.

▸ **Velocity**: If enabled, this sets the particle speed in world units per second.

▸ **Angle**: If enabled, this sets the particle emission angle in degrees.

▸ **Rotation**: If enabled, this rotates the particle textures by the given value, in degrees.

▸ **Wind**: When enabled, a horizontal force in world units per second is applied to the particles.

▸ **Gravity**: When enabled, a vertical force in world units per second is applied to the particles.

▸ **Tint**: This multiplies the texture color by the set color. As previously mentioned, grayscale textures give the best results.

▸ **Transparency**: This is an alpha value that the particles will adopt over time.

▸ **Additive**: When checked, the additive blending mode will be used to render the particles, which results in a high color range and is good for the effects.

▸ **Attached**: If enabled, the existing particles will follow the movement of the emitter.

▸ **Continuous**: When checked, the emitters will automatically restart every time they are finished.

> ▸ **Aligned**: When enabled, textures will be rotated to face the direction of each particle's movement.

Some properties feature an expand (**>**) button that, when clicked, adds another value input. When expanded, the first input becomes the minimum value, while the second input represents the maximum value. The effect will then adopt a random value within the range. This can be disabled by clicking on the collapse (**<**) button, as shown in the following screenshot:

Other particles include a chart that can be expanded or collapsed with the **+** and **–** buttons, respectively. The x axis represents the lifetime in percentage, while the vertical axis shows the property value. These charts provide great power to control how our systems behave over time and achieve awesome results. The user can add new nodes by clicking on a segment, and delete them with a double click. It is pretty easy to shape up the chart the way we want just by dragging the nodes around:

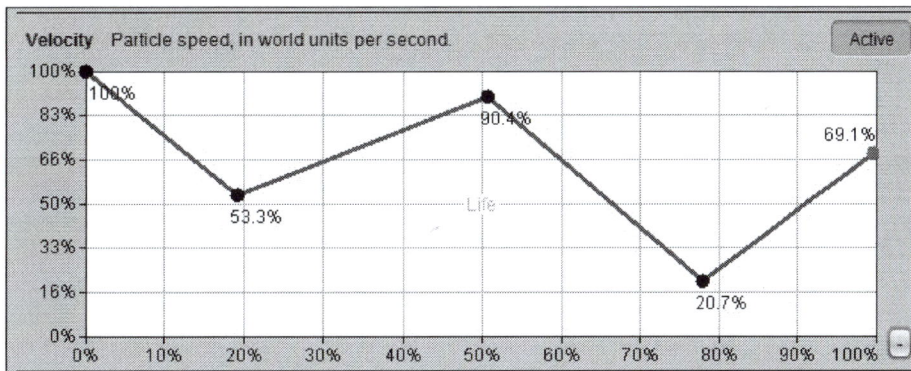

It is perfectly normal to feel a bit scared with such a vast variety of options. For those who are not visual effects artists, at the end of the day, it is just a matter of experimentation with the properties and a constant check of the results in the previewer.

There's more...

Surely you appreciate that our example is quite easy. Even though this approach works flawlessly for most situations where we occasionally fire a single one-shot effect, it does not scale well enough. Games such as space shooters or action platformers might require dozens of simultaneous onscreen effects at a given time. Constantly creating and deleting `ParticleEffect` objects is not sustainable, especially when it comes to mobile devices, because of the tremendous stress the garbage collector will go through. It is not rare to experience severe stalls every few seconds, and you do not want that now, do you?

Luckily enough, Libgdx comes with a **particle pooling** mechanism that elegantly takes care of our concerns. The `ParticleEffectPool` class instantiates a number of `PooledEffect` objects. Any time, we can request the pool for an effect and use it normally. Once we are done, we put it back in the pool. Since the pool allocates all the objects upfront, there are exactly zero runtime allocations and garbage collection operations.

`PooledEffectsSample.java` illustrates how to use particle pooling. The user can click/touch the screen to spawn explosions and can do so repeatedly without any memory overhead or additional allocation. We will limit ourselves to commenting the differences with our previous example.

First, add `ParticleEffectPool` and a collection of `PooledEffect` references to keep track of the active effects:

```
private ParticleEffectPool pool;
private Array<PooledEffect> activeEffects;
```

Pools can only have instances of the same effect, and we need to provide some sort of a model when initializing them. In the `create()` method, we first instantiate and load our explosion particle effect from the `explosion.particle` file. Then, we call the `ParticleEffectPool` constructor passing in `explosionEffect`, the initial number of allocated effects, and the maximum number of effects the pool can expand to:

```
ParticleEffect explosionEffect = new ParticleEffect();
explosionEffect.load(Gdx.files.internal("data/explosion.particle")
  , Gdx.files.internal("data"));
pool = new ParticleEffectPool(explosionEffect, 10, 100);
activeEffects = new Array<PooledEffect>();
```

Within our `render()` method, we iterate through the active effects and check whether they have finished playing. If they have, we delete them from the list and put them back into the pool with the `free()` method. If they are still playing, we update and draw them, just like before:

```
float deltaTime = Gdx.graphics.getDeltaTime();

batch.setProjectionMatrix(camera.combined);
batch.begin();

for (int i = 0; i < activeEffects.size; ) {
  PooledEffect effect = activeEffects.get(i);

  if (effect.isComplete()) {
    pool.free(effect);
    activeEffects.removeIndex(i);
  }
  else {
    effect.draw(batch, deltaTime);
```

```
        ++i;
    }
}
```

```
    batch.cnd();
```

Every time the user clicks or touches the screen, we try to fetch a new effect from the pool using the `obtain()` method of `ParticleEffectPool` and add it to the active collection. As we saw before, the pool initially allocates memory for 10 instances. If we try to obtain more than this, it will make the pool grow, though never exceeding its maximum size, which, in this case, is 100 elements. We then convert the interaction coordinates into world space units and set the offset position.

```
    public boolean touchDown (int screenX, int screenY, int pointer, int
    button) {
        PooledEffect effect = pool.obtain();

        if (effect != null) {
            touchPos.set(screenX, screenY, 0.0f);
            camera.unproject(touchPos);

            activeEffects.add(effect);
            effect.setPosition(touchPos.x, touchPos.y);
        }

        return true;
    }
```

Following this method, we can end up with a situation like the one shown in the following screenshot, with very little overhead. Let the fireworks begin!

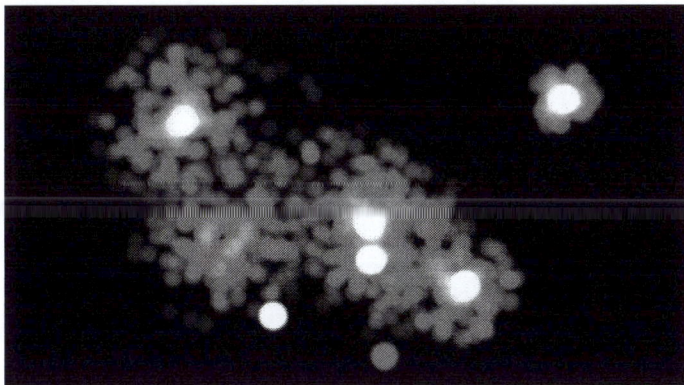

See also

▶ You can also achieve great effects using shaders. If you want to know more, read the *Welcome to the world of shaders* recipe.

Frame buffers and image composition

Knowing how to render textures, animated characters, and particle effects at arbitrary positions already gives you great power to build incredibly rich and elaborate game worlds. However, some effects may be tricky to achieve, if not impossible, just by using these tools.

Let's imagine you want to implement smooth crossfade screen transitions in your game. When we talk about screens, we are referring to the main menu, game, victory, and so on. We will progressively decrease the alpha value of the old screen, while the new screen comes into play with an increasing alpha value. This cannot be accomplished by passing the corresponding transparency value to each screen, simply because the second we encounter overlapping elements with various alpha values, artifacts will start to appear.

A possible solution involves rendering each screen to a temporary render surface and then mixing the two with our calculated alpha values. These auxiliary targets are known as **frame buffer objects** (**FBO**). The following diagram illustrates the process:

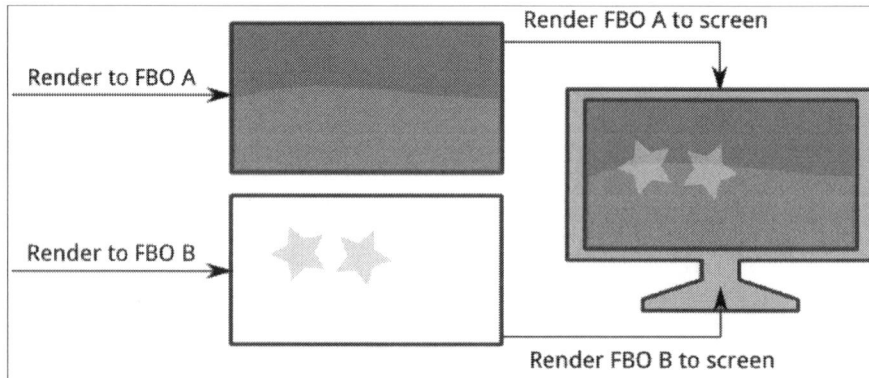

With this approach, you can take screenshots and generate a mini map. There are countless possibilities, and you can probably come up with a few more.

> The process of rendering to FBOs is also known as **render to texture**.

Throughout this recipe, we will show how to use Libgdx FBOs to create a small image gallery with transitions from one picture to the next.

Getting ready

We will work with one of the sample applications found in the [cookbook]/samples folder distributed along with this book. Import all the projects under this folder into your Eclipse workspace.

Find the images for your gallery in the JPG format under the [cookbook]/samples/samples-android/assets/data/gallery folder.

How to do it...

You will find the FBO example in the `FrameBufferSample.java` file that contains a classic `ApplicationListener` implementation. First, we have an `enum` that will define the two possible states, `PICTURE` and `TRANSITIONING`, of our application:

```
private enum GalleryState {
  PICTURE,
  TRANSITIONING,
}
```

A few self-explanatory constants follow, representing the number of pictures that make the gallery, the time that we spend on each picture before transitioning, and the duration of the transitions:

```
private static final int GALLERY_NUM_PICTURES = 4;
private static final float GALLERY_PICTURE_TIME = 3.0f;
private static final float GALLERY_TRANSITION_TIME = 2.0f;
```

The list of members starts with the well-known `camera`, `viewport`, and `batch` and continues with an array of `TextureRegion` references that will point to the gallery images and two `FrameBuffer` objects, one to hold the old picture and another to have the one we are transitioning to, to help with transitions. Finally, we keep the index of the current picture, the time we have spent in the current state so far, and the gallery state we are in:

```
private TextureRegion [] gallery;
private FrameBuffer currentFrameBuffer;
private FrameBuffer nextFrameBuffer;

private int currentPicture;
private float time;
private GalleryState state;
```

The `create()` method is responsible for instantiating and initializing our members as we are already used to. We iterate the gallery array creating new `TextureRegion` objects with the paths for each picture. The `FrameBuffer` constructor takes the color format (8 bits per RGB channel, in our case) and dimensions (our virtual screen size), and decides whether it uses a depth buffer (which we do not need since we work in a 2D space):

```java
public void create() {
...

    gallery = new TextureRegion[GALLERY_NUM_PICTURES];

    for (int i = 0; i < GALLERY_NUM_PICTURES; ++i) {
      gallery[i] = new TextureRegion(new
        Texture(Gdx.files.internal("data/gallery/gallery" + (i + 1)
        + ".jpg")));
    }

    currentFrameBuffer = new FrameBuffer(Format.RGB888,
      VIRTUAL_WIDTH, VIRTUAL_HEIGHT, false);
    nextFrameBuffer = new FrameBuffer(Format.RGB888, VIRTUAL_WIDTH,
      VIRTUAL_HEIGHT, false);

    currentPicture = 0;
    time = 0.0f;
    state = GalleryState.PICTURE;

    camera.position.set(SCENE_WIDTH * 0.5f, SCENE_HEIGHT * 0.5f,
      0.0f);
}
```

Some cleanup needs to be done within the `dispose()` method, as `batch`, all our textures, and the FBOs require us to deallocate resources. Note that we can access the texture a region points to through its `getTexture()` method:

```java
public void dispose() {
  batch.dispose();

  for (TextureRegion background : gallery) {
    background.getTexture().dispose();
  }

  currentFrameBuffer.dispose();
  nextFrameBuffer.dispose();
}
```

As we usually do in our `render()` method, we clear the screen and set the batch projection matrix. Then, we increment our `time` variable according to the time that has passed since the last frame, and call `updateStatePicture()` or `updateStateTransitioning()`, depending on the current state:

```
public void render() {
...

  time += Gdx.graphics.getDeltaTime();

  switch (state) {
  case PICTURE:
    updateStatePicture();
    break;
  case TRANSITIONING:
    updateStateTransitioning();
    break;
  }
}
```

We use the `drawTexture()` and `drawRegion()` utility methods to render our backgrounds.

During the time a picture is being shown, we normally render it on the screen. We need to check whether enough time has passed for us to kick off a transition. If it has, we change the state and proceed to render the two pictures involved in our FBOs.

To tell OpenGL that an FBO is now the active render target, we need to call its `bind()` method. Then, we can work with `batch` like we always do. If we call `bind()` on the next FBO, the latter will become the active render target. Once we want to go back to rendering on the screen, we call the `unbind()` static method of `FrameBuffer`.

We render the current picture to `currentFrameBuffer`, increase the `currentPicture` counter, and render the next counter to `nextFrameBuffer`.

Note that we flip the region around its *y* axis with `flip(false, true)`. Since everything that we render is mirrored around the *y* axis, we need to compensate for this. `SpriteBatch` does it automatically for us:

```
private void updateStatePicture() {
  TextureRegion region = gallery[currentPicture];

  batch.begin();
  drawRegion(gallery[currentPicture]);
  batch.end();

  if (time > GALLERY_PICTURE_TIME) {
    time = 0.0f;
```

```
        state = GalleryState.TRANSITIONING;

        region.flip(false, true);

        currentFrameBuffer.bind();

        Gdx.gl.glClearColor(0.0f, 0.0f, 0.0f, 1.0f);
        Gdx.gl.glClear(GL20.GL_COLOR_BUFFER_BIT);

        batch.begin();
        drawRegion(region);
        batch.end();

        region.flip(false, true);

        currentPicture = (currentPicture + 1) % GALLERY_NUM_PICTURES;

        region = gallery[currentPicture];
        region.flip(false,  true);

        nextFrameBuffer.bind();

        Gdx.gl.glClearColor(0.0f, 0.0f, 0.0f, 1.0f);
        Gdx.gl.glClear(GL20.GL_COLOR_BUFFER_BIT);

        batch.begin();
        drawRegion((gallery[currentPicture]));
        batch.end();
        nextFrameBuffer.unbind();

        region.flip(false, true);
    }
}
```

Finally, we reach the function that manages the transitioning state. The transition is simply a linear interpolation of the alpha channel that initially shows the first full picture and progressively crossfades to the next one.

We can now render our FBOs to the screen using `batch`. In order to retrieve an FBO's texture data, we simply need to call its `getColorBufferTexture()` method. Lastly, we make sure we change to the PICTURE state when appropriate:

```
private void updateStateTransitioning() {
    float alpha = Math.min(time / GALLERY_TRANSITION_TIME, 1.0f);
```

```
batch.begin();
batch.setColor(1.0f, 1.0f, 1.0f, 1.0f - alpha);
drawTexture(currentFrameBuffer.getColorBufferTexture());

batch.setColor(1.0f, 1.0f, 1.0f, alpha);
drawTexture(nextFrameBuffer.getColorBufferTexture());
batch.end();

if (time > GALLERY_TRANSITION_TIME) {
  time = 0.0f;
  state = GalleryState.PICTURE;
}
}
```

After running the example, you should be seeing something similar to the following illustration:

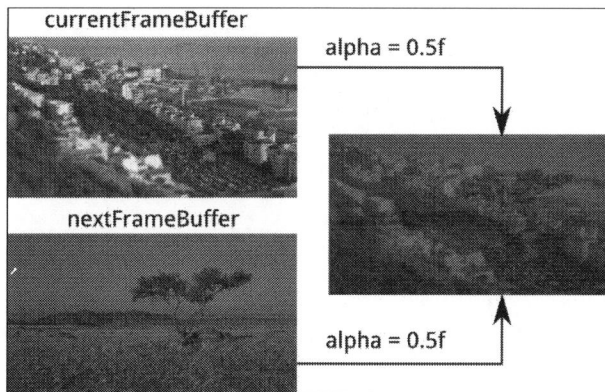

How it works...

`FrameBuffer` objects simply hold a `Texture` instance. Through `bind()`, we ask the OpenGL 2.0 API to use it as a target for all the following draw calls. Once we call `unbind()`, FBO asks OpenGL 2.0 to restore the screen as the target for all draw calls.

There's more...

Drawing particles with transparencies on a dark background generally produces excellent results; however, they start looking pretty bad the second we introduce brighter environments, as shown in the following left hand-side picture. **Additive blending** adds overlapping pixel color values, resulting in areas that are unnaturally bright.

In `FrameBufferParticleEffectSample.java`, we render explosions to a black and fully transparent FBO. This FBO is then rendered on top of the background, producing the result shown in the following right hand-side picture:

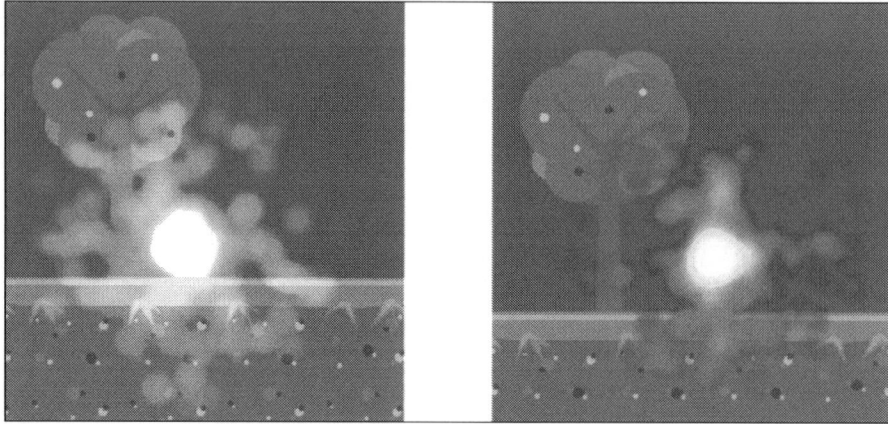

We need to create the `FrameBuffer` object so that it supports alpha channel, which is why we use `Format.RGBA8888` as opposed to `Format.RGB888`:

```
particleBuffer = new FrameBuffer(Format.RGBA8888,
  Gdx.graphics.getWidth(), Gdx.graphics.getHeight(), false);
```

Feel free to dive into the sample code; the `render()` process sticks with the following pattern:

1. Set the render target to `particleBuffer`, calling its `bind()` method.
2. Clear the FBO with `Color(0.0f, 0.0f, 0.0f, 0.0f)`, which means black but fully transparent.
3. Render the particle effects to the FBO using `batch`.
4. Call `FrameBuffer.unbind()`.
5. Clear the screen with the solid black `Color(0.0f, 0.0f, 0.0f, 1.0f)`.
6. Render the background and the FBO's texture using `batch`. Remember to flip the FBO around its *y* axis.

Welcome to the world of shaders

Shaders are small computer programs that give us more control over what is rendered by letting us communicate more closely with the GPU. This is a broad field and cannot be possibly covered in great detail within this book's scope, but nonetheless, it's absolutely essential to graphics programming. We will try to provide some introductory guidelines so as to start working with them; you can later check the several shader programming-specific books available.

Throughout this and the following recipes, we will dig into **OpenGL Shading Language** (**GLSL**). As a first contact, we will postprocess an image by adding the grayscale, sepia, and inverted color filters.

Getting ready

Once more, make sure the sample projects are ready to be used in your Eclipse workspace.

Shader scripts are loaded at runtime. For this recipe, you will need the following files:

▸ [cookbook]/samples/samples-android/assets/data/shaders/
   grayscale.vert

▸ [cookbook]/samples/samples-android/assets/data/shaders/
   grayscale.frag

▸ [cookbook]/samples/samples-android/assets/data/shaders/
   sepia.vert

▸ [cookbook]/samples/samples-android/assets/data/shaders/
   sepia.frag

▸ [cookbook]/samples/samples-android/assets/data/shaders/
   inverted.vert

▸ [cookbook]/samples/samples-android/assets/data/shaders/
   inverted.frag

How to do it...

Here is what we will achieve in this recipe: kick off a Libgdx application that renders the jungle background we used in the past articles. As the user clicks or taps on the screen, we will cycle through a collection of shaders and apply them to the background. The example can be found in ShadersSample.java.

First, we define a constant containing the number of shaders:

```
private static final int NUM_SHADERS = 4;
```

At this point in time, rendering a simple texture should be straightforward. Precisely, we use the camera, viewport, batch, and background texture references. This time, we add an array of ShaderProgram references, a list of their names, and the index of the active shader in the array:

```
private ShaderProgram shaders[];
private String shaderNames[];
private int currentShader;
```

In the `create()` method, we construct and initialize our members. To create a `ShaderProgram` object, we need to pass in the file handles of the vertex shader and the fragment shader scripts. More details on these will follow. We do this for all our shaders, except for the first one, which we leave as `null`, which means no postprocessing will be done when this index is active.

Make sure you tell the input system to send input events to the main class with `Gdx.input.setInputProcessor()`:

```
public void create() {
    ...

    shaders[1] = new
      ShaderProgram(Gdx.files.internal("data/shaders/grayscale.
      vert"), Gdx.files.internal("data/shaders/grayscale.frag"));
    shaderNames[1] = "Grayscale";


    ...
}
```

`ShaderProgram` objects allocate resources that require to be freed once we stop needing them. In the `dispose()` method, we iterate the array, cleaning all the valid shaders:

```
public void dispose() {
    batch.dispose();
    background.dispose();

    for (ShaderProgram shader : shaders) {
      if (shader != null)
        shader.dispose();
    }
}
```

Our render method is exactly the same as the sprite batch example; we simply render our background normally.

The interesting bit comes in the `touchDown()` event because it's here that we set the active shader. Every time the user clicks on the mouse or touches the screen, we increment the `currentShader` index and call `setShader()` on `batch`. This tells the batch which `ShaderProgram` to use for rendering; the default is `null`:

```
public boolean touchDown (int screenX, int screenY, int pointer, int
button) {
    currentShader = (currentShader + 1) % shaders.length;
    batch.setShader(shaders[currentShader]);

    Gdx.app.log("ShaderSample", "Switching to shader " +
      shaderNames[currentShader]);

    return true;
}
```

> Every time you call `setShader()`, the `SpriteBatch` is forced to flush the currently cached draw calls and send them to the GPU, which is quite expensive. Be careful not to switch shaders unnecessarily.

Naturally, the interesting action takes place inside the shader scripts. Every `ShaderProgram` contains a vertex and a fragment shader, and each one of them must have a `main()` function.

- **Vertex shaders**: These operate on every vertex that is drawn. Each shader has associated extra information, such as a 3D point, color (RGBA), and a set of texture coordinates. Typically, they are more relevant in 3D applications, but they are also used in 2D, as mentioned in the *Texture rendering with SpriteBatch* recipe of *Chapter 2*, *Working with 2D Graphics*, to render images when we use quads (4-vertex polygons) with linked texture coordinates.

- **Fragment shaders**: These shaders are also known as pixel shaders because they operate on a per-pixel basis. After being run, they output an RGBA color.

> Shaders are written in plain text files. Typically, we use the `.vert` and `.frag` extensions for vertex and fragment shaders, respectively.

The Libgdx default vertex shader projects the current vertex on the screen using the view matrix, while the default fragment shader uses the corresponding color from the bound texture for the current fragment.

The following diagram summarizes the basic shader pipeline:

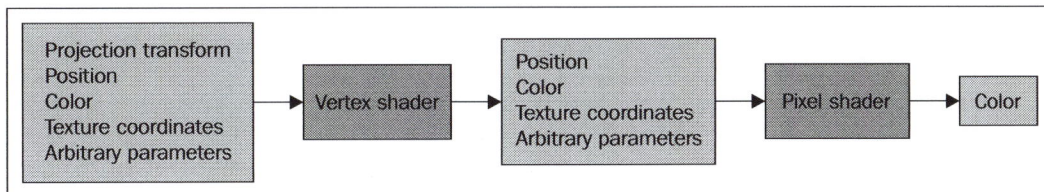

The following code snippet corresponds to the grayscale vertex shader. As you can see, the syntax looks very much like that of C. Do not worry too much about the details as we will get into them later; just try to observe the code from an algorithmic point of view.

To summarize, the script takes the projection transform (`u_projTrans`), vertex position (`a_position`), texture coordinates (`a_textCoord0`), and color (`a_color`) as inputs, and it does calculations and passes the same parameters to the fragment shader.

The texture coordinates and color are passed along untampered. However, we need to transform the 2D space coordinates given by the batch to the 3D world space. This is why we apply the projection transform to obtain `gl_Position`:

```
uniform mat4 u_projTrans;

attribute vec4 a_position;
attribute vec2 a_texCoord0;
attribute vec4 a_color;

varying vec4 v_color;
varying vec2 v_texCoord;

void main() {
    gl_Position = u_projTrans * a_position;
    v_texCoord = a_texCoord0;
    v_color = a_color;
}
```

The fragment shader does a bit more work since it is the one that is actually responsible for transforming RGBA pixel colors into grayscale. It uses a texture sampler (`u_texture`), a color (`v_color`), and texture coordinates (`v_texCoord`) as inputs to produce the resulting pixel color (`gl_FragColor`).

Quite a few options are available when it comes to grayscale conversion. We can just take one of the RGB components or perform some blending between the three. Color perception and grayscale studies conclude that the best results are obtained when we blend and combine the components using the weights `0.299, 0.587, 0.114`. The following image illustrates these three approaches:

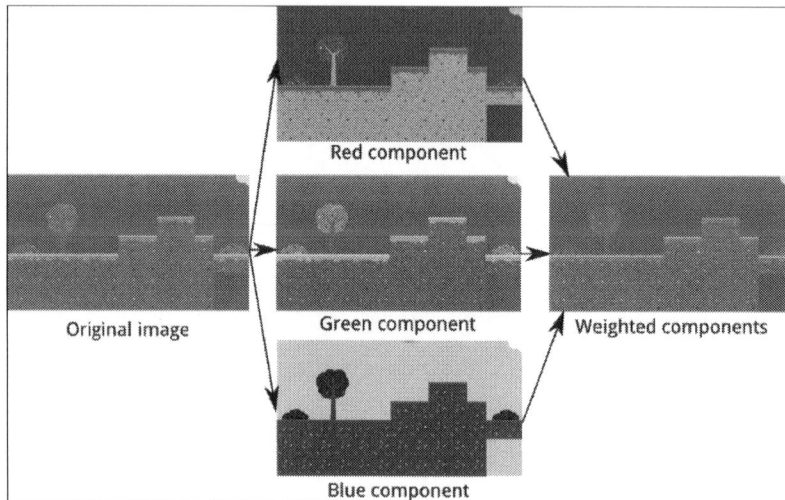

We define the weights in the `grayScaleMultiplier` three-element array constant and use the `dot()` function to combine it with `texColor`. As the name points out, the function calculates the dot product of two vectors. The result is a `float` value, which we set as the three components of the grayscale vector.

The color is obtained by calling `texture2D()` that takes the texture sampler and the coordinates and returns the corresponding pixel color. Finally, we set `gl_FragColor` as the RGB grayscale components and the alpha from the original pixel:

```
#ifdef GL_ES
precision mediump float;
precision mediump int;
#else
#define highp;
#endif

uniform sampler2D u_texture;

varying vec4 v_color;
varying vec2 v_texCoord;

const vec3 grayScaleMultiplier = vec3(0.299, 0.587, 0.114);

void main() {
  vec4 texColor = texture2D(u_texture, v_texCoord);
  vec3 gray = vec3(dot(texColor.rgb, grayScaleMultiplier));
  gl_FragColor = vec4(gray.r, gray.g, gray.b, texColor.a);
}
```

You now have your first working shader, congratulations!

How it works...

Let's shed some light on the GLSL syntax and conventions so that it becomes a bit easier to understand simple scripts. For the complete language reference, refer to http://www.opengl.org/documentation/glsl.

Data types

Here is a list of the most essential data types used in GLSL:

- `float`: The floating point value
- `vec2`: This is a 2-component float array, typically used to represent 2D points
- `vec3`: This is a 3-component float array used to represent 3D points or RGB colors
- `vec4`: This is a 4-component float array, typically used to store RGBA colors

- ▶ `int`: The classic integer
- ▶ `vec2i`, `vec3i`, and `vec4i`: These are the equivalents to `vec2`, `vec3`, and `vec4`, respectively, but they hold integers rather than float values
- ▶ `sampler2D`: This is used to work with textures

There are several ways we can declare, initialize, and use variables of these types:

```
int a = 5;
float b = 5.5; // using 5 can result in a compile error
vec2 c = vec2(1.0, -4.4);
vec3 d = vec3(1.0, -4.4, 0.0);
vec3 e = vec3(c, 1.5); // from a vec2 and an additional component
vec4 f = vec4(1.0, 1.0, 1.0, 1.0);
vec4 f = vec4(e, 1.0); // from a vec3 and an additional component
vec4 g = vec4(1.0); // equivalent to vec4(1.0, 1.0, 1.0, 1.0);
```

Vectors are like low-level arrays, but can be accessed and assigned in interesting manners:

```
vec3 otherColor = color.rgb;
vec3 otherPosition = vector.xyz;
otherPosition.xy = otherPosition.yz; // swaps x and y components
vec2 texCoords = vector.st; // texture coordinates are given as stpq
float x = otherPosition.x;
float y = otherPosition[1];
```

The `rgba`, `xyzw`, and `stpq` accessors are always valid as long as they are not mixed up together.

Constants have to be declared using the `const` keyword before the data type; this works exactly as in other languages, such as C++.

Vertex attributes

Vertex attributes are read-only variables set by external systems to be used by the vertex shader. Keep in mind that they are provided on a per-vertex basis, not globally for all vertices. They are defined with the `attribute` keyword preceding the type.

Uniforms

Uniforms are read-only variables that are set from Java code and can be retrieved from either the vertex or the fragment shader, but not both. These are set globally and affect all vertices and fragments. To declare one, we just need to add the `uniform` keyword before the type. In our grayscale fragment shader, we have the `u_projView` uniform, which is set by the `SpriteBatch` and takes the value of its combined transformation matrix. Remember how we used to set it using the camera matrix?

This is a really powerful feature as we can dynamically modify the result of our shaders using application states such as user input and time, among many others.

OpenGL ES precision specifiers

Android, WebGL, and iOS use an OpenGL variant called OpenGL ES, which is aimed at embedded hardware. Most of the time, there is no need to worry about this, but shaders is one of the most sensitive topics.

OpenGL ES forces us to specify the **precision** of our float, int, and derived arrays in the fragment shader. The three different precision types that exist are lowp, mediump, and highp. Obviously, the greater the precision, the better the results for finely grained calculations, but at a significant computational cost. Some devices do not even support highp.

The classic OpenGL does not use precision qualifiers, but the syntax accepts them just to maintain compatibility with the mobile version. Therefore, we need to take special care of the desktop version. We can use preprocessor directives to tell the GLSL compiler which precision we want to use by default. Preprocessor directives, just like in C/C++, are resolved at compile time and can strip out code.

The following code snippet tells the compiler to use the mediump precision for both int and float types, when under OpenGL ES. If the shaders are being compiled under OpenGL, both lines will be completely taken out.

```
#ifdef GL_ES
precision mediump float;
precision mediump int;
#else
#define highp;
#endif
```

Check the official OpenGL ES documentation for further information at http://www.khronos.org/opengles.

Now that you have a better overview of the basics of shaders, you might want to take another look at the *How to do it...* section of this recipe.

There's more...

Many interesting effects can be achieved just by tweaking the color components of a fragment with simple operations. In this section, we will cover two additional shader programs: a sepia filter and inverted colors.

The sepia effect

Sepia is a brownish color, represented in our script by the `vec3(1.2, 1.0, 0.8)` constant. We get the fragment color, convert it to grayscale, multiply it by `sepia`, and use it to set `gl_FragColor`. This can be used to give your game a vintage style:

```
uniform sampler2D u_texture;

varying highp vec4 v_color;
varying highp vec2 v_texCoord;

const vec3 grayScaleMultiplier = vec3(0.299, 0.587, 0.114);
const vec3 sepia = vec3(1.2, 1.0, 0.8);

void main() {
  vec4 texColor = texture2D(u_texture, v_texCoord);
  vec3 gray = vec3(dot(texColor.rgb, grayScaleMultiplier));
  gl_FragColor = vec4(gray * sepia, texColor.a);
}
```

After running it, you should see something similar to the following screenshot:

Inverted colors

Inverting the colors of an image does not produce very pleasant results, but this might very well be your intent, depending on the situation. In this case, we grab the fragment color from the texture and calculate its inverse. Knowing that RGB components range from `0.0` to `1.0`, we can do the following:

```
uniform sampler2D u_texture;

varying highp vec4 v_color;
varying highp vec2 v_texCoord;

void main() {
  vec4 texColor = texture2D(u_texture, v_texCoord);
```

```
    vec3 inverted = 1.0 - texColor.rgb;
    gl_FragColor = vec4(inverted.r, inverted.g, inverted.b,
      texColor.a);
}
```

Feel free to check how inverted colors can be painfully beautiful!

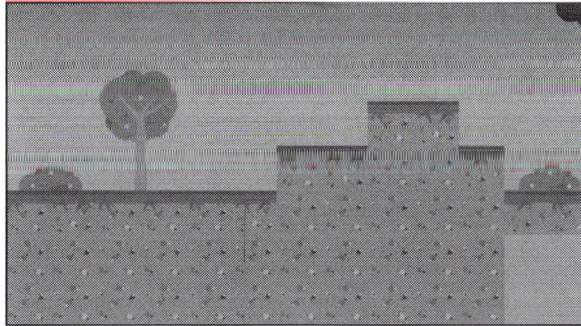

Passing parameters into shader programs

The shaders we have seen so far simply apply a non-configurable filter to a texture, and nothing more. You will most likely want to have richer effects in your applications, some that change over time and others that take into account external factors such as user input. This recipe is all about **uniforms**, which let us send parameters from the Java code into the vertex and fragment shader scripts.

We will add a vignette effect to our classic jungle background. The shader will create a circle in the center of the screen and darken everything that falls out of it. From the code, we will increase and decrease the circle's radius so that it looks like a scene transition. Refer to the following diagram for further clarity:

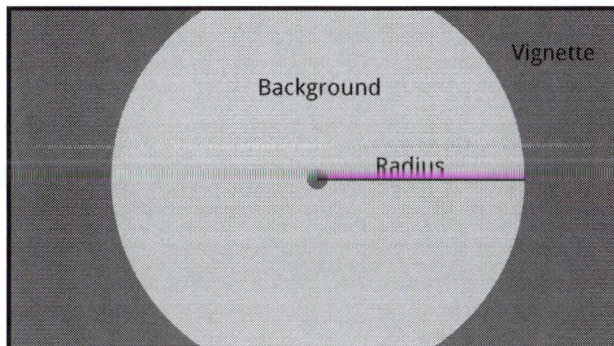

Getting ready

This recipe requires you to import the sample projects into your Eclipse workspace.

The code for the vignette shader is located in the following paths:

- `[cookbook]/samples/samples-android/assets/data/shaders/vignette.vert`
- `[cookbook]/samples/samples-android/assets/data/shaders/vignette.frag`

How to do it...

First, let's take a look at the vignette shader program. The vertex shader is exactly identical to the ones we have seen in the *Welcome to the world of shaders* recipe, so we will move on to the fragment shader, where the actual work takes place.

Two uniforms, `resolution` and `radius`, are defined, and we expect the values to be set from the Java code. The first uniform informs us about the current dimensions of the screen, and the second uniform establishes the radius of the vignette effect. You will also find two constants, `SOFTNESS` and `VIGNETTE_OPACITY`; the former is used to define the transition from dark to bright areas while the latter specifies how dark the areas outside of `radius` become:

```
uniform sampler2D u_texture;

varying vec4 v_color;
varying vec2 v_texCoord;

uniform vec2 resolution;
uniform float radius;

const float SOFTNESS = 0.1;
const float VIGNETTE_OPACITY = 0.9;
```

Take a look at the `main()` function. To create the circle, we need to figure out how far the current fragment is from the center of the screen and apply some kind of threshold, using the radius to decide whether it needs to be darkened.

We will work with positions ranging from `0.0` to `1.0`, using the center of the screen as the origin, hence `(gl_FragCoord.xy / resolution.xy) - vec2(0.5)`. We multiply the x component of the position by the aspect ratio to avoid having a squashed circle. The `length()` GLSL function returns the length of a vector, which, in our case, is the distance in relative terms (`0.0` to `1.0`) from the current fragment to the center of the screen.

The `smoothstep(low, high, value)` function returns `0.0` if the value is less than `low`, and `1.0` if it is greater than `high`. When it is somewhere in between, it uses the **Hermite cubic interpolation** function to return a value between `0.0` and `1.0`. We can also use `step(threshold, value)`, with either `0.0` or `1.0`, depending on whether `value` is less than or greater than `threshold`. However, we will have a very rough-edged circle in the end.

Finally, we take the color of the current pixel according to the texture sampler and the texture coordinates. The `mix(x, y, a)` function takes x, and y, and linear interpolates between the two, using a (ranging between `0.0` and `1.0`). `gl_FragColor` receives the resulting RGB color with the original alpha of the fragment:

```
void main() {
    vec2 position = (gl_FragCoord.xy / resolution.xy) - vec2(0.5);
    position.x *= resolution.x / resolution.y;
    float len = length(position);
    float vignette = smoothstep(radius, radius+SOFTNESS, len);
    vec4 texColor = texture2D(u_texture, v_texCoord);
    texColor.rgb = mix(texColor.rgb, texColor.rgb * vignette,
        VIGNETTE_OPACITY);
    gl_FragColor = vec4(texColor.r, texColor.g, texColor.b,
        texColor.a);
}
```

The Java code for this recipe is hosted in the `ShaderUniformSample.java` file, which contains a classic `ApplicationListener` implementation. To represent the different phases our application can go through, we define a `State` enum with the values `TransitionIn`, `TransitionOut`, and `Picture`:

```
private enum State {
    TransitionIn,
    TransitionOut,
    Picture,
}
```

Three constants are added to specify the duration of each state: a second to transition into the picture, half a second to transition out, and two seconds showing either the picture or a black screen:

```
private static final float TRANSITION_IN_TIME = 1.0f;
private static final float TRANSITION_OUT_TIME = 0.5f;
private static final float PICTURE_TIME = 2.0f;
```

The next step is to add our members. To render our background, we need a `camera`, a `viewport`, a `batch`, and the `background` `Texture` reference. To apply the effect, we also count with `ShaderProgram`, the current transition `state` and the `time` value we spent in the current state. Finally, we need to cache the current `resolution` in an array (to avoid runtime allocations) and the current `radius` of the vignette:

```
private Texture background;
private ShaderProgram shader;
private State state;
private float time;
private float resolution[];
private float radius;
```

Inside `create()`, we proceed to instantiate our `camera`, `viewport`, `batch`, `background`, and `shader`. For the latter, the `vignette.vert` and `vignette.frag` scripts are used. We then create the `resolution` array, set the sprite batch to use the vignette `shader`, and initialize the `state` and `time` variables:

```
public void create() {
    …
    background = new Texture(Gdx.files.internal("data/jungle-
      level.png"));
    shader = new ShaderProgram(Gdx.files.internal("data/shaders/
      vignette.vert"),
      Gdx.files.internal("data/shaders/vignette.frag"));
    resolution = new float[2]
    camera.position.set(VIRTUAL_WIDTH * 0.5f, VIRTUAL_HEIGHT * 0.5f,
      0.0f);
    batch.setShader(shader);
    state = State.TransitionIn;
    time = 0.0f;
}
```

As is customary, we get rid of the resources allocated by `batch`, `background`, and `shader` in the `dispose()` method:

```
public void dispose() {
    batch.dispose();
    background.dispose();
    shader.dispose();
}
```

Inside the `resize()` method, we update our `viewport` and `resolution` array with the current viewport dimensions.

The next step is to update `state`. For the transition states, we update the vignette `radius` using linear interpolation. The `radius` goes from `0.0f` (all black) to `1.0f` (all clear), so we only need to divide time over the corresponding transition duration so as to know how far through it we stand. For the outro, we go from a big radius to a small one, hence `1.0f - time / TRANSITION_OUT_TIME`.

Each state needs to check whether it is time to change to the next one, in which case we assign the new state to the `state` variable and reset `time`. Finally, we make sure `radius` is within our limits to avoid artifacts in the shader using `MathUtils.clamp()`, and we update time according to `Gdx.graphics.getDeltaTime()`:

```
switch(state) {
case TransitionIn:
  radius = time / TRANSITION_IN_TIME;

  if (time > TRANSITION_IN_TIME) {
    time = 0.0f;
    state = State.Picture;
  }

  break;
case TransitionOut:
  radius = 1.0f - time / TRANSITION_OUT_TIME;

  if (time > TRANSITION_OUT_TIME) {
    time = 0.0f;
    state = State.Picture;
  }

  break;
case Picture:
  if (time > PICTURE_TIME) {
    time = 0.0f;
    state = radius == 0.0f ? State.TransitionIn :
      State.TransitionOut;
  }
  break;
}

radius = MathUtils.clamp(radius, 0.0f, 1.0f);
time += Gdx.graphics.getDeltaTime();
```

The actual rendering is quite simple; nothing new on this aspect, except that this time, we need to pass `resolution` and `radius` through to the shader. This is achieved through the `setUniform2fv()` and `setUniformf()` methods in the `ShaderProgram` class. The first method is used for the `vec2` objects, while the second is needed for `float` uniforms:

```
viewport.update(Gdx.graphics.getWidth(), Gdx.graphics.getHeight());
camera.update();
batch.setProjectionMatrix(camera.combined);
batch.begin();
shader.setUniform2fv("resolution", resolution, 0, 2);
shader.setUniformf("radius", radius);
...
batch.end();
```

The following diagram illustrates all the transitions our sample goes through:

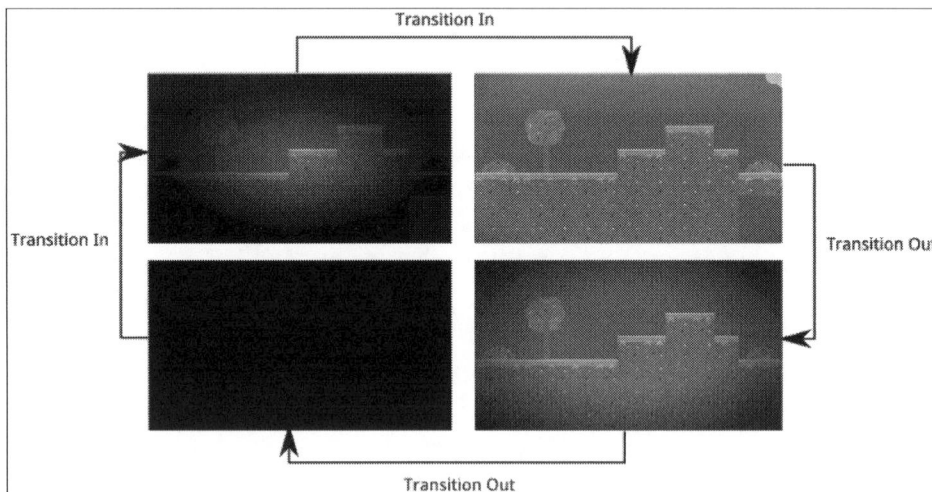

How it works...

The essence of this recipe is the uniform shader variables and how we set them from the Java code. So far, we have seen just two `ShaderProgram` methods available to do this. However, there are many other variants we must use, depending on the uniform type. For a complete list, check the official documentation at `http://libgdx.badlogicgames.com/nightlies/docs/api/com/badlogic/gdx/graphics/glutils/ShaderProgram.html`.

As you can see, they basically take the name of the uniform and a series of values, either of type `float` or `int`. This maps them directly to individual variables or arrays in GLSL. Notice how some other convenience methods are added to pass in `Vector2`, `Vector3`, or `Color` objects, which makes for more readable code:

```
void setUniformf(java.lang.String name, Vector3 values)
```

There's more...

As additional points of interest, we will learn how to detect shader compile errors and pass uniforms to the shader in a more efficient way.

Detecting shader compiler errors

Making mistakes is only human; everyone writes bad syntax at some point. Luckily enough, we have compilers that are sufficiently smart to tell us we have missed a semicolon or misspelled a variable name. Shader programs are compiled at creation time and, obviously, might contain these kinds of errors. However, if we do not explicitly check for the errors, our program will terminate with an exception the first time we try to render using the shader.

Libgdx provides an API that allows us to ask whether a shader was **successfully compiled** and, if there was a problem, to ask why. At least during development, it is highly recommended to do this on a per-shader basis. The `isCompiled()` method returns whether the compilation has been carried out with success, while `getLog()` gives us more information about the process:

```
if (!shader.isCompiled()) {
  Gdx.app.error("Shader", shader.getLog());
}
```

> Even if the shader compiles, it might be useful to print the log in debug builds to see if there are any warnings or hints.

If we remove the `SOFTNESS` constant definition from our `vignette.frag` script as an example, and try to run the sample, we will get the following error:

```
Shader: Fragment shader failed to compile with the following errors:
ERROR: 0:15: error(#143) Undeclared identifier SOFTNESS
ERROR: error(#273) 1 compilation errors.  No code generated
```

More efficient uniform settings

Every shader uniform has a location represented by an integer value, and this can be retrieved with:

```
int getUniformLocation(java.lang.String name)
```

`ShaderProgram` features equivalent `setUniform()` methods that accept a uniform location instead of a string with the name. This results in a performance improvement that might not be huge, but it does not cost us much to achieve. It is as simple as caching the locations of the uniforms we want to set at the same time we instantiate the shader.

2D depth of field shader

Shaders can help us achieve a huge amount of visually interesting effects and give your games the extra *something* to impress users. This recipe will tackle a very basic implementation of a **depth of field** postprocessing effect, which will reinforce a cinematic feeling.

The term depth of field comes from film and photography and refers to the distance between the nearest and furthest objects in a scene that appear reasonably sharp. Lenses can focus at a single distance, and the sharpness of objects will decrease as they are positioned away from the point. The human eye itself also works in a similar manner, although it can dynamically adjust the focus point much more easily.

The following diagram illustrates the depth of field effect:

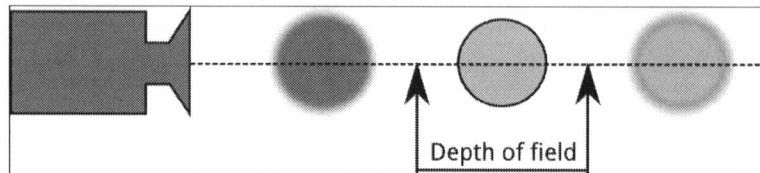

Depth of field

Computer graphics are not affected by this constraint, yet they constantly try to emulate it; why? The answer is rather simple; it gives the impression that a scene is being shown by a real-life camera lens rather than rendered as a computer simulation, which increases player immersion.

In this recipe, we will build a jungle scene where the camera focuses on a piece of the level and some characters. We will also have some blurred mountains in the distance and some blurred rocks right in front of the camera to give the impression that we are observing from inside a cave. A fragment shader implementing the **Gaussian blur** will be combined with frame buffers to create the effect. For further information, check `http://en.wikipedia.org/wiki/Gaussian_blur`.

Quite a few concepts are needed to fully grasp the Gaussian blur. Long story short, a Gaussian blur can be achieved in two passes, a horizontal blur followed by a vertical blur. Find the process divided in the steps shown in the following diagram:

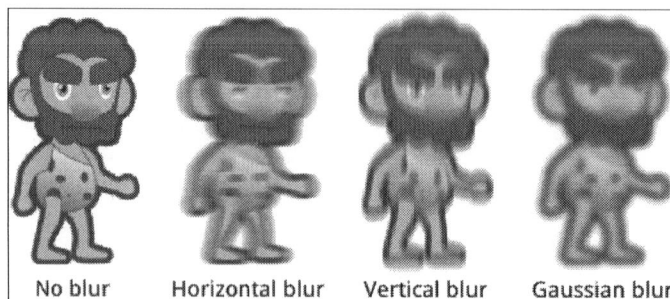

No blur   Horizontal blur   Vertical blur   Gaussian blur

Getting ready

For the sake of simplicity, we will avoid using texture packing this time. All the PNGs needed to build the scene can be found in the `[cookbook]/sample/sample-android/assets/data/blur` folder. The two shader scripts used in this sample are:

- `[cookbook]/sample/sample-android/assets/data/shaders/blur.vert`
- `[cookbook]/sample/sample-android/assets/data/shaders/blur.frag`

As usual, you need to import the sample projects into your Eclipse workspace.

How to do it...

Let's take a look at the `blur.frag` code as its vertex counterpart is exactly the same as in previous recipes, it just passes all the information with no modifications. First, we define varying variables for the color and texture coordinates that come from the vertex shader. Then, we add uniforms that will be set on Java's side. The texture to be used is set by Libgdx, but we also have the screen's `resolution`, `radius` of the blur effect in pixels, and `dir` (either horizontal or vertical):

```
varying vec4 v_color;
varying vec2 v_texCoord;

uniform sampler2D u_texture;
uniform float resolution;
uniform float radius;
uniform vec2 dir;
```

The main idea behind each fragment shader pass is to grab the current pixel along eight neighbors as far from the original pixel as the radius indicates, and mix them together using a set of predefined weights. The closer the neighbor is to the original pixel, the higher its impact is on the combined color.

The `radius` uniform comes in pixel units, but the `texture2D()` function uses values from `0.0` to `1.0`, so we need to divide by `resolution`. The result is stored in the `sum` variable and finally assigned to `gl_FragColor`:

```
void main() {
  vec4 sum = vec4(0.0);
  vec2 tc = v_texCoord;

  // Number of pixels off the central pixel to sample from
  float blur = radius/resolution;
...
  // Blur direction
  float hstep = dir.x;
```

```
    float vstep = dir.y;
...
    // Apply blur using 9 samples and predefined gaussian weights
    sum += texture2D(u_texture, vec2(tc.x - 4.0*blur*hstep, tc.y -
       4.0*blur*vstep)) * 0.006;
    sum += texture2D(u_texture, vec2(tc.x - 3.0*blur*hstep, tc.y -
       3.0*blur*vstep)) * 0.044;
    sum += texture2D(u_texture, vec2(tc.x - 2.0*blur*hstep, tc.y -
       2.0*blur*vstep)) * 0.121;
    sum += texture2D(u_texture, vec2(tc.x - 1.0*blur*hstep, tc.y -
       1.0*blur*vstep)) * 0.194;

    sum += texture2D(u_texture, vec2(tc.x, tc.y)) * 0.27;

    sum += texture2D(u_texture, vec2(tc.x + 1.0*blur*hstep, tc.y +
       1.0*blur*vstep)) * 0.194;
    sum += texture2D(u_texture, vec2(tc.x + 2.0*blur*hstep, tc.y +
       2.0*blur*vstep)) * 0.121;
    sum += texture2D(u_texture, vec2(tc.x + 3.0*blur*hstep, tc.y +
       3.0*blur*vstep)) * 0.044;
    sum += texture2D(u_texture, vec2(tc.x + 4.0*blur*hstep, tc.y +
       4.0*blur*vstep)) * 0.006;

    gl_FragColor = sum;
}
```

The Java code lies within the `BlurSample.java` file. We have our typical `camera`, `viewport`, and `batch` accompanied by a bunch of `Texture` references to represent the objects in our scene.

To preserve alpha values, we blur out collections of objects that lie in a common plane rather than individual ones; so, we need to render them to `FrameBuffer`. Depth of field is achieved in two steps, and we cannot perform it directly onscreen as we might blur the wrong objects. This is why horizontal blur is performed on an additional offscreen buffer, and it goes through the vertical blur stage while being rendered onscreen:

```
    private ShaderProgram shader;
    private FrameBuffer fboA;
    private FrameBuffer fboB;
```

The following diagram illustrates this process:

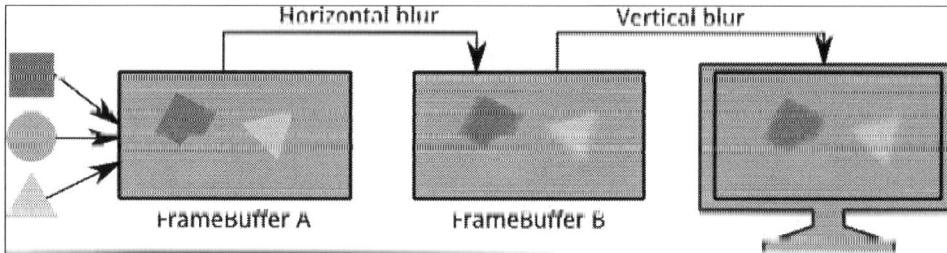

The `create()` method is used to instantiate all our members the way we have been doing, so check the sample code for specifics. However, take a look at how we initialize the uniforms in our shader between calls to its `begin()` and `end()` methods:

```
shader.begin();
shader.setUniformf("dir", 0.0f, 0.0f);
shader.setUniformf("resolution", VIRTUAL_WIDTH);
shader.setUniformf("radius", 0.0f);
shader.end();
```

> For clarity, we have set uniforms by name, but you should use the integer location for performance reasons.

Remember to free all the allocated resources in the `dispose()` method. This involves the sprite batch, both FBOs, the shader program, and all the textures.

The sky background will not be blurred, so it is rendered directly to the screen with the default shader. The mountain texture is the first layer that will be blurred, so we render it to `fboA`, and then call `applyBlur()`, which does the rest. The foreground and the characters are exactly what the camera is focusing on, so there is no need to blur them out. Finally, the cave is completely out of focus, so we repeat the same process we followed for the mountains:

```
public void render() {
...
  batch.begin();

  // Draw background as-is
  batch.setShader(null);
  drawTexture(background,  0.0f, 0.0f);
  batch.flush();

  // Draw blurred mountains
  fboA.begin();
  Gdx.gl.glClearColor(0.0f, 0.0f, 0.0f, 0.0f);
```

```
Gdx.gl.glClear(GL20.GL_COLOR_BUFFER_BIT);
batch.setShader(null);
drawTexture(mountains, 0.0f, 0.0f);
batch.flush();
fboA.end();
applyBlur(3.0f);

// Draw foreground and characters without blur effect
batch.setShader(null);
drawTexture (foreground, 0.0f, 0.0f);
drawTexture (caveman, 100.0f, 150.0f);
drawTexture (dinosaur, 600.0f, 245.0f);
batch.flush();

// Draw blurred rock
fboA.begin();
Gdx.gl.glClearColor(0.0f, 0.0f, 0.0f, 0.0f);
Gdx.gl.glClear(GL20.GL_COLOR_BUFFER_BIT);
batch.setShader(null);
drawTexture(rock, 0.0f, 0.0f);
batch.flush();
fboA.end();
applyBlur(5.0f);

batch.end();
}
```

The `applyBlur()` method takes the blur amount in pixels, and it applies the horizontal blur from `fboA` to `fboB` and the vertical blur from `fboB` to the screen. By now, you should be acquainted with how uniforms are set from the Java code using one of the `setUniform()` family methods:

```
private void applyBlur(float blur) {
    // Horizontal blur from FBO A to FBO B
    fboB.begin();
    batch.setShader(shader);
    shader.setUniformf("dir", 1.0f, 0.0f);
    shader.setUniformf("radius", blur);
    Gdx.gl.glClearColor(0.0f, 0.0f, 0.0f, 0.0f);
    Gdx.gl.glClear(GL20.GL_COLOR_BUFFER_BIT);
    drawTexture(fboA.getColorBufferTexture(),  0.0f, 0.0f);
    batch.flush();
    fboB.end();

    // Vertical blur from FBO B to the screen
```

```
    shader.setUniformf("dir", 0.0f, 1.0f);
    shader.setUniformf("radius", blur);
    drawTexture(fboB.getColorBufferTexture(), 0.0f, 0.0f);
    batch.flush();
}
```

When the same scene is rendered with a well-configured depth of field effect, the results are quite obvious and effective if the cinematic look and feel is what we pursue:

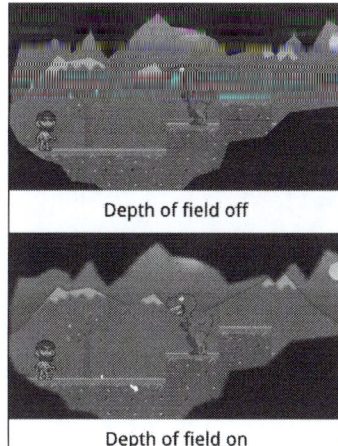

Depth of field off

Depth of field on

There's more...

Truth be told, everything we have produced so far in this recipe can be obtained much more efficiently with pre-blurred textures. However, before you ask for your money back, give it some thought. Generating the depth of field effect as a postprocessing effect clearly has its perks because it enables us to change the plane the camera is focusing on whenever we please.

Taking the previous scene as an example; we can make the camera focus on the cave to show another caveman observing what is happening out there. Transitions between camera focus can be smoothed by interpolating the blur radius of each plane in the scene. This is a really powerful narrative tool, and tons of high-profile games, both 2D and 3D, make constant use of it.

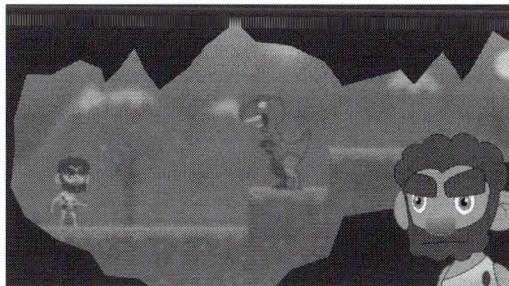

> ▶ The last three recipes on shaders should have given you a basic understanding of GLSL and what can be produced with it. You can now continue reading the *Embedding a Libgdx window into a Java desktop application* recipe.

Embedding a Libgdx window into a Java desktop application

Developing a medium-sized game takes an unholy amount of time. Logically, this makes your **toolset** a crucial factor because the tools' productivity and your mastery over them will dramatically affect the process. Most areas are already covered by brilliant tools: tiles for level editing, spine for skeletal animation, Physics Editor to create rigid bodies, the Libgdx particle editor, and the list goes on.

However, you might have certain requirements that no existing software features yet. Beware, the *never reinvent the wheel* advice is really good advice. Think about it; if the tool closest to what you need is open source, it is probably more convenient to check out the repository and add such a feature yourself. The community will probably be quite grateful for this and you will get public recognition!

Alright, if you really need something completely different, the best option can end up being implementing a new tool from scratch. This tool can typically have a bunch of UI controls (buttons, panels, tick boxes, sliders, and so on) and a previewer to see live results of our work. How can we code this?

In this recipe, we will learn how to embed a Libgdx canvas into a **Swing** application, which is the main Java GUI toolkit. As an example, we will create an application that lists all the samples in this book on the right and runs them on the left, without launching additional windows.

Note that this is not an introductory article about Swing; some previous knowledge on the matter is advisable.

Getting ready

This time, you only need to make sure that the sample projects are in your Eclipse workspace.

How to do it...

For obvious reasons, this exercise focuses exclusively on desktop platforms, so take a look at the code within the `samples/desktop` folder. More specifically, open up the `SwingCanvasSample.java` file.

`SwingCanvasSample` derives from `JFrame`, a top level Swing container. It also implements `SampleLauncher`, a custom utility interface to help us launch our samples. The `LwjglAWTCanvas` member is the entry point to our Libgdx application—it contains an OpenGL surface on an AWT `Canvas`. As you might suspect, an AWT `Canvas` is a component that can be added to a `JFrame` layout. `SampleList` is a custom `JPanel` containing a list with all the book samples and a button to launch them:

```
public class SwingCanvasSample extends JFrame implements
SampleLauncher {
  LwjglAWTCanvas canvas;
  SampleList list;


  ...
}
```

In the constructor, we instantiate `SampleList`, passing the `SampleLauncher` implementation as a parameter, and we add it to the content pane on the left. We set the size of `JFrame`, make it visible and nonresizable, and then we set the title. Finally, we establish that `System.exit(0)` is called when the window is closed. The canvas will not be created until the **Run Sample** button is pressed (inside `SampleList`):

```
public SwingCanvasSample() {
  list = new SampleList(this);
  list.setSize(320, 540);

  Container container = getContentPane();
  container.add(list, BorderLayout.WEST);

  setSize(1280, 540);
  setVisible(true);
  setResizable(false);
  setTitle("Libgdx Game Development Cookbook Samples");

  addWindowListener(new WindowAdapter() {
    public void windowClosed (WindowEvent event) {
      System.exit(0);
    }
  });
}
```

The SampleLauncher interface declares the launchSample() method. It gets called whenever the user picks a sample from the left-hand side panel and clicks on **Run Sample**. What we need to do is remove the previous Libgdx sample using remove(), if it exists, and instantiate the new sample. GdxSamples is a static class that maps sample names to the ApplicationListener classes. Its newSample() method makes sure that the corresponding ApplicationListener is given a name that we can use to create a new LwjglAWTCanvas and embed into the content pane:

```
public boolean launchSample(String sampleName) {
  Container container = getContentPane();

  if (canvas != null) {
    container.remove(canvas.getCanvas());
  }

  ApplicationListener sample = GdxSamples.newSample(sampleName);

  canvas = new LwjglAWTCanvas(sample, true);
  canvas.getCanvas().setSize(960, 540);
  container.add(canvas.getCanvas(), BorderLayout.EAST);

  pack();

  return test != null;
}
```

The main method simply creates a new SwingCanvasSample:

```
public static void main (String[] args) {
  SwingUtilities.invokeLater(new Runnable() {
    @Override
    public void run () {
      new SwingCanvasSample();
    }
  });
}
```

With this method, you can easily embed as many Libgdx canvases as you wish into your Swing applications. The result for our sample is illustrated in the following figure:

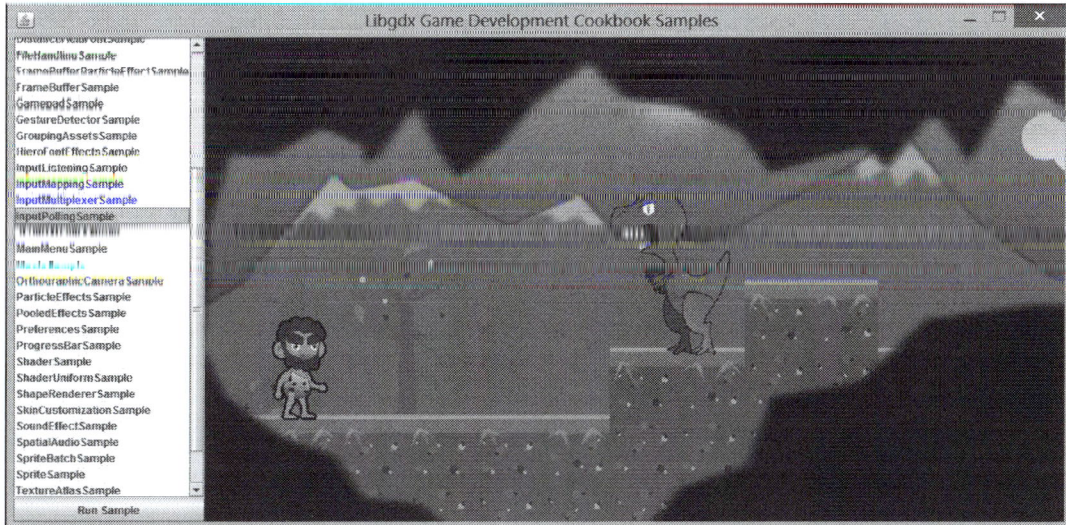

How it works...

To put things into perspective, let's regress to the *Understanding the project structure and application life cycle* recipe, where we examined the Libgdx projects' architecture. Every supported platform had a backend that implemented the `Application` interface and a launcher to instantiate them passing through an `ApplicationListener` object.

In our current situation, `LwglAWTCanvas` is a different backend and our `JFrame` acts as the launcher. Do not trust these words; as an exercise, feel free to examine the Libgdx source code, and see for yourself how everything fits together nicely.

There's more...

An alternative to creating a tool with Swing and embedding a Libgdx canvas in it is to build a Libgdx-only application using its **Scene2D UI** API, which is easily extensible and feature rich. Spine, the popular skeletal animation editor, took this approach.

Like everything in life, both methods have their drawbacks. Using an OpenGL canvas in Swing reduces performance, though this might not be a deal breaker as per your requirements. On the other hand, the Libgdx Scene2D UI makes it a bit more difficult to design layouts.

See also

▶   Move on to *Chapter 8, User Interfaces with Scene2D,* and its opening recipe, *Introducing the Scene2D API,* to find out more about alternatives to embedding Libgdx canvases into Swing applications for tool development.

4
Detecting User Input

In this chapter, we will cover the following recipes:

- ▶ Detecting user input via event polling
- ▶ Detecting user input via event listening
- ▶ Managing multiple listeners at once
- ▶ Detecting more complex gestures
- ▶ Introducing the controllers API
- ▶ Input mapping for cross-platform development

Introduction

Games are fundamentally different from other kinds of modern media: they are interactive. The player adopts an active role and jumps into the action of what is happening on the other side. This is a true marvel and one of the reasons why people feel so engaged.

For a game to be enjoyable, interaction needs to be seamless and fluid. The user should not feel a barrier or any disconnection between what they want to do and what actually happens. Good controls are required for your game to succeed!

Throughout this chapter, we will discuss the myriad of ways to detect user input within Libgdx and the extra utilities you can use to make your life easier.

Detecting user input via event polling

Typically, there are a couple of approaches when it comes to detecting user input. The most straightforward approach is **event polling**, which involves actively querying the state of a specific input peripheral whenever we want to make a decision based on it. This can happen either in every frame or on demand for specific bits of game logic.

Throughout this recipe, we will work with an example where you will learn how to query the keyboard, mouse, accelerometer, and compass of the device. The updated state of these devices will be shown on the screen.

Getting ready

The sample projects are required to follow this recipe; please make sure that you already have them in your Eclipse workspace.

How to do it...

The code for this recipe is found in the `InputPollingSample` class. We have the classic members to support regular rendering: camera, viewport, and sprite batch. Besides these, we add a `BitmapFont` object to draw the state of the input devices on the screen, rather than using logging and spamming the console in every frame. In the `create()` method, we instantiate our members and in the `dispose()` method, we deallocate the batch and font resources.

> Take a peek at *Chapter 6, Font Rendering*, for more details on how `BitmapFont` works.

The actual polling takes place inside the `render()` method, which means it will run in every frame. We will proceed on a per device basis; you will see that this is extremely simple.

We can retrieve the mouse or touch coordinates with `Gdx.input.getX()` and `Gdx.input.getY()`. Keep in mind that they come in screen space, so you have to call `unproject()` on your camera to transform them into world space. Computer mice typically have three buttons: left, right, and middle. We can check the state of these buttons with `Gdx.input.isButtonPressed()`, passing in the appropriate constant. Alternatively, on mobile devices, you can use `Gdx.input.isTouched()`.

Screen space means the actual pixels on your device's screen, while world space refers to the virtual units you use to model your game world. A camera knows how to convert between the two spaces. Refer to *Chapter 2, Working with 2D Graphics*, for more details.

Have a look at the following lines of code:

```
float mouseX = Gdx.input.getX();
float mouseY = Gdx.input.getY();
boolean leftPressed = Gdx.input.isButtonPressed(Buttons.LEFT);
boolean rightPressed = Gdx.input.isButtonPressed(Buttons.RIGHT);
boolean middlePressed = Gdx.input.isButtonPressed(Buttons.MIDDLE);
```

Since they lack buttons, touch events in phones and tablets correspond to the `Buttons.LEFT` constant. The reason behind this is simply convenience.

To know whether a given key is pressed or not, we can use the `Gdx.input.isKeyPressed()` method, passing in the corresponding constant, as shown in the following lines of code. These constants live inside the `Keys` static class; please check the official documentation at `http://libgdx.badlogicgames.com/nightlies/docs/api/com/badlogic/gdx/Input.Keys.html` to access the whole list.

```
boolean wPressed = Gdx.input.isKeyPressed(Keys.W);
boolean aPressed = Gdx.input.isKeyPressed(Keys.A);
boolean sPressed = Gdx.input.isKeyPressed(Keys.S);
boolean dPressed = Gdx.input.isKeyPressed(Keys.D);
```

Most tablets and phones come with accelerometers. These sensors detect the device acceleration along the three axes relative to the Earth's gravitational field. Axes are queried separately using methods similar to `Gdx.input.getAccelerometerX()`. The values we obtain lie within the [-10.0, 10.0] range:

```
float accelerometerX = Gdx.input.getAccelerometerX();
float accelerometerY = Gdx.input.getAccelerometerY();
float accelerometerZ = Gdx.input.getAccelerometerZ();
```

Other devices also feature a compass, which is often used for map applications such as Google Maps. The `Gdx.input.getPitch()` function returns the device's orientation in degrees around its *x* axis, where positive *x* points to the west. The `Gdx.input.getRoll()` function returns the *y* axis rotation in degrees, where positive *y* points to the north. Finally, `Gdx.input.getAzimuth()` gives us the *z* axis rotation in degrees, where positive *z* points to the Earth's center:

```
float pitch = Gdx.input.getPitch();
float roll = Gdx.input.getRoll();
float azimuth = Gdx.input.getAzimuth();
```

The following diagram illustrates a phone's axes:

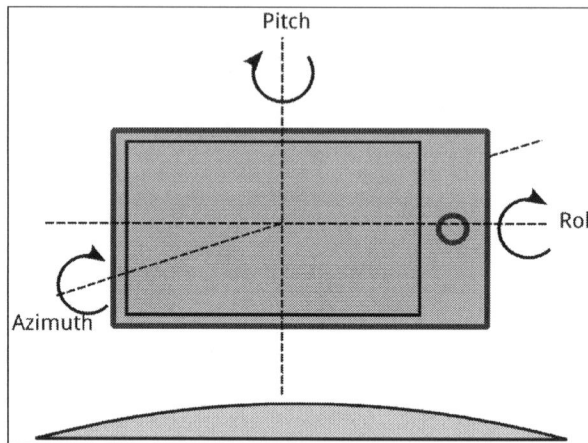

The result of each one of the queries we have made is shown on the screen using the `draw()` method in the `BitmapFont` class. Check the sample source code for more details.

How it works...

The input is one of the Libgdx main subsystems and is statically accessible from the `Gdx` environment class. Every backend is responsible for implementing all the functionality offered by the interface. Feel free to dig in to the Libgdx repository to find out on your own, but here is how each backend achieves it:

- ▶ **Desktop**: This uses the **LWJGL** framework, which provides input features. The `Input` implementation is `LwjglInput`.
- ▶ **Android**: The **Android SDK** is used by the `AndroidInput` class.
- ▶ **HTML 5**: The `GWTInput` class uses the **GWT** input systems.
- ▶ **iOS**: The `IOSInput` class uses the `cocoatouch` module in **RoboVM**.

Peripherals can be disabled or enabled using the configuration parameters that are passed to the launcher class. See the *Understanding the project structure and application life cycle recipe* of *Chapter 1, Diving into Libgdx*, for more details.

There's more...

A couple of extra useful things that you can do with the input interface is check the peripheral availability and show or hide the on-screen keyboard.

Checking input availability

Desktop platforms always have a keyboard and a mouse, but they tend to lack touch screens and definitely do not have a compass or an accelerometer. On the other hand, smartphones typically have a compass and an accelerometer. It would not be rare to find yourself with the need to check whether a particular peripheral is available or not at runtime.

This is really easy to achieve with the `Gdx.input.isPeripheralAvailable()` method, passing in a constant that represents the device in question. The following code fragment has been added to `InputPollingSample` in order to check for input availability:

```
Gdx.input.isPeripheralAvailable(Peripheral.Accelerometer);
Gdx.input.isPeripheralAvailable(Peripheral.Compass);
Gdx.input.isPeripheralAvailable(Peripheral.HardwareKeyboard);
Gdx.input.isPeripheralAvailable(Peripheral.MultitouchScreen);
Gdx.input.isPeripheralAvailable(Peripheral.OnscreenKeyboard);
Gdx.input.isPeripheralAvailable(Peripheral.Vibrator);
```

Showing the on-screen keyboard

Phones and tablets may not have a hardware keyboard, but we can make them display an on-screen one if need be. In order to control whether or not such a keyboard should be active, you can use the following line of code:

```
Gdx.input.setOnScreenKeyboardVisible(boolean visible);
```

Detecting user input via event listening

Rather than asking the input system about the state of a certain peripheral in every single frame, we can let the input system know that we are interested in certain user-generated events and we can get notified whenever they occur. This is known as **event listening**, and it is better known in the design patterns world as **Observer**.

> It is important to know the most common design patters and when to apply them. To learn more about this topic, we recommend that you take a look at the book *Design Patterns: Elements of Reusable Object-Oriented Software, Erich Gamma, Addison-Wesley Professional*, or the freely available *Game Programming Patterns, Robert Nystrom, Apress* (http://gameprogrammingpatterns.com).

In this recipe, we will tell Libgdx to notify our sample application of the input events and show them all as a list on the screen. Examples of input events are mouse movements, touch dragging, scrolling, touching/clicking, key presses and releases, and character typing.

Getting ready

Once again, make sure that the sample projects are available from your Eclipse workspace.

How to do it...

This time round, please direct your attention towards the `InputListeningSample.java` file, where the code for this recipe lives. We have a `MESSAGE_MAX` constant that defines the maximum number of input events we can show at once on the screen:

```
private static final int MESSAGE_MAX = 45;
```

The list of events is nothing more than an array of string objects, holding each message, as shown in the following code. As we did in the previous recipe, we need an orthographic camera to render these messages, a rectangle to represent our viewport, a sprite batch, and a bitmap font object:

```
private Array<String> messages;
```

The `create()` method details should be fairly easy to understand at this point. However, it is worth mentioning that in order to tell Libgdx that the current object is interested in receiving input events, we use `Gdx.input.setInputProcessor()`, which takes an `InputProcessor` interface implementation.

> Be aware that only one input processor can be active at a time using this method.

Have a look at the following code:

```
public void create() {
...

    Gdx.input.setInputProcessor(this);
}
```

> The `InputListeningSample` class inherits from
> `GdxSample`, which in turn extends `InputAdapter`.
> Finally, `InputAdapter` is just a stub implementation
> of the `InputProcessor` interface.

Next one up is the `render()` method, where we iterate over all the messages and use the bitmap font to draw the message on the screen. We do so at a fixed location on the x axis, while we decrease the value of y axis at each step so as to stack messages on top of each other.

Here is the complete `InputProcessor` interface, which `InputListeningSample` implements. For every method, we make a call to the `addMessage()` method, shown later on, passing in some string with the event information:

```
Public interface InputProcessor {
    public boolean keyDown (int keycode);
    public boolean keyUp (int keycode);
    public boolean keyTyped (char character);
    public boolean booleanbn (int boolea, int boolea, int pointer,
        int button);
    public boolean boolean (int boolea, int boolea, int pointer, int
        button);
    public boolean touchDragged (int boolea, int boolea, int
        pointer);
    public boolean mouseMoved (int boolea, int boolea);
    public boolean scrolled (int amount);
}
```

The methods' names are quite self-explanatory. Nevertheless, please find a detailed list as follows:

- `keyDown()`: Whenever the user presses a hardware or on-screen key, this method receives a value from the `Key` static class.
- `keyUp()`: Whenever the user releases a previously pressed key, this method also receives a value from the `Key` static class.
- `keyTyped()`: This is fired up under the same circumstances as `keyUp()`, only it takes the character that the user pressed.

- ► `touchDown()`: This is called whenever the user touches the screen or clicks on the screen with the mouse/touchpad. It gets the screen coordinates, the pointer, and the button code from the `Buttons` static class.

- ► `touchUp()`: This is identical to `touchDown()`, but it fires whenever the user releases the finger or the mouse button.

- ► `touchDragged()`: This fires every time the mouse or finger position changes while clicking on or touching the screen. It receives the new screen coordinates and the pointer that caused the event.

- ► `mouseMoved()`: Every time the user moves the mouse, the method takes the new cursor coordinates in screen space. Note that this will fire regardless of whether or not the user is clicking.

- ► `scrolled()`: This is fired whenever the user activates the mouse wheel.

> The term **pointer** makes sense when we think about multitouch screens since it refers to the index of the finger that causes the event. Naturally, this is not really necessary in desktop applications, but it is necessary for mobile/tablet applications.

Whenever `addMessage()` is called, we call `add()` on the messages array with the new string and a timestamp. We just need to make sure that the array's size does not exceed `MESSAGE_MAX`, in which case, we remove the first element, which is the oldest event in the collection. This is shown in the following code:

```
private void addMessage(String message) {
  messages.add(message + " time: " + System.currentTimeMillis());

  if (messages.size > MESSAGE_MAX) {
    messages.removeIndex(0);
  }
}
```

It would be really good to experiment with events and see for yourself under which conditions they fire. This example will give you a better insight on how input listening works on Libgdx.

Event polling versus event listening

Which approach is better? Polling or event listening? An excellent question, but unfortunately, there is no immediate answer. It really depends on the situation that you are facing. If you simply want to occasionally make a decision depending on the state of some input device, polling might be the best approach. On the other hand, if what you want is to react to individual actions, event listening could be the way to go as it tends to be more efficient. If you need to check the state of a key when the user clicks the mouse, then you can use a combination of the two.

With input polling, you might miss inputs. If the user presses a key and releases it during the same frame, those events will be lost.

At the end of the day, what matters is to write efficient code while maintaining readability and ease of modification.

How It works...

Event listeners are typically implemented in a very similar way across engines and frameworks, as follows:

1. The interested party registers itself as a listener of certain events with a manager.

2. The manager detects an event whenever it takes places and informs the registered listener. This is achieved with method invocation.

3. As soon as the listener is no longer interested, it unregisters itself with the manager.

Libgdx's `Input` backend implementations handle the specifics of when to call the `InputProcessor` event handlers while achieving uniform behavior across platforms.

There's more...

Android devices have the Back and Menu keys with default behaviors. The Back key goes up one slot in the `Activity` stack, and the Menu key directly takes us to the launcher. Our Libgdx games may have different screens, but they are not implemented as different `Activity` objects, which means that both the Back and Menu keys will take us out of the application. Surely, we do not want this!

Using Libgdx, we can prevent such behavior and implement your response. As an example, the Back key could take us from the game screen to the level selection screen, whereas the Menu key could show an exit confirmation dialog.

To intercept the Back and Menu keys, we need to use the following methods (the Android Home key behavior cannot be overridden for security reasons):

```
Gdx.input.setCatchBackKey(boolean catchBack);
Gdx.input.setCatchMenuKey(boolean catchMenu);
```

Later on, we can react to these keys using their corresponding codes inside the `keyDown` event handler as shown in the following snippet:

```
public boolean keyDown (int keycode) {
  if (keycode == Keys.MENU) {

  }
  else if (keycode == Keys.BACK) {
```

```
    }

    return true;
}
```

The following screenshot shows a game running on an Android phone with the Back, Menu, and Home keys visible:

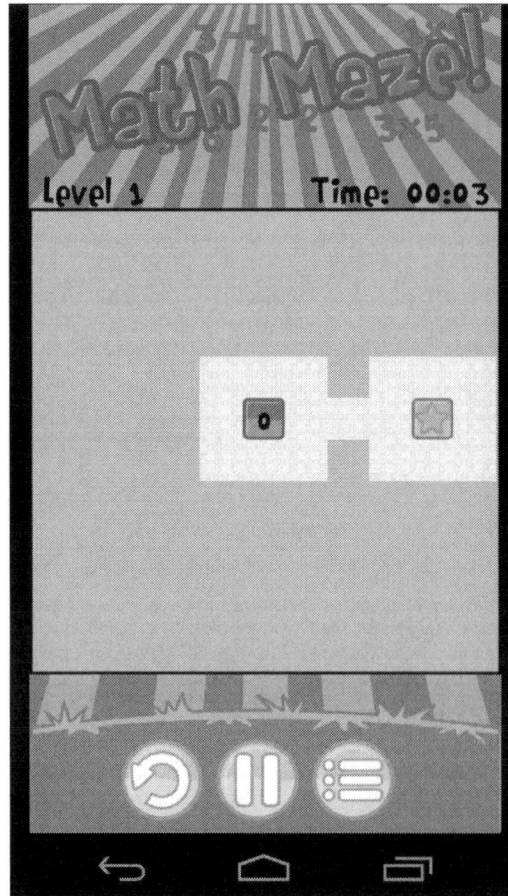

Managing multiple listeners at once

So far, we have studied the two basic mechanisms that Libgdx provides when it comes to handling user input. An event-based approach can be quite useful to respond to certain actions. However, only one `InputListener` can capture events at a given time.

Often, you will find yourself with two separate subsystems that are interested in different events. Maybe the player input controller, UI system, and game screen all want to be informed whenever the user does something. How will you tackle this limitation then?

You will be pleased to know that Libgdx also comes with a way to achieve this with minimal hassle. Throughout this recipe, we will cover **input multiplexing** and will have two classes listening to events at once.

Getting ready

For this recipe, it is recommended that you have the sample projects available from the Eclipse workspace.

How to do it...

Take a look at the `InputMultiplexerSample` class, which looks very similar to the sample from the previous recipe. At the bottom of the file, we have two inner classes called `InputHandlerA` and `InputHandlerB`. Both of these extend the `InputAdapter` stub class. However, each one of them overrides different methods; while `A` is interested in the key-related events, `B` only cares about touch- and mouse-related events.

Two `InputProcessor` objects can handle the same event through a multiplexer.

The following listing illustrates our description. Implementation details have been stripped for reasons of space. They simply call the `addMessage()` method of `InputMultiplexerSample`, providing the event data for logging purposes:

```
private class InputHandlerA extends InputAdapter {
  public boolean keyDown (int keycode);
  public boolean keyUp (int keycode);
  public boolean keyTyped (char character);
}

private class InputHandlerB extends InputAdapter {
  public boolean touchDown (int screenX, int screenY, int pointer,
    int button);
  public boolean touchUp (int screenX, int screenY, int pointer,
    int button);
  public boolean touchDragged (int screenX, int screenY, int
    pointer);
  public boolean mouseMoved (int screenX, int screenY);
  public boolean scrolled (int amount);
}
```

To distinguish between the two systems more clearly, we have a `ScreenLogMessage` class, which simply holds a string message and a color. `InputHandlerA` uses yellow, while `InputHandlerB` goes for green, shown as follows:

```
private class ScreenLogMessage {
  public final String message;
  public final Color color;

  public ScreenLogMessage(String message, Color color) {
    this.message = message;
    this.color = color;
  }
}
```

Our `InputMultiplexerSample` class starts from where `InputListeningSample` left, and it adds a `InputMultiplexer` object and an array of `ScreenLogMessage` references. The multiplexer will hold references to both our listeners and will distribute all input events between them:

```
private InputMultiplexer multiplexer;
private Array<ScreenLogMessage> messages;
```

In the `create()` method, we need to pay attention to what we do with the multiplexer. We set it as our input processor in the Libgdx input system and then add new instances of our `InputHandler` classes to the multiplexer:

```
public void create() {
  ...

  messages = new Array<ScreenLogMessage>();
  Gdx.input.setInputProcessor(multiplexer);
  multiplexer.addProcessor(new InputHandlerA());
  multiplexer.addProcessor(new InputHandlerB());
}
```

Let's quickly move on to the `render()` method. Here, we simply iterate through the `ScreenLogMessage` objects, rendering them on the screen using our bitmap font. Messages are displayed at a fixed location along the x axis while we decrease our y axis value so as to stack them on top of each other:

```
public void render() {
  ...

  batch.begin();
  for (int i = 0; i < messages.size; ++i) {
    ScreenLogMessage message = messages.get(i);
    font.setColor(message.color);
```

```
        font.draw(batch, message.message, 20.0f, VIRTUAL_HEIGHT -
          15.0f * (i + 1));
    }
    batch.end();
}
```

Whenever an event is caught by one of the handlers, it calls the `addMessage()` method of the enclosing class. This basically adds the message to the array and removes the oldest one if in case there are too many elements already:

```
private void addMessage(String message, Color color) {
    messages.add(new ScreenLogMessage(message, color));

    if (messages.size > MESSAGE_MAX) {
        messages.removeIndex(0);
    }
}
```

Feel free to run the sample; after a few movements of the mouse and keystrokes, you will see which processor handles each event.

How it works...

`InputMultiplexer` is nothing more than a special `InputProcessor` interface implementation; feel free to see this by yourself in the Libgdx source code. Your own `InputProcessor` implementations can be registered with it and removed when required. The multiplexer will simply channel all the events to the registered listeners.

There is one subtlety to take into account though. You may have noticed how event handlers are supposed to return a Boolean value. If a handler returns `true`, it means that the event has been processed and will not be sent to the next processor. Intuitively, if it returns `false`, the notification process will carry on as normal:

```
public boolean keyDown (int keycode)
```

Consequently, the order in which the `InputProcessor` objects are added to a multiplexer matters. Do you want your UI system to have the chance to decide whether or not it is interested in a certain event before the player controller takes over? This can also happen within a complex UI system, where some widgets can capture an event and prevent it from being broadcasted. We will cover this in *Chapter 8, User Interfaces with Scene2D*.

See also

- ▶ After this recipe, most of your input processing related needs should be pretty much covered. Going further, topics are slightly more complex but also exciting. Carry on and read the *Detecting more complex gestures* recipe.

Detecting more complex gestures

Control and user experience should receive a strong focus when you are working on applications in general and games in particular. It is essential that your target audience finds your product to be smooth and flawless. Many elements impact the user experience, such as UI or sound, although a truly crucial one is controls.

Tapping, double tapping, pinching, panning, zooming—there are a myriad of **gestures** that have almost become an accepted convention. For better or worse, users now expect a certain behavior when they perform an action on a specific game element.

For instance, it is normal for the camera to be moved around when you swing your finger over a map so that the displayed section changes.

Libgdx offers an easy way to detect and react to the most typical gestures. In this recipe, you will learn how to do it through a sample application. We will capture user gestures and show a log on the screen, as we have done in previous input-related recipes.

Getting ready

Before we continue, please double check that you have the sample projects available from your Eclipse workspace.

How to do it...

The code for this recipe is located in the `GestureDetectorSample.java` file. First, we define a few constants that we will use further ahead, as follows:

```
private static final int MESSAGE_MAX = 30;
private static final float HALF_TAP_SQUARE_SIZE = 20.0f;
private static final float TAP_COUNT_INTERVAL = 0.4f;
private static final float LONG_PRESS_DURATION = 1.1f;
private static final float MAX_FLING_DELAY = 0.15f;
```

`GestureDetector` will do all the necessary heavy lifting to detect gestures for us, letting us enjoy our lives. We also have an array of messages to keep events' information. Naturally, our sample also requires a camera, batch, viewport, and a bitmap font to use when rendering the log messages:

```
private GestureDetector gestureDetector;
private Array<String> messages;
```

The `create()` method has nothing special except for the instantiation of our gesture detector. It takes a few parameters to configure, as follows:

- `float halfTapSquareSize`: This denotes half the width (in pixels) of the square of the initial touch event. If the user moves their finger/mouse further than this, it will stop being considered as a long press.
- `float tapCountInterval`: This denotes the time (in seconds) for consecutive taps to be considered as part of the same sequence; otherwise, the tap counter will reset.
- `float longPressDuration`: This denotes the time (in seconds) that the user has to press for the long press event to fire.
- `float maxFlingDelay`: This denotes the time between the detection of a fling gesture and it being reported as an event.

The `GestureDetector` constructor also takes a `GestureListener` interface implementation as a parameter. In our case, we pass in a new instance of the `GestureHandler` inner class, which is defined later. Our newly created gesture detector will be set as the input processor, as it turns out, it conveniently implements such interfaces. This is shown in the following code:

```
public void create() {
  …

  gestureDetector = new GestureDetector(HALF_TAP_SQUARE_SIZE,
    TAP_COUNT_INTERVAL, LONG_PRESS_DURATION, MAX_FLING_DELAY, new
    GestureHandler());
  Gdx.input.setInputProcessor(gestureDetector);
}
```

Let's move on to the `render()` method because there is nothing to do in `dispose()`. To render the event information, we iterate the log array, calling the bitmap font's `draw()` method:

```
public void render() {
  …

  batch.begin();
  for (int i = 0; i < messages.size; ++i) {
    font.draw(batch, messages.get(i), 20.0f, VIRTUAL_HEIGHT -
      22.0f * (i + 1));
  }
  batch.end();
}
```

Our `GestureHandler` class implements the `GestureListener` interface and makes every method call `addMessage()` with a string containing the event information. This is the `GestureListener` interface definition:

```
public class GestureHandler implements GestureListener
{
  public boolean touchDown(float x, float y, int pointer, int
    button);
  public boolean tap(float x, float y, int count, int button);
  public boolean longPress(float x, float y);
  public boolean fling(float velocityX, float velocityY, int
    button);
  public boolean pan(float x, float y, float deltaX, float
    deltaY);
  public boolean panStop(float x, float y, int pointer, int
    button);
  public boolean zoom(float initialDistance, float distance);
  public boolean pinch(Vector2 initialPointer1, Vector2
    initialPointer2, Vector2 pointer1, Vector2 pointer2);
}
```

Just like in the previous examples, the `addMessage()` method is quite simple. It takes a string and adds it to the `messages` array. Whenever we exceed the maximum number of messages, we delete the oldest one:

```
private void addMessage(String message) {
  messages.add(message + " time: " + System.currentTimeMillis());

  if (messages.size > MESSAGE_MAX) {
    messages.removeIndex(0);
  }
}
```

The result, while not spectacular, makes the point that it is really easy to integrate rich gestures in your Libgdx applications. This approach is certainly legitimate for all platforms. Nevertheless, gestures such as zooming or pinching only make sense with multitouch screens.

How it works...

We have mentioned before that `GestureDetector` is simply an `InputProcessor` implementation with some internal logic to identify a set of the most common gestures. Whenever a gesture is detected, the corresponding method in its `GestureListener` reference is called with the appropriate data. Again, a gesture detector only accepts one listener.

You should be careful when using `GestureDetector` in combination with `InputMultiplexer`. A single gesture relies on several events, and it will be a bad idea to have one `InputProcessor` stop an event from being propagated to the `GestureDetector` constructor.

Earlier in this recipe, we have listed the `GestureListener` methods, but here is a more detailed explanation:

- `tap()`: This is called every time the user touches and lifts their finger without dragging it outside the tap square. It receives the screen coordinates, the number of taps in the current sequence, and the button used to tap.

- `longPress()`: This is called whenever the user touches the screen for a long period of time and takes the screen coordinates.

- `fling()`: This is called when the user drags and lifts their finger or the mouse. This receives the velocity along the *x* and *y* axis in pixels per second.

- `pan()`: This is called when the user drags a finger across the screen. It takes the last known screen coordinates and the deltas for both axes since the last pan event.

- `panStop()`: This is called when the user stops panning. It takes the screen coordinates, the finger pointer, and the button.

- `zoom()`: This is called when the user performs a zoom gesture with two fingers. It takes the initial and final distances of the zoom.

- `pinch()`: This is called when the user pinches; it takes the initial and final positions in screen space of the two involved fingers.

All these methods are quite intuitive. However, in order to fully understand them, the best way is to play around with the recipe sample and see which ones get called as well as seeing when and what kind of data they receive.

There's more...

In this section, we will cover some additional features that the Libgdx gesture detection system can provide you.

Gesture polling

The `GestureDetector` class also has a few methods that we can use to poll its state. Both versions of `isLongPressed()` return a Boolean value whether or not the user has had their finger on the screen for longer than a certain amount of time. The first one uses the default long press time, while the second one takes a custom duration. Finally, `isPanning()` tells us whether the user is currently performing a panning action:

```
boolean isLongPressed()
boolean isLongPressed(float duration)
boolean isPanning()
```

Introducing the controllers API

Controllers play a big role in gaming as they are the kings of home consoles. Interestingly, they are also gaining followers among PC users, who had originally praised the mouse. Lots of people have a desktop connected to their living room television just to play from their couches using controllers. Not to mention that some games, such as sports titles, are simply better experienced with gamepads.

After diving into keyboard, mouse, and touch inputs, it is time to pay some attention to such an important icon of games. Libgdx provides a fully featured **controllers API**; however, it does not belong to the core framework. Instead, it is distributed as an extension, which means that you will not include it in your project unless you actually need it.

Throughout this recipe, we will cover the main aspects of the controllers API, which will be shown in the accompanying sample.

> The controllers extension is only supported on the desktop, Android (3.1 or greater), and GWT backends. The iOS backend comes with a stub implementation with no functionality.

Getting ready

For the controllers example, you need to import the sample projects into your Eclipse workspace.

How to do it...

There are quite a few sides to this extension. First, we will see how to include the controllers extension in an existing project, then we will move on to how to enumerate which controllers are connected, and finally we will explain how to do polling and event listening.

Everything in the controllers API is accessible through the `Controllers` singleton.

Including the controllers extension

Controllers is a Libgdx extension, so you need to edit your Gradle build file to add the new dependency. We already covered this in the *Updating and managing project dependencies* recipe of *Chapter 1, Diving into Libgdx*.

Enumerating controllers

Several players can have their controllers plugged in at the same time, and we can query this information with the getControllers() method, which returns an array of the Controller objects:

```
for (Controller controller : Controllers.getControllers()) {
  Gdx.app.log("Controllers: ", controller.toString());
}
```

Controller state polling

The Controller interface is implemented by the corresponding backends. Once we have the Controller instance that we are interested in, we can use it to poll its state with the following methods, which we will explain later:

```
public interface Controller {
    public boolean getButton (int buttonCode);
    public float getAxis (int axisCode);
    public PovDirection getPov (int povCode);
    public boolean getSliderX (int sliderCode);
    public boolean getSliderY (int sliderCode);
    public Vector3 getAccelerometer (int accelerometerCode);

    ...
}
```

Controller event listening

We can register a class to be notified on every controller event quite easily, as long as it implements the ControllerListener interface. There are two ways of doing this, depending on whether we are interested in all controllers' events or just those for a specific one.

To listen to events coming from all controllers, you need to register with the Controllers class, as follows:

```
Controllers.addListener(new ControllerListener() {
...
});
```

If you only care about a specific controller, you need to register with a specific instance:

```
Controller player1Controller =
  Controllers.getControllers().get(0);
player1Controller.addListener(new ControllerListener() {
...
});
```

The `ControllerListener` interface looks like the following code snippet:

```
public interface ControllerListener {
  public void connected(Controller controller);
  public void disconnected(Controller controller);
  public boolean buttonDown (Controller controller, int
    buttonCode);
  public boolean buttonUp (Controller controller, int buttonCode);
  public boolean axisMoved (Controller controller, int axisCode,
    float value);
  public boolean povMoved (Controller controller, int povCode,
    PovDirection value);
  public boolean xSliderMoved (Controller controller, int
    sliderCode, boolean value);
  public boolean ySliderMoved (Controller controller, int
    sliderCode, boolean value);
  boolean accelerometerMoved (Controller controller, int
    accelerometerCode, Vector3 value);
}
```

Our sample application, located in `GamepadSample.java`, logs event messages pretty much like the other input samples.

How it works...

Controllers come in all flavors and colors, each with different button layouts and a wide range of components such as buttons, axes, accelerometers, and so on and so forth. The controller interface is supposed to abstract a generic gamepad with the following concepts:

- **Buttons**: These are the classic *A*, *B*, *X*, and *Y* buttons as well as some triggers, such as *Start* and *Select*. Each button has a code represented by an integer value and can trigger the `buttonDown()` and `buttonUp()` events.

- **Axes**: These are analog sticks; their value ranges from -1 to 1, where 0 is the middle. Each axis has an integer code, and its use triggers the `axisMoved()` events.

- **POVs**: These are directional inputs such as digital pads. The `povMoved()` event takes the pov ID and a `PovDirection` value, which is simply an `enum` containing a list of directions such as `north` or `southEast`.

- **Sliders**: These are controller-specific sliders along the *x* and *y* axis.

- **Accelerometer**: This is represented by a vector, indicating the acceleration in m/s2 along each axis.

> Controller event handlers return true or false depending on whether the event should be distributed to other listeners or not. This is consistent with the `InputProcessor` interface. However, a controller supports several listeners, so there is no need for multiplexers.

There's more...

Integrating gamepad controls in your game is actually far from simple. While the Libgdx API is quite nice and clean, the variety of devices makes it really hard to handle all the cases. Keep this in mind when trying to officially support controllers in your game.

Controller mappings

As a game programmer, you cannot be aware of the controller your users will plug into the game machine. It could be an Xbox controller, a PlayStation 3, OUYA, or a generic one. Each one of these assigns different buttons and axes to their physical components. The horizontal axis of the right stick will not have the same code across devices and platforms. This can be an awful nightmare!

The `com.badlogic.gdx.controllers.mappings` package hosts classes with static values representing codes for known controllers. As of now, the only available one is the OUYA mapping set. Obviously, you are free to add support for other controllers in your game following this method:

```
public class Ouya {
   public static final String ID = "OUYA Game Controller";
   public static final int BUTTON_O;
   public static final int BUTTON_U;
   public static final int BUTTON_Y;
   public static final int BUTTON_A;
   ...
}
```

The following picture illustrates only a fraction of the controllers' variety in the market:

This approach can be really good if you are only going to support a specific controller, such as the OUYA one, if you are releasing on that platform. However, if you want to support a wide range of controllers, it is not feasible to check for each of the mappings whenever an event fires. In this case, the best approach is usually to provide a controller configuration screen, where the user picks the button or axis of his choice for every action in the game.

Handling disconnections

Detecting when a controller is plugged in or gets disconnected is tricky. You need to listen to the `connected()` and `disconnected()` events, but it only works on Android. Whenever possible, it is always good to handle this in the game by triggering a pause screen or something similar.

See also

Most aspects of Libgdx's input system have already been covered. Please find the following related content:

 ▸ The *Input mapping for cross-platform development* recipe covers how to elegantly handle input in a cross-platform project

 ▸ *Chapter 11, Third-party Libraries and Extras*, offers a collection of other Libgdx extensions

Input mapping for cross-platform development

Managing inputs in a relatively complex game that targets several platforms with different peripherals can become a massive headache. Keys, touch, mouse, gestures, analog sticks, on-screen sticks, and so on, the variety is just too overwhelming, not to mention that controllers by different manufacturers do not have the same button codes. Sometimes, device codes vary even across platforms!

Without an additional system to aid us in user-input issues, the game's logic code will become a sea of conditional blocks to handle each possibility.

Quite rapidly, an additional layer becomes imperative to spare us the need to worry about which user input peripheral is currently being used and to gain a few years of life expectancy. This recipe introduces a barebones system to achieve this goal. It makes use of concepts such **actions** and **states**, which keys are mapped to. The user could potentially configure the said mapping to their taste. Moreover, the system allows different input contexts, because we care about different events when the user is browsing the menu or playing the actual game.

The present recipe explains the concepts, design, and implementation details of the aforementioned system and provides a direction to expand on it.

Getting ready

The input mapping sample requires you to import the sample projects into your Eclipse workspace.

How to do it...

All the code for this recipe can be found in the `InputMappingSample.java` file and the `com.cookbook.samples.inputmapping` package. However, before we jump into the inner workings of the system, we are going to pause for a moment and explain some of its fundamental concepts.

Our whole input mapping system is data-driven; interactions are defined in an XML configuration file whose format we will examine later on in this section.

> The implementation of this input mapping system is too big to be directly included in this text, so we will only show important snippets. Please refer to the sample code for a full implementation.

Input contexts

An **input context** defines a set of interactions that the user can trigger for as long as such context is active. For instance, while the player navigates the character selection menu, he or she may go forward or backward, select a character, or return to the previous screen. However, while the game is active, these inputs become invalid, and now, the user may be able to jump, move around, shoot, and so on.

> For the purpose of this recipe, we only process keyboard events. However, extending it will be fairly straightforward.

We can classify the various kinds of inputs that a user can enter within a context in different categories, as follows:

- **Action**: These are one-time events such as jumping and shooting.
- **State**: These are the persistent properties, such as the character wanting to move forward.

This is the skeleton of our `InputContext` class. It has a name, a set of action listeners, and dictionaries to keep track of the states as well as actions:

```
public class InputContext extends InputAdapter {
  private String name;
  private ArrayMap<String, Integer> keyStates;
  private ArrayMap<Integer, String> keyActions;
```

```
        private ObjectSet<InputActionListener> listeners;

        public InputContext() {}

        public void load(Element contextElement) {}

        public void addListener(InputActionListener listener) {}
        public void removeListener(InputActionListener listener) {}

        public boolean getState(String state) {}
        public String getName() {}

        public boolean keyDown(int keycode) {}
    }
```

The `load()` method takes an XML element and populates the context with the appropriate data. The `addListener()` and `removeListener()` methods are pretty self-explanatory; they just add or remove a listener to or from the set, respectively. To check whether a **state** is active, we use the `getState()` method, passing in the name of the state. This state simply checks the `keyStates` dictionary for its corresponding `keycode` and checks whether or not the said key is pressed:

```
    public boolean getState(String state) {
        Integer keycode = keyStates.get(state);

        if (keycode != null) {
            return Gdx.input.isKeyPressed(keycode);
        }

        return false;
    }
```

> XML and JSON serialization and deserialization will be covered in the *The XML parsing primer* and *JSON serialization and deserialization* recipes of *Chapter 5, Audio and File I/O*.

Let's take a look at the `keyDown()` event handler. It tries to see if there is an action associated with this key and then notifies all the registered listeners:

```
    public boolean keyDown(int keycode) {
        boolean processed = false;

        String action = keyActions.get(keycode);

        if (action != null) {
            for (InputActionListener listener : listeners) {
                processed = listener.OnAction(action);
```

```
        if (processed) {
          break;
        }
      }
    }

    return processed;
}
```

Input profiles

An **input profile** contains a set of **input contexts** and defines a complete configuration instance of potential user interactions. It keeps a dictionary from `Strings` to `InputContext` as well as the active context. The constructor takes a `FileHandle` pointing to the configuration XML file, which we will examine soon.

When the game switches between screens, you could call the `setContext()` method, passing in the desired context name to adopt the new high-level control scheme. We can get the current context with `getContext()` or get an arbitrary context by name with `getContextByName()`.

All the event handlers simply defer onto the current context by passing through the event. Consider the following code:

```
public class InputProfile implements InputProcessor {
  private ArrayMap<String, InputContext> contexts;
  private InputContext context;

  public InputProfile(FileHandle handle) {}

  public void setContext(String contextName) {}
  public InputContext getContext() {}
  public InputContext getContextByName(String name) {}

  public boolean keyDown(int keycode) {}
  public boolean keyUp(int keycode) {}
  public boolean keyTyped(char character) {}
  public boolean touchDown(int screenX, int screenY, int pointer,
    int {}
  public boolean touchUp(int screenX, int screenY, int pointer,
    int button) {}
  public boolean touchDragged(int screenX, int screenY, int
    pointer) {}
  public boolean mouseMoved(int screenX, int screenY) {}
  public boolean scrolled(int amount) {}
}
```

Alright, this is all very good, but where is the file that defines an **input profile**? Let's take a look at the `profile.xml` file in the `[cookbook]/android/assets/data/input/` folder:

```
<InputProfile>
  <context name="Game">
    <states>
      <state name="Crouch"><key code="DOWN"/></state>
      <state name="LookUp"><key code="UP"/></state>
      ...
    </states>
    <actions>
      <action name="Jump"><key code="A"/></action>
      <action name="Shoot"><key code="S"/></action>
    </actions>
  </context>
  <context name="MainMenu">
    ...
  </context>
</InputProfile>
```

Event notifications with InputActionListener

States are polled, but we need a mechanism for other systems to subscribe to **action** events. They can do so by implementing the `InputActionListener` interface, which only contains the `OnAction()` method:

```
public interface InputActionListener {
  public boolean OnAction(String action);
}
```

Input mapping in action

We have seen how our small input mapping system works internally, but it is now time to see it in action. Take a look at the `InputMappingSample.java` file. Note that the `InputMappingSample` class implements the `InputActionListener` interface.

Events will be logged on the screen, so we are going to keep an array of strings for them:

```
private static final int MESSAGE_MAX = 15;
private Array<String> messages;
```

Besides our usual base setup, we add two `InputProfile` and `InputContext` references:

```
private InputProfile profile;
private InputContext gameContext;
```

In the `create()` method, we initialize our keys' mappings and create a new `InputProfile`, passing in our configuration XML file. We then set the `Game` context and cache it off for ease of use later on. Finally, we tell the context to send action events to the `InputMappingSample` instance, as follows:

```
public void create() {
  ...
  KeyCodes.init();
  profile = new
    InputProfile(Gdx.files.internal("data/input/profile.xml"));
  profile.setContext("Game");
  gameContext = profile.getContext();
  gameContext.addListener(this);
  Gdx.input.setInputProcessor(profile);
}
```

The `render()` method is quite simple. We first draw the current state at the top using the `getState()` method on the context and the latest messages at the bottom:

```
public void render() {
  ...
  batch.begin();

  font.draw(batch, gameContext.getState("Crouch") ? "crouching" :
    "not crouching", 50.0f, SCENE_HEIGHT - 20.0f);
  ...

  int numMessages = messages.size;
  for (int i = 0; i < numMessages; ++i) {
    font.draw(batch, messages.get(i), 50.0f, SCENE_HEIGHT - 160.0f
      - 30.0f * i);
  }

  batch.end();
}
```

Every time an **action** event is fired, we add the message to the queue:

```
public boolean onAction(String action) {
  addMessage("Action -> " + action);
  return false;
}
```

When we reach the limit of the message queue, we need to delete the oldest queue:

```
private void addMessage(String message) {
  messages.add(message);

  if (messages.size > MESSAGE_MAX) {
    messages.removeIndex(0);
  }
}
```

Now it is a good time to run the sample and play around with it. See how it is easier now to handle game events and states? Rather than dealing with key codes, you can just stick purely to gameplay concepts such as *jump* or *shoot*.

How it works...

The following diagram illustrates the class hierarchy of the previously explained system:

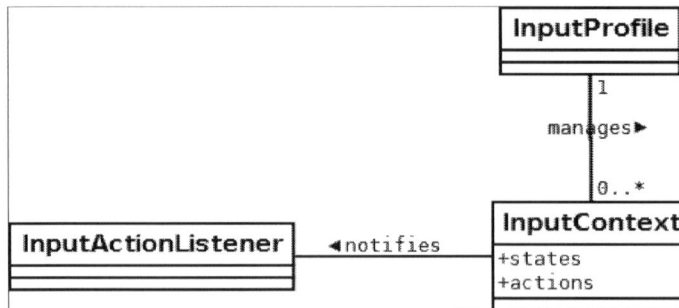

There's more...

As we have seen, we only work with keyboard inputs for simplicity reasons. However, this does not make this system very useful for real-life applications. A good way to put your newly acquired skills to practice is to extend the code so that it can handle mouse clicks, touch events, and gamepad inputs.

Going further, you could map gestures to specific actions! There are many possibilities.

Naturally, you need to add elements to `profile.xml` and modify the code that parses it as well as add new event handlers.

This input mapping system does not support more than one local player either, which could be a nice addition you may want to work on yourself.

Other important issues that need taking into account in a production environment are gamepad connections and disconnection events. What happens when a new player joins? Even trickier, what happens when someone accidentally plugs out his or her controller?

5

Audio and File I/O

In this chapter, we will cover:

- ▶ Playing short sound effects
- ▶ Audio streaming for background music
- ▶ Optimizing audio files to reduce download sizes
- ▶ Procedural audio generators
- ▶ Engine sounds with dynamic audio
- ▶ The 2D space sound system
- ▶ The first approach to file handling in Libgdx
- ▶ Using preferences to store game states and options
- ▶ The XML parsing primer
- ▶ JSON serialization and deserialization

Introduction

Audio plays an essential role in building a game's atmosphere. Every single title that intends to immerse you in its world puts a great deal of attention on sound effects and music, especially in classic horror games. You are in a corridor, it is dark, and you can barely see. The appropriate combination of sounds will make you want to turn off the console immediately, in a good way. Moreover, sound also gives the player feedback and extra information of the game world. It is important to let the player know that their actions have a consequence, even during menu navigation. Every time they tap, swing, or use an element, there should be some kind of audio cue confirming the interaction has taken place.

This chapter tackles how to add both sound effects and background music to your Libgdx applications in an effective manner. We will start from the ground up so as to end with more complex creations such as dynamic and spatial sound effects.

Later in the chapter, we will dive into the Libgdx file's input/output system. This will enable us to load levels and save a player's progress, configuration profiles, and other useful information. The data-driven approach is always considered good practice as it enables non-programmer team members to modify a game's behavior quite easily.

Playing short sound effects

We will get started with the Libgdx sound system by playing short sound effects, also known as **SFX**. Often, effects go unnoticed, and this is really unfair towards them! As an exercise, try turning the effects' volume down in an action shooter and see how much you enjoy it. It is not the same experience at all, is it?

The sample shown in this recipe will illustrate how to play, pause, resume, and stop sounds. We will map the number keys from *1* to *7* to different sounds. The *P* key will pause the sounds, *R* will resume playback, and *S* will stop playback.

Getting ready

Make sure the sample projects are in your Eclipse workspace to follow this recipe.

How to do it...

The code for this recipe will be found in the `SoundEffectSample` class. Follow these instructions to master how to play back sound effects:

1. Unsurprisingly, the class through which we will work is called `Sound`. An `IntMap` of `Sound` instances will help us manage the sound collection of our sample. The effects will be played when the user presses the number keys from *1* to *7*:

   ```
   private IntMap<Integer, Sound> soundKeys;
   ```

2. We use the `create()` method to construct our collections and populate them. `Sound` objects are instantiated through the `Gdx.audio.newSound()` method passing in the appropriate file handle; we instantiate with all seven effects under the `data/sfx` folder. The key sound dictionary will contain the key code from `Keys.NUM_1` to `Keys.NUM_7`, pointing to the corresponding entries in the sound arrays. Finally, we set our `SoundEffectSample` class as the input processor and show the sample controls on the console output:

   ```
   public void create() {
     sounds = new IntMap<Sound>();
   ```

```
sounds.put(Keys.NUM_1, Gdx.audio.newSound
  (Gdx.files.internal("data/sfx/sfx 01.wav")));

...

Gdx.input.setInputProcessor(this);

Gdx.app.log("SoundEffectSample", "Instructions");

...
}
```

3. Sound objects need disposing when they are no longer needed so as to avoid nasty resource leaks. We iterate over the sound collections calling dispose() on all of the entries:

```
public void dispose() {
  for (Sound sound : sounds.values()) {
    sound.dispose();
  }
}
```

4. A Sound object can be used to play several instances of itself at the same time. Every time we call its play() method, the effect will be played and we will get a playID handle back, which we can use to refer to the instance later.

5. Effect operations are performed from within the keyDown() event handler. When a user presses the S key, we need to stop playing all sounds. Calling the stop() method on a Sound object will halt all effects that were played from it:

```
if (keycode == Keys.S) {
  for (Sound sound : sounds.values()) {
    sound.stop();
  }

  Gdx.app.log("SoundEffectSample", "Sounds stopped");
}
```

6. Upon pressing the P key, we simply pause all instances by calling the pause() method:

```
else if (keycode == Keys.P) {
  for (Sound sound : sounds.values()) {
    sound.pause();
  }

  Gdx.app.log("SoundEffectSample", "Sounds paused");
}
```

7. If the user presses *R*, we call the `resume()` method and all the instances to resume the paused sounds:

```
else if (keycode == Keys.R) {
  for (Sound sound : sounds.values()) {
    sound.resume();
  }

  Gdx.app.log("SoundEffectSample", "Sounds resumed");
}
```

8. When the pressed key is none of the above, we perform a lookup in the `sounds` dictionary to see whether there is a sound we should play using the `play()` method:

```
else {
  Sound sound = sounds.get(keycode);

  if (sound != null)
  {
    sound.play();
    Gdx.app.log("SoundEffectSample", "Playing sound");
  }
}
```

9. To add basic support for touchscreens, we play a random `Sound` instance from the array whenever the user touches the screen:

```
public boolean touchDown (int screenX, int screenY, int
  pointer, int button) {
  Sound sound = sounds.get(MathUtils.random(sounds.size -
    1));
  sound.play();

  Gdx.app.log("SoundEffectSample", "Playing sound");
  return true;
}
```

10. You should now be able to run the sample, play around with it, and check for yourself.

How it works...

Libgdx offers an audio interface to let us work with sound effects and music in a platform-agnostic way. Each backend implements it using different resources, as follows:

▶ The desktop backend uses **OpenAL**

▶ The Android backend uses the official **Android SDK**, mostly `SoundPool`, `AudioManager`, and `MediaPlayer`

- The HTML5 backend uses the **sound tag**, and falls back to **Flash** if the former does not work
- The RoboVM backend also uses **OpenAL**

Several formats are supported for sound effects in Libgdx. Make your choice depending on your needs: WAV, MP3, and OGG (unsupported in iOS).

There's more...

Quite a few goodies are available to us in the Sound interface.

Handling sounds individually

We already mentioned that the `play()` method returns a handle that we can store to manage effect instances individually later on. The other methods are as follows:

```
long soundID = sound.play();
sound.pause(soundID);
sound.resume(soundID);
sound.stop(soundID);
```

Note that if the effect of the handle references has finished playing, anything that we do with its handle will have no effect and fail silently.

Changing the volume

Volume is represented with a float ranging from `0.0f` to `1.0f`. We can set an effect's volume by doing the following:

```
sound.setVolume(soundID, volume);
```

Creating looping sounds

To play a sound effect that will keep playing indefinitely, you can make use of the `loop()` method, which also returns a handle to reference the instance later on:

```
long soundID = sound.loop();
```

You can change your mind at any time and tell an effect to stop looping; in this case, you will have to call `setLooping()` with the corresponding handle:

```
sound.setLooping(soundID, false);
```

Managing effect priorities

There is a limit on how many sound effects can be played at a time, but such limits are configurable on Android and desktops at application startup time, through the configuration objects passed to the application instance:

```
AndroidApplicationConfiguration.maxSimultaneousSounds
LwglApplicationConfiguration.audioDeviceSimultaneousSources
```

If your game environment is rich and complex, it is not rare to exceed the sound limit at times. However, you might be quite keen on making sure that very specific instances play above all others. For instance, in an RPG, you might not care if the cow in the background moos, as long as the NPC that gives the player a new quest is properly heard.

Libgdx lets us give the sound system hints on how important an effect request is:

```
sound.setPriority(soundID, priority);
```

Priorities are set using integer values indicating their positions on the sound queue, so sounds with a *smaller priority will be considered first* if the queue is full.

See also

> ▶   We tackled how to play short sound effects. For longer audio files, read the *Audio streaming for background music* recipe

Audio streaming for background music

The Sound interface gives us a great deal of flexibility. However, it's not suitable for all needs due to one fundamental reason: sounds are fully loaded in memory before playback can start. This is not a problem for short effects, but it rapidly becomes one if we try to use it to play our soundtracks, especially in memory-limited devices such as phones. While effects lie around the order of tens to hundreds of KB, reasonably decent-quality song files can take up around 10 MB, even if they are not very long.

How do we solve this dire situation? **Streaming** is the answer. This technique only needs to keep in memory the next chunk of file that needs to be played, which makes for an epic win. However, not everything is happiness. Streaming means we need to decode the audio files as we go, rather than at load time. This inevitably has a CPU-wise performance impact that we did not suffer from with SFX. Still, streaming is the preferable way when it comes to playing long audio files.

Throughout this recipe, we will discover how to wield audio streaming to play background music with Libgdx. The presented sample consists of a very minimalistic music player, without an interface. The user can use some keys to control playback and select the next or previous song.

Getting ready

You will need the sample projects in your Eclipse workspace before going ahead.

How to do it...

This sample is hosted by the `MusicSample.java` file. Follow the next steps to learn how to play music files:

1. First, we define a constant representing the value by which the volume is going to change every time the user presses the appropriate keys:

```
private static final float VOLUME_CHANGE = 0.2f;
```

2. Libgdx uses the `Music` interface to allow us to stream and play audio from disk. Our sample counts with an `Array` of `Music` objects accompanied by the index of the instance that is currently playing. We also keep track of the current volume level. Finally, we have `SongListener`, which is a custom implementation of the `OnCompletionListener` interface that we will examine later:

```
private Array<Music> songs;
private int currentSongIdx;
private float volume;
private SongListener listener;
```

3. The `create()` method is quite simple; we initialize our members and populate the `songs` array with the files inside the `data/music` folder. We register our sample as the current `InputProcessor`, log the instructions, and play the first song with a custom `playSong()` method:

```
public void create() {
  listener = new SongListener();

  songs = new Array<Music>();
  songs.add(Gdx.audio.newMusic(Gdx.files.internal(
    "data/music/song_1.mp3")));
  ...

  currentSongIdx = 0;
  volume = 1.0f;

  Gdx.input.setInputProcessor(this);

  Gdx.app.log("MusicSample", "Instructions");
  ...

  playSong(0);
}
```

4. Before we exit the application, we need to ensure the `Music` objects are disposed to avoid memory leaks:

```
public void dispose() {
  for (Music song : songs) {
    song.dispose();
  }
}
```

5. The `playSong()` method gets the `Music` reference pointed by `songIdx` from the array and plays it. In order to do this, it needs to fetch the previous reference and call `stop()` on it. Music objects are played with the `play()` method. We also set the current volume on the objects with `setVolume()`, and tell each object we want to be notified when it is done with our listener:

```
void playSong(int songIdx) {
  Music song = songs.get(currentSongIdx);
  song.setOnCompletionListener(null);
  song.stop();

  currentSongIdx = songIdx;
  song = songs.get(currentSongIdx);
  song.play();
  song.setVolume(volume);
  song.setOnCompletionListener(listener);
}
```

> Unlike `Sound`, we cannot have multiple instances of the same `Music` object playing at the same time.

6. The `OnCompletionListener` interface has only one method, `onCompletion()`, that gets called when the `Music` instance we are listening to is over. In our case, we simply play the next song, going back to the start of the array, if necessary:

```
private class SongListener implements OnCompletionListener {
  @Override
  public void onCompletion(Music music) {
    playSong((currentSongIdx + 1) % songs.size),
    Gdx.app.log("MusicSample", "Song finished, play next
      song");
  }
}
```

7. In order to change the volume, we provide the convenience method, `changeVolume()`. It simply makes sure the volume we pass in is between `0.0f` and `1.0f`, calls `setVolume()` on the current song, and caches the current volume:

```
void changeVolume(float volumeChange) {
  Music song = songs.get(currentSongIdx);
  volume = MathUtils.clamp(song.getVolume() + volumeChange,
    0.0f, 1.0f);
  song.setVolume(volume);
}
```

8. The `keyDown()` event handler checks which key has been pressed. If the user presses *P*, we call `pause()` on the current song.

```
if (keycode == Keys.P) {
  songs.get(currentSongIdx).pause();
  Gdx.app.log("MusicSample", "Song paused");
}
```

9. Upon the *R* key-down event, we resume the current song's playback with the `play()` method. Note that as we cannot play the same `Music` object twice, this will have no effect if it is already playing:

```
else if (keycode == Keys.R) {
  songs.get(currentSongIdx).play();
  Gdx.app.log("MusicSample", "Song resumed");
}
```

10. Whenever the user presses the Up or Down arrow keys, we call `changeVolume()`, passing in positive or negative VOLUME_CHANGE, respectively:

```
else if (keycode == Keys.UP) {
  changeVolume(VOLUME_CHANGE);
  Gdx.app.log("MusicSample", "Volume up");
}
else if (keycode == Keys.DOWN) {
  changeVolume(-VOLUME_CHANGE);
  Gdx.app.log("MusicSample", "Volume down");
}
```

11. The user can use the Right and Left arrow keys to play the next and previous song, respectively, for which we call `playSong()` with the appropriate argument:

```
else if (keycode == Keys.RIGHT) {
  playSong((currentSongIdx + 1) % songs.size);
  Gdx.app.log("MusicSample", "Next song");
}
else if (keycode == Keys.LEFT) {
```

```
        int songIdx = (currentSongIdx - 1) < 0 ? songs.size - 1 :
          currentSongIdx - 1;
        playSong(songIdx);
        Gdx.app.log("MusicSample", "Previous song");
      }
```

12. Not to discriminate against touchscreens, we added a `touchDown()` handler that simply plays the next song, as shown in the following code. We could have used `GestureDetector` to add full controls, but decided not to do so for the sake of briefness:

```
public boolean touchDown (int screenX, int screenY, int
    pointer, int button) {
    playSong((currentSongIdx + 1) % songs.size);
    Gdx.app.log("MusicSample", "Next song");
    return true;
}
```

As you can see, getting Libgdx to play background music is fairly straightforward. Run the sample and play around with the controls to see the effects of your little sample.

How it works...

The `Music` interface lies with `Sound` inside the Libgdx `Audio` module. Backends use the same underlying methods they used for `Sound` to support `Music`.

There's more...

We covered the basic operations you can perform with a `Music` object. However, there are a couple more things you can do.

Checking the playback state

The `isPlaying()` method returns whether or not our `Music` instance is currently being played. You can also check for how long the file has been playing in milliseconds with `getPosition()`.

Looping the background music

The background music can be set to loop indefinitely with the `setLooping(boolean isLooping)` method. This can be useful if your soundtrack is not long, and some situations can be active for longer than the audio file lasts. The looping state of a `Music` object can be checked at any point in time with the `isLooping()` method.

See also

Now that you know how to manage SFX and background music with Libgdx, feel free to move on to the following recipes:

- *Optimizing audio files to reduce download sizes*
- *Procedural audio generators*

Optimizing audio files to reduce download sizes

When it comes to packing the release build for your shiny new game, you will realize that graphics and audio contribute the most to its final size. Sound effects and music definitely get the first prize in the race to make your download heavier.

As long as you only care about desktop, this should not be a problem. Nowadays, Internet connections are decent enough for people not to mind about moderately big downloads. However, if you plan on releasing for iOS, Android, and/or browsers, you should seriously stop and think about your package size. People are getting progressively more used to instantaneous experiences, but at the moment, not everyone has an unlimited data plan. Even if they do, their speed is usually far from great.

Take a look at how big your package is. In case you think it is over what you deem to be good enough, go through the collection of audio files and try to reduce their weight while ensuring your quality standards.

How? Well, this is exactly what we will explain in this recipe.

Getting ready

We need a tool to tweak and process our audio files, and **Audacity** will do the job just fine. Audacity is a fully featured cross-platform audio editing tool. It is open source and free, so you will not lose anything by giving it a try.

If you are a Windows or Mac user, go to the official website and download the latest version. If you use GNU/Linux, you can probably find Audacity in your software repository. For further information, check out `http://audacity.sourceforge.net`.

How to do it...

Let's see what you can do to reduce your audio file sizes while keeping a reasonable quality level. What follows is a series of things you can try. However, it really depends on the nature of the file, the size of which you are trying to reduce; some tinkering might be necessary. Execute the following steps:

1. Start by running Audacity. Then, click on **File**, select **Import**, and finally select **Audio**. Pick the audio file you want to work with and accept. After the process is over, the sound wave in your work area looks as shown in the following screenshot:

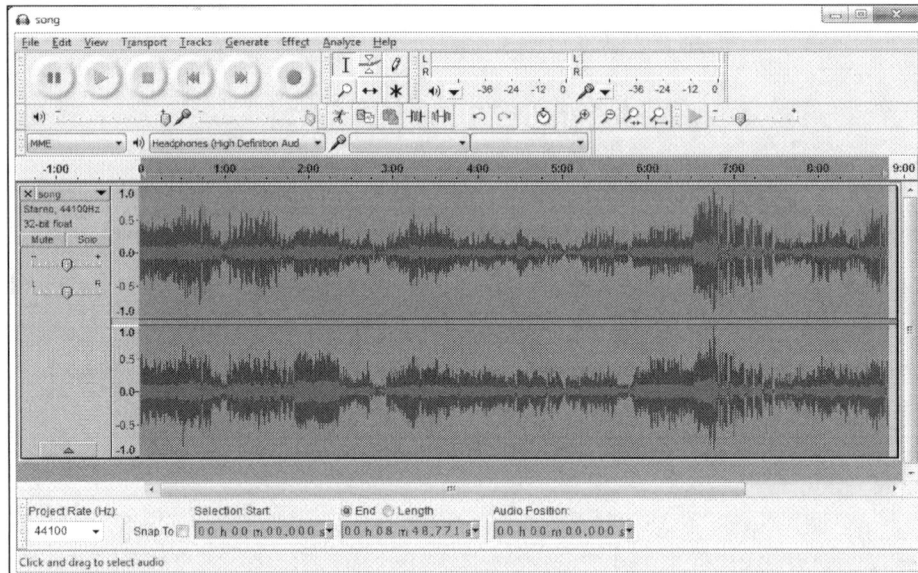

2. Open the **Preferences** panel inside the **Edit** menu and go to the **Quality** entry.

3. Here, you can change the values of **Default Sample Rate** and **Default Sample Format**. Try reducing them, but do not go any lower than 11,025 Hz for the former. You can probably get away with low values here for voice files, but music files will require higher values to sound good. Another option is to use mono rather than stereo, which will probably go unnoticed in some devices.

4. Another option is to directly click on the arrow next to the track name and select **Set Rate** and **Set Sample Format**.

5. Once you are happy with the result, we can proceed with the export process. Click on **File** and then **Export**.

6. Now, it is time to select the output format. **WAV** files are uncompressed raw data and therefore help avoid quality loss. **OGG Vorbis** and **MP3** are compressed and inevitably incur some quality loss. They also require some more computation power for on-the-fly decoding, but they take up less space.

> As long as you are not targeting iOS, we recommend that you favor OGG Vorbis over MP3 as the latter might be subject to patent issues. On the other hand, OGG Vorbis is an open format, ready for you to use freely, absent of limitations of any kind. They both offer similar results anyway!

7. If you select OGG, you can click on the **Options** buttons and select an output quality level with a slider. When choosing MP3, you can click on the same button to select the output bit rate. It is recommended to start at 128 Kbps and only increase when needed.

8. Finally, hit **Save** and manually check the quality of the resulting file. Tweak the previously mentioned values, as necessary, until you are happy with it.

How it works...

We tweaked a few parameters of our audio files. They are quite simple, but let's see what they actually mean:

▶   **Sample rate**: Digital audio cannot keep the wave amplitude in a continuous manner as this will require an infinite amount of data. Digital audio only stores samples at discreet steps in time. The sample rate is the frequency of these samples. We measure it in Hertz (Hz), which is the number of samples per second.

▶   **Sample format**: A value is stored for every audio sample. The amount of information in bits per sample defines the sample format.

▶   **Bit rate**: The number of bits per second of compressed audio. This applies to formats such as OGG Vorbis and MP3.

There's more...

Now that you have installed Audacity, it will be a shame not to explore the possibilities of this rather powerful free audio suite.

With Audacity, you can import or record audio onto tracks. You can then cut, copy, paste, and mix them however you fancy. Moreover, you can add many effects and distortions to make your work sound more interesting. It is too big a piece of software to cover in this book, so refer to the official tutorials for more insight, available at http://audacity.sourceforge.net/manual-1.2/tutorials.html.

See also

► Move on to the *Procedural audio generators* recipe to learn how to prototype sound effects and music quickly so that your game can have audio from the very beginning.

Procedural audio generators

Developers tend to oversee audio and leave it for the later stages of production, which is a tremendous mistake because audio greatly contributes to the feel of the game. When there is good sound, it feels right. However, when the sound is bad or there is none at all, the game loses many points straightaway.

It is important to take audio into account from the very beginning. Use it to create a mood and provide constant feedback to the player.

Understandably, you might not have an audio artist or a musician on board throughout the whole project. So, what can you do if you lack sound design or composing skills? Worry no more, **procedural effect generators** can rescue you!

They are perfect for quick prototyping and game jams. In no time, with a little bit of tweaking, you can have a **placeholder** sound effect ready to be included in your game logic. The sound designer can replace it later with a more up-to-the-standard version.

In this recipe, we will take a tour around **Sfxr**, one of the procedural sound effect generators.

Getting ready

Before you start experimenting with Sfxr, you need to download it. Fortunately, the tool is free, open source, and cross-platform. Visit its creator's website at `http://www.drpetter.se/project_sfxr.html` and choose the download link that suits your purposes best.

If you are interested in taking a peek into the source code, Sfxr's repository is hosted in Google Code available at `https://code.google.com/p/sfxr`.

How to do it...

Sfxr does not require installation. Once you have downloaded and uncompressed it, you can run it normally. The user interface might seem cluttered because it presents all options on a single screen, but it is actually very easy to use.

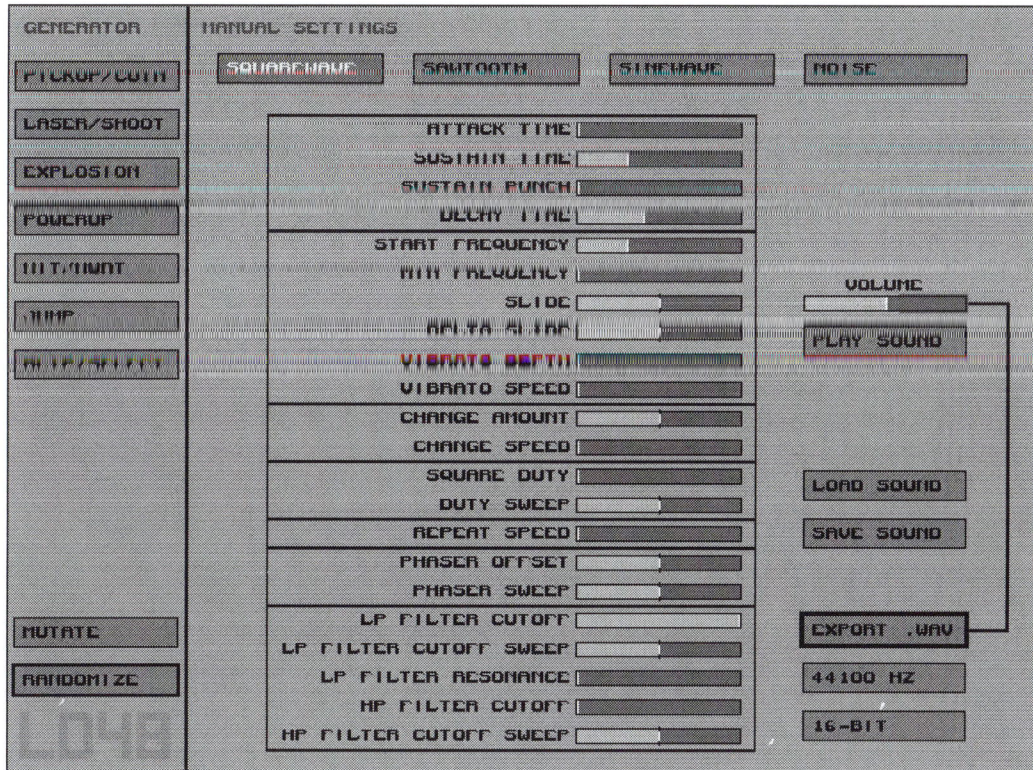

Follow these steps to generate cool sound effects lightning fast:

1. From the **GENERATOR** panel, you can choose the kind of sound effect you want: shot, power-up, jump, hit, and so on. Every time you click on an effect, it will generate a new random sound and play it.

2. Feel free to keep clicking until you get something similar to what you are after.

3. Once you have a base sound, the **MANUAL SETTINGS** panel will let you customize its properties further. You can change the wave shape as well as the myriad of parameters you can see in the screenshot. Every time you make a change, it is advisable to click on the **PLAY SOUND** button to check how the setting affects the result.

4. If you want to stop working on a sound and continue later, you can hit **SAVE SOUND**. This will generate a file Sfxr understands. The next time you run the application, you can get it back with **LOAD SOUND**.

5. The sample frequency is customizable, so you can switch between 44 KHz and 22 KHz.

6. You can also alternate between 8 bit and 16 bit for the sample size.

7. When you are happy with the sound you have, click on the **EXPORT .WAV** button to generate a sound file that is playable in Libgdx.

Great, now you have a sound effect you can use in your game straightaway. Easy!

How it works...

There is no need for any explanation here, as there is no need to explain the Sfxr internals.

There's more...

Sfxr is not the only procedural sound generation tool out there, although it is extremely popular and widely used for prototyping and game jams such as Ludum Dare. Here is a list of derived and alternative tools:

▶ **Bfxr**: This is very similar to Sfxr but with a wider range of settings, available at `http://www.bfxr.net`

▶ **AS3fxr**: An Action Script 3 version of Sfxr; this can be used from browsers and is available at `http://www.superflashbros.net/as3sfxr/`

▶ **Sfxr for Android**: This is a free mobile version of Sfxr, available at `https://play.google.com/store/apps/details?id=be.minimal.sfxr`

▶ **Abundant music**: This is a free browser-based procedural music generation tool, available at `http://abundant-music.com`

Additionally, it is worth mentioning **SunVox**, a free, cross-platform, graph-based tool for music composing. It does not do procedural music generation, but it is a simple enough tool to use for a non-expert to achieve decent results. It is available at `http://www.warmplace.ru/soft/sunvox`.

See also

▶ Move forward and discover how you can create more realistic and engaging experiences in the *Engine sounds with dynamic audio* recipe.

Engine sounds with dynamic audio

Some effects have a dynamic nature and cannot be achieved by simply playing a plain audio file. Imagine a car engine; the sound it makes depends on many factors such as the type of engine and the revolutions per minute it is running at. Since a user can accelerate or hit the brake at any point in time, developers need to play audio in an adaptive manner.

Many games also have a dynamic soundtrack. *Shadow of the Colossus* (PlayStation 2, 2005) comes to mind when thinking of music that adapts to gameplay. In this game, the player has to defeat a series of giant beasts by climbing on them and striking weak spots. Music would smoothly change to accompany the mood of the moment. We are not talking about changing music tracks when the player reaches a point via script, but blending tracks in and out depending on things such as player performance.

Throughout this recipe, we will show you how to reproduce a car sound as it moves at different speeds. Obviously, we will do so with a rather simplistic approach. Do not expect modern racing simulator quality!

Getting ready

As usual, make sure the sample projects are in your Eclipse workspace. We will use a couple of sound effect files:

- `[cookbook]/samples/android/assets/data/sfx/car-engine.wav`
- `[cookbook]/samples/android/assets/data/sfx/car-idle.wav`

How to do it...

The user will be able to use the Space key or the touchscreen to hit the gas pedal of an imaginary car. When the car is not being accelerated, friction will reduce its speed. Under the hood, we'll make the engine sound effect adapt to the current state of the car.

The code for this recipe is inside the `CarEngineSample` class. Follow these steps to learn how to dynamically manipulate audio:

1. First, define a set of constants such as the maximum speed in km/h, acceleration, friction, and a threshold from which we no longer consider the car to be stationary to configure the car's behavior:

   ```
   private final static float MAX_SPEED = 200.0f;
   private final static float ACCELERATION = 25.0f;
   private final static float FRICTION = 15.0f;
   private final static float IDLE_THRESHOLD = 0.1f;
   ```

2. Then, add a few members such as the current car speed, a sound effect for when the car is moving, and another for when it is idling. Finally, we have the `soundId` of the effect instance that is playing at the moment so as to be able to access it and modify it on the fly:

   ```
   private float speed;
   private Sound engine;
   private Sound idle;
   private long soundId;
   ```

3. Besides instantiating our viewport, camera, font, and batch in the `create()` method, we also load our `.wav` files and start playing the idle engine sounds in a loop:

```
public void create() {
    ...
    idle = Gdx.audio.newSound(Gdx.files.internal
        ("data/sfx/car-idle.wav"));
    engine = Gdx.audio.newSound(Gdx.files.internal
        ("data/sfx/car-engine.wav"));
    soundId = idle.play();
    idle.setLooping(soundId, true);
}
```

4. Always make sure to dispose of your resources if you want to avoid memory leaks:

```
public void dispose() {
    ...
    engine.dispose();
    idle.dispose();
}
```

5. The `render()` method is quite simple; we only draw the current car speed and control instructions. The interesting work is done by `updateEngine()`:

```
public void render() {
    ...
    updateEngine(Gdx.graphics.getDeltaTime());

    camera.update();
    batch.setProjectionMatrix(camera.combined);
    batch.begin();
    font.draw(batch, "Speed: " + speed + "km/h", 20.0f,
        200.0f);
    font.draw(batch, "Press SPACE or touch to accelerate",
        20.0f, 150.0f);
    batch.end();
}
```

6. Let's take a look at `updateEngine()`. It first figures out whether the car should accelerate or decelerate, depending on whether the user is pressing space or touching the screen. It then increases the current car speed by `acceleration` times `delta` (time since the previous frame), while making sure it stays within the bounds.

7. The next step is to detect whether the car just started moving or has stopped, in which case we need to switch the active sound and set it to loop.

8. Finally, if the car is in motion, we need to update the engine effect so that it matches its current speed. In order to do so, we will play around with the sound's pitch. The faster the car runs, the higher the pitch will be. We modify the pitch using the `setPitch()` method, passing in the sound ID and a value between `0.5f` and `1.0f`:

```java
private void updateEngine(float delta) {
    boolean wasIdle = speed < IDLE_THRESHOLD;

    float acceleration = -FRICTION;

    if (Gdx.input.isKeyPressed(Keys.SPACE) || Gdx.input.
isButtonPressed(Buttons.LEFT)) {
        acceleration = ACCELERATION;
    }

    speed = MathUtils.clamp(speed + acceleration * delta, 0.0f, MAX_
SPEED);

    boolean isIdle =  speed < IDLE_THRESHOLD;

    if (wasIdle && !isIdle) {
        idle.stop();
        soundId = engine.play();
        engine.setLooping(soundId, true);
    }
    else if (!wasIdle && isIdle) {
        engine.stop();
        soundId = idle.play();
        idle.setLooping(soundId, true);
    }

    if (!isIdle) {
        float pitch = 0.5f + speed / MAX_SPEED * 0.5f;
        engine.setPitch(soundId, pitch);
    }
}
```

It is now time to run the sample, get our imaginary car to move at different speeds, and notice how the sound changes to reflect its state.

> Currently, the `setPitch()` method will have no effect in the HTML backend due to a browser's sound limitations. Take this into account when developing your project.

How it works...

Up until this point, we did not talk about sound for what it really is: just **waves**. Technically speaking, sound is a vibration that propagates as a **mechanical wave** of pressure and displacement through a medium such as air or water. We do not hear sounds in outer space because vibrations cannot propagate in a vacuum!

Relax, do not start sweating; this is not going to be a physics lecture. However, we do need to mention some basic concepts as they are relevant to this recipe. Take a look at the following figure showing a sound wave over time:

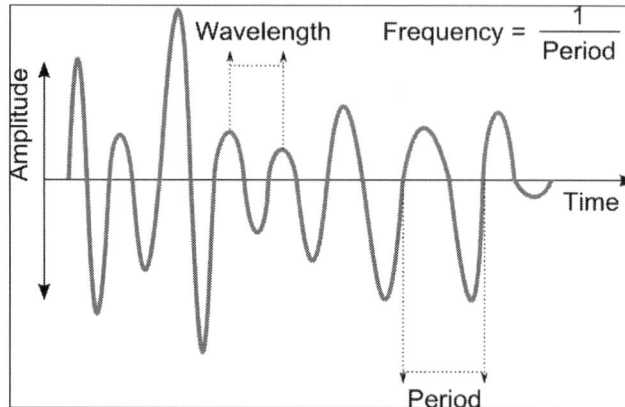

We can highlight the following features:

- ▶ **Amplitude**: This is the distance between the crest and the still position
- ▶ **Wavelength**: This is the distance between two crests
- ▶ **Period**: This is the duration of one wave cycle
- ▶ **Frequency**: This is the number of wave cycles per unit of time, that is, the inverse of period

Let's focus on the frequency, which is closely related to the **pitch**, the value we tweaked in our car engine simulation toy.

Pitch is a perceptual property that allows us to distinguish between different sound frequencies. It is related to frequency, but strictly speaking, it is not a physical property. As you might be used to hearing, pitches are compared as *higher or lower*.

There's more...

Here are a couple of extra things you can do with dynamic sound.

Controlling direction through panning

Another interesting Sound instance property we can tweak is the **pan**, which determines the location the sound is coming from. A pan of -1.0f means the sound is coming from the left, while a pan of 1.0f indicates it is placed on the right. The following diagram shows the pan an explosion can have in relation to the listener. Obviously, multispeaker systems are needed to appreciate the effect as they use two independent audio channels.

The following diagram illustrates panning; the orange marker indicates the listener position and direction.

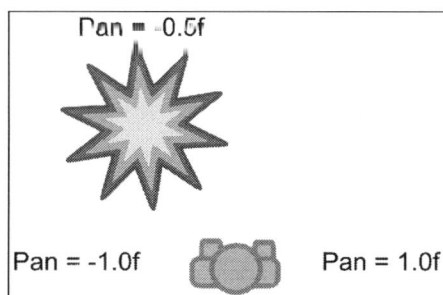

We can set the pan of a sound instance with the following method:

```
void setPan(long soundId, float pan, float volume)
```

Music transitions

Something you can look towards to expand your dynamic audio knowledge is mixing music tracks. Some sort of MusicManager will take requests to change from one track to another, and it will handle transitions and timing. The only thing it really needs to do is smoothly decrease the volume of the previous track while increasing that of the incoming one, as shown in the following diagram:

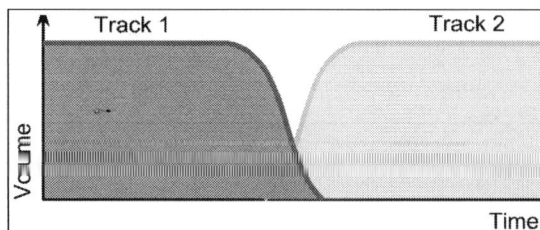

See also

► You are now very familiar with Libgdx audio, which is great! In *The 2D space sound system* recipe, you will learn how to use audio to improve immersion by making it space aware.

The 2D space sound system

Modern games do not simply play sounds and forget about them; they usually feature a full-blown **spatial audio system**.

Effects have a position in the game, which makes them play differently depending on the camera position. The further away the camera moves from the source, the fainter the effect will be perceived. Moreover, they usually take into account the angle between the camera and the effect so as to produce a stereo effect. Some engines implement really complicated sound models to produce the most realistic results possible.

Not only do these systems play an important role in immersion, they also greatly contribute to gameplay in many occasions. In a stealth game, for instance, it is crucial to know where a sound is coming from as it may hint the position of nearby enemies. You can surely come up with many other examples where sound positioning is relevant to gameplay.

In this recipe, we will cover the full implementation of a simple 2D spatial sound system as well as its usage. Keep in mind that this will be a rather simplistic approach; however, the results are pretty decent, extensible, and ready to be used in your games.

Getting ready

Make sure the sample projects are in your Eclipse workspace to follow this recipe. We will also reuse some of the sound effects from the *Playing short sound effects* recipe.

How to do it...

First, we will cover the spatial sound system classes and see how they fit together, and then move on to an example. For space reasons, implementation details will be omitted, unless they are not trivial, in which case they will be accompanied with appropriate explanations.

Find the spatial audio system classes under the `com.cookbook.audio` package.

The `Listener` class holds information about the entity that receives the sounds. For now, we need `position` and `direction` as well as getters and setters for them:

```
public class Listener {
    private Vector2 position = new Vector2();
    private Vector2 direction = new Vector2();

    public Listener();
    public Vector2 getPosition();
    public Vector2 getDirection();
    public void update(Vector2 position, Vector2 direction);
}
```

`SoundData` models a sound effect archetype; it holds a reference to the sound, its duration in seconds, the distance in world units at which it starts fading out, and the maximum distance at which it can be heard. The getter methods are self-explanatory.

The following illustration shows the aforementioned `SoundData` properties:

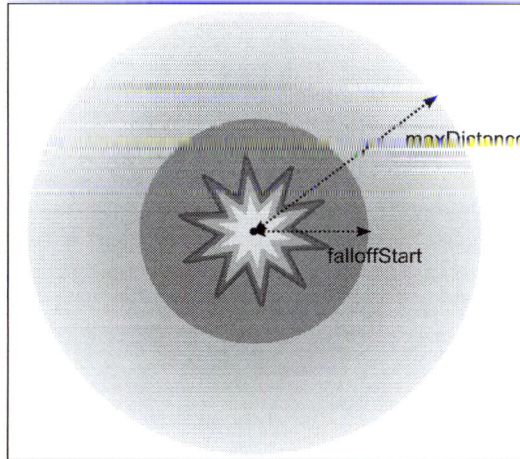

Here is the code:

```
public class SoundData {
    private Sound sound;
    private float duration;
    private float falloffStart;
    private float maxDistance;

    public SoundData(Sound sound, float duration, float
        falloffStart, float maxDistance);
    public Sound getSound();
    public float getDuration();
    public float getFalloffStart();
    public float getMaxDistance();
}
```

> Unfortunately, neither does Libgdx provide any method to know the length of a sound strip nor does it notify when an instance finishes playing. This is why we need to provide the information manually.

Playing effects are represented by the `SoundInstance` class. It contains a reference to the `SoundData` instance it belongs to, the `id` of the SFX instance, its current `position`, and the time it started playing, so we can figure out whether it is complete:

```
public class SoundInstance {
    private SoundData data;
    private long id;
    private Vector2 position;
    private long startTime;
    private Vector2 tmp;

    public SoundInstance(SoundData data);
    public Vector2 getPosition();
    public void setPosition(Vector2 position);
    public boolean update(Listener listener);
    public boolean isFinished();
    private void play();
}
```

`SoundInstance` objects play their referenced effect at creation time by internally calling the private `play()` method. It simply calls `play()` on the `Sound` object, caching off the resulting `id` and recording the current time in milliseconds:

```
private void play() {
    id = data.getSound().play();
    startTime = TimeUtils.millis();
}
```

The `update()` method takes a `Listener` instance and is responsible for updating the effect's volume and panning. It returns a Boolean value indicating whether the instance has finished playing, so we check this first:

```
if (isFinished()) {
    return true;
}
```

The first step to calculate the correct panning for the playing sound is to get the normalized direction from the listener to the source positions:

```
Vector2 listenerPos = listener.getPosition();
Vector2 listenerDir = listener.getDirection();

tmp.set(position).sub(listenerPos).nor();
```

Then, we get the angle between the listener direction and the direction from the listener to the source. We need to know whether the source is on the right or the left of the listener, for which we check the sign of the cross-product between the two vectors:

```
float angle = Math.abs(listenerDir.getAngleRad()
   tmp.getAngleRad());
boolean isRight = tmp.crs(listenerDir) > 0.0f;
```

The next step is to use linear interpolation and the angle to get the right pan value. Remember that a pan of -1.0 indicates the sound is on the left, while 1.0 means it is on the right:

```
float pan = 0.0f;

if (angle > MathUtils.PI * 0.5f) {
  angle -= MathUtils.PI * 0.5f;
  pan = Interpolation.linear.apply(isRight ? 1.0f : -1.0f, 0.0f,
    angle / (MathUtils.PI * 0.5f));
}
else {
  pan = Interpolation.linear.apply(0.0f, isRight ? 1.0f : -1.0f,
    angle / (MathUtils.PI * 0.5f));
}
```

See the following diagram to understand how this calculation works:

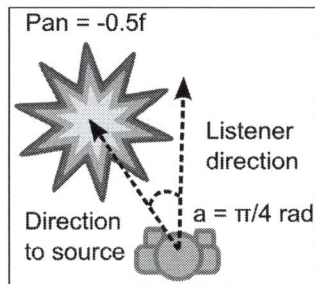

Obtaining the right volume is a lot simpler. The first volume calculation gives us a value between 0.0 and 1.0 as long as the distance falls within `falloffStart` and `maxDistance`. We need to clamp it to make sure this remains in the domain:

```
float distance = position.dst(listenerPos);
float falloffStart = data.getFalloffStart();
float volume = 1.0f - (distance - falloffStart) /
  (data.getMaxDistance() - falloffStart);
float volume = MathUtils.clamp(volume, 0.0f, 1.0f);
```

> As a small optimization, we can work with squared distances, using the dst2 method in Vector2 to save some square root computations in each update call.

To apply the results, we call the setPan() method using id as well as the resulting pan and volume:

```
data.getSound().setPan(id, pan, volume);
return false;
```

We can instantiate SoundData objects manually and give them properties from the Java code. However, it is a lot cleaner to keep logic and data separate. This way, we can reuse the system for different projects without tampering with the code. In this case, the list of SoundData definitions is in the data/sfx/spatial-audio.json file:

```
[ { name : "data/sfx/sfx_01.wav", duration : 4, falloffStart : 1,
  maxDistance : 10 } ... ]
```

The SoundManager class orchestrates the whole process. It loads the JSON file with the collection of sound definitions we can choose from and keeps track of the active sound instances. The play() method takes the sound's filename and returns the instance upon success, which is useful to update the source positions if they are not static. The updateListener() method takes the new listener location and direction so that it can make accurate calculations on the following update. The update() method iterates over the collection of playing sounds, calling their update() function and removing them from the collection when done:

```java
public class SoundManager implements Disposable {

    private Listener listener;
    private Array<SoundInstance> sounds;
    private ObjectMap<String, SoundData> soundsData;

    public SoundManager(FileHandle handle);
    public void dispose();

    public SoundInstance play(String soundName) {
        SoundData data = soundsData.get(soundName);

        if (data != null) {
            SoundInstance instance = new SoundInstance(data);
            instance.update(listener);
            sounds.add(instance);
            return instance;
        }

        return null;
    }
```

```
    public void updateListener(Vector2 position, Vector2 direction);

    public void update() {
      for (int i = 0; i < sounds.size; ) {
        SoundInstance instance = sounds.get(i);

        if (instance.update(listener)) {
          sounds.removeIndex(i);
        }
        else {
          ++i;
        }
      }
    }

    private void loadSoundData(FileHandle handle);
}
```

> Another potential optimization will be to use numerical
> IDs for sounds rather than String objects to avoid
> expensive comparisons.

The SpatialAudioSample class makes use of our newly created 2D audio system. We will
create several sound emitters represented by small circles and a user-controlled entity to
be the listener. The *W*, *A*, *S*, and *D* keys control the circles' motion, while the mouse pointer
determines their direction.

This is what you will be creating:

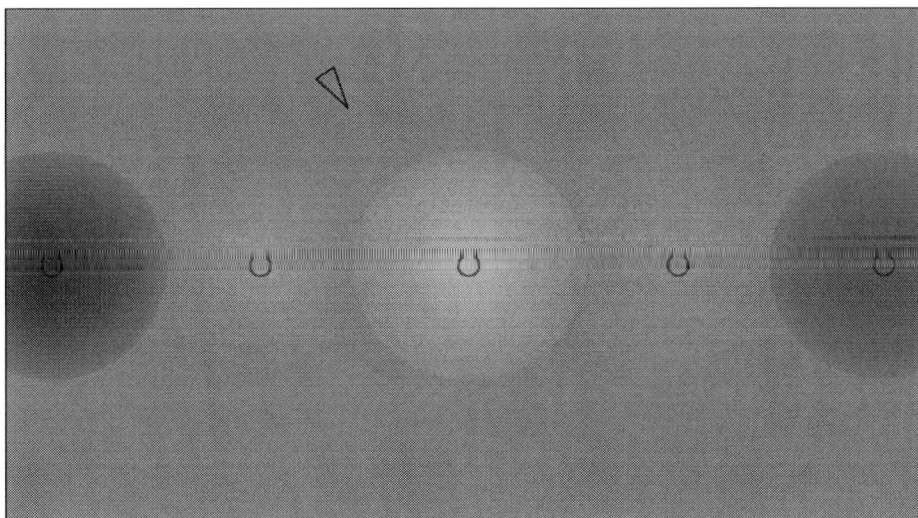

Our sample will then have a SoundManager, a collection of SoundEmitter objects, and a player:

```
private SoundManager soundManager;
private TextureRegion emitterTexture;
private TextureRegion playerTexture;
private Player player;
private Array<SoundEmitter> emitters;
```

In the create() method, soundManager is passed our spatial-audio.json file; we load the textures and instantiate all the emitters as well as the user-controlled entity:

```
public void create() {
    ...
    soundManager = new SoundManager(Gdx.files.internal
      ("data/sfx/spatial-audio.json"));
    emitterTexture = new TextureRegion(new
      Texture(Gdx.files.internal("data/sfx/emitter.png")));
    playerTexture = new TextureRegion(new
      Texture(Gdx.files.internal("data/sfx/player.png")));
    player = new Player();
    createSoundEmitters();
}
```

We need to remember to dispose all our resources, including soundManager:

```
public void dispose() {
  soundManager.dispose();
  batch.dispose();
  emitterTexture.getTexture().dispose();
  playerTexture.getTexture().dispose();
}
```

The SoundEmitter inner class is fairly simple; it contains the name of the sound it plays, a position, a color, and its corresponding sound instance. It simply keeps playing the same sound in a loop:

```
private class SoundEmitter {
  String name = new String();
  Vector2 position = new Vector2();
  Color color = new Color(Color.WHITE);
  SoundInstance soundInstance;

  public void update() {
    if (soundInstance == null || soundInstance.isFinished()) {
      soundInstance = soundManager.play(name);
    }
    soundInstance.setPosition(position);
  }
}
```

The `createSoundEmitters()` method is self-explanatory; it creates the `emitters` array and populates it with a few manually configured emitters:

```
private void createSoundEmitters() {
   emitters = new Array<SoundEmitter>();

   SoundEmitter emitter = new SoundEmitter();
   emitter.name = "data/sfx/sfx_01.wav";
   emitter.position.set(-18.0f, 0.0f);
   emitter.color = Color.BLUE;
   emitters.add(emitter);

   ...
}
```

The `Player` inner class is responsible for keeping track of and updating the user-controlled entity according to the inputs:

```
private class Player {
   final float speed = 10.0f;
   Vector2 position =  new Vector2();
   Vector2 direction = new Vector2(1.0f, 0.0f);
   Vector2 movement = new Vector2();
   Vector2 mousePos = new Vector2();

   public void update(float delta);
}
```

Finally, the `render()` method updates the manager, the player, and all the emitters. It also draws all the elements onscreen, using their corresponding texture region, current position, and direction:

```
public void render() {
   ...
   soundManager.updateListener(player.position, player.direction);
   soundManager.update();

   player.update(Gdx.graphics.getDeltaTime());

   for (SoundEmitter emitter : emitters) {
     emitter.update();
   }

   ...
}
```

Experiment with how some sounds fade out while others can be heard with more intensity as you move around. Now, you can add this feature to your next game!

How it works...

This is not required to be explained for this recipe as the system we implemented is explained thoroughly in the previous section.

There's more...

The spatial audio system you just implemented can be expanded in several interesting ways.

You can research sound propagation here, introduce a more realistic model for intensity decay, and introduce phenomena such as the Doppler effect. Compare the results, play around with both approaches in your game, and decide which one feels better. At the end of the day, games are not about simulating real life, but providing a good experience.

Additionally, you can extend the system to support 3D coordinates instead of just 2D ones. The necessary changes are straightforward, and it will still be usable for bidimensional games.

Finally, if you want to save some CPU time, it is not necessary to call the `update()` method for every frame.

See also

> ▶ As far as our cookbook is concerned, we are done with the Libgdx sound system. If you think you did not understand all the concepts well, we invite you to review the recipes and play around with the samples as an exercise. Otherwise, feel free to move on to the I/O system with the *The first approach to file handling in Libgdx* recipe.

The first approach to file handling in Libgdx

As our first contact with the Libgdx **filesystem**, we will learn about the types of files available to us. We will also show you how to read from and write to both binary and text files. Moreover, this recipe will show you how to extract information from entries such as whether it is a file or a directory as well as its size, name, and extension. Finally, you will also discover how to traverse a directory tree hierarchy.

This will settle the grounds for you to include features such as save game states and configuration files in your projects.

Getting ready

Once again, make sure the sample projects are in your Eclipse workspace before continuing.

How to do it...

Jumping straight into the topic at hand, everything explained throughout this recipe is illustrated in the `FileHandlingSample` class within the `samples/core` project.

In order for us to work with a file in Libgdx, we need a `FileHandle` instance that points to said file or folder. This class takes care of all the platform-specific details, offering us a clean, simple API to carry out a wide set of operations.

To obtain an appropriate `FileHandle`, we can call `getFileHandle()`, which is a static method in the `Files` interface. Such an interface is accessible through `Gdx.files`:

```
FileHandle getFileHandle(java.lang.String path, Files.FileType
    type)
```

`FileType` is an enum listing the different kinds of files available in Libgdx. All of them will be covered in detail in this recipe:

```
public enum FileType { Absolute, Classpath, External, Internal,
    Local};
```

The `Files` interface also provides convenient methods to retrieve file handles:

```
FileHandle handle = Gdx.files.absolute("test.txt");
FileHandle handle = Gdx.files.classpath("test.txt");
FileHandle handle = Gdx.files.external("test.txt");
FileHandle handle = Gdx.files.internal("test.txt");
FileHandle handle = Gdx.files.local("test.txt");
```

> Asking for a handle to an invalid or nonexistent file will not result in an exception being thrown. This allows us to obtain a handle to a file that does not exist, write to it, and thus effectively create the file.

Retrieving basic information from files

The `FileHandle` class provides a few methods to easily retrieve information from the files they point to:

▸ `handle.name()`: This returns the name of the file, including its extension but excluding the path to it, for example, `sfx_01.wav`

▸ `handle.nameWithoutExtension()`: This returns the name of the file with neither the extension nor the path to the parent folder, for example, `sfx_01`

▸ `handle.extension()`: This returns the extension of the file without the dot, for example, `wav`

- ▶ `handle.path()`: This returns the path to the file, for example, `data/sfx/sfx_01.wav`

- ▶ `handle.pathWithoutExtension()`: The same as the preceding method excluding the extension, for example, `data/sfx/sfx_01`

- ▶ `handle.lastModified()`: This returns the date and time the file was modified for the last time, in milliseconds, since epoch

- ▶ `handle.length()`: This returns the size of the file in bytes

- ▶ `handle.isDirectory()`: This indicates whether the handle points to a directory or a plain file

Traversing tree structures

The `FileHandle` class provides a `list()` method that returns an array of `FileHandle` instances containing its children. Using this, we can walk a tree hierarchy with a very simple recursive function. If the handle points to a regular file and not a directory, `list()` will return an empty array:

```
private void traverseTree(FileHandle handle) {
  doSomething(handle);

  for (FileHandle child : handle.list()) {
    traverseTree(child);
  }
}
```

> Listing a directory is not supported in desktop platforms; take this into consideration when developing your games. It works during development when running from your IDE. However, it will not work from a packed `.jar` file. A quick-and-dirty solution will be to call and parse the output of commands, such as `ls` or `dir`.

Writing to and reading from files

File writing can be achieved through any of the `write()` method variants the `FileHandle` class has; we will only cover a couple of them. Creating a new file and adding a string to it is as easy as is shown in the following code. The second parameter indicates whether to append at the end or write at the beginning (truncating the file):

```
Gdx.files.external("test.txt").writeString("This is a test file",
    false);
```

On the other hand, you might want to treat the file as binary and write a stream of bytes to it:

```
byte[] bytes = new byte[] {'T', 'e', 's', 't'};
Gdx.files.external("test").writeBytes(bytes, false);
```

The same options to read from a file are also available. We can put all the contents of a file on a `String` object with the following snippet:

```
String string = Gdx.files.external("test.txt").readString();
```

We can also get the whole content of the file as an array of bytes by executing this:

```
String bytes = Gdx.files.external("test.txt").readBytes();
```

Check out the official API documentation for a comprehensive list of mechanisms for file reading and writing, available at `http://libgdx.badlogicgames.com/nightlies/docs/api/com/badlogic/gdx/files/FileHandle.html`.

Copying and deleting files and directories

Libgdx offers additional file and directory manipulation through the following `FileHandle` functions.

To copy a file or folder, use `copyTo()` to pass the handle of the destination handle:

```
void copyTo(FileHandle dest)
```

You can erase files or directories with `delete()`. The operation will fail if the handle points to a non-empty directory or a location where the user cannot delete files. If you want to delete a directory and its contents recursively, call the `deleteDirectory()` method instead:

```
boolean delete()
boolean deleteDirectory()
```

Lastly, you might want to erase the contents of a directory without removing the directory itself. Use the `emptyDirectory()` function in this case. The `preserveTree` parameter tells the handle whether to delete recursively, or delete only the files at this level:

```
void emptyDirectory(boolean preserveTree)
```

How it works...

We mentioned the different file types briefly earlier in this recipe; it is really important to understand their differences and quirks because there are many platform-specific details to take into account. Here is a more detailed description of each one of them:

- ▶ **Absolute**: These are fully qualified paths. They should be avoided whenever possible for the sake of portability as it is harder to rely on users that have specific directory structures. Absolute files are not available in the HTML backend.
- ▶ **Classpath**: These are files inside the source directory of your Java application, which are strictly read only and cannot be used within HTML applications.

> ▶ **Internal**: This is relative to the working directory on desktop platforms, the `assets` folder on Android, and the `war/assets` directory in HTML projects. It's available on all platforms, but is also only read only. This is where we typically store all our game files, such as audio, graphics, and gameplay data.

> ▶ **External**: This is relative to the home directory of the current user on desktop platforms and the root of the SD card on Android (requires special permissions in the manifest file). It can be written as well as read, although not from the HTML backend. It is best suited for saving downloaded files and other similar activities.

> ▶ **Local**: This is basically equivalent to internal files on a desktop, but relative to private storage on Android. It can be both read only and write files, but it's not supported from the HTML backend. It is typically used for small game-save data.

As we just mentioned, some kinds of files are not available on all platforms. To check for this, you can make use of the following methods. Keep in mind that it's best not to use absolute or classpath files:

```
Gdx.files.isExternalStorageAvailable();
Gdx.files.isLocalStorageAvailable();
```

There's more...

As you have seen already, the `Files` interface is quite powerful. Here are a few quick extra things you can do with it.

Creating temporary files

We often need disposable files with unique names for certain operations so that they do not collide with other files in the system. We can create a temporary directory or file in the `FileHandle` class with the following static methods. The parameter is used as the prefix for the name:

```
FileHandle tempDir = FileHandle.tempDirectory("temp");
FileHandle tempFile = FileHandle.tempFile("temp");
```

Filtering directory listings

Another common situation is to iterate over the files in a directory, but only be interested in files that match a certain criteria. Rather than adding an `if` condition every time you traverse a tree, why not just pass a `FileFilter` or `FileNameFilter` instance to the `list()` function? This approach is cleaner and avoids code duplication.

`FileFilter` and `FileNameFilter` are interfaces in the Java standard library. Provide your own implementation with the required criteria in each case:

```
public interface FileFilter {
  boolean accept(File pathname);
```

```
  }

  public interface FileNameFilter {
    boolean accept(File dir, String name);
  }
```

File streaming

Libgdx supports streaming for large files. Take a look at the `read()` and `write()` method overloads that take or return streams at `http://libgdx.badlogicgames.com/nightlies/docs/api/com/badlogic/gdx/files/FileHandle.html`.

See also

▶ Move on to the *Using preferences to store game states and options* recipe to learn more about files in Libgdx.

Using preferences to store game states and options

Being able to read and write both text and binary files in your Libgdx projects already gives you all the flexibility you will ever require to handle game saves and configuration files. However, binary files might not be very convenient to store key-value pairs.

Do not worry! Libgdx always keeps a hidden ace. If all you need is to store a set of key-value pairs to keep track of basic player progress or game settings, there is a small utility that will make your day. The `Preferences` class offers an extremely simple API for you to store things such as top scores, the desired music volume, and so on.

This brief recipe will show you how to use this utility to your advantage.

Getting ready

Very quickly, import the samples projects into your Eclipse workspace.

How to do it...

Every `Preferences` instance points to an internal file. Creating or loading an existing file is as easy as calling the `getPreferences()` method in the `Application` interface:

```
Preferences preferences = Gdx.app.getPreferences("preferences");
```

The string you need to pass through might be used to determine the filename, so make sure it is valid and unique (it depends on the platform implementation). A good idea is to use the current package or fully qualified class name:

```
Preferences preferences =
   Gdx.app.getPreferences(PreferencesSample.class.getName());
```

The entries stored in a `Preferences` instance are identified by unique keys, and the values can either be integers, floats, Booleans, strings, or longs. In order to add new values or modify existing ones, use one of the following methods:

```
void putBoolean(String key, boolean val)
void putFloat(String key, float val)
void putInteger(String key, int val)
void putLong(String key, long val)
void putString(String key, String val)
```

Reading previously stored values is equally straightforward; you only need to call the corresponding `get` method, supplying the desired key and an optional default value. If no default value is supplied, and the entry does not exist, a built-in default value will be returned:

```
boolean getBoolean(String key, boolean defValue)
float getFloat(String key, float defValue)
int getInteger(String key, int defValue)
long getLong(String key, long defValue)
String getString(String key, String defValue)
```

Adding an entry does not immediately result in the `Preferences` instance saving everything out to the filesystem; the new values stay in memory instead. In order to trigger a save-to-disk operation, you need to call the `flush()` method on said instance.

How it works...

After running `PreferencesSample` on the desktop, you will have a `com.cookbook.samples.PreferencesSample` file inside a `.prefs` folder in your user directory. The file is just XML and has a very basic schema:

```
<?xml version="1.0" encoding="UTF-8" standalone="no"?>
<!DOCTYPE properties SYSTEM
   "http://java.sun.com/dtd/properties.dtd">
<properties>
  <entry key="difficulty">10</entry>
  <entry key="effectsVolume">0.0</entry>
  <entry key="playerName">8</entry>
  <entry key="showTips">false</entry>
  <entry key="musicVolume">0.0</entry>
</properties>
```

There is no encryption whatsoever, which may not make `Preferences` suitable for more sensitive data such as private keys, sensitive user data, or game records that should be validated against a server (trophies, best scores, and so on). No one likes cheats!

A workaround is to encrypt the stored keys and values.

There's more...

You can retrieve the whole set of options as an associative array indexed by strings and containing arbitrary objects through the following method:

```
Map<String, ?> get()
```

Similarly, you can push a whole batch of preferences into a `Preferences` instance through the following method:

```
void put(Map<String, ?> vals)
```

You might encounter a situation where an entry is no longer needed; to get rid of it, just call the following:

```
void remove(String key)
```

See also

When the `Preferences` class just does not cut it, you can discover how to deal with more powerful file formats in the following recipes:

▸ The *The XML parsing primer* recipe

▸ The *JSON serialization and deserialization* recipe

The XML parsing primer

XML stands for **Extensible Markup Language**, and it is a standard that defines a set of rules to encode information created by the **World Wide Web Consortium (W3C)**. The major advantage of XML is that it is both human and machine readable, which contributes to its success not only on the Web but also in game development.

We assume you have basic knowledge of XML, but take a look at the W3C introduction tutorial if this is the first time you have come across the standard. It is available at `http://www.w3schools.com/xml/xml_whatis.asp`.

XML's flexibility and hierarchical tree-oriented nature made many game studios use it to represent their data, such as configuration files, level layout, animation, and so on. Keeping the code separated from data makes it more reusable, allows rapid iteration through hot reloading, and lets nontechnical people tweak aspects of the game.

As you might have expected, Libgdx features its own XML parsing utilities, and we will show you how to leverage them in this recipe.

Getting ready

Import the sample projects into your Eclipse workspace.

How to do it...

An example of how to proceed can be found in the XMLParsingSample class, which parses the data/credits.xml file. This document contains nothing more than the credits for this book. Here, we will provide you with an insight into how to read arbitrary XML documents:

```
<Credits>
  <Book year="2014" pages="300" >Libgdx Game Development
    Cookbook</Book>
  <Publisher>PACKT Publishing</Publisher>
  <Authors>
    <Author>David Saltares</Author>
    <Author>Alberto Cejas</Author>
  </Authors>
  <Reviewers>
    <Reviewer>Manuel Palomo</Reviewer>
    <Reviewer>Simon Fleming</Reviewer>
    ...
  </Reviewers>
</Credits>
```

To open and parse an XML file, you will need an instance of the XMLReader class and to call its parse() method. In the following example, we pass FileHandle through to the parser; however, it can take an input stream, a reader, or just a string:

```
XmlReader reader = new XmlReader();
Element root =
  reader.parse(Gdx.files.internal("data/credits.xml"));
```

> You might want to be careful here because if anything goes wrong during the parsing process, the parse() method will throw an IOException. Watch out for missing files or malformed XML.

The reader will return a reference to the tree's root element, which you can use to get the information you want. Once you have an element, retrieving its name is simple, as follows:

```
String elementName = root.getName();
```

You can also get the text that an element encloses using the following code:

```
String elementText = root.getText();
```

Elements can have attributes, which you can retrieve using their names. The following methods return the attribute identified by the given name or the contents of a child node with that tag name. When nothing is found, `defaultValue` is returned. The second parameter is optional in every case.

```
String get(String name, String defaultValue)
float getFloat(String name, float defaultValue)
boolean getBoolean(String name, boolean defaultValue)
int getInt(String name, int defaultValue)
```

Let's take a look at the following XML element:

```
<Book year="2014" pages="300" >Libgdx Game Development
    Cookbook</Book>
```

The `getName()` method will return `Book`, while the `getText()` method will give us `Libgdx Game Development Cookbook`; easy peasy! To get the year, we will intuitively call `getInt("year")`.

> Pay special attention to files with special characters and make sure they are encoded in the UTF-8 format, which Libgdx is ready to handle without any problems.

Iterating over the children of an element is a simple enough job:

```
int numChildren = element.getChildrenCount();

for (int i = 0; i < numChildren; ++i) {
  Element child = element.getChild(i);
}
```

Sometimes, you might be interested in a child with a specific name; do not iterate over all the children because Libgdx can do it for you if you ask using the following functions:

```
Element getChildByName(String name)
Element getChildByNameRecursive(String name)
```

This will return the first occurrence of a child or descendant (in the recursive version) that matches the given name. Oh, you say you want them all? If so, then use the following versions, which return an array of `Element` references:

```
Array<Element> getChildrenByName(String name)
Array<Element> getChildrenByNameRecursively(String name)
```

These mechanisms will give you enough power to traverse a tree, fetching the data you need.

What about modifying an existing tree? You can set the text of an element as well as add or modify existing attributes with the following methods:

```
void setAttribute(String name, String value)
void setText(String text)
```

Once you are done modifying the document tree, you will probably want to save it off to persistent memory. Such a task is as simple as grabbing a new file handle pointing to the file we want and writing the text representation of the tree. To obtain it, just call the `toString()` method on the root node. Optionally, you can pass the indent string (either a few spaces or a tab character):

```
FileHandle handle = Gdx.files.external("data.xml");
handle.writeString(root.toString('   '));
```

> Make sure you can write to the selected file handle. As mentioned in the *The first approach to file handling in Libgdx* recipe, not all file types on all platforms are writeable.

How it works...

`XMLReader` supports a subset of the full XML specification so as to be able to provide lightweight and faster document processing. This subset includes elements, attributes, text, CDATA (text that should not be parsed), and so on. Namespaces are simply considered part of the element or attribute name. Doctypes and schema declarations are completely ignored.

When it comes to games, performance and simplicity are usually preferred over correctness or sticking to strict standards.

There's more...

We covered how to parse an XML file, modify it, and save it to disk, but what about creating a new tree from scratch? This is when the `XMLWriter` class comes into play. First and foremost, you need to instantiate it:

```
StringWriter writer = new StringWriter();
XmlWriter xml = new XmlWriter(writer);
```

All operations on an `XmlWriter` object return a reference to the same instance, which allows chaining (as seen in the following code). To add a new element to the tree, we call the `element()` method. Every subsequent operation will be performed on the element; whenever we want to go back up one level in the hierarchy, we have to call `pop()`. Attributes can be added with the `attribute()` method.

Imagine that we want to recreate the following document:

```
<Credits>
  <Book year="2014" pages="300" >Libgdx Game Development
    Cookbook</Book>
</Credits>
```

Here is the code snippet that will achieve it:

```
xml.element("Credits")
  .element("Book", "Libgdx Game Development Cookbook")
    .attribute("year", "2014")
    .attribute("pages", "300")
  .pop()
.pop();
```

Piece of cake! To finally save the document off to disk, we can do the following:

```
FileHandle handle = Gdx.files.external("credits.xml");
handle.writeString(writer.toString());
```

See also

- Some people love XML for its hierarchical structure and readability when compared with binary files. However, XML can sometimes be slightly verbose, in which case, you might be interested to know about JSON. Read more about this format in the *JSON serialization and deserialization* recipe.

JSON serialization and deserialization

JSON stands for **JavaScript Object Notation** and it is an open standard, human readable format to transmit objects formed by attribute-value pairs. It has become very popular to transmit data between clients and servers, but it is also heavily used in games as an alternative of XML.

Originally, it came from JavaScript, although it is actually language agnostic as there are many utilities to write and read JSON in virtually every widely used language. Being less verbose than XML and easier to parse are probably its main advantages when compared to the aforementioned format.

JSON is really awesome, but in order to be able to follow this recipe, make sure you are familiar with the basics. Check out `http://www.json.org` for more details.

In this recipe, you will learn how to deserialize (read) Java objects from JSON files and serialize them back to JSON.

Getting ready

Make sure you have the sample projects in your Eclipse workspace.

How to do it...

The code for this recipe can be found in the `JSONParsingSample` class. We will work with the `data/character.json` file, which defines an RPG-like character with some typical attributes and his inventory:

```
{
  name: "David",
  experience: 2534,
  strength: 6,
  dexterity: 8,
  intelligence: 6,
  inventory : [{ name: "iron-sword", number: 1 },
    { name: "wooden-shield", number: 1 },
    { name: "leather-armor", number: 1 },
    { name: "leather-boots", number: 1 },
    { name: "healing-potion", number: 3 },
    { name: "poison-herbs", number: 2 }]
}
```

The two following classes will model our character in code:

```
public class Item {
  private String name;
  private int number;
}
public class Character {
  private String name = "";
  private int experience = 0;
  private int strength = 1;
  private int dexterity = 1;
  private int intelligence = 1;
  private Array<Item> inventory = new Array<Item>();
}
```

Now that we have the basics, it is time to learn how to deal with the Libgdx JSON API. We will start with reading, then proceed to writing, and finally, we will cover some advanced aspects.

Reading objects from JSON

The `Json` class can recreate objects automatically from a JSON-formatted string:

```
Json json = new Json();
```

It associates the keys in the file with member names in the corresponding class using reflection. This works wonderfully for basic data types, but it gets slightly more complicated when objects contain other objects. In our case, we can have a problem with the `items` array. There are two ways to handle this:

► The item entries in the file should say which class they belong to:

```
{ class: com.cookbook.samples.JSONParsinSample.Item:
  "wooden-shield", number: 1 }
```

► We tell the `Json` object that the `"inventory"` element inside `Character` contains objects of type `Array<Item>`:

```
json.setElementType(Character.class, "inventory",
  Array<Item>.class);
```

Once we have cleared out these potential conflicts, we can safely instantiate a new `Character` object from the file:

```
Character character = json.fromJson(Character.class,
  Gdx.files.internal("data/character.json"));
```

Magic! We managed to create a `Character` instance from the JSON file with very little hassle.

Writing objects to JSON

We can now work with our `Character` object, increase the experience level, add a few items, and modify some of the attributes. The player might reach a save point, so we need to serialize `character` and save it off to disk. Luckily enough, this is simple. Consider the following code:

```
FileHandle handle = Gdx.files.external("character.json");
String string = json.toJson(character);
string = json.prettyPrint(string);
handle.writeString(string);
```

The `toJson()` method produces a compact but not very readable result. We call `prettyPrint()` on the result so as to get proper indentation.

Manual JSON parsing

Sometimes, you might need to do manual parsing for some objects in your game. Imagine you have an `enemy.json` file that defines all the attributes for an enemy in your game and uses a string to identify the texture the character should use. The `Enemy` class will have a `Texture` member, but it will just be a string in the file. In this case, you will have to read the texture name and instantiate a `Texture` object with the result.

First, you need to parse the file and get the `JsonValue` root object:

```
JsonReader reader = new JsonReader();
JsonValue root =
  reader.parse(Gdx.files.internal("data/enemy.json");
```

The `JsonValue` class models elements in a document, which can be of different types such as string, integer, Boolean, float, array, or object. Checking the value type is simple; call one of the following methods: `isArray()`, `isBoolean()`, `isNumber()`, `isString()`, `isObject()`, or `isNull()`.

To retrieve the contents of a `JsonValue` object, you can use one of the following: `asBoolean()`, `asFloat()`, `asInt()`, `asArray()`, or `asString()`.

When `JsonValue` instances are objects, they might have children that you can easily retrieve. Call `has()`, passing in the name to make sure a child of the given name exists. Once you are sure, use one of the following, simple that `defaultValue` can be omitted:

```
JsonValue get(String name)
String getString(String name, String defaultValue)
bool getBoolean(String name, bool defaultValue)
float getFloat(String name, float defaultValue)
int getInt(String name, int defaultValue)
```

Iterating over an array element is easy with the `JsonIterator` class:

```
for (JsonValue item : items) {
    …
}
```

This will give you enormous flexibility when it comes to parsing JSON documents.

How it works...

Libgdx's JSON implementation does not strictly follow the standard; it is a bit more forgiving. Firstly, value names do not need to be quoted. Officially, it should be `"name": "David"` rather than `name: "David"`. Secondly, it allows C-style comments in case developers want to document complicated formats inline.

There's more...

The Libgdx JSON library is rather powerful and has a few extra goodies to help you with serialization.

The Serializable interface

When an object is particularly complicated, such as our previous Enemy example, you might want to make it implement the Serializable interface so that you can customize the process:

```
public class Enemy implements Serializable {
  public void read(Json json, JsonValue jsonData) { ... }
  public void write(Json json) { ... }
}
```

The Serializer interface

Making your classes responsible for their own serialization might be seen as polluting them. Do not panic though, you can still customize serialization without touching the serializable class with a different class that implements the Serializer interface:

```
public class EnemySerializer implements Serializer<Enemy> {
  public Enemy read(Json json, JsonValue jsonData, Class type) {
    ... }
  public void write(Json json, Enemy object, Class knownType) {
    ... }
}

Json json = new Json();
json.setSerializer(Enemy.class, new EnemySerializer());
```

See also

- We have covered all Libgdx features related to file handling, and you should have a pretty clear understanding of how to introduce save and configuration files in your project. This will be the time to revisit areas that you did not understand very well. Otherwise, move on to Chapter 6, Font Rendering.

6
Font Rendering

In this chapter, we will cover the following recipes:

- ► Generating and rendering bitmap fonts
- ► Baking effects into fonts using Hiero
- ► Scaling friendly font rendering with distance fields
- ► Dynamic font effects using distance fields

Introduction

Depending on the genre of your awesome game project, you may need to show the user more or less text. Role-playing games and some adventures tend to be very text-heavy, while action games ... well, they let the guns do the talking. However, in all likeness, all of these will require some font rendering, even if it is just for the menus or the game scores.

This chapter will start with the very basics of how to generate a Libgdx-compatible font and render some text with it on the screen. We will then move on to effects such as drop shadows or outlines, both using prebaked techniques and shaders. Additionally, we will tackle the font-scaling problem and offer a practical solution using distance field fonts.

By the time you finish reading and practicing with the samples, you will be able to handle most font rendering issues in your game without too much trouble.

Generating and rendering bitmap fonts

While you may be most familiar with **TrueType Fonts** (**TTF**), they are not the best supported approach when it comes to font rendering in games; this also applies to the Libgdx environment. Rendering text from a TTF is a costly process because it involves rasterizing the vector representation of the font onto a texture.

Instead, TTF files are baked into textures or **bitmap fonts** using an offline tool, such as Hiero, as you will see later in this recipe. This way, the graphics system only needs to load a texture and the location of each contained character. Rendering text becomes a lot simpler: rendering multiple regions using additional logic for correct character positioning. Don't worry, Libgdx does all of this for us!

In this recipe, we will create bitmap fonts from TTF files using **Hiero**, a tool distributed with the Libgdx package. Then, we will use the result to render text in various ways within a Libgdx application.

> Libgdx features a FreeType extension that allows the user to generate bitmap fonts on the fly from TTF files, but it is not compatible with the HTML backend.

Getting ready

To get a hold of Hiero, get the latest Libgdx package and unzip it somewhere in your hard drive (`http://libgdx.badlogicgames.com/releases`).

For our recipe, we will use the `data/fonts/play.fnt` file to render text on the screen. We will also be using the `samples` projects, as usual.

How to do it...

We are going to subdivide the process for this recipe in two steps. First, we will generate our font texture with Hiero, and then, we will cover the rendering process with Libgdx.

Using Hiero to generate bitmap font files

Perform the following steps to run Hiero and generate a bitmap font texture:

1. Open a command-line window and access the unpacked Libgdx download folder.
2. Windows users have to enter the following command:

```
java -cp gdx.jar;gdx-natives.jar;gdx-backend-lwjgl.jar;gdx-
backend-lwjgl-natives.jar;extensions\gdx-tools\gdx-tools.jar com.
badlogic.gdx.tools.hiero.Hiero
```

If you use either Linux or Mac, you need to replace backslashes with forward slashes:

```
java -cp gdx.jar:gdx-natives.jar:gdx-backend-lwjgl.jar:gdx-
backend-lwjgl-natives.jar:extensions/gdx-tools/gdx-tools.jar com.
badlogic.gdx.tools.hiero.Hiero
```

The following screenshot shows the Hiero bitmap font tool:

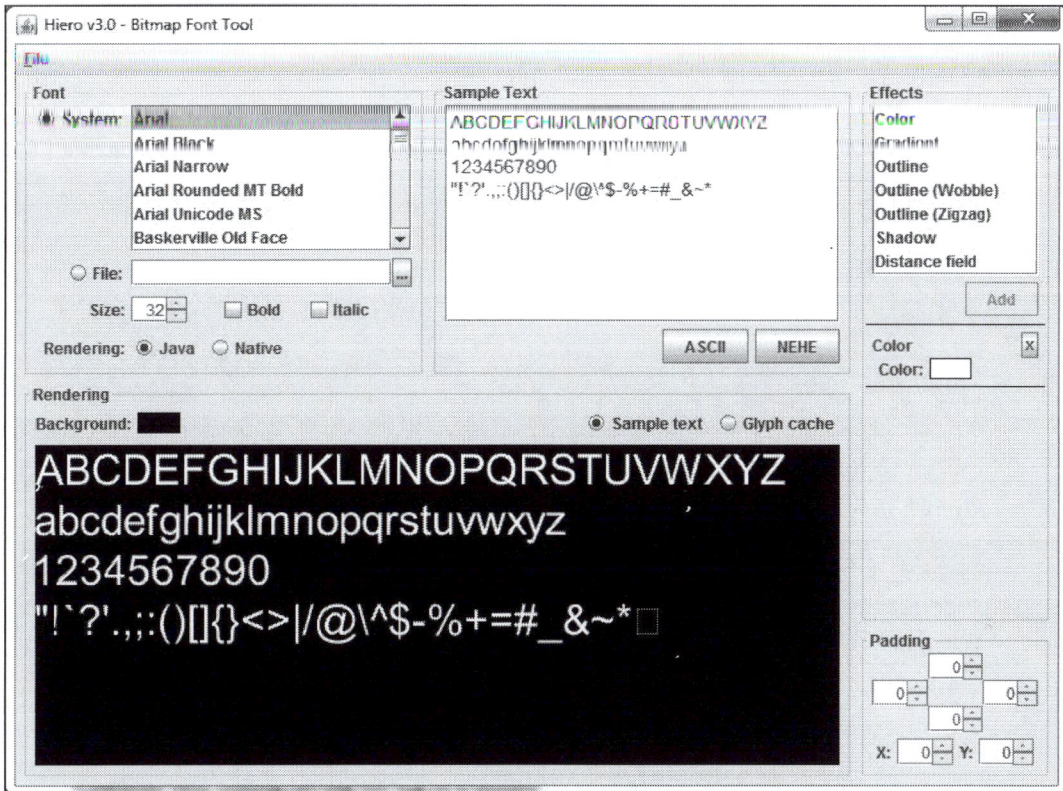

3. Take a look at the **Font** panel and select the font you want to work with. You can either choose from the ones in your **System** option or pick a TTF file with the **File** option.

4. Now, select **Size** in pixels and whether the resulting font should have the **Bold** or **Italic** style.

5. The **Sample Text** box shows the characters that the bitmap will contain. Add the characters you require, keeping in mind that this will not suffice for languages that could potentially have thousands of characters, such as Chinese or Korean. The texture will be too big and unsupported by most GPUs.

6. The **Rendering** panel contains a preview of the final result. You can change the color with the **Color** selector in the **Effects** panel, but it is advisable that you keep it white and change it dynamically from the code, just as we do with regions.

7. If you want to stop and carry on later, you can always click on **File** and **Save Hiero settings file…**. This will let you save the current project, which can be opened by clicking on **File** and then on **Open Hiero settings file…**.

8. Once you are done, click on **File** and **Save BMFont files (text)…** to generate the texture and a text file that indicates the location of each character within this texture.

Fantastic! You can now generate bitmap fonts.

Rendering bitmap font files with Libgdx

The code for this example is inside the `BitmapFontSample` class. First, we add our classic `Viewport`, `OrthographicCamera`, and `SpriteBatch` classes. This time, we will also need `BitmapFont`, the class that handles the loading and rendering of texture-based fonts.

The font is loaded inside the `create()` method, simply by passing in the `data/fonts/play.fnt` file:

```
font = new BitmapFont(Gdx.files.internal("data/fonts/play.fnt"));
```

By default, a bitmap font will allocate and own its texture, so you need to dispose of it appropriately. We do so in the `dispose()` method:

```
font.dispose();
```

The meaty part takes place inside the `render()` method, between the calls to `begin()` and `end()`. The most straightforward way to render text is through the `draw()` function in `BitmapFont`. It takes `SpriteBatch`, the string you want to render, and a pair of (*x*, *y*) coordinates:

```
font.draw(batch, "This is a one line string", 20.0f, VIRTUAL_HEIGHT -
50.0f);
```

You can also draw several lines in one go using the `drawMultiline()` method. It takes the same parameters as `draw()`, but it looks for line break characters, \n:

```
font.drawMultiLine(batch, "This is a\nmultiline string", 20.0f,
VIRTUAL_HEIGHT - 150.0f);
```

Sometimes, you will have limited space to render your text and you do not want to insert line breaks manually because that could be a pain. It is possible to wrap your text so that it fits within a given width, through the `drawWrapped()` method:

```
font.drawWrapped(batch, "[...]", 20.0f, VIRTUAL_HEIGHT - 400.0f,
900.0f);
```

> Please note that the `drawWrapped()` method is CPU-intensive; consider rendering it to a `FrameBuffer` object to cache the result.

While working with Hiero, we intentionally made our texture white so that we could change the rendered color programmatically. This can be achieved with the `setColor()` function, but beware as it is a state-changing procedure, meaning that all subsequent draw calls will have this color applied:

```
font.setColor(Color.RED);
```

You can also change the color of a string within a single draw call using special markup:

- `[color-name]`: This sets the current color by name from a predefined list
- `[#RRGGBBAA]`: This sets the color by a hexadecimal value; AA defaults to `0xFF`
- `[]`: This sets the current color to the previous one
- `[[`: This escapes the `[` character

To enable this feature, you need to call the `setMarkupEnabled(true)` method on the font reference. Here are a couple of examples of how to render a multicolor string:

```
font.draw(batch, "[PURPLE]This [BLUE]is [GREEN]a [YELLOW]cool [ORANGE]
multicolor [RED]string", 0.0f, 0.0f);
font.draw(batch, "[#ff00ff]This [#0000ff]is [#00ff00]a [#66ff00]cool
[#ffff00]multicolor [#ff0000]string", 0.0f, 0.0f);
```

The `BitmapFont` instances can also be scaled using the `setScale()` method; keep in mind that this is also a state-changing operation:

```
font.setScale(1.5f);
```

The following screenshot illustrates the results of this sample. Now, you can add awesome text to your game!

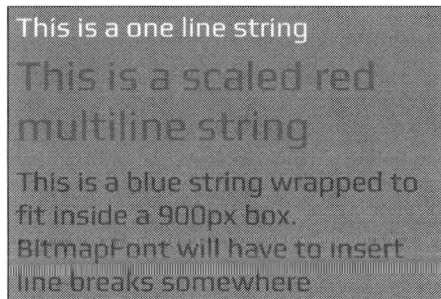

How it works...

Even though it makes life so much easier for us, `BitmapFont` actually works in quite a simple way. It loads a `font.fnt` file, which is nothing more than a plain text file pointing to a texture. The file contains information of where the characters are located inside the texture and additional font metrics. This data is used to render characters together in a way that makes sense and feels pleasant.

Here is an extract of `data/arial-15.fnt`:

```
info face=Arial,Normal size=15 bold=0 italic=0 charset="" unicode=1
stretchH=100 smooth=0 aa=1 padding=0,0,0,0 spacing=1,1
common lineHeight=17 base=14 scaleW=1024 scaleH=1024 pages=1 packed=0
page id=0 file=arial-15_00.png
chars count=190
char id=33 x=957 y=12 width=1 height=11 xoffset=2 yoffset=3 xadvance=5
page=0 chnl=0
```

Fonts have a set of metrics associated with them; let's take a look at the basics:

▸ **Baseline**: This is the line to which the characters are bottom-aligned.

▸ **Ascent**: This is the distance between the normal height (the cap height) and the top of the tallest glyph.

▸ **Descent**: This is the distance between the baseline and the bottom of the lowest glyph.

▸ **Font height**: This is the total height of the font; it is used to calculate the distance to the next line. It is also known as line height.

The following diagram illustrates the main features of a font:

Libgdx lets you query metrics from a font using the following methods:

```
font.getAscent();
font.getDescent();
font.getCapHeight();
font.getLineHeight();
font.getSpaceWidth();
```

You can actually check how much space a piece of text will take on the screen with the given string, using the getBounds() and TextBounds objects it takes. A TextBounds object only has two fields: width and height:

```
void getBounds(CharSequence str, TextBounds bounds);
```

There's more...

Although Hiero will serve you well, you might want to take a look at a few alternatives:

*   **DMFont**. This is a Windows-only tool that uses FreeType under the hood. It can produce better results at smaller sizes, but it does not support effects. For more information, you can refer to http://www.angelcode.com/products/bmfont.
*   **gdx-fontpack**: This is a tool that uses Libgdx and its TTF extension internally; it supports effects and multiple other parameters. For more information, you can refer to https://github.com/mattdesl/gdx-fontpack.
*   **JMonkeyEngine**: The JMonkeyEngine also has a bitmap font generation tool. For more information, you can refer to http://hub.jmonkeyengine.org/forum/topic/font-creator-for-jmp.

You might want to consider packing the font texture with your other sprites in order to reduce the number of texture switches when rendering the scene.

See also

Congratulations! You now know how to create bitmap fonts and render them with Libgdx. It is time to explore some of the fancy effects discussed in the following recipes:

*   The *Baking effects into fonts using Hiero* recipe
*   The *Dynamic font effects using distance fields* recipe

Baking effects into fonts using Hiero

Let's be completely honest: the standard fonts generated with Hiero are pretty boring, and the quality is not bad but they don't stand out. Certainly, these will do just great for bulk of text in an RPG-like conversation scene but will look slightly boring as menu headers. Typically, user interface designers add effects such as drop shadows or strokes to important pieces of text in order to make them stand out.

In this recipe, we will show you how to create a font texture with Hiero, with an outline and shadow effect, and add it to your game.

Getting ready

This time we will use the `data/fonts/lobster.fnt` file. Hiero is also needed; download the latest Libgdx package from `http://libgdx.badlogicgames.com/releases` and unzip it somewhere safe.

Additionally, you will need the `samples` projects.

How to do it...

The process is really simple, and the results can be great—an easy win! Perform the following steps:

1. Open up Hiero from the command line. Linux and Mac users only need to replace semicolons with colons and back slashes with forward slashes:

   ```
   java -cp gdx.jar;gdx-natives.jar;gdx-backend-lwjgl.jar;gdx-
   backend-lwjgl-natives.jar;extensions\gdx-tools\gdx-tools.jar com.
   badlogic.gdx.tools.hiero.Hiero
   ```

2. Click on the **...** button next to the **File** entry and select the `LobsterTwo-Regular. ttf` file.

3. Inside the **Rendering** panel, select a gray background so that you're able to visualize the result better. This will not affect the output texture.

4. Direct your attention towards the **Effects** panel. Effects are applied in order, from top to bottom. Remove the existing color effect with the **x** button.

5. Add a black **Outline** effect with a width of `2.0`.

6. Add a black **Shadow** effect with `0.6` as **Opacity** and `2.0` as the **X** and **Y** distance.

7. Add the previously removed white color.

8. Increase the padding in the **Padding** panel so that the characters have enough space to accommodate the newly added effects.

9. Feel free to tweak the values as well as add or remove effects until the results fit your needs.

10. Once you are happy with the result, generate the font by going to **File | Save BMFont files (text)....** We will save it as `data/lobster.fnt` inside the Android `assets` folder.

The following screenshot shows the Hiero UI with some effects applied to a font:

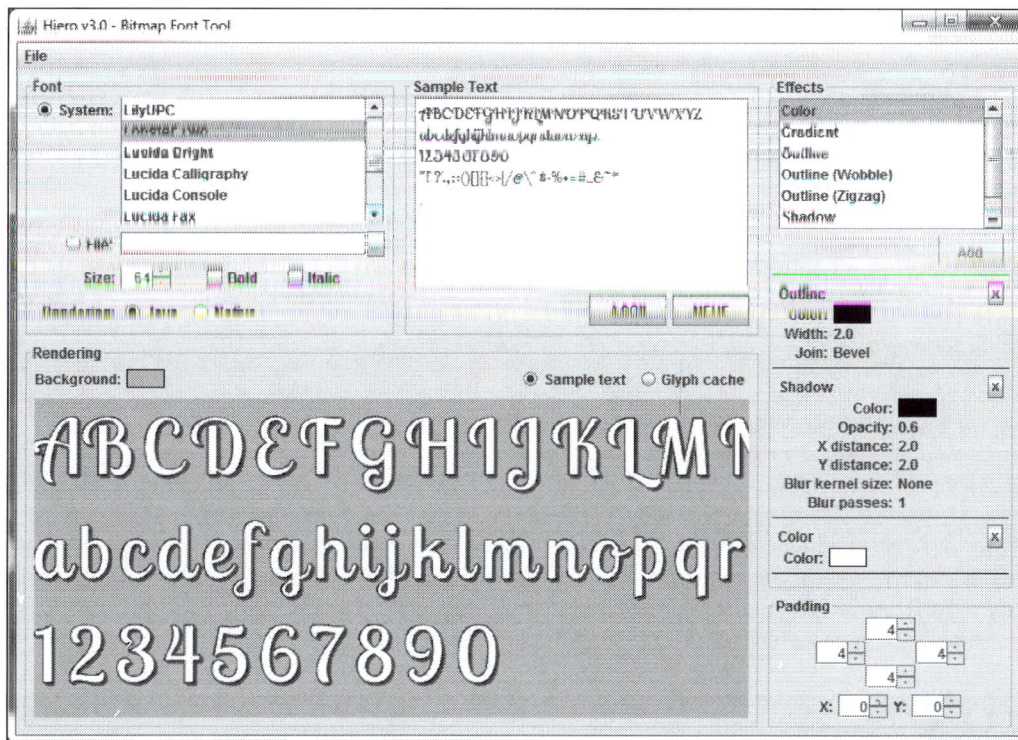

The code for this recipe can be found in the `HieroFontEffectsSample.java` file, and it is practically identical to `BitmapFontSample` from the *Generating and rendering bitmap fonts* recipe. However, this time, we load `data/fonts/lobster.fnt` as well as `data/fonts/play.fnt` so that we can compare both the fonts. We have a camera, viewport, and batch and two `BitmapFont` objects; the rendering process stays the same.

The following screenshot clearly illustrates the differences between the two fonts. Use the effects wisely!

How it works...

All font texture generators operate in a similar manner, including Hiero. They use a library to render characters from TTF files onto a texture. The rendering process can be configured, normally by selecting a font color, size, padding, and so on.

This time round, we also add effects. Internally, this can be achieved using shaders. For instance, the tool can fairly easily render the font on a semi-transparent black color onto a texture and add it to the result, creating a shadow. Everything is baked into the output texture for you convenience:

A quick and dirty alternative to achieving effects such as shadows or outlines directly in the code is to render the same text twice using different colors, sizes, and positions. Take a look at the previous screenshot; to get this result, we could render *Libgdx* in semi-transparent black and then the same text in opaque red, just a bit up and to the left. While this might give you what you want, you should be aware that it is significantly worse performance-wise. It also results in messier code!

See also

> ▸   Read the *Dynamic font effects using distance fields* recipe if you don't want prebaked effects and prefer on-the-fly ones instead.

Scaling friendly font rendering with distance fields

As a bitmap font is scaled up, it becomes blurry due to linear interpolation. It is possible to tell the underlying texture to use the nearest filter, but the result will be pixelated. Additionally, until now, if you wanted big and small pieces of text using the same font, you would have had to export it twice at different sizes. The output texture gets bigger rather quickly, and this is a memory problem.

Distance field fonts is a technique that enables us to scale monochromatic textures without losing out on quality, which is pretty amazing. It was first published by Valve (Half Life, Team Fortress...) in 2007. It involves an offline preprocessing step and a very simple fragment shader when rendering, but the results are great and there is very little performance penalty. You also get to use smaller textures!

In this recipe, we will cover the entire process of how to generate a distance field font and how to render it in Libgdx.

Getting ready

For this recipe, we will load the `data/fonts/oswald-distance.fnt` and `data/fonts/oswald.fnt` files. To generate the fonts, Hiero is needed, so download the latest Libgdx package from `http://libgdx.badlogicgames.com/releases` and unzip it.

Make sure the `samples` projects are in your workspace.

How to do it...

First, we need to generate a distance field font with Hiero. Then, a special fragment shader is required to finally render scaling-friendly text in Libgdx.

Generating distance field fonts with Hiero

1. Open up Hiero from the command line. Linux and Mac users only need to replace semicolons with colons and back slashes with forward slashes:

   ```
   java -cp gdx.jar;gdx-natives.jar;gdx-backend-lwjgl.jar;gdx-
   backend-lwjgl-natives.jar;extensions\gdx-tools\gdx-tools.jar com.
   badlogic.gdx.tools.hiero.Hiero
   ```

2. Select the font using either the **System** or **File** options.

3. This time, you don't need a really big size; the point is to generate a small texture and still be able to render text at high resolutions, maintaining quality. We have chosen **32** this time.

4. Remove the **Color** effect, and add a white **Distance field** effect.

5. Set the **Spread** effect; the thicker the font, the bigger should be this value. For Oswald, `4.0` seems to be a sweet spot.

6. To cater to the spread, you need to set a matching padding. Since this will make the characters render further apart, you need to counterbalance this by the setting the **X** and **Y** values to twice the negative padding.

7. Finally, set the **Scale** to be the same as the font size. Hiero will struggle to render the charset, which is why we wait until the end to set this property.

8. Generate the font by going to **File | Save BMFont files (text)...**.

The following is the Hiero UI showing a font texture with a **Distance field** effect applied to it:

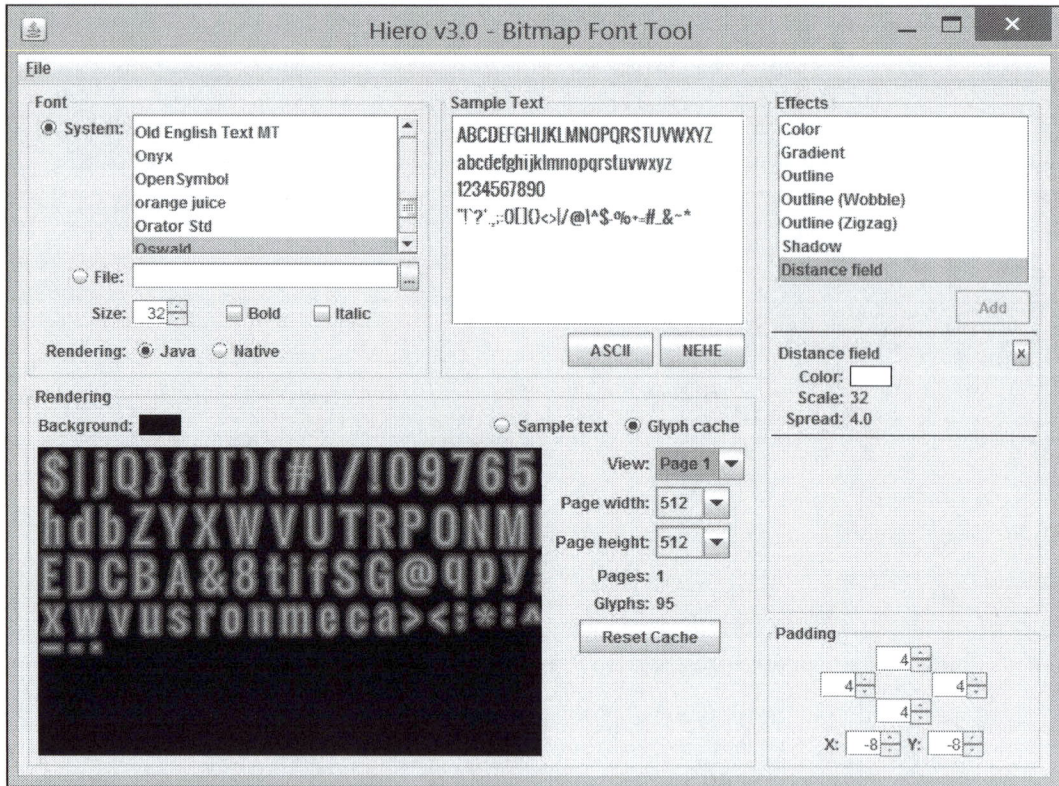

Distance field fonts shader

We cannot use the distance field texture to render text for obvious reasons—it is blurry!
A special shader is needed to get the information from the distance field and transform it into the final, smoothed result. The vertex shader found in `data/fonts/font.vert` is simple, just like the ones in *Chapter 3, Advanced 2D Graphics*. The magic takes place in the fragment shader, found in `data/fonts/font.frag` and explained later.

First, we sample the alpha value from the texture for the current fragment and call it `distance`. Then, we use the `smoothstep()` function to obtain the actual fragment alpha. If `distance` is between `0.5-smoothing` and `0.5+smoothing`, Hermite interpolation will be used. If the distance is greater than `0.5+smoothing`, the function returns `1.0`, and if the distance is smaller than `0.5-smoothing`, it will return `0.0`. The code is as follows:

```
#ifdef GL_ES
precision mediump float;
precision mediump int;
#endif
```

```
uniform sampler2D u_texture;

varying vec4 v_color;
varying vec2 v_texCoord;

const float smoothing = 1.0/128.0;

void main() {
    float distance = texture2D(u_texture, v_texCoord).a;
    float alpha = smoothstep(0.5 - smoothing, 0.5 + smoothing,
distance);
    gl_FragColor = vec4(v_color.rgb, alpha * v_color.a);
}
```

> The `smoothing` constant determines how hard or soft the edges of the font will be. Feel free to play around with the value and render fonts at different sizes to see the results. You could also make it `uniform` and configure it from the code.

Rendering distance field fonts in Libgdx

Let's move on to `DistanceFieldFontSample.java`, where we have two `BitmapFont` instances: `normalFont` (pointing to `data/fonts/oswald.fnt`) and `distanceShader` (pointing to `data/fonts/oswald-distance.fnt`). This will help us illustrate the difference between the two approaches. Additionally, we have a `ShaderProgram` instance for our previously defined shader.

In the `create()` method, we instantiate both the fonts and shader normally:

```
normalFont = new BitmapFont(Gdx.files.internal("data/fonts/oswald.
fnt"));
normalFont.setColor(0.0f, 0.56f, 1.0f, 1.0f);
normalFont.setScale(4.5f);

distanceFont = new BitmapFont(Gdx.files.internal("data/fonts/oswald-
distance.fnt"));
distanceFont.setColor(0.0f, 0.56f, 1.0f, 1.0f);
distanceFont.setScale(4.5f);

fontShader = new ShaderProgram(Gdx.files.internal("data/fonts/font.
vert"),
 Gdx.files.internal("data/fonts/font.frag"));

if (!fontShader.isCompiled()) {
   Gdx.app.error(DistanceFieldFontSample.class.getSimpleName(),
"Shader compilation failed:\n" + fontShader.getLog());
}
```

We need to make sure that the texture our `distanceFont` just loaded is using linear filtering:

```
distanceFont.getRegion().getTexture().setFilter(TextureFilter.Linear,
TextureFilter.Linear);
```

Remember to free up resources in the `dispose()` method, and let's get on with `render()`. First, we render some text with the regular font using the default shader, and right after this, we do the same with the distance field font using our awesome shader:

```
batch.begin();
batch.setShader(null);
normalFont.draw(batch, "Distance field fonts!", 20.0f, VIRTUAL_HEIGHT
- 50.0f);

batch.setShader(fontShader);
distanceFont.draw(batch, "Distance field fonts!", 20.0f, VIRTUAL_
HEIGHT - 250.0f);
batch.end();
```

The results are pretty obvious; it is a huge win of memory and quality over a very small price of GPU time. Try increasing the font size even more and be amazed at the results! You might have to slightly tweak the `smoothing` constant in the shader code though:

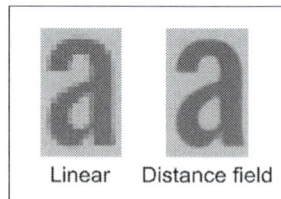

Linear   Distance field

How it works...

Let's explain the fundamentals behind this technique. However, for a thorough explanation, we recommend that you read the original paper by Chris Green from Valve (`http://www.valvesoftware.com/publications/2007/SIGGRAPH2007_AlphaTestedMagnification.pdf`).

A distance field is a derived representation of a monochromatic texture. For each pixel in the output, the generator determines whether the corresponding one in the original is colored or not. Then, it examines its neighborhood to determine the 2D distance in pixels, to a pixel with the opposite state. Once the distance is calculated, it is mapped to a `[0, 1]` range, with `0` being the maximum negative distance and `1` being the maximum positive distance. A value of `0.5` indicates the exact edge of the shape. The following figure illustrates this process:

Within Libgdx, the `BitmapFont` class uses `SpriteBatch` to render text normally, only this time, it is using a texture with a **Distance field** effect applied to it. The fragment shader is responsible for performing a smoothing pass. If the alpha value for this fragment is higher than `0.5`, it can be considered as **in**; it will be **out** in any other case:

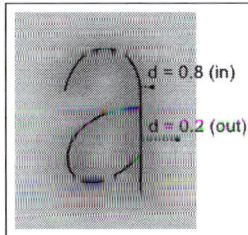

This produces a clean result.

There's more...

We have applied distance fields to text, but we have also mentioned that it can work with monochromatic images. It is simple; you need to generate a low resolution distance field transform. Luckily enough, Libgdx comes with a tool that does just this.

Open a command-line window, access your Libgdx package folder and enter the following command:

```
java -cp gdx.jar;gdx-natives.jar;gdx-backend-lwjgl.jar;gdx-backend-lwjgl-
natives.jar;extensions\gdx-tools\gdx-tools.jar com.badlogic.gdx.tools.
distancefield.DistanceFieldGenerator
```

The distance field font generator takes the following parameters:

- `--color`: This parameter is in hexadecimal RGB format; the default is `ffffff`
- `--downscale`: This is the factor by which the original texture will be downscaled
- `--spread`: This is the edge scan distance, expressed in terms of the input

Take a look at this example:

```
java [...] DistanceFieldGenerator --color ff0000 --downscale 32 --spread
128 texture.png texture-distance.png
```

Alternatively, you can use the gdx-smart-font library to handle scaling. It is a simpler but a bit more limited solution (`https://github.com/jrenner/gdx-smart-font`).

Dynamic font effects using distance fields

Interestingly, the distance fields technique from the previous recipe can be exploited to achieve font effects dynamically, such as **outlines**, **glows**, and **drop shadows**. Can this technique get any more awesome?

No need to generate yet another font texture with prebaked effects; you can turn them off or on as well as tweak and tween their parameters completely at runtime. Consequently, you will be able to achieve a much richer and engaging experience. Moreover, the performance penalty is negligible—you can go crazy!

Just keep in mind that every time you set a shader on a SpriteBatch object, the latter is automatically flushed with the consequent draw call.

In this recipe, we will start off with an existing distance field font and write a configurable fragment shader to obtain outline and glow effects.

Getting ready

This time, we will use the data/fonts/pacific-distance.fnt file as well as the data/fonts/font-effects.frag and data/fonts/font-effects.vert shaders. Additionally, you need the samples projects to be in your workspace.

How to do it...

First, let's get our fragment shader sorted; make sure to check data/fonts/font-effects.frag for the full source. We are going to control the outline and glow parameters from the code, so we need to define a few uniform variables, as follows:

```
uniform vec4 u_outlineColor;
uniform vec4 u_glowColor;
uniform int u_enableOutline;
uniform int u_enableGlow;
uniform vec2 u_outline;
uniform vec2 u_glow;
```

The u_outline and u_glow vector uniform variables contain the minimum and maximum distance values for which those effects should be visible; this way, we can configure their position and width. We require u_outline to be closer to the center than u_glow for the shader to work correctly.

Then, we get the `distance` value from the texture and initialize our `alpha` variable. Remember that a distance of `1.0` means right inside the font, while `0.0` marks the greatest distance possible:

```
float distance = texture2D(u_texture, v_texCoord).a;
float alpha = 1.0;
```

When the **Outline** effect is enabled, we check whether the distance for the current fragment falls within our configured outline boundaries. If so, we need to check whether the fragment is either in the inner or outer falloff area and use the same smoothing function to calculate the alpha value, as we did in our previous recipe:

```
if (u_enableOutline > 0 && distance >= u_outline.x && distance <= u_outline.y) {

    if (distance <= u_outline.x + smoothing) {
        alpha = smoothstep(u_outline.x - smoothing, u_outline.x + smoothing, distance);
    }
    else {
        alpha = smoothstep(u_outline.y + smoothing, u_outline.y - smoothing, distance);
    }

    gl_FragColor = vec4(u_outlineColor.rgb, alpha * v_color.a * u_outlineColor.a);
}
```

When the **Outline** effect is disabled but the glow effect is enabled, we need to readjust the boundaries to avoid a gap between the font edge and the start of the glowing area:

```
vec2 glow = u_glow;
glow.y = max(u_outline.y, glow.y);
```

Then, we check whether the glow effect is enabled and the fragment is within the correct range. If so, we get the appropriate alpha and fragment color using the glow effect color:

```
if (u_enableGlow > 0 && distance >= glow.x && distance < glow.y) {
    alpha = smoothstep(glow.x - smoothing, glow.y + smoothing, distance);
    gl_FragColor = vec4(u_glowColor.rgb, alpha * u_glowColor.a);
}
```

Finally, if either no effects are enabled or the current fragment belongs to the actual text, we use the same approach as in the distance fields recipe:

```
else {
    alpha = smoothstep(threshold - smoothing, threshold + smoothing,
distance);
    gl_FragColor = vec4(v_color.rgb, alpha * v_color.a);
}
```

We are now done with the fragment shader; let's move on to the Java side of this sample, which is located inside the `DistanceFieldEffectsSample.java` file. First, we define a few constants to configure the color and size of our effects:

```
private static final Color OUTLINE_COLOR = new Color(0x00222b);
private static final Color GLOW_COLOR = new Color(0xffe680);
private static final Vector2 OUTLINE = new Vector2(0.45f, 0.55f);
private static final Vector2 GLOW = new Vector2(0.00f, 0.45f);
```

Naturally, we need a camera, a viewport, a batch, our font, and a shader object. Both the `create()` and `dispose()` methods are very similar to the ones in the previous recipe:

```
public void create() {
    ...
    font = new BitmapFont(Gdx.files.internal("data/fonts/pacifico-
distance.fnt"));
    font.setColor(new Color(0x5fbcd3));
    font.setScale(3.0f);
Texture texture = font.getRegion().getTexture();
    texture.setFilter(TextureFilter.Linear, TextureFilter.Linear);
    fontShader = new ShaderProgram(Gdx.files.internal("data/fonts/font-
effects.vert"), Gdx.files.internal("data/fonts/font-effects.frag"));

}
```

We are going to render several pieces of text with different effects enabled. We need to pass the uniform values to the shader:

```
fontShader.setUniformf("u_glow", GLOW);
fontShader.setUniformf("u_outline", OUTLINE);
fontShader.setUniformf("u_glowColor", GLOW_COLOR);
fontShader.setUniformf("u_outlineColor", OUTLINE_COLOR);
```

Before calling the `draw()` method of the bitmap font, we enable or disable the effects at wi If the next draw call uses different shader parameters, we need to make sure that the batch sends the current draw instructions to the GPU; otherwise, the parameters will be overwritten. In order to do so, we call its `flush()` method. Be careful though; flushing the batch is a costly operation, so you should group draw calls that use the same shader parameters together:

```
fontShader.setUniformi("u_enableGlow", 1);
fontShader.setUniformi("u_enableOutline", 1);
font.draw(batch, "Outline and glow", 20.0f, VIRTUAL_HEIGHT - 500.0f);
batch.flush();
```

> Remember that you can set uniforms by index rather than name, which is considerably faster. Querying a uniform index is easy; just call `getUniformLocation()`.

The results are quite good; here is some text with an outline:

We can also render glowing text:

Finally, it is also possible to combine both the effects:

Brilliant! Now you can introduce awesome, dynamically generated font effects in your game.

ks...

...ious section, this follows the same principles as explained in the *Scaling*
...ing with distance fields recipe. We determine whether or not we should
...ent using the distance field and 0.5 as the threshold.

...hat we take to add effects is simple; it is possible to use different thresholds and
...o render specific areas of the letters in a particular way. Just before the edge of the
..., the outline color kicks in, whereas, the glow color does the same from the outer edge
...nwards, progressively fading away.

There's more...

Drop shadows is an additional effect that you can achieve using the distance field information.
Instead of sampling the texture once in the fragment shader, you will have to do it twice, with
an offset for the second one. Feel free to experiment and try to implement this effect yourself.

Since we are configuring our shader using uniforms, we can make the color and size of the
effects vary over time in interesting ways.

7
Asset Management

In this chapter, we will cover the following recipes:

- ▶ Getting to know AssetManager
- ▶ Asynchronous asset loading
- ▶ Creating custom asset loaders
- ▶ Managing groups of assets for bigger games

Introduction

Assets are an intrinsic part of games in the sense that their mixture defines the final game experience and highly contributes to players' opinions.

Most modern and successful games make use of a variety of assets such as textures, fonts, music, sound effects, skins, particle effects, maps, physics, and so on. The asset ecosystem can be very demanding of memory resources.

In this chapter, we will learn how to efficiently manage any kind of asset in your Libgdx applications through the built-in `AssetManager` class, even when the amount of resources increases unexpectedly. In this way, we will save valuable time and memory. Moreover, you will learn how to interact with the user while the load is in progress.

At the beginning, you will find `AssetManager` an extra complication, but later, you will think of it as a faithful ally. Your code will be more readable and succinct because it will be independent of data.

It is an essential feature whose flexibility allows you to customize its usage according to your needs.

At the end of this chapter, I suggest you go beyond and try to put it into practice.

Getting to know AssetManager

One of the main advantages of using `AssetManager` is that resources will be *reference counted*. This means that they will be allocated in memory just once; it doesn't matter how many times you use it in code. This also includes safe dependency disposal; for instance, if an asset X depends directly on another asset Y, the latter will not be deleted until the former has been disposed of.

In terms of organization and clarity, it is a good point to gather all resources in the same place, so it is a recommended practice to always include `AssetManager`.

Obvious, but not less important, is the fact that `AssetManager` allows us to load resources whenever we need them, neither before nor after. We have to bear in mind that Libgdx's target platform can include mobile devices, not only desktop, so we must be aware of the resources and not deliberately waste them.

Getting ready

The sample projects are required to follow this recipe; make sure you already have them in your Eclipse workspace. Right-click on the **Package Explorer** panel, select **Import**, and then click on **Gradle Project**. They are under the `[cookbook]/samples` folder. If you have any problems, feel free to reread *Chapter 1, Diving into Libgdx*.

How to do it...

The code for this recipe can be found in the `AssetManagerSample` class. By default, Libgdx comes with an out-of-the-box `AssetManager` class that we need to declare:

```
AssetManager manager;
```

We place its initialization on the `create()` method, followed by an asset loading:

```
public void create() {
    ...
manager =  new AssetManager();
manager.load("data/loading_screen/background.png", Texture.class);
    ...
}
```

When calling the constructor of `AssetManager`, its instance is set up, which is capable of loading any kind of built-in Libgdx asset type, such as `Texture`, `BitmapFont`, `TextureAtlas`, `Music`, `Sound`, `Skin`, and `ParticleEffect`. Once the manager is initialized, we enqueue the asset load by calling `load()`, which doesn't perform the actual load operation yet, the background texture asset to be brought from disk to memory by calling `load()`. Each type of `AssetLoader` implements the two methods `loadAsync(...)` and `loadSync(...)`. The difference between them is the thread where the load is performed. Do not panic, we will dig into this later.

[A thread is an execution context for a set of instructions.]

In the way that is written in the previous code, we can load any other type of resource, for instance:

```
manager.load("data/font.fnt", BitmapFont.class);
manager.load("data/music.mp3", Music.class);
manager.load("data/pack", TextureAtlas.class);
manager.load("data/skin.json", Skin.class);
manager.load("data/particle.p", ParticleEffect.class);
```

Alternatively, extra parameters, related to the type itself, can be passed to `Texture`, `BitmapFont`, `TextureAtlas`, `Skin`, and `ParticleEffect` loaders:

```
BitmapFontParameter param = new BitmapFontParameter();
param.flip = true; // To turn over the font image
param.magFilter = TextureFilter.Linear; // See Texture filters in
Chapter 2
manager.load("data/font.fnt", BitmapFont.class, param);
```

There are several cases, such as loading or splash screens, where you will need to make sure that all queued assets have been properly loaded into memory. To achieve this, we can call:

```
manager.finishLoading();
```

[Note that the `finishLoading()` method blocks as it runs on the thread it is being called from. So, the program execution will wait until all the resources are allocated from the disk. This is okay, since we're only loading a few resources in the previous example, and they will not take a long time to be allocated.]

In the rest of the cases, you must use `update(...)` to tick and query whether the load is done or not in the context of the rendering thread. In the next recipe, we will provide a proper example of this.

As a Libgdx program does not live by loads alone, we need to be able to retrieve the instance of any asset anywhere in the code. To carry this out, we make use of the `get(...)` method:

```
Texture background = manager.get("data/loading_screen/background.png",
Texture.class);
```

We can also simply use the following:

```
Texture background = manager.get("data/loading_screen/background.
png");
```

> Be aware that while not supplying the class parameter is more convenient, there is a performance penalty due to the need to look for the asset in a larger number of resource containers.

Be aware of the existence of the resource that you are trying to retrieve because it can lead you to a `GdxRuntimeException` if it is not stored in memory.

In order for you not to be in danger and ensure that the asset has been loaded, you can use the following:

```
if(manager.isLoaded("data/background.png")) {
    // Let's have some fun with the asset
    background = manager.get("data/loading_screen/background.png",
    Texture.class);
}
```

To check the asset, you can use the following:

```
if(manager.contains(background)) {
    // Let's have some fun with the asset
}
```

Once the asset is not needed anymore, you must free it to avoid memory leaks. Here is where you say: "oh yes! `dispose()`! I have read about it ten times already!" I am sorry to inform you that when using `AssetManager`, it is slightly different:

```
manager.unload("data/loading_screen/background.png");
```

The reason why we use `AssetManager` to unload resources is the famous reference count, which gets into action, making the former unload ineffectively until the reference count for the asset is set to zero or, in other words, it is not directly or indirectly used anywhere else in the program at the moment. Consequently, it is totally advised not to dispose of assets manually while using `AssetManager`.

It is interesting to point out that we might want to free all assets, no matter whether queued or loaded, at once, instead of doing it one by one. It is as easy as shown in the following code:

```
manager.clear();
```

Nevertheless, by using the `clear()` method, `AssetManager` is still alive. What about getting rid of all resources plus the manager itself?

```
manager.dispose();
```

Writing the preceding line of code in the `dispose()` method of your container class is usually a good idea.

You should now be able to run the sample, play around with it, and check for yourself.

How it works...

Assets follow a simple life cycle. There are two possible locations for the assets: memory and disk. The transition between the two states relies on dependencies and referencing counting. The following figure illustrates this:

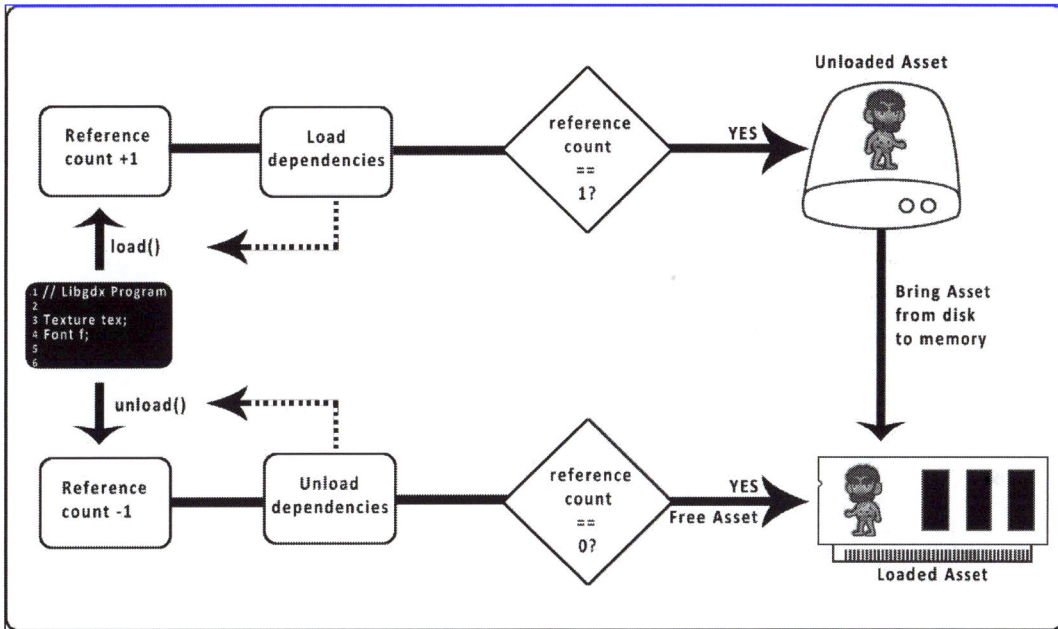

In a Libgdx program, you can load or unload assets through `AssetManager`. These operations will always modify the reference count. Sometimes, it might require loading other linked assets. This happens, for instance, with map files that usually depend on different images.

However, the actual transition of the asset from disk to memory is only effective for the first time `load` is called, since the reference count's value is one. Likewise, the asset is freed up from memory whenever the reference count stores a zero.

At this point, you have a decent understanding of what you are capable to do with `AssetManager`. However, there is still some hidden black magic that has not shown up on these pages.

Is it not kind of weird that we only supply a `String` object and we get the asset? Where does Libgdx search for the file? As you will know from the *The first approach to file handling in Libgdx* recipe of *Chapter 5, Audio and File I/O*, the `FileHandleResolver` interface is responsible for this. More precisely, the `resolve(String file)` method returns `FileHandle` that represents the specified file.

As you already understand, we can set an instance from a class that implements the `FileHandleResolver` interface as the default way to go for asset loaders:

```
AssetManager manager = new AssetManager(new
LocalFileHandleResolver());
```

There's more...

Undoubtedly, you liked the reference count feature of the built-in `AssetManager` class, but sometimes, you might have oversights unloading resources at some part of the code, so the reference count is never zeroed and, consequently, your tasty memory bytes are occupied.

A quick and simple solution to this problem can be:

```
int refCount = manager.getReferenceCount("data/myfont.fnt");
```

Easy! We can compare how many references there should be and the actual references at a certain part of the code, but what if `myfont.fnt` is not the direct leaker? Maybe it depends on some other file:

```
Array<String> dependencies = manager.getDependencies("data/myfont.
fnt");
```

Finally, it might be that we do not have a clue of what asset is causing the leak, so we need a general overview:

```
String diagnostics = manager.getDiagnostics();
```

The `diagnostics` string will now contain the reference count and dependency information for all assets in the manager.

See also

▶ After a complete overview of the `AssetManager` class, it is a good idea to carry on and keep reading the *Asynchronous asset loading* recipe in order understand how to interact with the player while `AssetManager` is processing.

Asynchronous asset loading

After focusing on loads with synchronous methods, this recipe is in charge of making asynchronous heavy loads totally clear.

For a while, imagine what will happen if a Triple-A RPG game has to load a graphically awesome world where the final boss is waiting for you while spitting tons of different hungry flunkies. In the context of this chapter, it is a 10 second loading time with a decent machine. The player is freaking out because of the hype generated by his friends. You cannot disappoint him with an eternal black screen, or he will panic thinking the game is broken. However, if you satisfy him a little by providing a dynamic loading screen where some kind of teaser is revealed, his adrenaline will start pumping. What's the moral of the story? The player needs to receive continuous feedback. Nonresponsive interfaces are not okay.

The sample shown in this recipe will illustrate how to take advantage of loading resources asynchronously by displaying a reactive loading screen while our `AssetManager` class is working on it.

Getting ready

This recipe is mostly based on practical content. It is a good idea to take a look at the sample projects that go with this book by importing them through the Gradle Plugin. If you need to do it from scratch, refer back to *Chapter 1, Diving into Libgdx*, to get some help. You will find the projects under the `[cookbook]/samples` folder.

How to do it...

This sample is hosted by the `ProgressBarSample.java` file. In order to build a reactive loading screen, you must make the player feel that something is changing and, at the same time, show the progress of the change, making its end clear. To this purpose, a progress bar will do the trick.

Next, we will explain a very easy and simple way to develop a progress bar by rendering a gray base image container; on top of this, we have the real progress bar image setting its width to the current progress of load.

First and foremost, let's declare all variables that will go into action:

```
private Texture progressBarImg, progressBarBaseImg;
private Vector2 pbPos;
private AssetManager manager;
```

The trivial matter is that `progressBarBaseImg` will contain the gray base image bar; `progressBarImg` will contain the front width-changing bar. Since the only dynamic element on screen will be the related-to-progress width of the actual loading bar, it is a good idea to cache its coordinates, `pbPos.x` and `pbPos.y`, instead of calculating them for every frame.

The next figure illustrates what we intend to do:

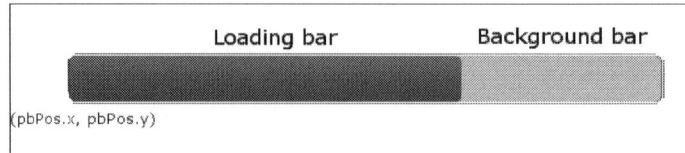

Within the `create()` method, once `AssetManager` is instantiated, just load the aforementioned textures:

```
manager.load("data/progress_bar.png", Texture.class);
manager.load("data/progress_bar_base.png", Texture.class);
```

The images used to draw the progress bar need to be loaded synchronously before starting to bring the required resources for the next screen from the disk, on another thread. Consequently, we should not forget to write the following line of code:

```
manager.finishLoading();
```

Then, retrieve the textures:

```
progressBarImg = manager.get("data/progress_bar.png");
progressBarBaseImg = manager.get("data/progress_bar_base.png");
```

It is a good idea to display elements relatively to other components on the screen in order to fit any resolution. In this case, the loading scene will contain a Libgdx logo that will be placed in the center, taking into account the application's width and height. The progress bar will be positioned below the logo:

```
pbPos.set(logoPos.x, logoPos.y- (logo.getHeight());
```

To close the `create()` method, queue the real bulk of resources needed for the next screen:

```
manager.load("data/1.png", Texture.class);
manager.load("data/2.png", Texture.class);
```

The next step is to draw the progress bar, but this is not that simple. To carry out the visual effect, it is necessary to know the current loading progress. This is achievable in two different ways. The first way is more laborious, but also more interesting. It starts by adding a `private int loaded` field to your class. Add the following code to your `create()` method after calculating the coordinates of the progress bar:

```
loaded = manager.getLoadedAssets();
```

The reason to do this is to know how many assets have been loaded only for the loading screen. It allows us to get the current progress by using the following code:

```
int currentAssets = manager.getLoadedAssets();
 float percent = Math.min(1, currentAssets - loaded) /
((float) (currentAssets + manager.getQueuedAssets() - loaded));
```

As you can see, we introduced a new method called getQueuedAssets() that returns the number of currently queued assets.

The second way of getting percent is as follows:

```
float percent = manager.getProgress();
```

Regardless of the way you choose, percent will store a float between 0.0 and 1.0 with the loading progress. Now that the real-time value is known, all we have to do is render, but with a slightly different method from SpriteBatch:

```
void draw(Texture texture, float x, float y, float width, float
height)
```

Apply the following code to the context and at the end of render():

```
batch.begin();
...
batch.draw(progressBarBaseImg, pbPos.x, pbPos.y);
batch.draw(progressBarImg, pbPos.x, pbPos.y,
    progressBarImg.getWidth()*manager.getProgress(),
    progressBarImg.getHeight());
batch.end();
```

Note that the order of drawing is important to keep the progress bar rendered on top of the base container.

To conclude, still within render() and right after drawing the progress bar, you must make sure that the loading screen does not last forever and it gives way to the next screen. The update() method will return true, once the progress bar reaches 100 percent:

```
if(manager.update()) {
    // Go to next screen
}
```

In the meantime, you have a wide range of possibilities to keep the player's attention. Lots of games understand the loading screen as a fantastic moment to show some gameplay tips or relate story bits. Other games such as *Call of Duty* prefer to take advantage of the space by displaying a mission briefing. FIFA titles offer an interactive training mode; classic load screens such as *Metal Gear Solid 4*'s warns against smoking.

How it works...

Reading a resource from disk is slow, and during the time the computer takes to retrieve a few of them, it can keep executing other code so that the load is made in another thread.

It is important to make two key concepts highly bound to this chapter clear:

> ▶ **Synchronous**: Here, the application will wait for the load process to finish in order to carry on with the execution. All the action takes place on the rendering thread.

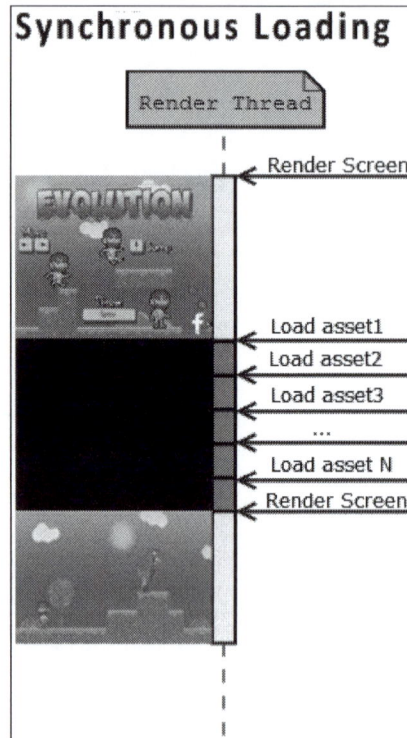

Note that the black area in the preceding diagram is drawn to make the diagram simpler to understand, but it does not mean that the screen has to be black during synchronous asset loading. It will just keep the last rendered scene.

> ► **Asynchronous**: Here, some parts of the asset are loaded on a worker thread, and the OpenGL descendant part is performed on the rendering thread. Most of the load is managed in the background so that it is a nonblocking task, keeping your application responsive. The example scenario is illustrated in the following figure:

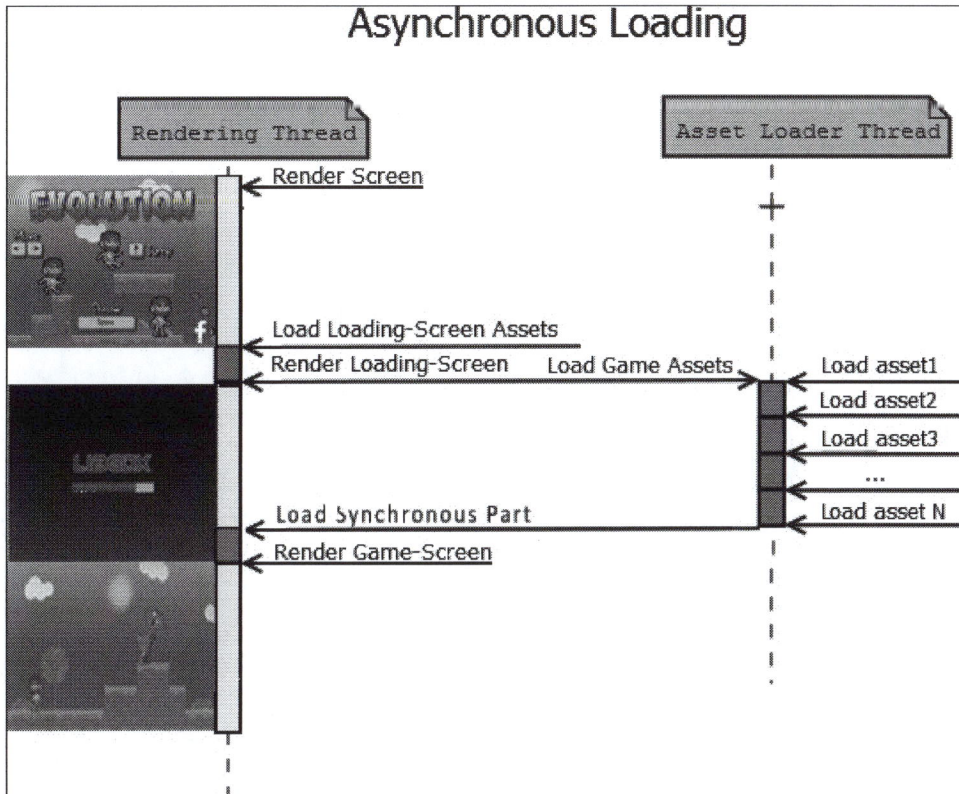

Every asset that you queue into the manager is treated as a task, or called `AssetLoadingTask` in Libgdx. It implements the `AsyncTask` interface that entails a public `call()` method to submit it to `AsyncExecutor`. This class is in charge of allowing asynchronous executions of `AsyncTask` instances on a worker thread.

The `AsyncExecutor` class internally relies on the `java.util.concurrent` package to manage threads. It is widely used in concurrent programming.

The `AssetLoadingTask` class is ruled by its `update()` method, which, if the asset is asynchronously loaded, calls the `loadAsync(...)` function from the loader on a separate thread. At the end of its execution, the rest of the asset is loaded on the rendering thread by calling `loadSync(...)`.

The `TextureLoader` class is a good example of loading the asset, making use of both methods. The asynchronous concept loads the pixel data, whereas `Texture` is created synchronously. Do not hesitate to take a look at its source code, which is available on `https://github.com/libgdx/libgdx/blob/master/gdx/src/com/badlogic/gdx/assets/loaders/TextureLoader.java`.

There's more...

So far, we have covered the usual flow of managing assets in a general application, but in some cases, you might want to offer support to pause and resume the app. It means that some assets must be reloaded whenever the user restarts playing, since OpenGL-context was lost. This issue is seen in Android when sending the app to the background by pressing the home button or receiving an incoming phone call, causing all OpenGL-associated resources (such as textures) to be deleted.

Resuming the app can take a few seconds, so why not give some feedback and say what the app is doing through a loading screen? You can carry out this once you have instantiated your `AssetManager` class and call the next function for each asset type:

```
Texture.setAssetManager(manager);
```

As seen in *Chapter 3, Advanced 2D Graphics*, Libgdx give us a `resume()` method when implementing the `ApplicationListener` interface. This is the place to locate your call to the loading screen and wait until `update()` returns true.

If you decide not to manage this scenario with `AssetManager`, all resources will be reloaded on the rendering thread, causing your app to be unresponsive for some seconds.

See also

Now that you know how to manage assets synchronously and asynchronously, feel free to move on to the following recipes:

- ▶ *Creating custom asset loaders*
- ▶ *Managing groups of assets for bigger games*

Creating custom asset loaders

Other than the already mentioned default loaders for the built-in asset types in Libgdx, you can implement your own loaders for other asset types you need to manage. When beginning work on this recipe, it is a good exercise to think about what types of custom assets you might need to define.

Some games require their actors to interact with each other and the environment. They are perfect candidates to make use of physics properties and bodies.

2D/3D animations are also a good example. It is necessary to store frames, duration, and so on.

The possibilities are endless. The preceding information about physics and animation can be stored in files in such a way as to load it at runtime.

Creating custom assets might seem complex, but contrary to first impressions, it will make your code more readable as well as save you a lot of time.

In this recipe, we will focus on a 2D animation sprite loader because it will only make use of concepts that were mentioned in previous chapters.

Getting ready

Remember to have the sample projects imported into your Eclipse workspace by right-clicking on the **Package Explorer** panel, selecting **Import**, and then clicking on **Gradle Project** again. Go back to *Chapter 1, Diving into Libgdx*, if you need some assistance.

How to do it...

The code for this recipe is in the `CustomLoaderSample.java` file within the `[cookbook]/samples` folder. It will lean on the `com.cookbook.animation` package.

The initial decision to make is whether your type will be loaded synchronously or asynchronously. As mentioned in the preceding recipes, using the synchronous loader means blocking the application (rendering thread) until the resource is loaded. On the other hand, an asynchronous loader allows your game to be responsive because the load will be performed on a secondary thread. Base your decision on the loading speed of your asset.

To carry out the implementation of custom loaders, Libgdx provides us with two abstract classes to extend, `AsynchronousAssetLoader<T, P>` and `SynchronousAssetLoader<T, P>`, where `T` represents the type to load, and `P` an extended type of the `AssetLoaderParameters` interface. As mentioned in the first recipe of this chapter, `AssetLoaderParameters` class allows you to load the data type with some initialization parameters.

A custom `SynchronousAssetLoader` class will have to override the `load(...)` method, whereas `AsynchronousAssetLoader` will do likewise with `loadAsync(...)` and `loadSync(...)`.

It is important to understand that the example shown in this recipe is just to illustrate, with a practical case, the process to follow when creating your custom asset loader. Focusing on the idea is the best perspective to adopt in the next sections.

Writing our own asset type

It is highly recommended to package your asset content into a specific asset class. It will make your life easier while writing your loader and using an asset in your application. The SpriteAnimationData class will be the container storing useful animation information:

```
public class SpriteAnimationData {
...
Texture texture = null;
int rows = 0;
int columns = 0;
float frameDuration = 0.0f;
ObjectMap<String, Animation> animations = new ObjectMap<String,
Animation>();
Animation defaultAnimation = null;
```

Later, you will understand how we will fill these fields in.

Writing our own asset loader

As you can imagine, our 2D animation sprite loader will extend AsynchronousAssetLoader. So, it will begin with:

```
public class SpriteAnimationLoader extends AsynchronousAssetLoader<Spr
iteAnimationData, SpriteAnimationLoader.AnimationParameter> {
...
}
```

We must define a static public parameter class within SpriteAnimationLoader to fit the previous template, even if we don't really need it, and it remains empty:

```
Static public class AnimationParameter extends AssetLoaderParameters<S
priteAnimationData> { }
```

Do not forget to declare and initialize the variable where the content data is being stored to null:

```
private SpriteAnimationData animationData = null;
```

Since we define an asset loader, it needs FileHandleResolver when being constructed. In this way, the resolve() method can be used, which makes it clear where to look for the files:

```
public SpriteAnimationLoader(FileHandleResolver resolver) {
    super(resolver);
}
```

Due to the strictly asynchronous nature of our loader, the synchronous method will just retrieve the animation data as is:

```
@Override
public SpriteAnimationData loadSync(AssetManager manager, String
filename, FileHandle, AnimationParameter parameter) {
    return animationData;
}
```

Fitting the suggested AsynchronousAssetLoader interface is something that you must accomplish, but now is when the real deal goes into action. The loadAsync(...) method has to parse a JSON file (it can be any other type, such as XML, but it is a good idea to get familiar with it after its explanation in *Chapter 5, Audio and File I/O*). A simple example JSON file for our animation format can be:

```
{
    "rows": "2",
    "columns": "5",
    "frameDuration": "0.025f",
    "animations" : [
      {
        "name": "walk",
        "frames": "0,1,2,3,4,5,6"
      }
    ]
}
```

As you can see, it contains almost all the information that SpriteAnimationData demands. Once this information is extracted, we have to organize it along with the animation sheet within the class. At the end of the loadAsync(...) method, all the required data will be stored in the animationData variable.

The animation-related code will add too much complexity and will divert the real goal of this recipe. If you are interested, take a look at the source code that comes together with this book; more specifically, check out the SpriteAnimationLoader.java file.

Summarizing...

In order to ensure that you know the real process to follow when creating a custom asset loader, use these steps:

1. Create your custom data type.
2. Decide whether your loader will work synchronously, asynchronously, or both.
3. Extend your loader class with the proper abstract class depending on its type: AsynchronousAssetLoader<T, P>, or SynchronousAssetLoader<T, P>.
4. Override the load() method for synchronous loaders and the loadAsync() and loadSync() methods for asynchronous loaders. Be aware of the dependencies.

How it works...

Both `AsynchronousAssetLoader` and `SynchronousAssetLoader` extend the `AssetLoader` abstract class, which is really the one in charge of calling the `resolve(...)` method from its set `FileHandleResolver`, already discussed in the first recipe of this chapter.

Here is a table with a classification of built-in type loaders:

Asynchronous	Synchronous
TextureLoader	MusicLoader
BitmapFontLoader	ParticleEffectsLoader
ModelLoader	TextureAtlasLoader
SkinLoader	ModelLoader
SoundLoader	
PixmapLoader	
I18NBundleLoader	

`TextureLoader` is an OpenGL-descendant part that is performed on the rendering thread. `BitmapFontLoader`, `SkinLoader`, `TextureAtlasLoader`, and `ModelLoader` are `AssetManagers` that will load its dependencies before the actual asset.

As seen in *Chapter 4, Detecting User Input*, note that music resources are streamed, so it won't have to load the whole thing.

There's more...

Custom asset loading is not fully covered in this chapter because there are some particular cases where dependencies exist between resources. To deal with this scenario, the assets loader abstract classes provide us with the `getDependencies(...)` method, which when applied to the `SpriteAnimationLoader` context, result in the following:

```
@Override
public Array<AssetDescriptor> getDependencies( String filename,
fileHandle file, AnimationParameter parameter) {
    Array<AssetDescriptor> dependencies = new Array<AssetDescriptor>();
    dependencies.add(new AssetDescriptor<Texture>(stripExtension(filena
me) + ".png", Texture.class));

    return dependencies;
    ...
}
```

The first thing to pay attention to here is the dependency on the animation sheet image file. However, if you look beyond it, there is a seemingly new concept to describe, and this is `AssetDescriptor`. As its name suggests, it describes an asset with its filename, type, and parameters, which will be used in the asset's subsequent load. In fact, it is not new at all as it is used in the already mentioned `AssetLoadingTask` class. Moreover, this class contains two methods, `handleSynchLoader` and `handleAsynchLoader`, which are in charge of injecting the dependencies.

See also

> ▸ The content of this recipe is hard to master without taking a look at the whole source code of the Libgdx loaders or implementing your own. Check out `https://github.com/libgdx/libgdx/tree/master/gdx/src/com/badlogic/gdx/assets/loaders`.

Managing groups of assets for bigger games

I am pretty sure that you will find yourself an authentic master of the Libgdx `AssetManager` class after going over this chapter as you are now able to load and unload whatever you want, whenever you want, but wait! It means that you will have to manage all the resources that will appear in your game one by one. Definitely, masters don't like to work on repetitive tasks that can easily lead to errors.

Undoubtedly, the answer is to group assets. This is why we will tweak the default Libgdx `AssetManager` class a little bit in this recipe. Group organization might vary depending on the scope and type of game, so it is up to you to decide whether you will group per level, characters, menus, and so on, and what will you stream on the spot.

You can still put the icing on top of the cake by adopting a data-driven approach. It consists of describing your asset groups in an XML or JSON file in such a way as to modify your code the least possible when adding/removing resources to groups or simply changing names.

Mixing the grouping idea with the data-driven approach definitely helps you to organize assets more efficiently, keep memory consumption under control, and save a lot of time.

Getting ready

As usual, make sure the sample projects are easily accessible which are under the `[cookbook]/samples` folder, to fiddle with the code of this recipe. Make sure you have them imported into your Eclipse workspace. Just in case you need it, take a look at *Chapter 1, Diving into Libgdx*, where the process is explained step by step.

How to do it...

The code for this recipe is in the `GroupingAssetsSample` class, but it directly relies on the `com.cookbook.assetmanager` package that contains an enhanced `AssetManager` and `Asset` class to wrap any type of asset.

Giving shape to the idea

Before rolling your sleeves up, it is good to lay the groundwork so that you can have a global overview of the full recipe. I refer to the root content file from which the assets' information will be extracted at runtime. It must be organized in groups, which in turn contain their specific asset data. To carry on with the technologies used in this chapter, JSON will be the chosen notation standard:

```
{
    "base": [
      {
        "type": "com.badlogic.gdx.graphics.Texture",
        "path": "data/loading_screen/background.png"
      }
    ],
    "game_screen": [
      {
    "type": "com.cookbook.animation.SpriteAnimationData",
    "path": "data/caveman-sheet.json"
    }
    ]
}
```

In the preceding example, there are two groups with one asset each, for which type and path attributes must be specified. Besides them, there must be an extra option in our syntax; otherwise, we will be limiting the strength of `AssetManager`:

```
{
    "base": [
      {
        "type": "com.badlogic.gdx.g2d.BitmapFont",
        "path": "data/menu_screen/font_fnt"
        "parameters": {
           "flip": true
        }
      }
    ]
}
```

Now that you have an understanding of what we are working on, let's dig deeper.

Empowering AssetManager

A good approach to take in order to strengthen our AssetManager class is to create a new wrapper class that is composed of the built-in Libgdx `AssetManager` class and some extra functionality:

```
public class Assets implements Disposable, AssetErrorListener {
    private AssetManager manager; //composition relationship
    private ObjectMap<String, Array<Asset>> groups;

    ...
}
```

Following Libgdx's lead and being aware of the resources we have, we cannot forget to free memory, and this is why we implement the `Disposable` interface. In the same way, `AssetErrorListener` gives us the power of managing errors when the load is not successful.

Last but not least, the `groups` field will store an array of assets per string name. The `ObjectMap` class is a Libgdx unordered map where null keys are not allowed, and works very fast on consulting, removing, and retrieving content. The reason for choosing this data type is because we will initialize our custom `AssetManager` class once at the beginning of our application, and from that moment on, we will just load/unload assets from specified groups using calls to the `get()` method of `ObjectMap`.

> A map is a data structure consisting of a set of key-value pairs that can be quickly accessed through the key.

Make use of the `AssetErrorListener` interface to get notified about runtime errors related to `AssetManager`. Add support to custom data types, and then parse your asset files:

```
public Assets(String assetFile) {
    manager = new AssetManager();
    manager.setErrorListener(this);

    //Custom datatypes loaders
    manager.setLoader(MyCustomAssetType.class, new MyCustomAssetType
Loader(new InternalFileHandleResolver()));
    manager.setLoader(SpriteAnimationData.class, new
SpriteAnimationLoader(new InternalFileHandleResolver()));

    loadGroups(assetFile);
}
```

Adding the capability of loading user-created data types to the manager is achievable through the `setLoader()` method in which you specify your custom class jointly with your custom loader, and also select the desired `FileHandleResolver`.

The `loadGroups(String assetFile)` method will do the dirty work by parsing the file and filling the groups variable with the needed information. Don't hesitate to consult the `Assets.java` source code file to go further into JSON details.

The extra values generated come with the capability of loading groups:

```
public void loadGroup(String groupName) {
    Array<Asset> assets = groups.get(groupName, null);
    if(assets != null)
        for(Asset asset : assets)
            manager.load(asset.path, asset.type, asset.parameters);
}
```

The unloading function member code is only differenced by the call to unload:

```
public void unloadGroup(String groupName) {
    Array<Asset> assets = groups.get(groupName, null);
    if(assets != null)
        for(Asset asset : assets)
            if(manager.isLoaded(asset.path, asset.type)
                manager.unload(asset.path);
}
```

The rest of the base functionalities of `AssetManager` are implemented by calling the Libgdx built-in `AssetManager` methods, for instance:

```
public boolean update() {
    return manager.update();
}
```

The same happens with `getLoader(...)`, `isLoaded(...)`, `finishLoading()`, `getProgress()`, and `get(...)`. Remember that the default Libgdx `get()` methods for the `AssetManager` class include the synchronized keyword, which implies that it is not possible to execute it on one thread while it is being executed on another at the same time over the same object. The reason to use this is the fact that it is a good way to prevent thread interferences and memory-consistency errors.

Until now, our class has been listening for errors related to `AssetManager`, but we are not managing them. You only have to override the `error(...)` method from the `AssetErrorListener` interface:

```
@Override
public void error(AssetDescriptor asset, Throwable throwable) {
    //Manage errors however you want
}
```

The `Throwable` class is the Java superclass for errors and exceptions. If you want to know more about this, visit `http://docs.oracle.com/javase/7/docs/api/java/lang/Throwable.html`.

Finally, make use of the `Disposable` interface:

```
@Override
public void dispose() {
    manager.dispose();
}
```

Once our custom-enhanced `AssetManager` version is done, just use it this way in your main module:

```
manager = new Assets("data/assets.json");
manager.loadGroup("base");
manager.loadGroup("loading_screen");
```

How it works...

The group-loading feature is considerably easy to carry out, but undoubtedly, the `Asset` class simplifies things a lot, resulting in very generalized code, without treating each type of asset separately.

Consequently, the `Asset` data type is in charge of representing any type of asset by the previously mentioned three attributes: `type`, `parameters`, and `path`. It implements the `Json.Serializable` interface in order to create an instance of this class from a valid JSON string. The magic happens with the `public Class<?> type;` attribute in the overridden read method:

```
type = Class.forName(jsonData.get("type").asString());
```

There's more...

It seems like everything on `AssetManager` is covered in this chapter, but there are still some cool features that you can add to the developed implementation. Some ideas are:

 ▶ **Associate file extensions to asset types**: This means that you don't need to indicate the type of the asset as a string. For instance, it will just link the `.png` extension to texture data, adding some meta-information in the filename to deal with exceptions.

 ▶ **Automatically scan asset folders**: Not worrying about individual asset files, just look for folders and convert its contents into one group of assets.

> The `File.list()` method can cause issues while deploying on desktop platforms.

See also

▶ We will now move on to *Chapter 8, User Interfaces with Scene2D*, and *Chapter 10, Rigid Body Physics with Box2D*, which will feed your brain with new ideas about adding functionalities to `AssetManager`.

8
User Interfaces with Scene2D

In this chapter, we will cover the following recipes:

- ▶ Introducing the Scene2D API
- ▶ Widget collection overview
- ▶ Creating a basic menu screen using tables
- ▶ Skin customization
- ▶ Creating new widgets

Introduction

User interface refers to the methods and components through which a user will interact with your application, which may or may not be a game. To make your life easier, Libgdx provides you with a built-in variety of widgets and structural components you can use to create a scene graph, commonly known as Scene2D.

> A scene graph is basically a data structure to hierarchically organize the content of a scene. This implies that changes in parent nodes will be reflected on their children too.

Introducing the Scene2D API

Before getting your hands dirty, it becomes absolutely necessary to clear up some key concepts:

▶ **Actor**: This represents a node within the scene graph and its default properties are position, size, origin, scale, rotation, Z-index, and color. In the context of this chapter, a node can contain a widget or a group of them taking into account that it will work in its local coordinate system, which means that transformations are performed relative to its current coordinate frame's origin and axes. Apart from that, it knows how to draw itself.

> Z-index refers to the level of depth when rendering. In the next image, you can see that the square with the higher z-index overlaps the other two.
>
> Z - INDEX 1
> Z - INDEX 2
> Z - INDEX 3

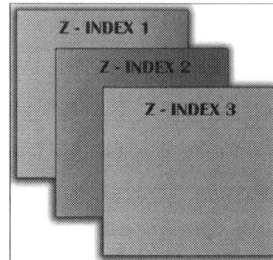

Scene2D actors can serve as any type of game element. However, they are often used for UI purposes (buttons, labels, checkboxes, and so on).

▶ **Action**: This consists of a progressive or immediate transformation to perform over an actor, for example, rotating a button or coloring an image.

▶ **Event**: This is launched when the user interacts with the Scene2D interface, for instance, by clicking/touching a widget. Actors will include listeners in order to handle them. There are plenty of event types that can be easily grouped into three self-explanatory names:

    ❑ `ChangeEvent`: This is fired when something has changed in an actor. This change is subject to the peculiarity of the actor itself, for instance, clicking a button or changing a `SelectBox` selection. It is specific to Scene2D and it is the most common within this context.

    ❑ `FocusEvent`: As its name suggests, this is fired when keyboard or scroll focus is gained or lost.

❑   `InputEvent`: This covers all input events from touch, mouse, keyboard, and scrolling. Some good examples might be a key press or a finger touch moving over an actor.

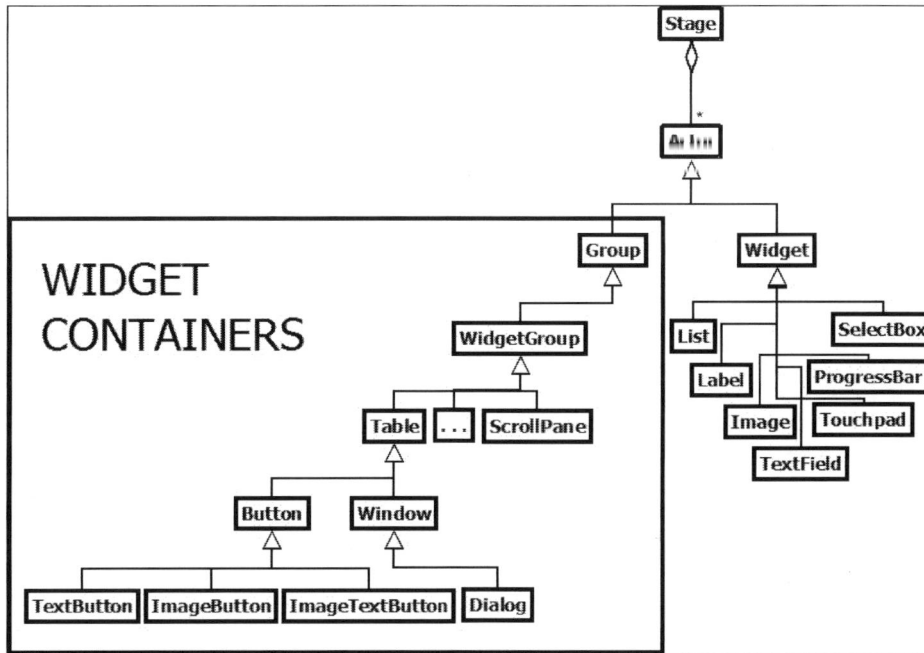

Scene2D tree nature diagram

Scene2D relies on a hierarchical organization of groupable actors that endows it with the following features:

►   **Action system**: This feature makes things simple and empowers your application with parallel or chained effects over the actors.

►   **Descendant transformations**: Any transformation applied to a group will affect all its children.

►   **Flexible event handling**: Actors can handle events before or after their parents do it through the two-step propagation phases: capture and regular, respectively.

►   **Individual simplified drawing**: Your sprite will be drawn in its local coordinate system whether it is rotated or scaled. Group drawing will render all the visible children.

> Remember that the default Libgdx coordinate system starts in the bottom-left corner at (0,0) with coordinates increasing in the up and right directions.

As a consequence of the model, a group is also an actor.

Almost every Scene2D UI is managed by a `Stage` instance. This class is in charge of receiving input events and firing them to the appropriate actors, generating the chance of handling them before their targets. You will get a better overview of this as you advance through this chapter.

Getting ready

The sample projects are required to follow this recipe, so make sure you already have them in your Eclipse workspace. Right-click on the **Package Explorer** panel, select **Import**, and then click on **Gradle Project**. They are located at `[cookbook]/samples`. In case you If you have any difficulty with this, feel free to re-read *Chapter 1, Diving into Libgdx*.

How to do it...

Once you finish this recipe, don't forget to visit the `ActorSample.java` source file, which contains a representative sample of a typical actor's life cycle with a wide range of manipulation options.

There are a lot of default actors that we will cover later on, but first we will create, manipulate, and render our own one.

Creating a custom actor

Please follow these steps to create your `Actor`:

1. First of all, define your custom actor class by extending the Libgdx one. Also, make it implement the `Disposable` interface to free the memory allocated by the texture:

    ```
    public class MyActor extends Actor implements Disposable {
       TextureRegion region = new TextureRegion( new
         Texture(Gdx.files.internal("data/myactor.png")) );

       public MyActor() {
         setPosition(SCENE_WIDTH * .5f,SCENE_HEIGHT * .5f);
         setWidth(1.61f);
         setHeight(0.58f);
       }

       public void dispose() {
         region.getTexture().dispose();
       }
    }
    ```

2. Even though it isn't mandatory, having `Stage` allows us to encapsulate the camera, manage event handling, and get a default root group. For this first recipe, we will not cover event listening on `stage` because we will just set our sample as `InputListener`, but remember from *Chapter 4, Detecting User Input*, that if you want to keep multiple input processors, you must go for `InputMultiplexer`. In this specific scenario, let's just initialize it; we will go beyond later on:

```
Stage stage = new Stage(viewport, batch);
```

3. Initialize myactor or instance with the previously defined constructor.

```
MyActor myactor = new MyActor();
```

4. Next, add your actor to the stage:

```
stage.addActor(myactor);
```

5. Note that the stage has to be disposed:

```
public void dispose() {
  batch.dispose();
  stage.dispose();
}
```

Rendering your custom actor

Render your actor as follows:

1. Override the `draw` method of your actor class to render the region, for example. Note that a long version of the `draw` method from the `Spritebatch` class is used. Otherwise, upcoming actions, such as rotating or scaling, will not be reflected at rendering:

```
public void draw(Batch batch, float alpha) {
  Color color = getColor();
  // Combine actor's transparency with parent's
    transparency
  batch.setColor(color.r, color.g, color.b, color.a *
    alpha);
  // Draw according to actors data model
  batch.draw(region, getX(), getY(), getOriginX(),
    getOriginY(), getWidth(), getHeight(), getScaleX(),
    getScaleY(), getRotation());
}
```

2. As a consequence of using `stage`, rendering becomes really simple, no matter the amount of actors that it contains. Just update each actor of `stage` and draw it:

```
public void render () {
    Gdx.gl.glClearColor(0, 0, 0, 1);
    Gdx.gl.glClear(GL20.GL_COLOR_BUFFER_BIT);

    stage.act(Gdx.graphics.getDeltaTime());
    stage.draw(); // This will call myactor's draw method
}
```

Manipulating an actor

On the one hand, immediate transformations can be performed over actors with the following methods:

Transformation	Methods
Rotation	`setRotation()` and `rotateBy()`
Translation	`setX()`, `setY()`, `setPosition()`, and `moveBy()`
Scale	`scaleBy()`, `setScale()`, `setScaleX()`, and `setScaleY()`
Size	`sizeBy()`, `setWidth()`, `setHeight()`, `setSize()`, and `setBounds()`

Parallel to these methods, you can retrieve data with `getRotation()`, `getX()`, `getY()`, `getWidth()`, `getHeight()`, `getScaleX()`, and `getScaleY()`.

Note that you cannot transform a `Group` by default. To enable it, you must call its `setTransform(true)` method so that `SpriteBatch` is transformed and children are drawn in their parents' coordinate system.

On the other hand, Libgdx provides you with actions. Here we will cover the principal built-in `Action` types, without digging into their variants (don't hesitate to visit the official API doc to get the complete picture), and how you can combine them.

In order to use these default actions, you can just instantiate them, giving values to their properties by calling their setters and finally adding it to the actor. The expected behavior will take place within the game render loop as shown in the following example code:

```
RotateByAction action = new RotateByAction();
action.setRotation(90f);
action.setDuration(5f);
myactor.addAction(action);
```

The next screenshot represents the preceding code so you can see what is really happening. The first box shows the actor before the action occurs. The second one covers the five-second process where the actor rotates by 90 degrees:

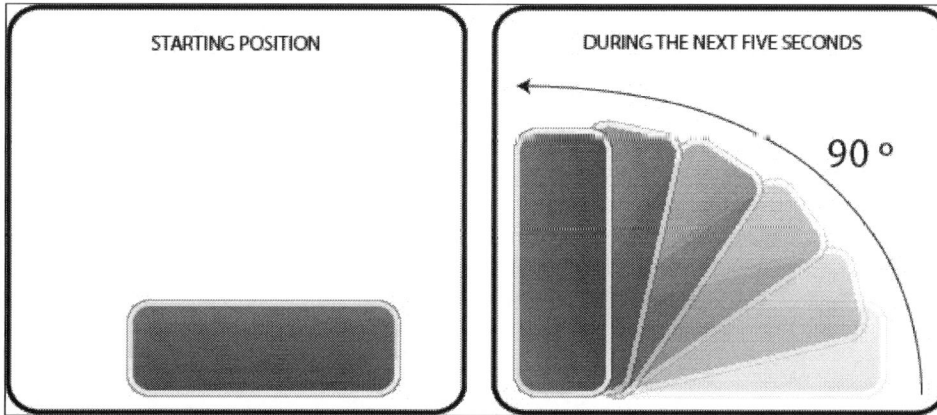

Nevertheless, this approach has a notable drawback consisting of allocating a new `RotateToAction` instance every time you need to perform it. Libgdx provides you with a `Pool` class to reuse objects:

```
Pool<RotateToAction> pool = new Pool<RotateToAction>() {
   protected RotateToAction newObject () {
      return new RotateToAction();
   }
};
RotateToAction action = pool.obtain();
action.setPool(pool);
... //Same as above
```

Actions can be divided into simple and complex.

Simple actions

Simple actions are atomic ones. An example of each type is described here:

1. A typical transformation is *rotation*. We can rotate our actor 90 degrees over five seconds, which can be achieved using the following code:

    ```
    myactor.addAction(rotateBy(90f, 5f));
    ```

2. You can get really cool effects using *alpha* actions. In this case, just make the actor appear in the scene smoothly:

    ```
    myactor.addAction(fadeIn(5f));
    ```

3. In order to *translate* your actor along the scene to a certain coordinate, let's use the following code:

    ```
    myactor.addAction(MoveTo(100f, 100f, 5f));
    ```

4. You can also specify the exact *size* of your actor by passing the desired width and height:

    ```
    myactor.addAction(sizeTo(100f, 33f, 5f));
    ```

5. Don't forget about the possibility of *scaling* your actor in both axes:

    ```
    myactor.addAction(scaleTo(2f, 2f, 5f));
    ```

> The last parameter is optional but common for all the previous examples; it represents the time spent to perform the action.

6. If your purpose is to *hide* your actor, you can use any of the following lines of code:

    ```
    myactor.addAction(hide());
    myactor.addAction(visible(false));
    ```

7. Or maybe you want to do the opposite:

    ```
    myactor.addAction(show());
    myactor.addAction(visible(false));
    ```

8. Another option is to *remove* your actor:

    ```
    myactor.addAction(removeActor());
    ```

Complex actions

You can also schedule a set of actions:

1. You can chain one action after another as a *sequence*, for instance, moving your actor and, once it is finished, rotating it by 90 degrees:

    ```
    myactor.addAction(sequence(moveTo(100f, 100f, 5f),
        rotateBy(90f, 5f)));
    ```

2. *Repeating* some task(s) a certain number of times is also possible:

    ```
    myactor.addAction(repeat(3, rotateBy(90f, 5f)));
    ```

3. To repeat it *forever*, you just have to write the following:

    ```
    myactor.addAction(forever(rotateBy(90f, 5f)));
    ```

4. As there is strength in numbers, performing actions *parallely* produces natural and dynamic effects that might catch the user's eye. Carrying this out is as simple as follows:

    ```
    myactor.addAction(parallel(moveTo(-200f, myactor.getY(),
        1.5f), fadeIn(1.75f)));
    ```

5. What if you want to execute one action only *after* the queued ones (at the moment `after()` is called) are done? A practical usage can be blocking a sequence.

```
myactor.addAction(sequence(fadeOut(5f), fadeIn(5f),
    rotateBy(-90f,5f), after(fadeIn(10f)), fadeOut(5f)));
```

6. It might happen that you cache your configured action into a variable that you just add to several actors, but the time taken to apply the action varies depending on the actor according to a *timescale* factor:

```
myactor.addAction(timescale(1.5f, rotateBy(90f, 5f)));
```

7. Finally, using the same scenario as before, let's say you want the same action to start at different times on different actors, in other words, you want a *delay*:

```
myactor.addAction(delay(5f, rotateBy(90f, 5f)));
```

How it works...

Behind the simplicity and practicality of the action usage approach, there is a background class, given it could not be any other way, named `Action`. This abstract class provides the skeleton for other intermediary to enclose the desired functionality or even for end actions. It relies on the setters of `Actor` to perform manipulations.

> You can also make use of this base API from the `Actor` class and modify its properties (which you can find in the first bullet point of the introduction to this chapter) without using actions, for instance, using `setPosition` or `setRotation`.

The spinal column is the `act` method, which supplies to subclasses a way to update the action based on time. Some of the main intermediate classes are:

- `DelegateAction`
- `EventAction`
- `ParallelAction`
- `TemporalAction`

As you can imagine through the self-explanatory names, they encompass some of the actions that have been already illustrated with examples in the previous section.

Undoubtedly, this wide hierarchy of action classes instigates flexibility and encourages the user to create its own ones either by extending or instantiating. If you still feel indecisive, a simple idea can be a sequence that flows into the switching of the screen. The following lines will generate a simple effect for transitions:

```
myactor.addAction(sequence(delay(0.5),parallel(fadeIn(2),rotateBy(
   360,1)),
   delay(0.5f), new Action() {
   @Override
   public boolean act(float delta) {
      myGdxSample.setScreen(new GameScreen());
      return true;
   }
})));
```

You might also have observed that you can pool any `Action`; this is because they implement the `Pool.Poolable` interface. This is a feature that you can apply to any class in your application that you want to reset for reuse, and in this way, you can avoid new allocations.

There's more...

At this point, you will have a good understanding of the `Actor` and `Action` APIs, but we can still go beyond on the second parcel.

If you have already visited the `ActorSample.java` code, you would have realized that I make use of `clearActions()` calls. This is a useful function to stop an action in process and empty the queue, keeping the actor as it is at that moment.

Diving into action types, you will also find `RunnableAction`, which allows you to execute some custom code once the action is finished:

```
actor.addAction(sequence(fadeOut(3), run(new Runnable() {
   public void run () {
      //Custom code
   }
})));
```

`TemporalAction` can also be tweaked in terms of interpolation, which defines the change rate of an action over time. It will use linear interpolation but it may not fit your needs appropriately. It means that, for example, in a 90 degrees over five seconds `RotateBy` action, you can have most of the time being spent on the first 70 degrees of rotation, slowing it down and then speeding up the rest of the rotation.

Libgdx provides you with an abstract base class, `Interpolation`, to extend in order to facilitate the creation of new ones. Apart from this, the following out-of-the-box implementations are also supplied:

- Bounce, BounceIn, BounceOut
- Elastic, ElasticIn, ElasticOut
- Exp, ExpIn, ExpOut
- Linear, LinearIn, LinearOut
- Swing, SwingIn, SwingOut

In the following picture, you can see some example function curves for the preceding `Interpolation` classes:

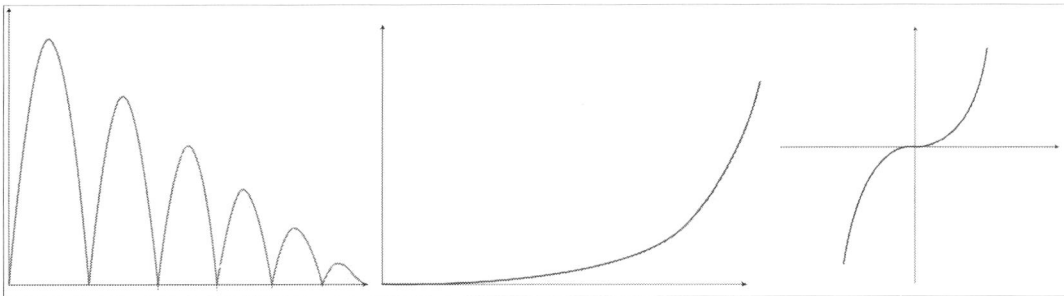

Classes ending with `in` make the interpolation faster at the beginning and decelerate as it progresses. There is an opposite effect with classes ending with `out`. You can put this into practice in the following way:

```
actor.addAction(fadeIn(4f, swingIn));
```

I highly recommend that you play around with them in order to familiarize yourself with their particular behavior because they really make applications look more professional.

See also

- Apart from Scene2D, you can also find some similar external libraries such as GridBagLayout, PageLayout, PnutsLayout, UIHierarchy, RiverLayout, FormLayout, MIGLayout, and DesignGridLayout.
- Once you understand the basis of the `Actor` class and how to interact with it, please continue to the *Widget collection overview* recipe to learn how to use the Libgdx built-in widgets.

Widget collection overview

Modern user interfaces allow people to interact with machines in a natural way within the context they are built upon. This is achieved through a wide variety of widgets (actors) designed with a specific purpose.

Having a well-cared interaction is also very important to immerse the user in your game experience.

Imagine the main menu for a shooter game with horror tinges where each and every detail counts: slightly lighted buttons with images, a nice gloomy font type for the main title, and a blunt gunshot sound when selecting the play option. The story doesn't end here because you must expand this environment to the settings screen where you might want to allow the user to change the volume through a custom-themed slider or set mutually-exclusive graphics options.

Libgdx provides you with a long list of customizable built-in widgets to save your valuable time, focusing your efforts on design. However, they are generic, so don't hesitate to implement your own version.

Getting ready

This recipe is mostly based on practical content. It is a good idea to take a look at the `WidgetSample.java` file from the `samples-core` project that comes with this book. You can import it through the Gradle plugin. If you need to do it from scratch, you can refer to *Chapter 1, Diving into Libgdx*. You will find the projects at `[cookbook]/samples`.

How to do it...

The Scene2D UI components extend the `Actor` class to acquire and expand its already explained functionality. You can easily frame them into two types:

- **Widgets**: This is the item with which the user will finally interact
- **Groups**: These are the structural actors used to organize widgets or other groups

Some of the components will require applying a user-defined style, which will vary according to the characteristics of the component. The style class will be contained within the widget class So, you can access it using `WidgetName.WidgetNameStyle`.

Before creating any widgets, we need to set up `Stage`:

1. The first step of this recipe is to initialize our `stage`, which will serve as the parent of all components:

   ```
   Stage stage = new Stage(viewport, batch);
   ```

2. In order for the `stage` instance to be able to capture events generated when interacting with the user, write the following:

```
Gdx.input.setInputProcessor(stage);
```

> Remember you can make use of an `InputMultiplexer` to set more than one `InputProcessor`.

In the next pages, you will find a complete tour through the built-in Libgdx UI components, their properties, and how to interact with them. These properties usually have self-explanatory names, but if you still have any queries, feel free to take a look at the Scene2D API at `http://libgdx.badlogicgames.com/nightlies/docs/api/com/badlogic/gdx/scenes/scene2d/ui/package-summary.html`

You can also simply play around with them in code terms.

After your widgets are defined, do not forget to add them to the stage or a group of your choice that is already in the scene, as follows:

```
stage.addActor(image);
stage.addActor(label);
stage.addActor(button);
...
```

Label

Label is the widget to use whenever you want to write any kind of text on the screen. You can set a style through the `LabelStyle` class where the font type must be specified while the font color and background image are optional. We can generate a label as follows:

1. Define what font we are using:

```
BitmapFont font =
    new BitmapFont(Gdx.files.internal("data/font.fnt"));
```

2. Next, create the style instance:

```
Label.LabelStyle labelStyle = new Label.LabelStyle(font,
    Color.WHITE);
```

3. Finally, call the `Label` constructor and set a position within the screen (by default, items are placed at (0,0) local stage coordinates):

```
label = new Label("This is a label", ls);
label.setPosition(x,y);
```

Keep in mind that Libgdx will use a, by default, linear `TextureFilter` when changing font size (scaling).

Image

As its name suggests, this widget will place a center-aligned image on the screen, by default. It can accept a `Drawable`, `NinePatch`, `Texture`, `TextureRegion`, or `TextureRegionDrawable` instance in the constructor. Only with the last one, Libgdx will keep the actor's properties (scale, rotation, and origin) when drawing.

> `NinePatch` permits drawing a texture in nine stretchable regions. In this way, they scale well for small sizes as well as big sizes. You can create your own `NinePatch` with the Android Draw 9-patch tool, which is available from `http://developer.android.com/tools/help/draw9patch.html`.
>
> `Drawable` contains objects that know how to draw themselves at a certain rectangular size. Its bounds are stored along with its minimum size in order to determine the space it must take up in a specific scene.
>
> `TextureRegionDrawable` is nothing more than a `TextureRegion` within a `Drawable` container.

The usage of this widget is easy:

1. Instantiate the `Image` class:

    ```
    Texture logo = new
       Texture(Gdx.files.internal("data/logo.png"));
    image = new Image(new TextureRegionDrawable( new
       TextureRegion(logo) ));
    ```

2. Place the image onto the screen with the `setPosition()` method. This step will be omitted from now onwards because it's common for all classes extending `Actor`.

Button

As you progress in this recipe, you will realize that you have multiple alternatives to choose from when including buttons in your game. This is the most general one.

It is a complex widget because it is internally implemented as a `Table`; an actor destined to organize elements on screen, which we will dive into later on. By its definition, you can infer that a button can contain other actors.

`Button` has no key properties, but you can specify a lot of optional details such as `Textures` or `Drawables` for `checked`, `checkedOver`, `disabled`, `down`, `up`, and `over` states through the `ButtonStyle` class, even the needed offset to press/release in both axes. In other words, you have a complete potpourri of options to contribute to the aforementioned game experience.

The resulting code for instancing a simple button can be as follows:

```
Texture actor = new
    Texture(Gdx.files.internal("data/button.png"));
Button.ButtonStyle buttonStyle = new Button.ButtonStyle();
buttonStyle.up = new TextureRegionDrawable(new
    TextureRegion(actor));
button = new Button( buttonStyle );
```

The following screenshot shows the example button:

TextButton

The TextButton class extends Button, adding a text Label within its internal table. As a consequence, the style includes everything belonging to the LabelStyle and ButtonStyle properties:

1. Start by defining the style, reusing the BitmapFont instance from the Label example:

```
Texture actor = new
    Texture(Gdx.files.internal("data/button.png"));
TextButton.TextButtonStyle tbs = new
    TextButton.TextButtonStyle();
tbs.font = font;
tbs.up = new TextureRegionDrawable( new TextureRegion() );
```

2. Finish by instancing the TextButton class:

```
textButton = new TextButton("TextButton", tbs);
```

The following screenshot shows the text button:

ImageButton

Changing a label for an image is the only difference between the ImageButton widget and the TextButton widget. This entails the inclusion of the ImageStyle and ButtonStyle properties within the ImageButtonStyle class.

It is a good idea to use this implementation when you want to place an icon over the button image.

The code is similar too. We can implement `ImageButton` as follows:

1. Construct the `ImageButtonStyle` property:

```
Texture accept = new
    Texture(Gdx.files.internal("data/icon.png"));
ImageButton.ImageButtonStyle ibs = new
    ImageButton.ImageButtonStyle();
// Background image
ibs.up = new TextureRegionDrawable( new TextureRegion(
    actor) );
// Icon image
ibs.imageUp = new TextureRegionDrawable( new
    TextureRegion(accept) );
```

2. Instantiate the `ImageButton` class:

```
imageButton = new ImageButton(ibs);
```

The following screenshot shows the image button:

ImageTextButton

The fat brother in the `Button` family is a mixture of the previous two widgets preserving properties from both:

1. As usual, define the style:

```
ImageTextButton.ImageTextButtonStyle itbs = new
    ImageTextButton.ImageTextButtonStyle();
itbs.font = font;
itbs.up = new TextureRegionDrawable( new TextureRegion(
    actor ) );
itbs.imageUp = new TextureRegionDrawable( new
    TextureRegion( accept ) );
```

2. Create an object:

```
imageTextButton = new ImageTextButton("ImageTextButton",
    itbs);
```

The following screenshot shows the imagc-text button:

CheckBox

Multiple or mutually exclusive options (commonly known as radio buttons, refer to the *There's more...* section for more) can be achieved through the CheckBox class. It is internally implemented extending the TextButton class. In order to instantiate it, you must set a Drawable instance to the checkboxOff and checkboxOn properties leaving checkboxOffDisabled, checkboxOnDisabled, and checkboxOver as optional.

The usage process would be as follows:

1. Set the style properties:

```
checkBoxOn = new Texture(
  Gdx.files.internal("data/scene2d/checkBoxOn.png"));
checkBoxOff = new Texture(
  Gdx.files.internal("data/scene2d/checkBoxOff.png"));
CheckBox.CheckBoxStyle cbs = new CheckBox.CheckBoxStyle();
cbs.checkboxOn = new TextureRegionDrawable( new
  TextureRegion( checkBoxOn ) );
cbs.checkboxOff = new TextureRegionDrawable( new
  TextureRegion( checkBoxOff ) );
cbs.font = font;
cbs.fontColor = Color.WHITE;
```

2. Create some new Checkbox objects through its constructor:

```
checkbox = new CheckBox("Checkbox", cbs);
checkbox = new CheckBox("Checkbox2", cbs);
```

The following screenshot shows the checkbox:

TextField

TextField is the widget to use whenever you need to get some input text from the user in a single line such as e-mail or password fields.

Selected text can be copied and pasted only under the desktop platform.

You must specify the `font` and `fontColor` properties, but it is a good idea to customize the `background`, `cursor`, `disabledBackground`, `disabledFontColor`, `focusedBackground`, `focusedFontColor`, `messageFont`, `messageFontColor`, and `selection` attributes to get a recognizable input appearance.

We can implement a password field as follows:

1. Set the style:

```
TextField.TextFieldStyle tfs = new
    TextField.TextFieldStyle();
tfs.font = font;
tfs.fontColor = Color.Black;

tfSelection = new
    Texture(Gdx.files.internal("data/tfSelection.png"));
tfBackground = new
    Texture(Gdx.files.internal("data/tfBackground.png"));
tfCursor = new
    Texture(Gdx.files.internal("data/cursor.png"));

// Blue background for selected text
tfs.selection = new TextureRegionDrawable(new
    TextureRegion(tfSelection));
// White background for text input
tfs.background = new TextureRegionDrawable(new
    TextureRegion(tfBackground));
// Cursor image
tfs.cursor = new TextureRegionDrawable(new
    TextureRegion(tfCursor));
```

2. Instantiate the component:

```
tf = new TextField("Enter password here");
```

3. Set the input type:

```
tf.setPasswordMode(true);
tf.setPasswordCharacter('*');
```

4. Listen for the user input:

```
tf.setTextFieldListener( new TextFieldListener() {
  public void keyTyped (TextField textField, char key) {
    // Do whatever...
    // For example: Hide screen keyboard if visible
    if(key == '\n')
      textField.getOnScreenKeyboard().show(false);
  }
});
```

The following screenshot shows `TextField`:

Enter password...

List

Commonly known as a listbox, this is a widget to display a sequence of strings, highlighting the selected one.

`ListStyle` needs `font`, `fontColorSelected`, `fontColorUnselected`, and `selection` to be defined while leaving it to the user whether or not to include a background. The usage process is as follows:

1. Customize `ListStyle`:

```
List.ListStyle listS = new List.ListStyle();
listS.font = font;
listS.fontColorSelected = Color.BLACK;
listS.fontColorUnselected = Color.GRAY;
listS.selection = new TextureRegionDrawable(new
   TextureRegion( tfBackground));
```

2. Instantiate the component:

```
list = new List<String>(listS);
```

3. Fill the container with the desired items:

```
Array<String> items = new Array<String>();
items.add("item1"); // One by one
items.add("item2", "item3", "item4"); // Or once for all
list.setItems(items);
```

4. Finally, as we have dynamically added content to the `List` widget, we need to call the `pack()` method in order to size it and fit the text bounds:

```
list.pack();
```

The following screenshot shows the `List` widget:

item1
item2
item3
item4

ScrollPane

Whenever you have a static space but a dynamic number of items to show, consider using the `ScrollPane` widget where all internal properties are optional but interesting to define. We can implement `ScrollPane` as follows:

1. In the same line as the rest, the first thing to do is customize the style:

```
ScrollPane.ScrollPaneStyle sps = new
  ScrollPane.ScrollPaneStyle();

Texture scroll_horizontal = new Texture(
  Gdx.files.internal( "data/scroll_horizontal.png" ) );
Texture knob_scroll = new Texture( Gdx.files.internal(
  "data/knob_scroll.png"));

// Background Image for each item
sps.background = new TextureRegionDrawable(new
  TextureRegion(tfBackground));
// Vertical Scroll container
sps.vScroll = new TextureRegionDrawable(new
  TextureRegion(scroll_horizontal));
// Vertical scroll current position knob
sps.vScrollKnob = new TextureRegionDrawable(new
  TextureRegion(knob_scroll));
```

2. Select an `Actor` to add the scrolling feature, for instance, a `List`, and instantiate the widget.

   Don't forget to call the `pack()` method to adapt the size of the `scrollPane` widget to its content:

```
scrollPane = new ScrollPane(list2, sps);
scrollPane.pack();
```

3. Set the component's height/width in order to take advantage of scrolling:

```
scrollPane.setHeight((float) (scrollPane.getHeight()*0.4));
```

The following screenshot shows the `ScrollPane` widget:

SelectBox

The `List` widget needs a relatively decent space within the screen to display all items, even when combined with a `ScrollPane` widget. However, we will not always have such luxury. `SelectBox` works in the same way but it will only display the selected item, showing the rest on clicking/touching the item. I am pretty sure that you must have seen it before with the name of the drop-down list.

Its style class is a bit different because it contains two other styles inside apart from the typical properties. This popularity becomes mandatory to define as well as `font`, `fontColor`, and `background`.

The inner styles are the already used `ListStyle` along with `ScrollPaneStyle`. We can implement `SelectBox` as follows:

1. The process starts by defining the style:

```
SelectBox.SelectBoxStyle sbs = new
   SelectBox.SelectBoxStyle();
sbs.listStyle = listS;
sbs.scrollStyle = sps;
sbs.background = new TextureRegionDrawable(new
   TextureRegion(new
   Texture(Gdx.files.internal("data/tfbackground.png"))));
sbs.font = font;
sbs.fontColor.set(Color.RED);
```

2. Fill `selectBox` with the desired items:

```
selectBox = new SelectBox<String>(sbs);
selectBox.setItems(items);
```

3. Size `selectBox` to bound the text:

```
selectBox.pack();
```

The following screenshot shows the `SelectBox` widget:

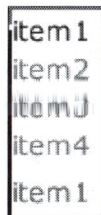

item 1
item 2
item 3
item 4
item 1

ProgressBar

Even though you already learned a way to implement this kind of UI component from scratch in *Chapter 6, Font Rendering*, Libgdx provides you with an out-of-the-box customizable progress bar.

It requires you to supply a background and a knob image. Nevertheless, you can also specify disabledBackground, disabledKnob, disabledKnobAfter, disabledKnobBefore, knobAfter, and knobBefore. Now, let's look at a practical example:

1. Start by feeding ProgressBarStyle:

```
Texture progress_bar = new
    Texture(Gdx.files.internal("data/progress_bar.png"));
Texture progress_bar_knob = new
    Texture(Gdx.files.internal("data/knob.png"));
ProgressBar.ProgressBarStyle pbs = new
    ProgressBar.ProgressBarStyle();
pbs.background = new TextureRegionDrawable(new
    TextureRegion(progress_bar));
pbs.knob = new TextureRegionDrawable(new
    TextureRegion(progress_bar_knob));
```

2. Then, instantiate the widget by passing the following to its constructor in the same order:

   ❑ Minimum and maximum value

   ❑ Size of each step in the progress

   ❑ Vertical (true) or horizontal (false) orientation

   ❑ Style

```
pb = new ProgressBar(0f, 100f, 1f, false, pbs);
```

3. Whenever you know the current point in the progress, use the following:

```
pb.setValue(currentPoint);
```

The following screenshot shows the ProgressBar widget:

Slider

An example of a slider is a sound volume selector. It allows, for instance, the user to move a knob along a bar, focusing more on the audio output than on the actual minimum-maximum value of volume, in order to detect the desired point.

This component only has two attributes that you must specify: background and knob. Suspicious right? In fact, Slider is an extension of ProgressBar with all the consequences that it entails. In the following example, we will just focus on its exclusive properties:

1. As usual, generate a slider style as follows:

```
slider_background = new Texture( Gdx.files.internal
    ("data/scene2d/slider_background.png"));
slider_knob = new Texture(
    Gdx.files.internal("data/scene2d/slider_knob.png"));

Slider.SliderStyle ss = new Slider.SliderStyle();
ss.background = new TextureRegionDrawable(new
    TextureRegion(slider_background));
ss.knob = new TextureRegionDrawable(new
    TextureRegion(slider_knob));
```

2. Instantiate the Slider widget taking into account that its constructor is similar to the constructor of the ProgressBar widget.

```
slider = new Slider(0f, 100f, 1f, false, ss);
```

The following screenshot shows the Slider widget:

Touchpad

There are some game genres, such as sports simulators, that usually do not fit gdx controllers as discussed in *Chapter 4*, *Detecting User Input*, so they must make use of a virtual touchpad.

Libgdx supports this widget with a circular movement area centered on its middle point. The background image must be specified, but it is recommended to define the knob image too.

Follow this process to create your own touchpad:

1. Define the style:

```
Touchpad.TouchpadStyle ts = new Touchpad.TouchpadStyle();
ts.background = new TextureRegionDrawable(new
    TextureRegion(new Texture(Gdx.files.internal
    ("data/touchpad_background.png"))));
ts.knob = new TextureRegionDrawable(new TextureRegion(new
    Texture(Gdx.files.internal("data/touchpad_knob.png"))));
```

2. Instantiate the widget, specifying the dead zone radius where the knob position will not be changed:

    ```
    touchpad = new Touchpad(10f, ts);
    ```

The following screenshot shows the example `Touchpad`:

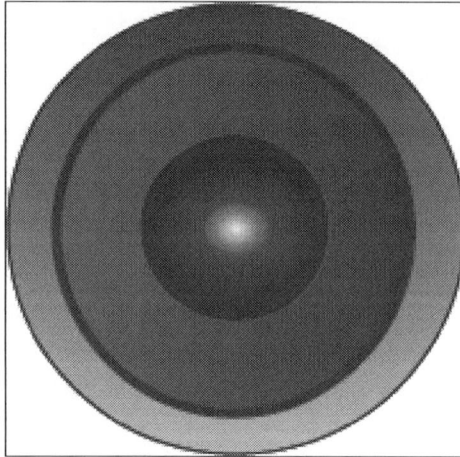

Stack

The `Stack` widget is a container where widgets are placed on top of each other, sizing all of its content to its bounds. The following is an example implementation:

1. Instantiate the class:

    ```
    stack = new Stack();
    ```

2. Add actors and set the desired size for the container:

    ```
    //Add first actor
    stack.add(button1);
    stack.pack(); // Sizes stack to button1's bounds
    //Add another actor
    stack.addActorAfter(button1, label1);
    ```

Tree

You can also organize your widgets hierarchically using the Scene2D `Tree` class, whose structure is composed of `Tree.Node`. Each of them has an icon and an actor, as well as zero or more children.

The mandatory properties of `TreeStyle` are the `minus` and `plus` images to expand or collapse the node. But it is also possible to decorate it with `background`, `selection`, and `over` images.

Next is an example implementation of its usage:

1. Set properties for your custom style:

```
Tree.TreeStyle treeS = new Tree.TreeStyle();
treeS.plus = new TextureRegionDrawable(new
  TextureRegion(new
  Texture(Gdx.files.internal("data/plus.png"))));
treeS.minus = new TextureRegionDrawable(new
  TextureRegion(new
  Texture(Gdx.files.internal("data/minus.png"))));
```

2. Instantiate the widget:

```
tree = new Tree(treeS);
```

3. Create and add nodes:

```
Label rootNode = new Label("Root-node", ls);
Label node1 = new Label("Child-node1", ls);
Label node2 = new Label("Child-node2", ls);
// parent
tree.add(new Tree.Node(node1));
// children
tree.getNodes().get(0).add(new Tree.Node(node1));
tree.getNodes().get(0).add(new Tree.Node(node2));
```

4. Expand to make all nodes visible and update the widget's bounds:

```
tree.expandAll();
tree.pack();
```

The following screenshot shows the Tree widget:

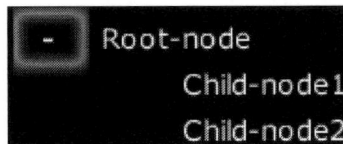

SplitPane

This is a structural component to store two widgets distributed either horizontally or vertically and separated by a specified handler image. Our example will contain two images. We can implement SplitPane as follows:

1. Define SplitPaneStyle:

```
SplitPane.SplitPaneStyle splitPaneS = new
  SplitPane.SplitPaneStyle();
splitPaneS.handle = new TextureRegionDrawable(new
  TextureRegion(new
  Texture(Gdx.files.internal("data/divider.png"))));
```

2. Instantiate the widget, passing both the actors, the orientation (vertical true, horizontal false), and the style to its constructor:

```
splitPane = new SplitPane(caveman1, caveman2, false,
    splitPaneS);
```

The following screenshot shows the `SplitPane` widget:

Window

Sometimes you will want to have your own customized windows within your app. Scene2D provides you with a built-in solution internally implemented as an extension of the `Table` class that will attract the attention of one of the subsequent recipes.

You must define what font you are using for the title of the `Window` widget and, subject to the programmer's preference, specify `background`, `stageBackground`, and `titleFontColor`.

The process to create a very simple `Window` widget is as follows:

1. Generate a new style:

```
Window.WindowStyle ws = new Window.WindowStyle();
ws.titleFont = font;
ws.titleFontColor = Color.WHITE;
```

2. Instantiate the `Window` class:

```
window = new Window("This is the title", ws);
```

3. Add some extra padding at the top to make some space for the title:

```
window.padTop(50f);
```

4. Add actors, for instance, a label and three random buttons. Every `row` call will place subsequent actors into a new row while `colspan(1)` calls indicate that it will have one column:

```
window.row().colspan(1); // 1 column row
window.add(label);
window.row().colspan(1);
window.add(firstButton);
window.row().colspan(1);
window.add(secondButton);
window.row().colspan(1);
window.add(thirdButton);
```

5. Use the `pack()` method to fit the content inside the bounds:

```
window.pack();
```

The following screenshot shows an example `Window` widget:

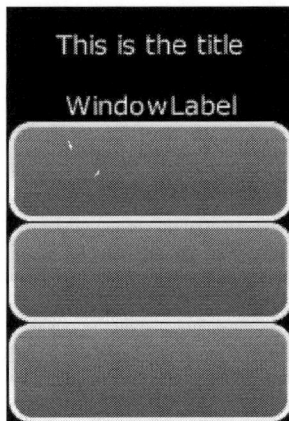

Dialog

The `Dialog` widget is a specific kind of `Window` due to the extended relationship that connects them. You can add any widget to it. The dialog will close if an inner button is clicked. Two `Table` instances organize the content of a `Dialog` widget. The first one is the content table, which is intended for storing labels. The second one is the button table whose obvious mission is to contain buttons.

`Dialog` makes use of `WindowStyle` to receive any style:

1. Create `WindowStyle`:

```
Window.WindowStyle ws2 = new Window.WindowStyle();
ws2.titleFont = font;
ws2.titleFontColor = Color.WHITE;
```

2. Instantiate `Dialog`:

```
Dialog dialog = new Dialog("Title", ws2);
```

3. We will disable clicks/touch on any other window/dialog apart from this by setting its modal property to `true`. Moreover, it will have a background image:

```
Texture dialog_background = new
    Texture(Gdx.files.internal("data/dialog_background.png"))

dialog.setModal(true); //User can only interact with this
    window
dialog.setBackground(new TextureRegionDrawable(new
    TextureRegion(dialog_background)));
```

4. Add a label so that the dialog shows a message:

```
dialog.getContentTable().row().colspan(1).center(); // 1
    row with 1 centered column
dialog.getContentTable().add(message);
```

5. Add two buttons created by you, for instance, `buttonYes` and `buttonNo`:

```
dialog().row().colspan(2); // 1 row, 2 columns
dialog.button(buttonYes);
dialog.button(buttonNo);
```

6. Pack the content as follows:

```
dialog.pack();
```

The following screenshot shows an example `Dialog` widget:

How it works...

If you have run the example code for this recipe, you must have realized that you can interact with each widget on the screen in one way or another. This happens because every actor can add `EventListeners` to its functionality and set its behavior. The available Scene2D listeners are:

▶ `ActorGestureListener`: This is fired when an actor is the subject of tap, long press, fling, pan, zoom, and pinch gestures.

- ► `ChangeListener`: This is a generic event that is fired whenever an actor receives some form of interaction.

- ► `ClickListener`: This is fired when the user clicks on the actor.

- ► `DragListener`: This is fired when mouse/finger dragging on an actor is detected.

- ► `DragScrollListener`: This is the same as the previous listener but will scroll through a scroll pane if needed.

- ► `FocusListener`: This is fired when losing or gaining focus.

- ► `InputListener`: This is a listener for touch, mouse, keyboard, and scroll inputs.

- ► `TextField.TextFieldClickListener`: This is a specific `InputListener` for text input. It can be useful to detect events such as typing or passing the cursor over `TextField`.

- ► `TextArea.TextAreaListener`: This is an extension of the previous listener.

A key method here from the Actor API is `hit()`, which returns the deepest *touchable* and *visible* actor where the interaction has occurred. Note that you can override it and decide when a hit is performed on your app.

There's more...

Individual behavior is explained along with this recipe, but you can still add some cohesion between several actors. This is the case of the `ButtonGroup` class, which allows you to group buttons in order to get the radio button's functionality. Refer to the following sample code:

```
ButtonGroup bg = new ButtonGroup();
bg.add(checkbox, checkbox2, checkbox3);
bg.setMaxCheckCount(1);
bg.setMinCheckCount(0);
```

See also

Once you are aware of all Scene2D possibilities, you should go for these recipes:

- ► The *Creating a basic menu screen using tables* recipe
- ► The *Skin customization* recipe

Creating a basic menu screen using tables

Until now, this chapter's recipes have been oriented to cover an enormous cut in the Scene2D API. From now on, you will find real cases to put the already explained concepts into practice with a few additional extras.

Almost every game has a main menu screen to allow the player to flow across the application. As it works as a facade, it must be neat so as not to give a bad first impression.

A very simple menu example will be explained in this recipe, but it can really serve you as a quick template to customize your own menu in a few minutes. To maintain chapter cohesion, it will make use of actions and some selected widgets.

Getting ready

This recipe is not an exception, so please import the sample projects into your Eclipse workspace. The source code for this recipe lives in the `MainMenuSample.java` file. It is a good idea to tweak that code at the same time that you learn the upcoming new concepts.

How to do it...

The content of this sample is now described step by step:

1. First of all, decide which components will appear in your menu screen. This example will contain the game title, some pictures of the main character, three buttons, and a slider to change the volume, as shown in the following screenshot:

2. Once you have your mental (or drawn) distribution of the screen space, declare your actors:

```
private Image gameTitle, hamsty1, hamsty2;
private TextButton btnPlay, btnSettings, btnExit;
private Slider slider;
```

3. Apart from visual components, you will also need some structural ones to organize and encapsulate your actors:

```
private Table table;
private Stage stage;
```

4. Within your `onCreate()` method, place the typical viewport stuff:

```
viewport = new FitViewport(VIRTUAL_WIDTH, VIRTUAL_HEIGHT);
```

5. Select your preferred font type:

```
BitmapFont font = new
  BitmapFont(Gdx.files.internal("data/font.fnt"));
```

6. Choose the images for the title and the main character. Note that an animation might be more suitable to get the player's attention, but for simplicity reasons, we will just use static images. Remember to dispose them all when the application exits:

```
Texture gameTitleTex = new Texture
  (Gdx.files.internal("data/gameTitle.png"));
Texture hamsty1Tex = new Texture
  (Gdx.files.internal("data/hamsty.png"));
Texture hamsty2Tex = new Texture
  (Gdx.files.internal("data/hamsty2.png"));

gameTitle = new Image(new TextureRegionDrawable(new
  TextureRegion(gameTitleTex)));
hamsty1 = new Image(new TextureRegionDrawable(new
  TextureRegion(hamsty1Tex)));
hamsty2 = new Image(new TextureRegionDrawable(new
  TextureRegion(hamsty2Tex)));
```

7. Define a common `TextButtonStyle` for all three buttons and instantiate them:

```
buttonUpTex = new Texture(
  Gdx.files.internal("data/scene2d/myactor.png"));
buttonOverTex = new Texture(
  Gdx.files.internal("data/scene2d/myactorOver.png"));
buttonDownTex = new Texture(
  Gdx.files.internal("data/scene2d/myactorDown.png"));

TextButton.TextButtonStyle tbs = new
  TextButton.TextButtonStyle();
tbs.font = font;
```

```
tbs.up = new TextureRegionDrawable(new
   TextureRegion(buttonUpTex));
tbs.over = new TextureRegionDrawable(new
   TextureRegion(buttonOverTex));
tbs.down = new TextureRegionDrawable(new
   TextureRegion(buttonDownTex));

btnPlay = new TextButton("PLAY", tbs);
btnSettings = new TextButton("SETTINGS", tbs);
btnExit = new TextButton("EXIT", tbs);
```

8. Repeat the process with `Slider`:

```
Slider.SliderStyle ss = new Slider.SliderStyle();
ss.background = new TextureRegionDrawable(new
   TextureRegion(new Texture(Gdx.files.internal
   ("data/slider_background.png"))));
ss.knob = new TextureRegionDrawable(new TextureRegion(new
   Texture(Gdx.files.internal("data/slider_knob.png"))));

slider = new Slider(0f, 100f, 1f, false, ss);
```

9. Instantiate the `Table` actor, which plays a key role in this recipe:

```
table = new Table();
```

10. Insert your first row, which will contain the game title. Don't worry about the details of the code because they will be explained in the upcoming *How it works...* section:

```
table.row();
table.add(gameTitle).padTop(30f).colspan(2).expand();
```

11. Add new rows to insert the remaining content. Pay special attention to the difference between `add()` and `addActor()`, as when using the former, the actors' position, size, and so on will be ignored when it is put inside a table:

```
table.row();
table.add(hamsty).padTop(10f).expandY().uniform();
table.add(hamsty2).padTop(10f).expandY().uniform();
table.row();
table.add(btnPlay).padTop(10f).colspan(2);
table.row();
table.add(btnSettings).padTop(10f).colspan(2);
table.row();
table.add(btnExit).padTop(10f).colspan(2);
table.row();
table.add(slider).bottom().colspan(2).expandY();
table.padBottom(30f);
```

12. Size the table to the stage:

```
table.setFillParent (true);
```

13. Pack our structural component to fit the bounds of its content:

```
table.pack();
```

14. One advantage of `Tables` is that they work as a group so that you can apply any `Action` over the whole set. Let's try a `fadeIn` animation, so the first thing is to hide the table by setting its transparency to 0:

```
table.getColor().a = 0f;

table.addAction(fadeIn(2f));
```

15. You can handle the user's interaction with the buttons as follows:

```
Gdx.input.setInputProcessor(stage);

// Play button listener
btnPlay.addListener( new ClickListener() {
  @Override
  public void clicked(InputEvent event, float x, float y) {
    Gdx.app.log(TAG, "PLAY");
  };
});
```

There are many types of `InputEvent`. Take a look at the Libgdx official documentation at `http://libgdx.badlogicgames.com/nightlies/docs/api/com/badlogic/gdx/scenes/scene2d/InputEvent.Type.html` to explore them.

16. Do the same with `Slider`:

```
slider.addListener(new InputListener() {
  @Override
  public void touchUp(InputEvent event, float x, float y,
    int pointer, int button) {
    Gdx.app.log(TAG, "slider changed to: " +
      slider.getValue());
    // Set volume to slider.getValue();
  }
  @Override
  public boolean touchDown (InputEvent event, float x,
    float y, int pointer, int button) {
    return true;
  };
});
```

If `touchDown` returns `true`, the listener is ready to receive `touchUp` and `touchDragged` events until the first one is executed. It will also prevent the event from feeding other listeners outside the stage.

17. To complete the `onCreate()` method, add the table to the stage:
```
stage.addActor(table);
```

18. Finally, update our stage and draw it on the `render` method:
```
stage.act(Gdx.graphics.getDeltaTime());
stage.draw();
```

19. Last but not least, remember to dispose the stage within the `dispose()` method:
```
public void dispose() {
   batch.dispose();
   font.dispose();
   stage.dispose();
}
```

How it works...

As mentioned earlier, `Table` becomes a really powerful and essential actor in the Scene2D ecosystem. It is even present internally on several of the other actors. It is mainly responsible for organizing the screen space to fit your needs without too much hardcoding. In this section, you will learn how to deal with this old enemy of UIs through the Libgdx interface.

`Table` is composed of `Cells`, which have a lot of interesting and tweakable properties related to space treatment.

Expand

The first way for a cell to occupy the space is by expanding its logical table's bounds up to the main table's bounds (stage). You will understand this quickly with the following screenshot:

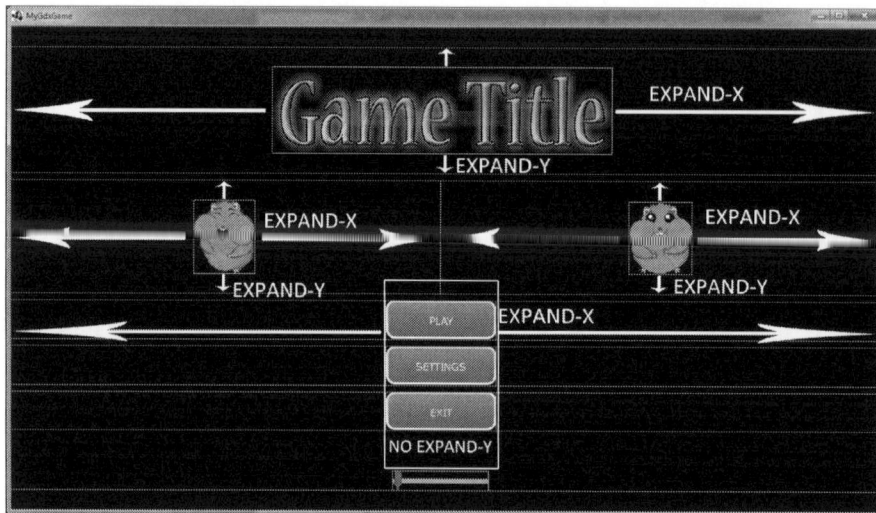

You can carry this out using these methods: expand(), expandX(), and expandY(), which only diffor on tho oxio thcy offcct.

In case we decide to avoid the expansion, we will get the following screenshot:

As you can see, the cells of the table are not expanded to the viewport limits but to the widest column, which is the one that contains the game title.

> If you have Box2DDebugRenderer enabled, you will see red, blue, and green lines. The red ones are the cell bounds, the blue ones are the stage limits, and the green ones delimit the space that a widget takes up.

Fill

We might want the content of a cell to fill its parent so the buttons become bigger over the *x* axis, just like the following screenshot:

Similar to the expand action, we can achieve this through `fill()`, `fillX()`, and `fillY()`.

> Note that stretching looks best when you use the `NinePatch` class.
>
> Take into account that fill methods are limited to the widget's maximum size. See the upcoming *Sizing* section in order to query and modify that size.

Uniform

In order to keep cells the same size, make use of the `uniform()` method. For instance, the two cells that contain a hamster image can be written as:

```
table.add(hamsty1).padTop(10f).expandY().uniform();
table.add(hamsty2).padTop(10f).expandY().uniform();
```

Sizing

You can also change a cell's width through `minWidth()`, `prefWidth()`, and `maxWidth()`, whose combined effect can be achieved with the `width()` method.

By default, a table takes the preferred width of a widget. But if it does not fit to a cell bound, they are scaled down to a value between its preferred size and its minimum size. If the widget does not fit yet with its minimum size, it might overlap with some other elements of the scene.

A widget will never take up a bigger space than its maximum width, not even through fill methods. This is the same with the height. You can factor width and height functions with the `size()` method. Cells or parent widgets may determine the size of child widgets according to the available space.

Padding and spacing

Both padding and spacing allow the designer to insert extra space around the edges of a cell, but the particularity is that padding will join adjacent spaces while spacing will take the biggest value. The following diagram will help to make things clearer:

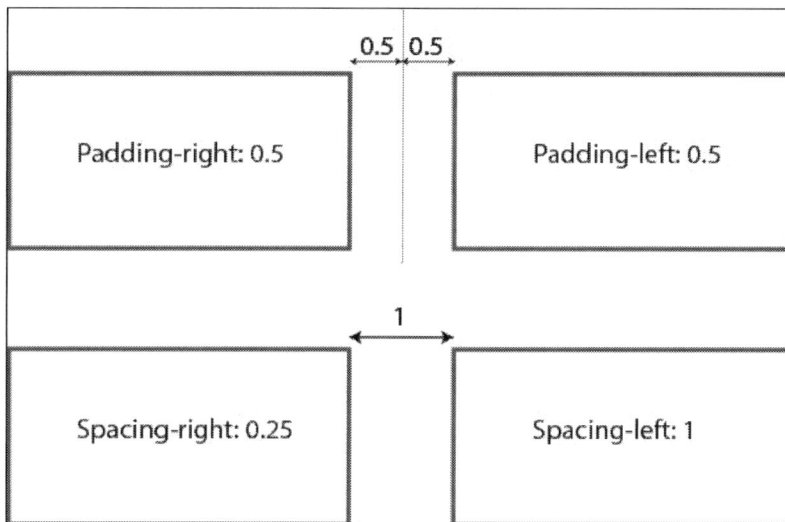

Some of the methods are `space()`, `spaceTop()`, `padBottom()`, `padLeft()`, and so on.

Alignment

You can align a widget within the cell itself by calling the `bottom()`, `right()`, `left()`, and `top()` methods.

Columns and rows

Whenever you want to have multiple columns, make use of the `colspan()` method. It receives the number of columns that a cell will take up as the argument.

The next screenshot shows a practical case:

As you can see, each hamster's cell occupies one column, whereas the game title's cell occupies just one. However, the game title column takes up the space of two columns. So, all we have to do is order the game title cell to span two columns:

```
table.add(gameTitle).colspan(2);
```

The next step is to add a new row. This can be carried out through the `row()` method:

```
table.row();
```

Finally, set the hamsters' cells to span just one column:

```
table.add(hamsty1).colspan(1);
table.add(hamsty2).colspan(1);
```

Or simply, do not specify any `colspan` because it will take one column by default.

> You might need a parallel method to get the same behavior in rows. It is not included, but you can still get it using nested tables.

Defaults

It is possible to set common attributes to all cells by default through the `table.defaults()` method. This gives you the chance of instantly applying any height, width, alignment, expansion, and more.

You can also do it only over columns with `table.columnDefault(numCol)` or over rows with `table.row()`

There's more...

The *Using ShapeRenderer for debug graphics* recipe in *Chapter 2, Working with 2D Graphics*, explains some really powerful and useful debug tools. However, Scene2D comes with its own debug system that really helps to get the desired UI.

All you need to do is make use of the following function call after instantiating a `Table` instance:

```
table.debug(); //Enables debug
```

> The `debug()` method can be applied generically (as shown in the previous example) or over tables, cells, or all widgets contained in the table itself.

Apart from debug utilities, there are some more features to enrich your table and consequently your UI, so I recommend that you take a walk through the table API.

See also

> ▶ Right now, you are very close to a real implementation of a UI in Libgdx, but it still lacks skin customization, so feel free to carry on and feed your neurons with tasty features in the *Skin customization* recipe.

Skin customization

Your current progress on the Scene2D topic allows you to develop a simple UI application without investing a huge effort. However, if you intend to program a more complex game with lots of UI shared assets, you will easily get yourself into a mess.

Skins are the wonderful solution to pack all your UI data into one simple JSON file adding to the aforementioned advantages of using an atlas.

As tends to happen with the data-driven approach, it requires an initial effort that turns into awesome commodities and facilities for the future.

Getting ready

The code for this recipe can be found in the `SkinCustomizationSample` class within the `samples-core` project. Please do not forget to visit it in order to run and play with the live example.

How to do it...

Skins can be created in two different ways, but both should make use of a `TextureAtlas` resource. The first one consists of loading a JSON file with the whole bulk of UI data. To help you to understand the process, an abstract syntax structure for this standard is shown here:

```
{
  Fully-qualified-Java-className: {
    Style-name: { Property-name: resource,
    ...},
    ...
  },
  ...
}
```

Next is a real simple piece of an example JSON file:

```
{
  com.badlogic.gdx.scenes.scene2d.ui.TextButton$TextButtonStyle:{
    default:{
      down:default-round-down,
      up:default-round,
      font:default-font,
      fontColor:white
    },
    toggle:{
      down:default-round-down,
      up:default-round,
      checked:default-round-down,
      font:default-font,
      fontColor:white,
      downFontColor:red
    }
  },
  com.badlogic.gdx.scenes.scene2d.ui.Slider$SliderStyle:{
    default-horizontal:{
      background:default-slider,
      knob:default-slider-knob
    }
  },
  com.badlogic.gdx.scenes.scene2d.ui.CheckBox$CheckBoxStyle:{
    default:{
      checkboxOn:check-on,
      checkboxOff:check-off,
      font:default-font,
      fontColor:white
    }
  },
  ...
}
```

As you can see, we are defining two different styles for TextButton with one of them named default, which means that if the style name is not specified in the code, this will be the default one. Unlike TextButtonStyle and CheckBoxStyle, SliderStyle is only defined for horizontal sliders.

It is not a coincidence that the properties of TextButtonStyle, for example, explicitly appear on the document. This is because Libgdx will build TextButtonStyle from those properties so that the style can be set to any TextButton. The same applies to any other type of widget.

If you want to familiarize yourself with the JSON skin definition, I highly recommend that you take a look at the uiskin.json file from the samples project. Be aware that such a file doesn't work on its own; it needs a uiskin.atlas, uiskin.png, and a .fnt file for each type of bitmap font defined. Here, you can see a Libgdx example uiskin.png file to make things clear:

It contains all the necessary graphical data to cover the widgets' properties.

So, the process of creating, using, and disposing a skin through a JSON file is as follows:

1. Create your .json file associating it to an atlas.

2. Instantiate a skin class in the code:

```
skin = new Skin(Gdx.files.internal("data/uiskin.json"));
```

3. Pass that instance to the widgets' constructor:

```
titleLabel = new Label("Skin Customization", skin);
button1 = new TextButton("SkinDefaultButton", skin);
slider = new Slider(0f, 100f, 1f, false, skin);
touchpad = new Touchpad(10f, skin);
```

4. Call the skin's dispose() method:

```
skin.dispose();
```

The preceding explanation is the most usual and recommended approach to deal with skins. However, you can still populate a skin programmatically by following these steps:

1. Instantiate a skin through its no-parameters constructor:

```
skin = new Skin();
```

2. Add regions from an atlas to your skin:

```
skin.addRegions(atlas);
```

3. Generate a custom style for any widget:

```
TextButtonStyle textButtonStyle = new TextButtonStyle();
textButtonStyle.up = skin.getDrawable("white"); // Explained below
textButtonStyle.down = skin.getDrawable("gray");
```

4. Add it to your skin:

```
skin.add("myTextButtonStyle", textButtonStyle);
```

5. Use the custom style:

```
button2 = new TextButton("SkinTweakedButton", skin, "
  myTextButtonStyle ");
```

6. Call the skin's `dispose()` method.

Now that you are almost in love with `Skin`, I will introduce you to its powerful and flexible methods to retrieve resources.

The first one is very similar to `get()` from `AssetManager`:

```
Texture icon = skin.get("icon", Texture.class);
```

You can also make use of some methods to retrieve the built-in type objects:

```
TextureRegion region = skin.getRegion("caveman");
Sprite sprite = skin.getSprite("sprite1");
BitmapFont font = skin.getFont("arial");
Color blue = skin.getColor("blue");
NinePatch ninepatch = skin.getPatch("ninepatch1");
TiledDrawable tiledDraw = skin.getTiledDrawable("tiledDraw1");
Drawable drawable = skin.getDrawable("gun");
```

As you will have already realized, `Drawable` implementation types define all image properties belonging to styles (for example, the `down` property from `TextButtonStyle`), which gives the application the feature of using any region on any widget within the application.

Another advantage of skins is the facility to convert between Libgdx image formats. Consider the following code for example:

```
Drawable drawable = skin.getDrawable("caveman");
Texture texture = skin.get("caveman", Texture.class);
TextureRegon region = skin.getRegion("caveman");
// Same for the rest of types as detailed in the above example but
  with the caveman source file
```

How it works...

The Skin class doesn't waste your bytes by instantiating the same resource twice. On the contrary, the get() methods will just return a reference to the instance of the asset itself. This means that if you change any of its properties, the changes will become effective on the rest of the context where it is being used.

If you don't want to globally modify the style, make use of the newDrawable() method so you got a copy of the aforementioned instance. This function has a variant that allows you to color any image so that you can reuse it:

```
textButtonStyle.over = skin.newDrawable("white", Color.YELLOW);
```

There's more...

Imagine that you are developing a trilogy where different skins have been used for the first and second parts and you want to enrich your third and last one with a new skin made by combining the other two. It is as simple as the following code:

```
skin3.load(Gdx.files.internal("data/skin1"));
skin3.load(Gdx.files.internal("data/skin2"));
```

Another possibility covered here is removing a resource from the skin, which can be done as follows:

```
skin.remove("caveman", Texture.class);
```

See also

▸ At this point, you dominate the fauna and flora of the Scene2D API. It is time to go beyond and read the *Creating new widgets* recipe.

Creating new widgets

It has been a long journey since you learned the basics of Scene2D, so you are now prepared for the fun part consisting of extending the library and generating your own content for personal projects or even for the community itself. With proper usage of the Skin class, you can perform a complete overhaul of your UI just by changing image assets. As you will know, software reuse becomes a booster in development companies so that you will not have to reinvent the wheel.

In this direction, you can easily create new widgets composed of simpler ones. Usually, the easiest way of approaching this is by extending a Table class and organizing inner widgets within it, but do not discard extending from WidgetGroup and using composition as a reliable alternative.

The possibilities for creating a new complex UI component are endless, but this recipe will cover a very simple and flexible level selector. The goal is being able to have a widget with a custom background, a level title, a descriptive image for the current level, left and right buttons to flow through the component, and a button to launch the game screen.

Getting ready

Do not forget to take a look at the sample projects from the [cookbook]/samples folder. You will need to import them correctly to your Eclipse workspace. Feel free to re-read *Chapter 1, Diving into Libgdx*, where the process is explained step by step.

How to do it...

The CustomWidgetSample.java and LevelSelector.java files contain all the source code that illustrates this recipe, so I highly recommend that you play around with them after your reading is done.

For you to have an idea of what you will have created at the end of this recipe, please take a look at the following screenshot:

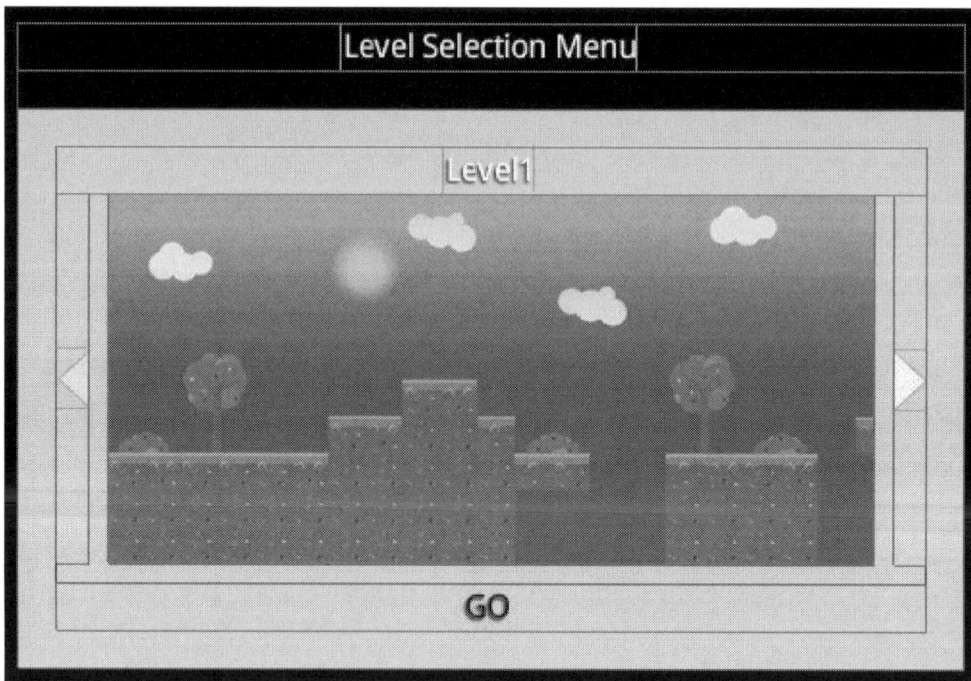

To accomplish the goal of implementing our own widget, its creation and usage is explained step by step in the upcoming sections.

Creating a widget

Make sure to start by following these instructions:

1. Define your `LevelSelector` class by extending the `Table` class:

```
public class LevelSelector extends Table {

    ...

}
```

2. Make sure to declare, if needed, an associated style, inner components, data containers, and auxiliary properties:

```
// Associated style
private LevelSelectorStyle style;
// Inner components
private Image buttonLeft, buttonRight;
private TextButton buttonGo;
// Data containers
private Array<Level> levels;
// Auxiliary properties
private int currentLevelIndex = 0; // current shown level
public float imageWidth = 400;// Normalized size for images
public float imageHeight = 195;
```

3. Before getting your hands dirty with the real deal, you need to know the attributes for our custom style:

```
static public class LevelSelectorStyle {
  /* Optional */
  public Drawable background;

  /* Must be defined */
  public Drawable leftArrow, rightArrow;
  public TextButtonStyle textButtonStyle;
  ...
}
```

4. Another inner class will be contained within `LevelSelector` in order to store information (title and image) about each level:

```
public static class Level {
  private Label title;
  private Image image;
  ...
}
```

The trivial matter is to implement constructors, getters, and setters for the `Level` class. Some ideas for the constructors are as follows:

```
public Level(CharSequence level_name, Skin skin)
public Level(CharSequence level_name, LabelStyle
  labelStyle)
public Level(CharSequence level_name, Image image, Skin
  skin)
public Level(CharSequence level_name, Image image,
  LabelStyle labelStyle)
```

Check the source code that comes along with this book if you have any doubts.

5. It is a good idea to provide a wide selection of constructors for your `LevelSelector` widget so that the user can determine which one fits their needs. Within our context, you can get the style through a skin, the raw style type, or even the separated properties that compose it. Another nonexclusive option is filling the container where we will store the levels in the constructor itself. Some of them are as follows:

```
// Initialize data content and extract style from skin
public LevelSelector(Array<Level> array, Skin skin) {
   super(skin);
   setStyle(skin.get(LevelSelectorStyle.class));
   initialize();
   setSize(getPrefWidth(), getPrefHeight());
   this.levels = new Array<Level>(array);
}

// Empty content and defined style via a skin
public LevelSelector(Skin skin, String styleName) {
   super(skin);
   setStyle(skin.get(styleName, LevelSelectorStyle.class));
   initialize();
   setSize(getPrefWidth(), getPrefHeight());
}

// Empty content and defined style via a style object
public LevelSelector(LevelSelectorStyle style){
   setStyle(style);
   initialize();
   setSize(getPrefWidth(), getPrefHeight());
}

// Empty content and defined style via separated properties
public LevelSelector(Drawable leftArrow, Drawable
   rightArrow, TextButtonStyle textButtonStyle) {
   this(new LevelSelector.LevelSelectorStyle(leftArrow,
      rightArrow, textButtonStyle));
}
```

6. Unexplained functions have been called while defining those constructors. The first one is `setStyle()`, which is responsible for applying the received style to the `LevelSelector` widget:

```
public void setStyle(LevelSelectorStyle style) {
  if (style == null) throw new
    IllegalArgumentException("style cannot be null.");

  this.style = style;
  this.buttonLeft = new Image(style.leftArrow);
  this.buttonRight = new Image(style.rightArrow);
  this.buttonGo = new TextButton("GO",
    style.textButtonStyle);
  setBackground(style.background); //Set table background
  invalidateHierarchy(); // Must be called whenever parent
    layout may change
}
```

7. The next method is `initialize()`, which is in charge of making the widget touchable, initializing the empty content data structure, and setting up the listeners for the arrows:

```
private void initialize() {
  setTouchable(Touchable.enabled);
  levels = new Array<Level>();

  buttonLeft.addListener(new ClickListener() {
    public void clicked (InputEvent event, float x, float
      y) {
      showPreviousLevel(); // Explained below
    }
  });
  buttonRight.addListener(new ClickListener() {
    public void clicked (InputEvent event, float x, float
      y) {
      showNextLevel();// Explained below
    }
  });
}
```

8. To complete the constructors, set the preferred width and height for the background as given by the `getPrefWidth()` and `getPrefHeight()` functions:

```
setSize(getPrefWidth(), getPrefHeight());
```

9. As it is a widget with a dynamic nature, you should also provide some methods to add new level(s). The `update` call will be explained in step 11:

```
// addLevel(level1);
public void addLevel(Level level) {
   if(level != null && !levels.contains(level,false))
      levels.add(level);
   update();
}

// addLevels(arrayLevels);
public void addLevels (Array<Level> array) {
   for(Level l : array)
      levels.add(l);
   update();
}

// addLevels(level1, level2, level3);
public void addLevels(Level...levelsvar) {
   for(Level level : levelsvar) {
      if(level != null && !levels.contains(level,false))
         levels.add(level);
   }
   update();
}
```

> Be aware that the `contains()` method will make use of the `equals()` operator of the `Level` class as its second parameter is `false`. Go to the source code to find out how to override it.

10. A key method needs to be called whenever the shown level changes. It will just rebuild the whole table with the new content. Do not hesitate to consult the first screenshot of this recipe in order to understand the next code snippet better:

```
private void update() {
   if(levels.size != 0) {
      clearChildren();
      Level currentLevel = levels.get(currentLevelIndex);
      row();
      add(currentLevel.getTitle()).colspan(3);
      row();
      add(buttonLeft).colspan(1).padRight(10f);
      add(currentLevel.getImage()).colspan(1).size(imageWidth
         , imageHeight);
      add(buttonRight).colspan(1).padLeft(10f);
```

```
    row();
    add(buttonGo).colspan(3).padTop(10f).fillX();
    row();
    pad(20f);
    pack();
  }
}
```

11. To move forward/backward across the selector, implement these methods:

```
private void showPreviousLevel() {
  if(currentLevelIndex > 0) {
    currentLevelIndex--;
    update();
  }
}
private void showNextLevel() {
  if(currentLevelIndex+1 < levels.size) {
    currentLevelIndex++;
    update();
  }
}
```

12. Finally, draw the widget:

```
public void draw(Batch batch, float parentAlpha) {
  validate(); //Ensures the actor has been laid out
  super.draw(batch, parentAlpha);
}
```

Using a widget

You can have a really cool widget, but users need to know how to use it. Next is a brief description for the `LevelSelector` class:

1. Making your widget come to life is pretty straightforward. Start by creating your title label and then generate the levels' content:

```
Label level_menu = new Label("Level Selection Menu", skin);
Array<LevelSelector.Level> levels = new
  Array<LevelSelector.Level>();
LevelSelector.Level level1 = new
  LevelSelector.Level("Level1", skin);

Texture jungleTex = new
  Texture(Gdx.files.internal("data/jungle-level.png"));
Texture mountainsTex = new
  Texture(Gdx.files.internal("data/blur/mountains.png"));
```

```
level1.setImage(
  new Image(new TextureRegionDrawable(new
  TextureRegion(jungleTex)))
);
//... Repeat it for the rest of levels
levels.addAll(level1, level2, level3);
```

2. Instantiate your component, populate the container, update the view, and add it to the main table:

```
final LevelSelector ls = new LevelSelector(skin);
ls.addLevels(levels);
table.add(ls);
```

3. You can start loading the selected level when the user clicks on the **GO** button:

```
ls.getButton().addListener( new ClickListener() {
  @Override
  public void clicked(InputEvent event, float x, float y) {
    Gdx.app.log(TAG, "LOADING LEVEL " +
      ls.getCurrentLevel());
  };
});
```

4. Remember to dispose the textures:

```
jungleTex.dispose();
mountainsTex.dispose();
```

How it works...

There is a bit missed out in the *How to do it...* section that consists of the JSON part. The skin can be generated quickly by packing your UI images into an atlas and setting the properties in the `.json` file. The properties for the `LevelSelector` class are as follows:

```
com.mygdx.game.LevelSelector$LevelSelectorStyle: {
  default: {
    leftArrow:left_arrow,
    rightArrow:right_arrow,
    background:goldDraw,
    textButtonStyle:default
  }
}
```

If you still don't really get on with this standard, please read the following paragraph.

It might be difficult to determine what is what within the JSON structure for the first time, so `leftArrow` is the property name in the code snippet while `left_arrow` is the filename, without the extension, of the image before being packed into the atlas.

In the code example, it is being used as a little trick to get background colors easily. As you read earlier, `goldDraw` is the selected resource. It is defined as follows:

```
com.badlogic.gdx.scenes.scene2d.ui.Skin$TintedDrawable: {
  goldDraw: { name: white, color: { r: 1, g: 0.84, b: 0, a: 1 } },
  ...
}
```

The highlighted word `white` is a white one-pixel image file included in the atlas, so you just tint it and color any surface uniformly.

There's more...

In order to keep a good grade of simplicity, a lot of details have been omitted, so you can improve this `LevelSelector` class in multiple ways.

Some quick ideas are hiding the arrow buttons when first or last levels are reached, populating the widget with a levels describer JSON file, allowing disabled levels, performance optimizations, adding the score for already played levels, and so on.

After the titan effort of learning the full Scene2D API, a question may fly around your head: can I develop a whole game using Scene2D? The answer is yes. However, you must have in mind an important consideration. Scene2D mixes models and views, and therefore, it makes it way harder to snapshot the game's state.

> In case you do not know, games with separate models and views can come back to a specific game state only by storing the model.

Developing a game with Scene2D might be worth it when you have a lot of UI or when it requires a bunch of actors to perform the same actions, such as card games.

Of course, you can implement only your UI with Scene2D and keep the rest without it.

9

The 2D Maps API

In this chapter, we will cover the following recipes:

- ▶ Creating maps with Tiled and loading them into Libgdx
- ▶ Adding and querying map metadata
- ▶ Developing your own map loaders and renderers

Introduction

Most games lay a collection of levels in front of the player for him or her to beat them. The design of those levels is crucial for the final result to be an enjoyable and engaging experience. If they are not challenging enough or too frustrating, the player will just throw away the controller or the phone and move on to something else!

We will not discuss level design; there are great specialized sources out there such as *The Art of Game Design*. You can refer to `http://artofgamedesign.com` for more details.

One thing is sure, though; level design involves loads of iterations including prototype, test, tweak, rinse and repeat. This makes it extremely important to use level editors that integrate well with your system, in order to be able to reduce the time from saving a level to testing it in the game.

Libgdx features a fantastic maps API that abstracts **level loading**, **querying**, and **rendering**. The **Tiled** and **tIDE** map editors are supported out of the box, but you can very easily extend it to achieve integration with the editor of your choice.

This chapter will provide you with everything you need to know about the Libgdx maps API, so you can succeed at making truly awesome levels with a streamlined pipeline.

Creating maps with Tiled and loading them into Libgdx

During our first contact with the Libgdx maps API, we will create a simple level with the Tiled map editor, load it into our game, and render it as part of our game loop. Tiled is a very popular, cross-platform, freely available, open source tile-based editor.

> Tile-based maps are levels made out of small texture blocks called tiles. Combining tiles from a reduced set, complex and interesting results can be achieved while saving texture memory.

There is not much you need to know to start working with Tiled maps in your game. You will soon realize how extremely simple the process is, as Libgdx, very kindly, does all the hard work for you!

Getting ready

Download and install the latest version of Tiled for your operating system from `http://www.mapeditor.org/download.html`.

We are going to use the Base tileset pack created by Kenney and available under the Creative Commons Zero license at `http://www.kenney.nl/assets`.

Make sure the `samples` projects are in your Eclipse workspace.

How to do it...

During the first part of this section we will briefly cover how you can create simple maps with Tiled and then we will move on to the basics of the Libgdx maps API.

Creating a basic map with Tiled

Perform the following steps:

1. Open Tiled and click on **File** and **New Map**.
2. We are going to work with **Orthogonal** maps although Tiled and Libgdx also support **Isometric** ones.
3. Our tileset is made out of `21 x 21` pixel blocks, so introduce those values in the **Tile size** panel.
4. Now, select **Map size** in tiles, in our case, we have chosen `30 x 12`. Do not worry, you can change it later if you need to. Click on the **OK** button when you are done.

5. You cannot go much further without an imported tileset. Click on **Map | New tileset** and select `data/maps/tileset.png`. The **Tile size** is 21 x 21 and in this case we have `1 px` for **Margin** and another one for **Spacing**. Click on **OK** when you are done.

6. Repeat the same process with `data/maps/backgrounds.png`.

7. Maps are organized in layers that are rendered from bottom to top. In the **Layers** panel, you can create, delete, rename, and rearrange layers. For our setup, we will be using three: background, terrain, and foreground.

8. To place tiles onto the map, make sure you are in the correct layer, select a tile from the **Tilesets** panel and pick the Stamp brush tool. Now you can "stamp" tiles onto the map.

9. The **Bucket Fill** tool will cover the isolated island with the selected tile.

10. For convenience, it is also possible to select several tiles from the set and stamp them all at once.

11. Play around with Tiled for a while and save the map when you are happy with it by clicking on **File** and then on **Save**. Our saved map will be located at `data/maps/tiled.tmx`.

The Tiled interface can be seen in the following screenshot:

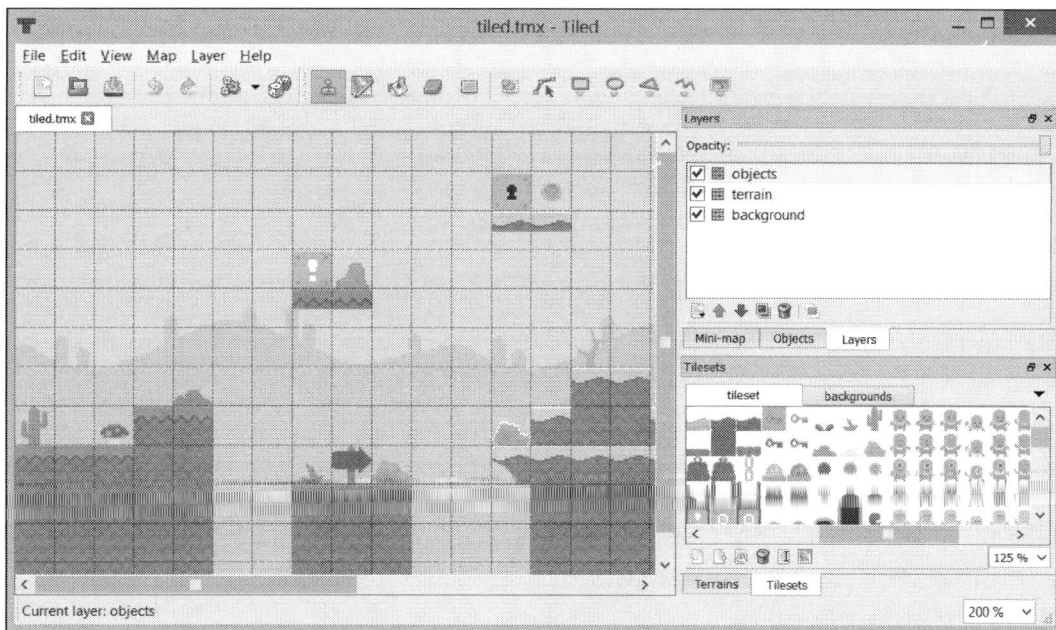

Loading and rendering a Tiled map in Libgdx

The code for this sample is in the `TiledMapSample.java` file. Follow these steps:

1. First of all, we define our viewport size using world units:

    ```
    private static final float VIRTUAL_WIDTH = 384.0f;
    private static final float VIRTUAL_HEIGHT = 216.0f;
    ```

2. To move the camera around, we will use the following constant, expressed in world units per second:

    ```
    private static final float CAMERA_SPEED = 5.0f;
    ```

3. We add a `TiledMap` object to carry all the information of our level. The `TmxMapLoader` class knows how to parse `.tmx` level files, which is the format used by Tiled. Additionally, we will use `OrthogonalTiledMapRenderer` to draw our `TiledMap` instance on the screen. Finally, we have a `direction` vector to control camera movement as well as a viewport and a camera:

    ```
    private TiledMap map;
    private TmxMapLoader loader;
    private OrthogonalTiledMapRenderer renderer;
    private Vector2 direction;
    ```

4. In the `create()` method, we instantiate the loader and call its `load()` method with our recently created map to obtain a `TiledMap` object. The renderer constructor takes a map and, optionally, a batch and the conversion scale from pixel to world units. When no batch is supplied, the renderer will create one of its own. You need to remember to dispose of both the map and the renderer whenever you stop needing them to avoid memory leaks:

    ```
    public void create() {
        ...
        loader = new TmxMapLoader();
        map = loader.load("data/maps/tiled.tmx");
        renderer = new OrthogonalTiledMapRenderer(map);
        direction = new Vector2();
    }
    ```

5. The `render()` method illustrates how simple it is to draw our map on the screen. First, we update the position of the camera according to the user's input. Then, we call `setView()` on the renderer passing in the camera so the renderer knows which section of the map the camera is looking at. Finally, we simply call the renderer function, `render()`:

    ```
    public void render() {
        Gdx.gl.glClearColor(0.8f, 0.8f, 0.8f, 1.0f);
        Gdx.gl.glClear(GL20.GL_COLOR_BUFFER_BIT);
    ```

```
    updateCamera();

    renderer.setView(camera);
    renderer.render();
}
```

> The `render()` method will go over all visible tile layers, drawing them from bottom to top. If you only want to render specific layers, you can use the `void render(int[] layers)` method, which takes an array of layer indices. This could be helpful when you want to render the level, your characters, and some overlay on top of them, such as fog or clouds.

6. The `updateCamera()` function is actually quite simple. First, we set the direction vector to zero (0, 0) and set it depending on whether the arrow keys are pressed or the user is touching near the edges of the screen. We then normalize the vector, which basically means scale it proportionally so its length equals 1. Finally, we scale it by the camera speed times the delta time and add it to the camera position:

```
direction.set(0.0f, 0.0f);

int mouseX = Gdx.input.getX();
int mouseY = Gdx.input.getY();
int width = Gdx.graphics.getWidth();
int height = Gdx.graphics.getHeight();

if (Gdx.input.isKeyPressed(Keys.LEFT) || (Gdx.input.isTouched() &&
mouseX < width * 0.25f)) {
    direction.x = -1;
}
else if (Gdx.input.isKeyPressed(Keys.RIGHT) || (Gdx.input.
isTouched() && mouseX > width * 0.75f)) {
    direction.x = 1;
}

if (Gdx.input.isKeyPressed(Keys.UP) || (Gdx.input.isTouched() &&
mouseY < height * 0.25f)) {
    direction.y = 1;
}
else if (Gdx.input.isKeyPressed(Keys.DOWN) || (Gdx.input.
isTouched() && mouseY > height * 0.75f)) {
    direction.y = -1;
}
```

```
direction.nor().scl(CAMERA_SPEED * Gdx.graphics.getDeltaTime());

camera.position.x += direction.x;
camera.position.y += direction.y;
```

7. We do not want the user to be able to scroll past the map limits, so we need to clamp the camera position accordingly. We can access the array of layers with `getLayers()` and then query the dimensions in tiles and size of each tile rather easily. The layer with index `0` corresponds to the bottom layer (background in our case):

```
TiledMapTileLayer layer = (TiledMapTileLayer)map.getLayers().
get(0);

float cameraMinX = viewport.getWorldWidth() * 0.5f;
float cameraMinY = viewport.getWorldHeight() * 0.5f;
float cameraMaxX = layer.getWidth() * layer.getTileWidth() -
cameraMinX;
float cameraMaxY = layer.getHeight() * layer.getTileHeight() -
cameraMinY;

camera.position.x = MathUtils.clamp(camera.position.x, cameraMinX,
cameraMaxX);
camera.position.y= MathUtils.clamp(camera.position.y, cameraMinY,
cameraMaxY);

camera.update();
```

That is all! Now you can work with Tiled maps from Libgdx. The following screenshot shows what you should be seeing on your screen. Magic!

You may observe some rendering artifacts when moving around. These are produced by imprecisions when dealing with the limits of each region in the atlas. Sometimes, showing a region might cause the edge of a neighboring region to appear. In order to solve the issue, you need to generate a tileset with **Edge padding**, as we have seen in the *More effective rendering with regions and atlases* recipe in *Chapter 2, Working with 2D Graphics*.

It is possible to load Tiled maps asynchronously with `AssetManager`. Please refer to *Chapter 7, Asset Management*, for more information on the subject:

```
assetManager.setLoader(TiledMap.class, new TmxMapLoader(new
InternalFileHandleResolver());
assetManager.load("data/maps/tiled.tmx", TiledMap.class);
...
map = assetManager.get("data/maps/tiled.tmx", TiledMap.class);
```

How it works...

The Libgdx 2D maps API is format-agnostic. Editor-specific systems can reuse and extend the classes provided by the API. Take a look at the base model in the following UML diagram:

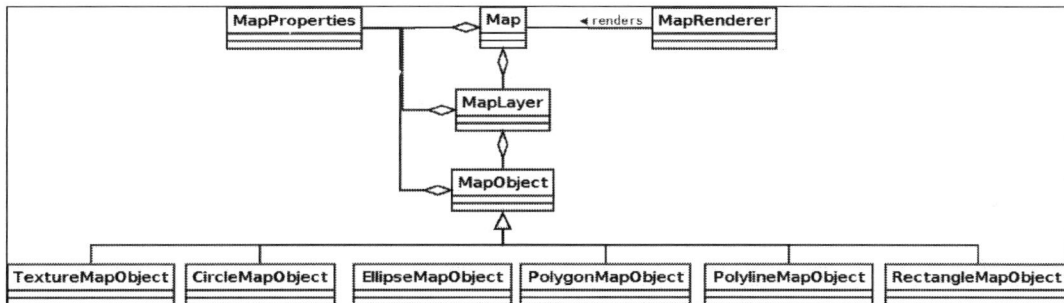

Here is a brief description of each class:

- `MapRenderer`: This is the base to render `Map` objects
- `Map`: This is the main class that contains a set of layers and properties
- `MapProperties`: This is a collection of key-value pairs to allow setting on different objects
- `MapLayer`: This is a collection of objects
- `MapObject`: This base map object has a name, opacity, visibility, and a collection of properties

Do not worry about all these classes just yet. Layers, objects, and properties will be covered in the next recipe. The `com.badlogic.gdx.maps.tiled` Libgdx package located at `http://libgdx.badlogicgames.com/nightlies/docs/api/com/badlogic/gdx/maps/tiled/package-frame.html` contains all the specialized classes to handle Tiled maps.

Tiled exports maps to `.tmx` files, but they are nothing more than easily readable plain old XML. As you can see, it contains all the information about tile sizes, dimensions, and layers. To save up space, layer data is represented in **Base64**, which the loader handles effortlessly:

```
<map version="1.0" orientation="orthogonal" width="30" height="12"
tilewidth="21" tileheight="21">
 <tileset firstgid="1" name="tileset" tilewidth="21" tileheight="21"
spacing="2" margin="2">
   <image source="tileset.png" trans="5e81a2" width="692"
height="692"/>
 </tileset>
 <tileset firstgid="901" name="backgrounds" tilewidth="21"
tileheight="21">
   <image source="backgrounds.png" trans="5e81a2" width="231"
height="189"/>
 </tileset>
 <layer name="background" width="30" height="12">
  <data encoding="base64">...</data>
 </layer>
 ...
</map>
```

> To change the layer format in Tiled, click on **Map** and then on **Map Properties** and expand the list. You can pick from XML, CSV, as well as Base 64, both compressed and uncompressed. Base 64 encoding is good because it considerably reduces the size of the file but it makes it less readable, so it is up to you to decide. Libgdx supports Base 64 and XML.

The `OrthogonalTiledMapRenderer` class is so awesome; you only need to supply the camera and it will handle everything else. Moreover, it is also really efficient as it will cull away tiles that wouldn't end up on the screen. Naturally, you still need to take a couple of details into consideration:

▶ Do not go too crazy with the number of layers; the renderer does not perform any kind of occlusion culling, and will have to render all the layers bottom to top

▶ You can use multiple tilesets but only use one texture per layer; otherwise, the render will cause costly texture switches on the GPU

There's more...

Although we truly believe Tiled is a fantastic piece of software that will meet the need of the vast majority of 2D game developers, it just might not be what you feel comfortable with. Luckily enough, Libgdx comes with built-in support for an alternative: tIDE Tile Map Editor, an open source Windows-only solution. Feel free to take a look at `http://tide.codeplex.com/`.

Libgdx also provides multiple renderers for Tiled maps; each one of them presents different features, advantages, and disadvantages. It is really up to you to decide which one to go for. They are as follows:

- `HexagonalTiledMapRenderer`: This is the render you should be using when working with hexagonal maps.

- `IsometricTiledMapRenderer`: This is ideal for regular isometric maps.

- `IsometricStaggeredTiledMapRenderer`: This is the appropriate solution when rendering staggered Tiled maps.

- `OrthoCachedTiledMapRenderer`: This is the alternative renderer for orthogonal maps. It uses a cached texture to avoid rendering large amounts of tiles every frame. However, it is very inefficient if the tiles change often as the cache needs to be rebuilt.

Adding and querying map metadata

You are now able to create, load, and render maps with Tiled and Libgdx. However, we have only been capable of showing backgrounds and little more. What about dynamic elements such as enemies, items, the player starting position, the level exit, and so on?

When designing a level, it is very typical to add special objects to represent events or dynamic entities. Once the level is loaded, the game code will have to query the map to retrieve this metadata and populate the world with the aforementioned special entities.

In this adventure around metadata land, you will learn how to add objects and set properties on them as well as load them later from a Libgdx game.

Getting ready

For this recipe, you will also need the Tiled editor and the following two tilesets: `data/maps/tileset.png` and `data/maps/backgrounds.png`. The `data/maps/tiled.tmx` map file will be needed as well. We will also use the `data/maps/sprites.atlas` file and the `data/music/song_1.mp3` audio file.

Additionally, we will work with the `samples` projects as usual.

How to do it...

Once again, we are going to split the process in two: Tiled editor and Java code.

Object layers and properties in Tiled

Run the Tiled editor and follow these steps:

1. To make things easier, click on **File | Open**, and select `data/maps/tiled.tmx`.

2. Remove the coins, key, and chest from the foreground layer, and we're going to replace them with objects.

3. Click on the new layer icon in the **Layers** panel and select **Add Object Layer**. Do this twice and name them `objects` and `physics` respectively.

4. We are going to use objects to define the player starting position, enemies, items and trigger areas. Triggers are a mechanism to fire events when the player enters their area of effect: exit, checkpoints, cinematic sequences. Use the **Insert Rectangle** button to place these elements.

5. Since we need to retrieve these objects later, it is necessary to give them meaningful names. To do so, right-click on them, select **Object Properties** and fill in the **Name** field:

   - Player starting position: `player`

   - Items: `item.type`, for example, `item.coin` or `item.key`

   - Enemies: `enemy`

   - Triggers: `trigger.name`, for example, `trigger.exit`

6. Almost any element has a set of properties in Tiled that can be set from the editor and retrieved at a later date from the game. This is useful to further configure our levels and entities. Perform the following steps:

   - To add map properties, click on **Map** and then on **Map Properties**. In this case, we will add a `music` property pointing to the `data/music/song_1.mp3` file. The game will read this information and play the song after loading the level.

   - To add layer properties, right-click on the layer and select **Layer Properties**.

   - To add tileset properties, click on the **Tileset Properties** button in the **Tileset** panel.

   - To add tile-specific properties, right-click on the tile and select **Tile Properties**.

   - Finally, for objects you have to right-click on it and select **Object Properties**.

7. We are not going to process the `physics` layer In code just yet but you can experiment with the possibilities of the approach. Try to add shapes to model the solid areas of the level.

8. When you are done, click on **File**, then on **Save As** and then select `data/maps/tiled-objects.tmx`.

This is how your Tiled editor should look at this point:

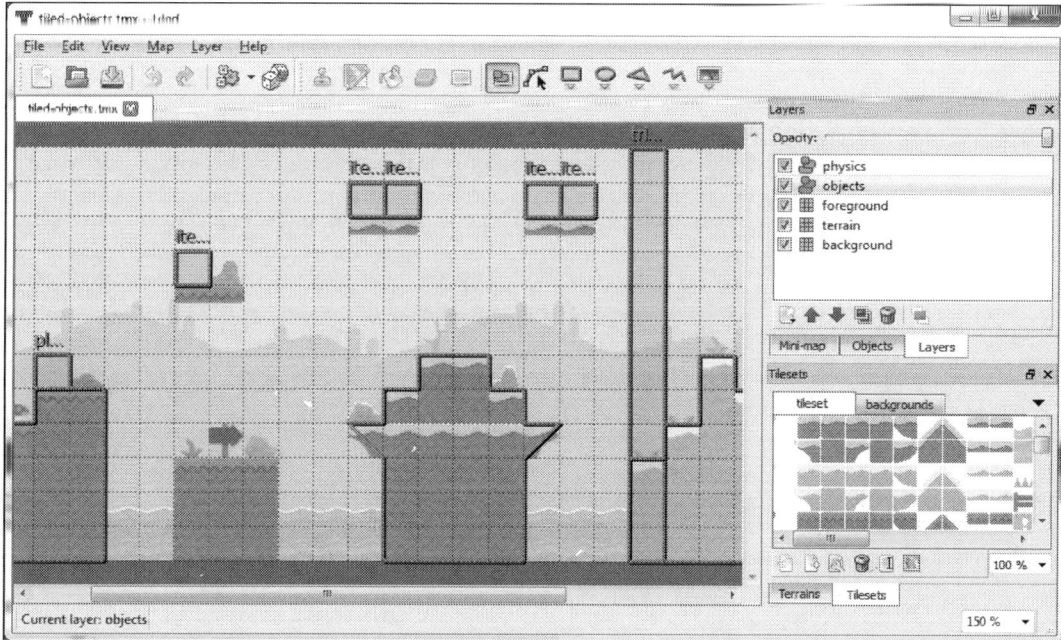

Querying map metadata from Libgdx

Allow us to direct your attention towards the `TiledMapObjectsSample.java` file. Here we load and render the `data/maps/tiled-objects.tmx` file very much like in the previous recipe. Additionally, we place the player, enemy, and items sprites as well as show the position and dimensions of triggers as per the map's objects. Finally, we also play the audio file in the map's properties.

This way you will see how easy it is to retrieve this information from a map object.

> We wanted to keep things simple in this recipe, but be aware that in a real-life situation, more complex entities would have been used rather than plain sprites. For example, we could have designed `Player`, `Enemy`, `Item`, and `Trigger` classes.

The `TiledMapObjectsSample` class simply adds code to `TiledMapSample`. Let's begin with some new members, arrays of sprites for the enemies, items and triggers, the player, a texture atlas, and a `Music` instance:

```
private Array<Sprite> enemies = new Array<Sprite>();
private Array<Sprite> items = new Array<Sprite>();
private Array<Sprite> triggers = new Array<Sprite>();
private Sprite player;
private TextureAtlas atlas;
private Music song;
```

Our `create()` method calls a `private processMapMetadata()` function, responsible for querying all the information from the level. We start off by retrieving the music property. Every object that has a set of properties (see the UML diagram in the previous recipe) will offer a `getProperties()` method. The `get()` method takes the property key, an optional default value, and the class of the value referenced by the key. The level song will serve as an example:

```
String songPath = map.getProperties().get("music", String.class);
song = Gdx.audio.newMusic(Gdx.files.internal(songPath));
song.setLooping(true);
song.play();
```

See the complete `MapProperties` class reference at `http://libgdx.badlogicgames.com/nightlies/docs/api/com/badlogic/gdx/maps/MapProperties.html` for more details and also how to add, remove, or modify the existing properties.

From a map, we can get a `MapLayers` object using `getLayers()` and then get individual layers by index or name with `get()`. We can even get all the layers of a given class with the `getByType()` method passing in the desired class. It is possible to iterate over all the layers using `iterator()` or a combination of `getCount()` and `get()`. You can find the full documentation at `http://libgdx.badlogicgames.com/nightlies/docs/api/com/badlogic/gdx/maps/MapLayers.html`.

Once we have a layer, we can retrieve its name, properties, opacity, visibility, and collection of objects. You can learn more about `MapLayer` at `http://libgdx.badlogicgames.com/nightlies/docs/api/com/badlogic/gdx/maps/MapLayer.html`

In our case, we want to get the list of objects contained in the `objects` layer:

```
MapObjects objects = map.getLayers().get("objects").getObjects();
```

The next step is to iterate over all the objects in the layer. Since our naming convention involved using . to separate between entity type and subtype (for example, item and coin), we need to split the name string. All our objects were rectangles, so we cast them to `RectangleMapObject` and retrieve the internal rectangle. Be careful because this code will crash if you bump into a nonrectangular object. Refer to the objects' documentation at `http://libgdx.badlogicgames.com/nightlies/docs/api/com/badlogic/gdx/maps/objects/package-frame.html` for more information.

Depending on the object name, we will create a sprite with a different region and add it to its corresponding collection. Note that we place the sprite at the (x, y) coordinates pointed by the object:

```
for (MapObject object : objects) {
    String name = object.getName();
    String[] parts = name.split("[.]");
    RectangleMapObject rectangleObject = (RectangleMapObject)object;
    Rectangle rectangle = rectangleObject.getRectangle();

    if (name.equals("enemy")) {
        Sprite enemy = new Sprite(atlas.findRegion("enemy"));
        enemy.setPosition(rectangle.x, rectangle.y);
        enemies.add(enemy);
    }
    else if (name.equals("player")) {
        player = new Sprite(atlas.findRegion("player"));
        player.setPosition(rectangle.x, rectangle.y);
    }
    else if (parts.length > 1 && parts[0].equals("item")) {
        Sprite item = new Sprite(atlas.findRegion(parts[1]));
        item.setPosition(rectangle.x, rectangle.y);
        items.add(item);
    }
    else if (parts.length > 0 && parts[0].equals("trigger")) {
        Sprite trigger = new Sprite(atlas.findRegion("pixel"));
        trigger.setColor(1.0f, 1.0f, 1.0f, 0.5f);
        trigger.setScale(rectangle.width, rectangle.height);
        trigger.setPosition(rectangle.x - rectangle.width * 0.5f,
rectangle.y + rectangle.height * 0.5f);
        triggers.add(trigger);
    }
}
```

Fantastic! Now you are able to define your game entities inside an editor and instantiate them at run time. It will be extremely easy to change their location, properties, and so on.

How it works...

Layers and properties are also stored as XML inside the map.tmx file. Object layers are represented by the `objectgroup` tag, while rectangles use the `object` tag, as shown in the following code snippet:

```
<objectgroup name="objects" width="30" height="12">
    <object name="player" x="63" y="126" width="21" height="21"/>
    <object name="item.chest" x="147" y="63" width="21" height="21"/>
    ...
</objectgroup>
```

Polylines are very useful to represent collision areas; they are represented by a combination of the `object` and `polyline` tags:

```
<object x="0" y="168">
    <polyline points="0,0 63,0 63,-21 105,-21 105,84 0,84 0,0"/>
</object>
```

When an element has set properties, it will contain a `properties` tag with a list of `property` entries:

```
<properties>
    <property name="music" value="data/music/song_1.mp3"/>
</properties>
```

Simple!

There's more...

As we mentioned before, in a real-life situation, we would like to spawn game entities by name. Imagine some sort of game-specific `IEntityFactory` interface implementation. A `create()` method would take the entity archetype name, its position in the world, and maybe a collection of properties. The factory would then instantiate an entity of the desired archetype at the right position with the appropriate configuration.

Using it would be quite comfortable; just iterate over your entities layer in the level and call the `create()` method for each object you find:

```
public interface IEntityFactory
{
    public Entity create(String name, Vector2 position, Properties
    properties);
}
```

Factory is a well-known design pattern. Read more about it at `http://en.wikipedia.org/w/index.php?title=Factory_method_pattern&oldid=608667321`.

Furthermore, you could have an `entities.json` file with the serialized prototype of all the entities in your game. Your `EntityFactory` interface would read this file and keep an instance of each type of entity and clone the corresponding one every time `create()` is called. This would make your entity tweaking completely data-driven.

At this point, you should have enough maps knowledge to achieve great things but surely you want more! Carry on reading to find out about the following recipes:

- The *Developing your own map loaders and renderers* recipe
- The *Building a physics world from level data* recipe in *Chapter 10*, *Rigid Body Physics with Box2D*, to integrate your levels with Box2D

Developing your own map loaders and renderers

What if Tiled or any of the other supported editors do not suit your needs? After all, they are all based on tiles and not all games use the same approach for their levels. Take the popular game *Braid*, for example, where levels are made of nonsquare images. You might want to use a different tool to edit levels or even roll out your own editor!

Luckily enough, Libgdx's 2D maps API is fully extensible. That is the beauty of this framework: simple, clean, and extensible. It does not impose a single way of doing things.

Throughout this recipe, you will learn how to easily add full support for bespoke level formats.

Getting ready

This recipe does not come with a code sample, so you do not need to prepare anything special before carrying on. Nevertheless, it is highly advisable that you understand all the concepts previously explained in this chapter.

How to do it...

Let's say you want to use an editor that is currently not supported by Libgdx. You will have to write your own `MapLoader` and `MapRenderer` implementations.

Let's cover level loading now. Pay attention to the features your editor supports and how the engine internal works. Once that is clear, ask yourself the following question: can I support everything I need with the built-in map classes?

The documentation for the `maps` package in Libgdx can be found by visiting `http://libgdx.badlogicgames.com/nightlies/docs/api/com/badlogic/gdx/maps/package-frame.html`.

If the answer is no, then you need to extend them and add new ones when necessary.

Now, imagine we have a custom-level editor we want to support in our Libgdx game. We create a `CustomMap` class that extends `Map`. You can add whatever `Map` is missing to support all the features your editor offers:

```
public class CustomMap extends Map {
    ...
}
```

We need a `CustomMapLoader` class that can give us `CustomMap` instances from `FileHandle`. It would also be nice to support `AssetLoader` for nice asynchrony and reference counting, so we will make it extend the `AssynchronousAssetLoader` class. For more details about asset handling, please refer to *Chapter 7, Asset Management*:

```
public class CustomMapLoader extends AsynchronousAssetLoader<CustomMap, CustomMapLoader.Parameter> {

public static class Parameter extends AssetLoaderParameters<CustomMap> {
...
    }

    public CustomMapLoader(FileHandleResolver resolver) {
        super(resolver);
    }

    public CustomMap load (String fileName, Gleed2DMapLoader.Parameters parameters) {
        ...
    }

    @Override
    public void loadAsync(AssetManager manager, String fileName, FileHandle file, Parameters parameter) {
        ...
    }

    @Override
    public CustomMap loadSync(AssetManager manager, String fileName, FileHandle file, Parameters parameter) {
        ...
    }

    @Override
    public Array<AssetDescriptor> getDependencies(String fileName, FileHandle file, Parameters parameter) {
        ...
    }
}
```

Finally, we need to tell our AssetManager class that CustomMapLoader is the one responsible for dealing with CustomMap objects:

```
assetManager.setLoader(CustomMap.class, new CustomMapLoader(new
InternalFileHandle));
```

Obviously, the actual loading of the level will depend on the format you are dealing with. Do not fear to dive into other Libgdx loaders at `https://github.com/libgdx/libgdx/blob/master/gdx/src/com/badlogic/gdx/maps/tiled/TmxMapLoader.java` to learn from them.

Great! You have your fantastic level loader and you are wondering how to get it on the screen. Add a CustomMapRenderer class that implements the MapRenderer interface.

The setView() method is typically used to set the SpriteBatch projection matrix. This will determine which parts of the map are going to be visible on the screen. It has two versions: one takes a camera while the other takes a projection matrix and the view bounds.

Override the render() method to draw all the visible layers by iterating through all their entities. It can take an optional array of layer indices that will determine the layers that will be rendered as well as the order in which that will happen. The code is as follows:

```
public class CustomMapRenderer implements MapRenderer {

    public CustomMapRenderer(CustomMap map) {
        ...
    }

    @Override
    public void setView(OrthographicCamera camera) {
        ...
    }

    @Override
    public void setView(Matrix4 projectionMatrix, float viewboundsX,
    float viewboundsY, float viewboundsWidth, float viewboundsHeight) {
        ...
    }

    @Override
    public void render() {
        ...
    }

    @Override
    public void render(int[] layers) {
        ...
    }
}
```

Keep in mind that you will have to be careful in order to make rendering fast enough. Something you should always try to achieve is to only render what is on screen. Do not try to draw all the objects in every layer every single frame, for that is absolute madness! Study other renderers at `https://github.com/libgdx/libgdx/blob/master/gdx/src/com/badlogic/gdx/maps/tiled/renderers/OrthogonalTiledMapRenderer.java` to see how they are implemented.

Brilliant! You just added full support to a new level format to Libgdx. Consider contributing back to the community!

There's more...

Here are a few options you might want to consider:

- **Gleed2D**: This is the open source Windows-only nontiled-based editor. The project is no longer active but you might make good use of it. The editor supports the standard lot: layers, properties, textures, and shapes. Levels are saved in an easy-to-read XML format. It is available at `http://gleed2d.codeplex.com/`.

- **Inkscape**: This is the open source cross-platform vector graphics editor. Besides the classic geometric shapes, you can import your own bitmaps as well. Additionally, it supports layering. Inkscape exports to SVG, which is nothing more than plain old XML. Be careful because the schema is not easy to handle. It is available at `http://www.inkscape.org`.

- **Ogmo**: This is the open source Windows-only tiled-based editor. It also saves its levels as XML. It is available at `http://www.ogmoeditor.com`.

10

Rigid Body Physics with Box2D

In this chapter, we will cover the following recipes:

- ▶ Introducing Box2D
- ▶ Introducing more complex shapes
- ▶ Introducing joints
- ▶ Real-life joints example – bike simulator
- ▶ Reacting to collisions
- ▶ Sensors and collision filtering
- ▶ Querying the world
- ▶ Building a physics world from level data
- ▶ Implementing a deferred raycaster
- ▶ The fixed timestep approach

Introduction

The path to reach this chapter has been long. Coding sessions and headaches have turned you into a master of the Libgdx subsystems, but there is still one important topic that resists your reign: Box2D physics.

Do not be afraid, brave knight, because as a man of action, this chapter brings you a lot of practical content to dominate and just the necessary theoretical physics concepts to rise you to develop the ultimate game.

Samples will be very interactive and enjoyable. Tweaking and adapting their code for your own purposes can be very useful for learning.

Introducing Box2D

Box2D is a physics engine that simulates realistic physical interactions between the bodies in your scene and allows you to interact with the objects by applying forces too. It was originally written in C++, but the Libgdx team made a thin Java wrapper which makes calls to the underlying C++ code.

Box2D's strengths have not gone unnoticed and hence it has a favorable reputation within the industry. Important physics-based games such as *Angry Birds* make use of this framework. Its author is Erin Catto who has worked in projects as renowned as *Diablo 3*.

This recipe is necessary to avoid putting the cart before the horse, so foundations are laid and we can focus on useful real-life physics situations along with the upcoming recipes.

Getting ready

You must add Box2D to your project as an extension in order to make use of its API. The process is described in the *Updating and managing project dependencies* recipe from *Chapter 1, Diving into Libgdx*. In your root folder where your projects are contained, make sure you add the dependencies to the `build.gradle` file.

As usual, remember that you will need to import the sample projects into your Eclipse workspace.

How to do it...

To whet your appetite, we will implement a really simple physics simulation where boxes and balls fall from the cursor/touch location to the ground. At the end of this recipe, do not forget to run and view the source code of the `Box2DSimpleSample.java` file. I recommend that you become familiar with this recipe before going ahead in this chapter because the basics will be omitted in the upcoming recipes for space and simplicity reasons.

The next screenshot introduces some basic concepts that you need to know through a typical scene from an adventure game:

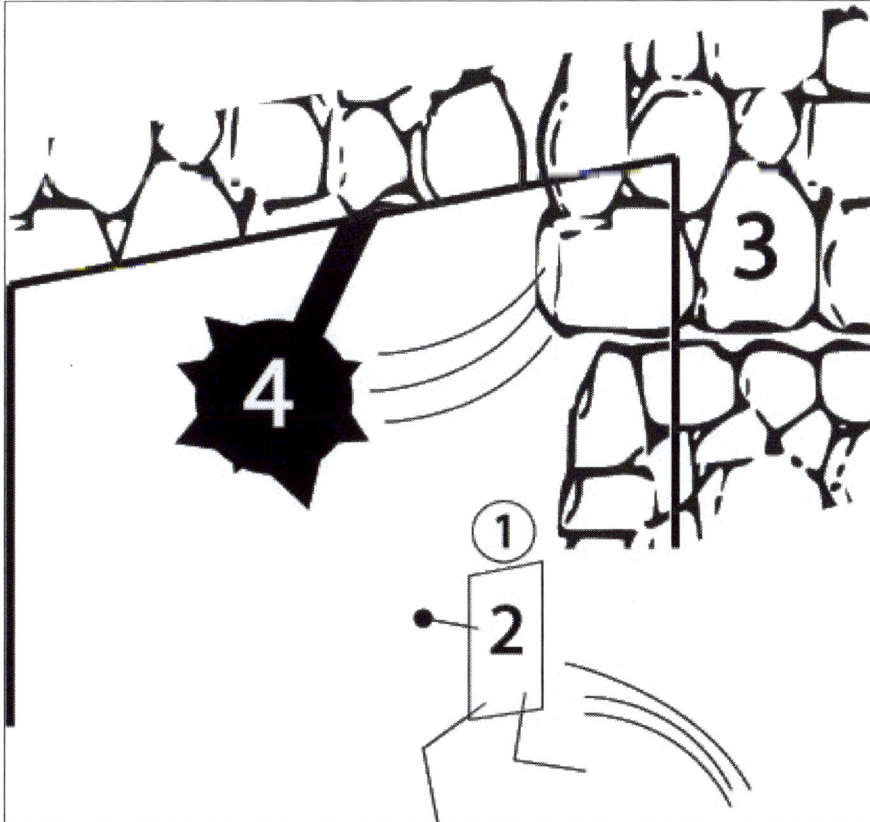

The intrepid hero's dynamic body is in the form of two fixtures. The first of them (**1**) has a circular shape while the second (**2**) is rectangular. The stone wall (**3**) is a static body and the mace (**4**) is implemented by constraining two bodies (the stick and the sharp sphere) with a joint. However, it is also interesting to read the *How it works...* section of this recipe in order to find a proper definition for each of these concepts.

We typically remember that we use the metric system. Consequently, we should take it into account for our game world.

1. To start with, let's define the visible width and height of the world:

```
private static final float SCENE_WIDTH = 12.8f; // 13 metres
    wide
private static final float SCENE_HEIGHT = 7.2f; // 7 metres
    high
```

2. As a common factor for this chapter, declare the Box2D `World` class and the `Box2DDebugRenderer`, which is in charge of drawing lines to represent your fixtures and joints:

```
World world;
Box2DDebugRenderer debugRenderer;
```

3. We will generate a dynamic body, either a ball or a box, on every mouse click, so we will cache shapes, fixture properties, and the final body definition. This information about fixtures and bodies is specified through a `BodyDef` or a `FixtureDef` object, respectively:

```
BodyDef defaultDynamicBodyDef;

// Box
FixtureDef boxFixtureDef;
PolygonShape square;

// Ball
CircleShape circle;
FixtureDef circleFixtureDef;
```

4. The current step and the next six steps take place in the `create()` method, so after instantiating the classic viewport, we translate the camera to the initial top-right corner:

```
// Center camera to get (0,0) as the origin of the Box2D world
viewport.update(WORLD_WIDTH, WORLD_HEIGHT, true);
```

5. The mandatory condition is to instantiate the physics world, setting its gravity and flag to indicate whether Box2D bodies are allowed to sleep and consequently are not simulated:

```
world = new World(new Vector2(0,-9.8f), true);
```

6. Instantiate `Box2DDebugRenderer` too as follows:

```
debugRenderer = new Box2DDebugRenderer();
```

> `Box2DDebugRenderer` is an awesome tool to display the desired debug information about physics objects. The existing options to draw are active bodies, inactive bodies, **Axis-aligned bounding box** (**AABB**), velocities, and contact points between two shapes and joints.
>
> **AABB** is the minimum axis-aligned square that contains all the shapes from a body.

7. Set the common body definition for the falling objects:

```
defaultDynamicBodyDef = new BodyDef();
defaultDynamicBodyDef.type = BodyType.DynamicBody;
```

8. Cache the shape and the physical properties of the boxes:

```
// Shape for boxes
square = new PolygonShape();
// 1 meter-sided square (0.5f is half-width/height)
square.setAsBox(0.5f, 0.5f);

// Fixture definition for boxes
boxFixtureDef = new FixtureDef();
boxFixtureDef.shape = square;
boxFixtureDef.density = 0.8f;
boxFixtureDef.friction = 0.8f;
boxFixtureDef.restitution = 0.15f;
```

9. Repeat the last step for the balls:

```
// Shape for circles
circle = new CircleShape();
// 0.5 metres for radius
circle.setRadius(0.5f);

// Fixture definition for our shapes
circleFixtureDef = new FixtureDef();
circleFixtureDef.shape = circle;
circleFixtureDef.density = 0.5f;
circleFixtureDef.friction = 0.4f;
circleFixtureDef.restitution = 0.6f;
```

10. Do not forget to listen for user clicks:

```
Gdx.input.setInputProcessor(this);
```

Now, override the touchDown method as explained in *Chapter 4, Detecting User Input*. Its mission will be to alternate between body creation function calls depending on a Boolean variable named buildmode. It is important to point out that touch coordinates have their origin in the upper-left corner and they grow as they advance to the lower-right corner. It is necessary to unproject touch coordinates to transform them into world units:

```
@Override
public boolean touchDown (int screenX, int screenY, int pointer,
int button) {
  if (button == Input.Buttons.LEFT) {
    //Translate screen coordinates into world units
```

```
      viewport.getCamera().unproject(point.set(screenX,
        screenY, 0));
      if(boxMode)
        createSquare(point.x, point.y);
      else // Ball mode
        createCircle(point.x, point.y);
      boxMode = !boxMode;
      return true;
    }
  return false;
}
```

11. I bet you want to know the content of those `create` functions. The next code snippet shows the box creation. For balls, simply create the fixture with the previously defined `circleFixtureDef`:

```
private void createSquare(float x, float y) {
    defaultDynamicBodyDef.position.set(x,y);

    Body body = world.createBody(defaultDynamicBodyDef);

    body.createFixture(boxFixtureDef);
}
```

> Note that the ground is a particular type of static body box whose `create` function will be omitted to avoid repeating code. However, it must be written to prevent boxes and balls from falling infinitely.

12. For every frame, we will update our physics world in a certain amount of time, commonly known as a timestep. This is a delicate matter that will be discussed in the final recipe of this chapter. For now, let's advance by 1/60 seconds on every iteration of the `render()` method. The other two parameters in the following method refer to velocity iterations and position iterations respectively. The higher they are, the most realistic simulation you will get in exchange for a performance cost:

```
world.step(1/60f, 6, 2);
```

> Box2D caps the maximum speed of bodies to n*2, where timestep is 1/n. In this way, the limit for the previous code is 120 meters per second (or 432 kilometers per hour) as 60 * 2 = 120. As you can see, it is a very high value, and it is necessary to have such a limit in order to avoid numerical problems.

13. Ask the `Box2DDebugRenderer` to draw the existing bodies using the matrix projection that has been already extracted from our viewport.

```
debugRenderer.render(world, viewport.getCamera().combined);
```

14. Last but not least, free up the memory:

```
public void dispose() {
  batch.dispose();
  square.dispose();
  circle.dispose();
  world.dispose();
}
```

15. After some clicks or touches, you will get something like this:

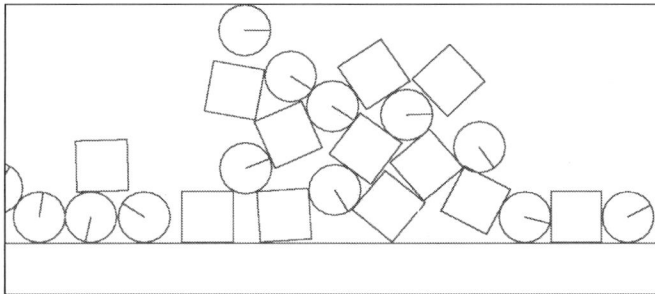

How it works...

As you can see, building a realistic physics environment is quite easy, but in order to understand the bowels of the current and upcoming demos, make sure you get fluent with the following Box2D base concepts:

- **Fixture**: This is a container that holds a shape, custom user data, physics properties such as density, friction, and restitution, and also whether it will physically react to collisions. Their mass (how heavy it is) is calculated by multiplying its area by its density.

  - **Density**: This is the amount of mass per unit volume. The possible value ranges from zero to any positive number. For instance, air is less dense than sand.

> Physically, the existence of a zero mass body is impossible but Box2D internally stores it in that way to simulate objects that cannot be moved. Paradoxically, those objects would have infinite mass in real life.
>
> Others bodies in the scene will still interact with zero mass bodies.

> ❑ **Friction**: This allows bodies to slide over other bodies when colliding. The minimal value is 0, which means no friction, and a positive value indicates friction; the higher it is, the more the friction will be.

> ❑ **Restitution**: This property will make your body able to bounce. The value 0 means no bounce, while 1 will keep the body bouncing forever with the same height. Higher values get higher height.

- ▶ **Bodies**: These are the main actors in the physics play; they can carry zero or more fixtures that will never collide between themselves. A body's total mass is the sum of all its fixtures. The way in which a body interacts with its environment directly depends on its type:

> ❑ **Static body**: These are nonmoving objects internally treated as zero mass bodies.

> ❑ **Kinematic body**: Opposite to the previous one, a kinematic body moves under simulation according to its velocity but it is not affected by forces. However, it is still stored as a zero mass body. In addition, it will not collide with other kinematic or static bodies.
>
> Because of these characteristics, it is ideal for being manually moved by the user.

> ❑ **Dynamic body**: It will interact with its entire environment, colliding with any other type of body and its velocity will be modified by forces.

- ▶ **Joints**: They are intended to constrain bodies to the world or to each other. Some typical usages are vehicles, ropes, chains, or rag dolls.

- ▶ **World**: All the simulated bodies will live in it, interacting between themselves just as defined and updating their physical properties according to a certain amount of time. The `World` class comes with tools to synchronously query as well as create and destroy bodies.

There's more...

The Box2D API for bodies this goes beyond and gives you many more possibilities to get your desired behavior.

Some bodies, such us dead ones, should not interact in certain moments of the simulation. This is very simple to set:

```
body.setActive(false);
```

When we instantiate our `World` class, we could specify whether we want to allow Box2D to sleep instead of simulating nonmoving bodies, which gives us a performance gain. Now, you can also decide this for each individual body as follows:

```
bodyDef.allowSleep = true;
```

If the body in question receives a collision from another body, the sleeping one will change its status and react with the expected behavior. Alternatively, you can force the body to wake up manually:

```
body.setAwake(true);
```

Other interesting properties are `linearVelocity` and `angularVelocity`, which allow you to change the uniform speed of a body for each axis or its angular displacement respectively. The pack also comes with `linearDamping` and `AngularDamping` to reduce the effect of the first two attributes. In other words, damping represents how much velocity will be lost over time. It can be a good way to fake air resistance or a body moving through water.

```
body.setLinearVelocity(20f, 0f);
body.setLinearDamping(.5f);
```

Position and rotation can also be explicitly set with `position` and `angle` properties. Rotation can even be fixed:

```
bodyDef.position.set(4f,2.4f);
bodyDef.angle = 45 * MathUtils.degreesToRadians;
bodyDef.fixedRotation = true;
```

Sometimes, the velocity of a body is so high that collisions are not processed, commonly known as tunneling, just like it happens in the following situation where the bullet does not collide with the wall image:

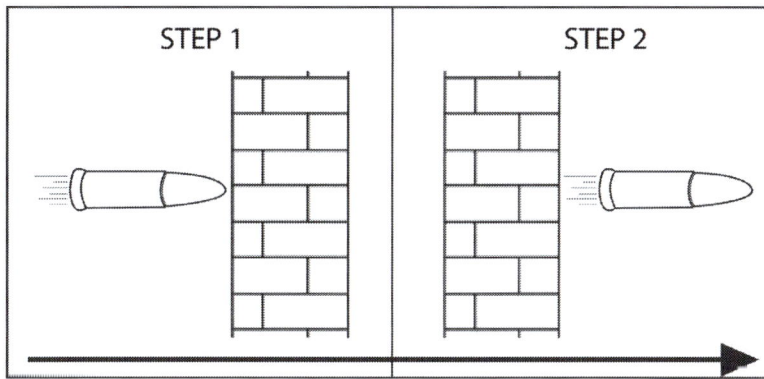

Being aware of the extra CPU usage, you can set the following flag to get continuous collision detection:

```
bodyDef.bullet = true;
```

Finally, you can scale the effect of gravity for some particular body as follows:

```
bodyDef.gravityScale = .5f;
```

▸ The *Introducing more complex shapes* recipe

Introducing more complex shapes

Basic shapes work great when you do not need high precision to detect collisions but sometimes you will require an extra level of detail where, for instance, your actors' head is a circle and the rest of the body is grouped into a rectangle.

Mixing basic shapes in order to get a more complex one is definitely a powerful tool but there are still some entities that you could not model, such as an empty glass where objects can fall into it.

Be aware that this significant precision improvement has consequences on CPU consumption, so try to keep your body as simple as possible.

Getting ready

To follow this sample, you will need the Box2D physics editor created by Aurelien Ribon, which is downloadable from `https://code.google.com/p/box2d-editor/downloads/list`.

Once you unzip it, simply run the `physics-body-editor.jar` file and the application window will show up.

You will also need the loader Java file, which is within the extracted folder or under the `aurelienribon.bodyeditor` package of the `sample-core` project.

Finally, have on hand the `/data/box2D/glass.png` file and the source code of this recipe, which is stored in the `Box2DComplexShapesSample.java` file. Now, you are ready to go on.

How to do it...

This recipe is split into two parts: the first will illustrate the process of generating encoded JSON files from an image while the second will parse that information and transform it into a precise physics shape for your games.

Generating JSON shape data

Once you have opened the physics editor, feel free to follow this technical roadmap:

1. Select **New Project** within the **Project Configuration** tab.
2. Save it wherever you want with your desired name. You are recommended to add the `.json` extension to maintain consistency with its content.
3. Click on the **New** button within the **Rigid Bodies** tab.

4. Type a name, in our case `glass`, for your new body and select an image, `glass.png`, for this example, whose size is not excessively big. Your application should look similar to the following screenshot:

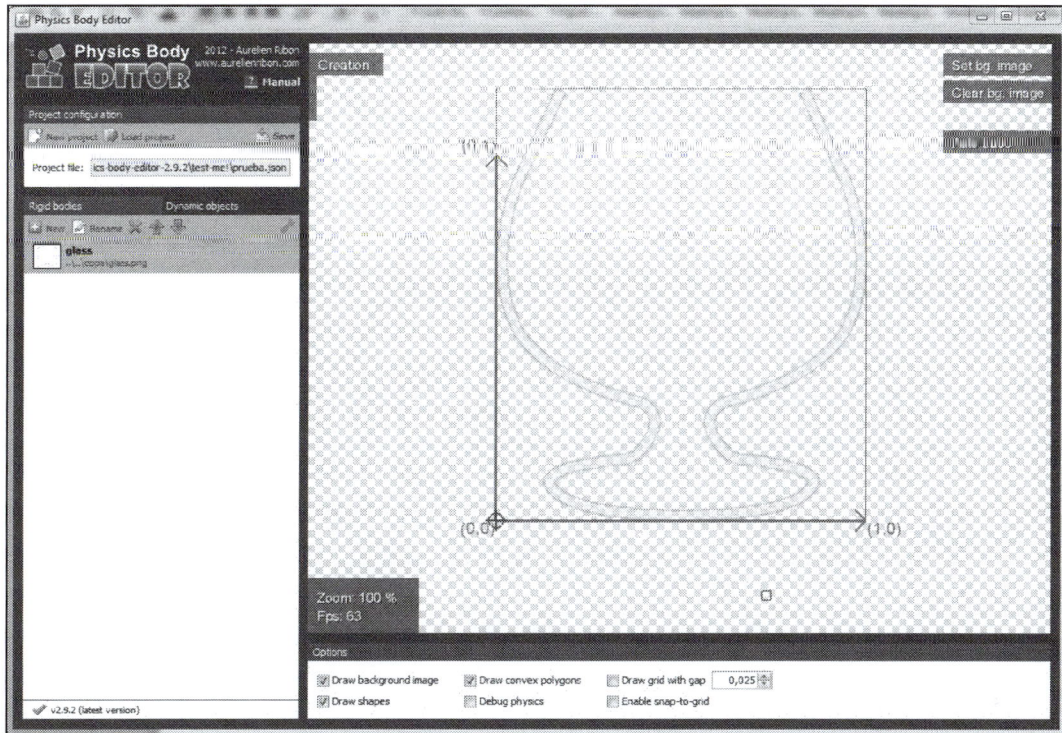

5. The next goal is to link points until the desired shape is formed. The quickest way is to select the **Auto-trace** option and tweak the generated polylines by adding, modifying, or removing points. The final result should be similar to this:

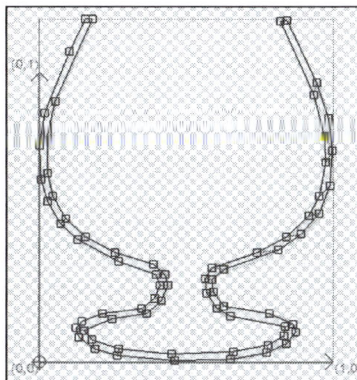

> 📝 Although the usage of the editor is quite intuitive, you can consult the manual at http://www.aurelienribon.com/blog/projects/physics-body-editor/.

6. Click on the **Save** option from the **Project Configuration** tab.

Loading JSON shape data into Libgdx

Once you have the shape data, the following steps will guide you through the simple and automatic process of importing it into your game:

1. Declare the body field and set a default width:

```
private Body glassBody;
private static final float GLASS_WIDTH = 3.0f;
```

2. Start the body creation process by instantiating `BodyEditorLoader`:

```
BodyEditorLoader loader = new BodyEditorLoader
  (Gdx.files.internal("data/box2D/glass.json"));
```

3. Create `BodyDef` and `FixtureDef` as explained in the former recipe.

4. Create the final body and attach the fixture to it:

```
// Create the glass body
glassBody = world.createBody(bd);

// Magic happens here!! Glass fixture is generated
  automatically by the loader.
loader.attachFixture(glassBody, "Glass", fixtureDef,
  GLASS_WIDTH);
```

5. As usual, step the world and render the debug lines.

How it works...

Behind the scenes, the editor generates a JSON file with the following sample structure:

```
{
  "rigidBodies": [
    {
      "name":"Glass",
      "imagePath":"glass.png",
      "origin":{"x":0,"y":0},
      "polygons":[[{"x":0.7387387156486511,
        "y":0.37837833166122437}, ... ]]
```

```
        "dynamicObjects":[]
      }
    ]
  }
}
```

The origin coordinates are represented by the red symbol located at the lower-left corner by default. The real meat of the file is the polygon section because it describes a set of vertices that forms a polygon and the union of them all gives way to the final shape.

As you would have already imagined, the loader parses this file with the purpose of getting the vertices information to generate a `PolygonShape`.

There's more...

The physics body editor is not the only way to generate a nonprimitive shape. The `ChainShape` class allows us to specify a set of vertices to automatically build a closed polygon. These objects are intended to be used as static geometry because self-intersection between instances from this class is not supported:

```
ChainShape chainShape = new ChainShape();

chainShape.createLoop(new Vector2[] {
  new Vector2(.0f, .0f),
  new Vector2(WORLD_WIDTH, .0f),
  new Vector2(WORLD_WIDTH, 1.5f),
  new Vector2(6f, 1.5f),
  new Vector2(3, 5.0f),
  new Vector2(1.5f, 1.5f),
  new Vector2(0, 1.5f),});
```

The `chainShape` variable is now ready to form part of the typical process to create a new body. The previous piece of code would result in something like the following screenshot:

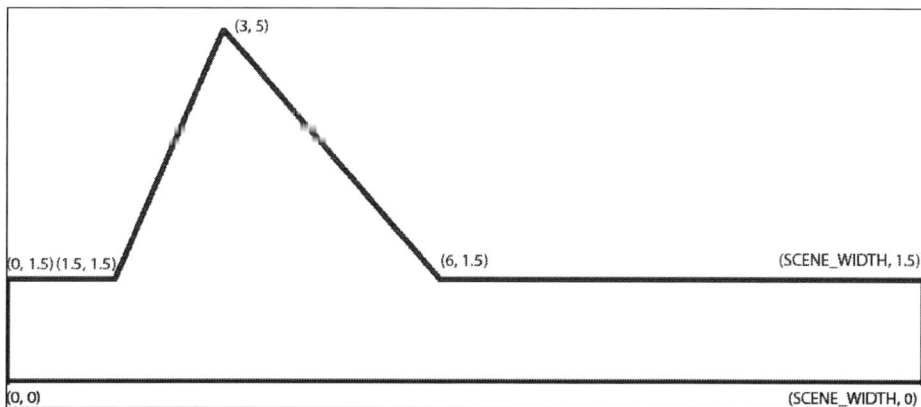

You can also build polygons with the `PolygonShape` class. However, they must be convex, which means that all edges joining two vertices in the interior should not cross any other edge of the polygon. Moreover, it must be a closed polygon of three or more vertices.

That is not all, you can group two fixtures in the same body. Before attaching the shape to `FixtureDef`, make use of the `setPosition(...)` method to set its local displacement from the body's origin. Adding both fixtures is a repetitive action:

```
body.createFixture(boxFixtureDef);
body.createFixture(circleFixtureDef);
```

An image is worth more than a thousand words:

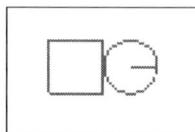

See also

▶   The *Introducing joints* recipe

Introducing joints

Box2D provides you with a powerful set of **joints** to connect bodies together or simply to the world with some particular constraints.

A wise usage of this tool can make the difference in your game with realistic physics behavior such as ragdolls, vehicles, ropes, and doors.

This recipe provides an explanation for each individual joint type. After reading it, you will be able to decide between a wide range of possibilities, which is the most suitable joint to achieve a specific real-life behavior. However, the best way to understand the upcoming explanation is to make a visit to the source code and run it.

Getting ready

Before getting on with it, one should mention that creating a joint follows the same line as creating bodies. We will make use of `JointDef` to construct the joint itself. In addition, you could build it through initialization functions, but they are only intended for prototyping purposes as defining the geometry directly makes the joint behavior more robust.

The `Box2DJointsSample.java` file contains the full source code; feel free to play around with it.

How to do it...

This recipe is not an exception so it needs the usual common steps to create your `SpriteBatch`, `Viewport`, `World`, `Box2DDebugRenderer`, and `groundBody` as explained previously. It will generate the necessary environment upon which this example is executed.

For simplicity and reusability reasons, we will make use of the next functions to easily construct circles and rectangles so we can focus on the important part:

```
Body createSphere(BodyType type, float x, float y, float density,
    float restitution, float friction, float radius)
Body createPolygon(BodyType type, float x, float y, float density,
    float restitution, float friction, float halfwidth, float
    halfheight)
```

Next, you will find a description and a usage example for each of the joint types.

WeldJoint

It is intended to glue two bodies together. A real-life example can take place in a dart game where darts stick to the dartboard.

It has a pretty simple execution:

1. Create two bodies.

2. Define `WeldJointDef`, specifying an anchor point for each body that will join them:

```
WeldJointDef weldJointDef = new WeldJointDef();
weldJointDef.bodyA=smallBall;
weldJointDef.bodyB=bigBall;
weldJointDef.localAnchorA.set(0,0);
weldJointDef.localAnchorB.set(.55f,0);
```

3. Add it to the physics world:

```
world.createJoint(weldJointDef);
```

DistanceJoint

This type of joint ensures that one point from `bodyA` keeps a fixed distance with another point from `bodyB`. It does not restrict any relative rotation.

1. Assuming that both bodies are already created, the process to implement it is quite simple. The key property here is `length`:

```
DistanceJointDef distanceJointDef = new DistanceJointDef();
distanceJointDef.bodyA=smallBall;
distanceJointDef.bodyB=bigBall;
distanceJointDef.length = 2.0f;
distanceJointDef.localAnchorA.set(0,0);
distanceJointDef.localAnchorB.set(0,0);
```

2. Do not forget to add the joint to the Box2D world:

```
world.createJoint(distanceJointDef);
```

RopeJoint

A rope joint works in the same way as the distance joint but instead of having a fixed separation, bodies are distanced for a maximum length, simulating an elastic rope. The steps are:

1. Firstly, create two bodies.

2. Connect them with a RopeJoint, setting a maximum length:

```
RopeJointDef ropeJointDef = new RopeJointDef();
ropeJointDef.bodyA=smallBall;
ropeJointDef.bodyB=bigBall;
ropeJointDef.collideConnected=true;
ropeJointDef.maxLength = 4.0f;
ropeJointDef.localAnchorA.set(0,0);
ropeJointDef.localAnchorB.set(0,0);
```

3. As usual, add it to the world:

```
world.createJoint(ropeJointDef);
```

FrictionJoint

Bodies can have top-down extra resistance (transactional and angular) when a `FrictionJoint` is attached.

We will just place a box in the air under the influence of a `FrictionJoint` so that it will take longer to reach the ground. The process to implement it on your game is simple:

1. Create two bodies, for instance, `squareBody` and `groundBody`.

2. Define `FrictionJointDef` and provide it with the previously created body along with the friction force. Unlike the previous examples and in order to tie up loose ends, we are going to use the `initialize(Body bodyA, Body bodyB, Vector2 anchor, Vector2 axis)` function, but remember it is advised against in the production code:

```
FrictionJointDef frictionJointDef = new FrictionJointDef();
frictionJointDef.initialize(groundBody, squareBody,
  new Vector2(SCENE_WIDTH*.5f,SCENE_HEIGHT*.5f));
frictionJointDef.collideConnected=true;
frictionJointDef.maxForce = 6.0f;
frictionJointDef.maxTorque = -.3f;
```

3. Do not forget to add `FrictionJointDef` to the world:

```
world.createJoint(frictionJointDef);
```

RevoluteJoint

A revolute joint allows you to define an anchor point per body so that they get connected with a single degree of freedom, which is their relative rotation. In the next diagram, you can see a static `bodyA` and a bigger dynamic `bodyB`, which rotates around the first one with the help of a motor force.

> A motor force within the joints context drives the motion of the bodies in question, according to the joint's degrees of freedom.

Please follow these steps to bring the `RevoluteJoint` to your game:

1. The code to implement it begins with the creation of both bodies:

```
Body smallBall = createSphere(BodyType.StaticBody, 0f,
  3.75f, 1f, 1f, 0f, .25f);
Body bigBall = createSphere(BodyType.DynamicBody, 0f,
  3.75f, 1f, 1f, 0f, .5f);
```

2. Then we declare and define `RevoluteJointDef` to connect the existing spheres through the anchor points defined in the upcoming diagram:

```
RevoluteJointDef revoluteJointDef = new RevoluteJointDef();
revoluteJointDef.bodyA=smallBall;
revoluteJointDef.bodyB=bigBall;
revoluteJointDef.localAnchorA.set(0,0);
revoluteJointDef.localAnchorB.set(-2.0f,);
revoluteJointDef.enableMotor=true;
revoluteJointDef.maxMotorTorque=360;
revoluteJointDef.motorSpeed=100*MathUtils.degreesToRadians;
```

3. Finally, add it to the world:

```
world.createJoint(revoluteJointDef);
```

You can also limit its upper and lower angle of rotation with the `upperAngle` and `lowerAngle` properties.

The previous code would result in something like this:

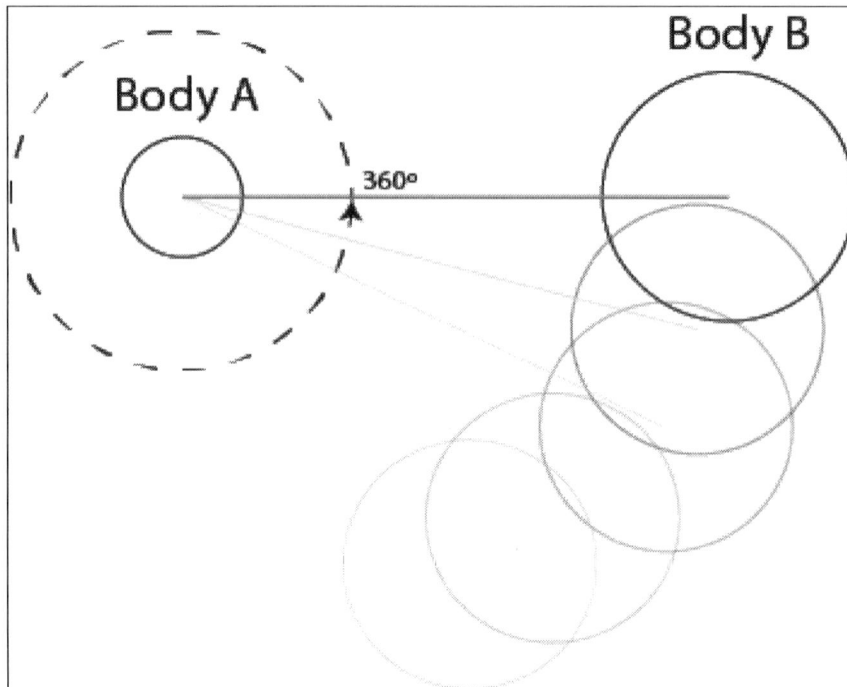

Revolute joints are good choices for wheels, chains, or swinging mace traps.

PrismaticJoint

A prismatic joint allows two bodies to move along a specified axis within a limited range without the capability of rotating. An elevator clearly illustrates this behavior because it is moved along the *y* axis with an upper and lower limit and there is no possible rotation.

Some other examples are sliding doors, dampers, or pistons.

Follow these steps to get a `PrismaticJoint` working under Libgdx:

1. Create two bodies, for instance, `squareBody` and `groundBody`.

2. Define the `PrismaticJointDef` object with the involved bodies, the selected axis to slide, and the range limits. Moreover, we will add a motor force. The motor speed is expressed in radians per second:

```
PrismaticJointDef prismaticJointDef = new
   PrismaticJointDef();
prismaticJointDef.initialize(groundBody, square,
   new Vector2(SCENE_WIDTH*.5f,SCENE_HEIGHT*.5f),
   new Vector2(SCENE_WIDTH*.5f+1f,0));
prismaticJointDef.lowerTranslation =-2;
prismaticJointDef.upperTranslation = 2;
prismaticJointDef.enableLimit = true;
prismaticJointDef.enableMotor = true;
prismaticJointDef.maxMotorForce = 100;
prismaticJointDef.motorSpeed = 20f *
   MathUtils.degreesToRadians;
```

3. Finally, we must add it to the world:

```
world.createJoint(prismaticJointDef);
```

PulleyJoint

Pulleys are extremely easy to carry out with the `PulleyJoint` class. The following diagram describes the process, which follows in the same line as the previous examples with some particularities such as the length of each segment of the rope:

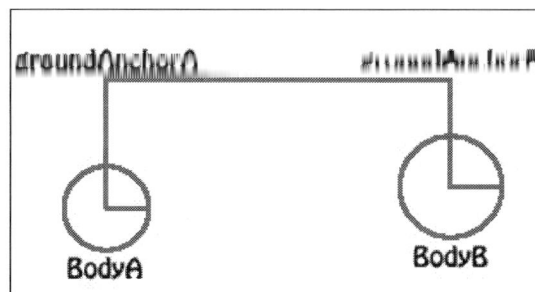

Please follow these steps to include this type of joint in your game:

1. First of all, create two bodies.

2. Initialize `PulleyJointDef` as illustrated in the previous image. You must also supply a `ratio` for setting how much one segment changes compared to the other:

```
PulleyJointDef pulleyJointDef = new PulleyJointDef();
pulleyJointDef.bodyA=smallBall;
pulleyJointDef.bodyB=bigBall;
pulleyJointDef.groundAnchorA.set(SCENE_WIDTH*.5f-1,
    SCENE_HEIGHT*.5f);
pulleyJointDef.groundAnchorB.set(SCENE_WIDTH*.5f+1f,
    SCENE_HEIGHT*.5f);
pulleyJointDef.localAnchorA.set(0,0);
pulleyJointDef.localAnchorB.set(0,0);
pulleyJointDef.lengthA = 0.7f;
pulleyJointDef.lengthB = 0.7f;
pulleyJointDef.ratio=1f;
```

3. As usual, add it to the world:

```
world.createJoint(pulleyJointDef);
```

GearJoint

As the name suggests, `GearJoint` provides you with a powerful and simple tool to create gears, avoiding the traditional inefficient method consisting of complex shapes and extra hassle to get the teeth to run smoothly. It is a complex joint because it links revolute and/or prismatic joints. Instead of modeling the aforementioned example, we will implement the scheme shown in the following diagram where the revolute joint angular movement linked to body A causes *y* axis translation on body B and vice versa:

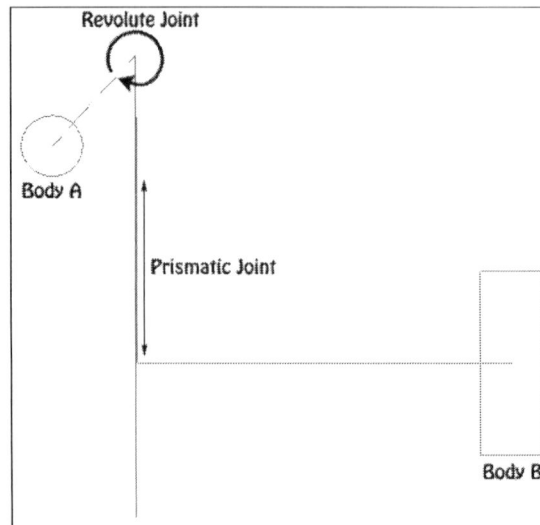

Take a look at the code to fully understand this example:

1. First of all, create bodyA (ball), bodyB (square), and groundBody.

2. Implement the first component of our mechanism: the RevoluteJoint as follows:

```
RevoluteJointDef revoluteJointDef = new RevoluteJointDef();
revoluteJointDef.bodyA=groundBody;
revoluteJointDef.bodyB=ball;
revoluteJointDef.localAnchorA.set(0f,5f);
revoluteJointDef.localAnchorB.set(1f,0f);
```

3. Continue to implement the second component: the PrismaticJoint as follows:

```
PrismaticJointDef prismaticJointDef = new
    PrismaticJointDef();
prismaticJointDef.initialize(groundBody, square,
    new Vector2(SCENE_WIDTH*.5f,5f),
    new Vector2(0f,1f));
prismaticJointDef.lowerTranslation = -2f;
prismaticJointDef.upperTranslation = .5f;
prismaticJointDef.enableLimit = true;
```

4. Add both components to the world and keep a reference to them:

```
Joint revoluteJoint = world.createJoint(revoluteJointDef);
Joint prismaticJoint =
    world.createJoint(prismaticJointDef);
```

5. Build GearJointDef and add it to the world too. Along with PulleyJointDef, you must supply a ratio. Take into account that this one is different because you are dealing with different terms as angular movement (revolute joint) and translations (prismatic joint) do not work in the same way:

```
GearJointDef gearJointDef = new GearJointDef();
gearJointDef.bodyA=ball;
gearJointDef.bodyB=square;
gearJointDef.joint1 = revoluteJoint;
gearJointDef.joint2 = prismaticJoint;
gearJointDef.ratio=(float) (2.0f * Math.PI / 0.5f);
world.createJoint(gearJointDef);
```

> GearJoint must be deleted before its two components to avoid unexpected behaviors.
>
> You can delete any joint through the destroyJoint() method of the World class. This action is usually followed by a call to destroyFixture() for each of the fixtures of the bodies that belong to the joint.

WheelJoint

The wheel joint is a good candidate to implement a car suspension model as it allows your body to translate along a fixed axis and, at the same time, rotate freely. So it is basically a `PrismaticJoint` without the rotation restriction. Follow these steps to add it to your game:

1. Create a spherical body.

2. Define `WheelJointDef`, which includes a motor. The suspension frequency can be specified through the `frequencyHz` field where `0` means no suspension. The damping ratio is also customizable and critical damping is enabled when the ratio value reaches one:

```
WheelJointDef wheelJointDef = new WheelJointDef();
wheelJointDef.bodyA=groundBody;
wheelJointDef.bodyB=wheel;
wheelJointDef.collideConnected=true;
wheelJointDef.localAnchorA.set(0,0);
wheelJointDef.localAnchorB.set(0,0);
wheelJointDef.motorSpeed = 5f;
wheelJointDef.enableMotor = true;
wheelJointDef.maxMotorTorque = 50f;
wheelJointDef.dampingRatio = 0.5f;
wheelJointDef.frequencyHz = 0.2f;
```

3. Add it to the world:

```
world.createJoint(wheelJointDef);
```

> Often, `WheelJoint` requires a lot of tweaking to get the desired effect.

There's more...

Apart from the classical joints, Box2D provides you with an extra one to manipulate bodies with the cursor: `MouseJoint`. It is intended to make a point of one body go towards the position of the cursor. This can be extremely useful for debugging purposes.

All you have to do is follow this process:

1. Declare a class field for the `MouseJoint` and `Body` to store a reference to the clicked object:

```
MouseJoint mouseJoint;
Body hitbody;
```

2. Instantiate a new MouseJoint whenever a click is processed. Take into account that two bodies are required and we have just defined one. The first one will be the body affected by the user's click/tap. The second is mandatory as MouseJoint extends the Joint class even if it is not used:

```java
public boolean touchDown (int x, int y, int pointer, int
  button) {
  // Mouse coordinates to box2D coordinates
  viewport.getCamera().unproject(point.set(x, y, 0));
  if(button == Input.Buttons.RIGHT) {
    //Make a query to get the clicked body (omitted for
      simplicity, see provided source code for details)
    hitBody = ...;
    ...
    MouseJointDef mouseJointDef = new MouseJointDef();
    mouseJointDef.bodyA = groundBody;
    mouseJointDef.bodyB = hitBody;
    mouseJointDef.collideConnected = true;
    mouseJointDef.target.set(point.x, point.y); //click
      coordinates
    mouseJointDef.maxForce = 1000.0f * hitBody.getMass();

    mouseJoint = (MouseJoint)
      world.createJoint(mouseJointDef);

  }
  ...
}
```

3. Update the target if the user is dragging the mouse:

```java
public boolean touchDragged (int x, int y, int pointer) {
  if (mouseJoint != null) {
    viewport.getCamera().unproject(point.set(x, y, 0));
    mouseJoint.setTarget(target.set(point.x, point.y));
  }
  ...
}
```

4. Delete the target when your mouse click is over:

```java
public boolean touchUp (int x, int y, int pointer, int
  button) {
  // if a mouse joint exists we simply destroy it
  if(button == Input.Buttons.RIGHT) {
    if (mouseJoint != null) {
```

```
        world.destroyJoint(mouseJoint);
        mouseJoint = null;
      }
    }
    ...
  }
```

See also

▸ The *Real-life joints example – bike simulator* recipe

Real-life joints example – bike simulator

Individual joints have no real value in a game by themselves. However, the mixture of some of them can enhance their final quality by simulating complex behaviors. Vehicles are good examples to illustrate the potential of joints.

In this recipe, you will learn how to build, step by step, the simplified model of a modern bike with suspension.

Getting ready

The process to implement the bike requires a good level of understanding about `PrismaticJoint` and `RevoluteJoint`. Make sure you feel fluent on these topics before carrying on.

The best way to take advantage of this recipe is to tweak the source code and understand how changes affect the final result. Therefore, feel free to take a look at the `Box2DBikeSimulatorSample.java` file.

How to do it...

Before diving into the code, it is a good idea to clarify the logic model of this complex mixture of physics bodies. For our purposes, we will divide this introduction into three components:

▸ **Wheels**: Each wheel is attached to a `RevoluteJoint` as it can rotate and move along the *x* axis.

▸ **Front damper**: Its main function is to connect the frame with the front wheel, but it must allow suspension too through a `PrismaticJoint`.

▸ **Back damper**: This is in charge of connecting the frame with the back wheel. However, it must make the structure react with a small rotation when the back wheel bounces.

The next diagram shows the bike structure that we will finally implement:

Anchor points are the local contact coordinates between the two bodies in a joint.

Once the model is clear, let's go into the real deal. Do not hesitate to review the code while going through these steps:

1. As is becoming the custom in this chapter, initialize `Viewport`, `SpriteBatch`, `World`, and `Box2DDebugRenderer` and create a ground.

2. The different parts of the code will refer to the size of each of the bike components. That is why we will cache those values in world units:

```
final float WHEEL_WIDTH = 1.25f;
final float BACKDAMPER_WIDTH = 1.13f, BACKDAMPER_HEIGHT =
  .39f;
final float FRONTDAMPER_WIDTH = .71f, FRONTDAMPER_HEIGHT =
  1.069f;
final float FRAME_WIDTH = 1.8f, FRAME_HEIGHT = 1.53f;
```

3. This example requires visual interaction. Consequently, several `Texture` instances must be created:

```
Texture frameTex = new
  Texture(Gdx.files.internal("data/box2D/frame.png"));
Texture backDamperTex = new
  Texture(Gdx.files.internal("data/box2D/backDamper.png"));
Texture frontDamperTex = new
  Texture(Gdx.files.internal("data/box2D/
  frontDamper.png"));
Texture wheelTex = new
  Texture(Gdx.files.internal("data/box2D/wheel.png"));
```

4. Now that we know the image bounds of each component, we create the physics bodies as usual—spheres for the wheels and rectangles for the rest:

```
Body frontWheelBody = createSphere(BodyType.DynamicBody,
   0f, 1f, 0.8f, 0f, 1.0f, WHEEL_WIDTH * .5f);
...
Body frameBody = createPolygon(BodyType.DynamicBody, 0f,
   3f, 1f, 0f, 0f, FRAME_WIDTH * .5f, FRAME_HEIGHT * .5f);
...
```

5. Once the puzzle is complete, it is time to join the pieces. The front damper connects with the frame through a `PrismaticJoint` whose translation axis is about 120 degrees inclined, hence it is the last vector passed to the `initialize` function. The next diagram can be of help to understand this better:

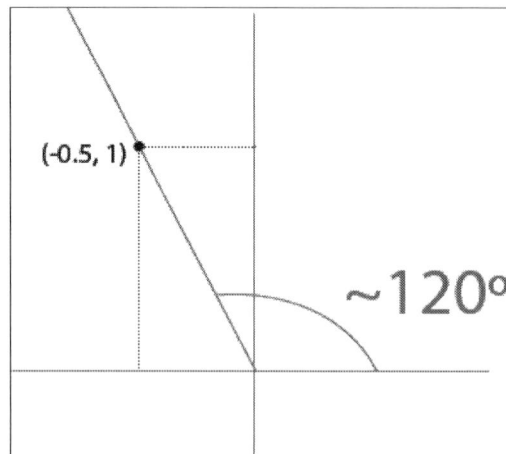

The movement range must be limited too. Anchor points are determined using the previously cached bounds and a little bit of trial and error:

```
PrismaticJointDef prismaticJointDef = new
   PrismaticJointDef();
prismaticJointDef.initialize(frontDamperBody, frameBody,
   new Vector2(0f,0f), new Vector2(-0.5f,1f));

prismaticJointDef.lowerTranslation =-.2f;
prismaticJointDef.upperTranslation = 0f;
prismaticJointDef.enableLimit = true;

prismaticJointDef.localAnchorA.set(-FRONTDAMPER_WIDTH * .5f
   * + 0.065f, FRONTDAMPER_HEIGHT * .5f);
prismaticJointDef.localAnchorB.set(FRAME_WIDTH * .5f -
   0.165f,0.1f);
```

```
prismaticJointDef.collideConnected=false;

Joint fDamperFrameJoint =
  world.createJoint(prismaticJointDef);
```

6. The next step involves connecting the front damper with the front wheel through a `RevoluteJoint` for the aforementioned reasons. The only complexity here is setting the proper anchor points:

```
RevoluteJointDef revoluteJointDef = new RevoluteJointDef();
revoluteJointDef.bodyA = frontDamperBody;
revoluteJointDef.bodyB = frontWheelBody;

revoluteJointDef.localAnchorA.set(FRONTDAMPER_WIDTH * .5f -
  0.065f,-FRONTDAMPER_HEIGHT * .5f);
revoluteJointDef.localAnchorB.set(0,0);

revoluteJointDef.collideConnected=false;

Joint fDamperFwheelJoint =
  world.createJoint(revoluteJointDef);
```

7. Another necessary `RevoluteJoint` connection is the one between the back damper and the frame. The rotation range must be generously limited in such a way that it bounces only a little bit when necessary, for instance, 30 degrees (the range between -4 and 26):

```
RevoluteJointDef revoluteJointDef2 = new
  RevoluteJointDef();
revoluteJointDef2.bodyA=backDamperBody;
revoluteJointDef2.bodyB=frameBody;

revoluteJointDef2.collideConnected=false;

revoluteJointDef2.localAnchorA.set(BACKDAMPER_WIDTH *
  .5f,0f);
revoluteJointDef2.localAnchorB.set(-FRAME_WIDTH * .5f +
  0.5f, -FRAME_HEIGHT * .5f + 0.25f);

revoluteJointDef2.lowerAngle = -4 *
  MathUtils.degreesToRadians;
revoluteJointDef2.upperAngle = 26 *
  MathUtils.degreesToRadians;
revoluteJointDef2.enableLimit = true;

Joint bDamperFrameJoint =
  world.createJoint(revoluteJointDef2);
```

8. The last joint of the model is in charge of connecting the back damper with the back wheel pretty much as the one explained in step 5 but taking into account that bikes are always powered by the back wheel, so we will add a motor force to improve the interaction:

```
RevoluteJointDef revoluteJointDef3 = new
  RevoluteJointDef();
revoluteJointDef3.bodyA=backDamperBody;
revoluteJointDef3.bodyB=backWheelBody;


revoluteJointDef3.collideConnected=false;


revoluteJointDef3.localAnchorA.set(-BACKDAMPER_WIDTH *
  .5f,-0.1f);
revoluteJointDef3.localAnchorB.set(0,0);


revoluteJointDef3.enableMotor = true;
revoluteJointDef3.maxMotorTorque = 100f;
revoluteJointDef3.motorSpeed = -135f *
  MathUtils.degreesToRadians;


Joint bDamperBwheelJoint =
  world.createJoint(revoluteJointDef3);
```

9. If you run the sample with the current progress, the front damper will not work as the frame body is colliding with the front wheel. This is due to the low precision physics shapes attached to the bodies as we are using rectangles for non-rectangular shapes.

Box2D collision filtering techniques (explained later in this chapter) would be the way to go but, in this case, and in order to keep recipes independent, we will use an easy-to-adapt method for our model to prevent collision between the frame and a wheel, creating MouseJoint instances:

```
MouseJointDef mjd1 = new MouseJointDef();
mjd1.bodyA = frameBody;
mjd1.bodyB = backWheelBody;
Joint frameBwheelJoint = world.createJoint(mjd1);


MouseJointDef mjd2 = new MouseJointDef();
mjd2.bodyA = frameBody;
mjd2.bodyB = frontWheelBody;
Joint frameFwheelJoint = world.createJoint(mjd2);
```

10. Update the physics world and render the textures:

```
world.step(1/60f, 6, 2);

batch.begin();
batch.setProjectionMatrix(viewport.getCamera().combined);

batch.draw(
    wheelTex,
    frontWheelBody.getPosition().x - (WHEEL_WIDTH*.5f),
    frontWheelBody.getPosition().y - (WHEEL_WIDTH*.5f),
    WHEEL_WIDTH*.5f, WHEEL_WIDTH*.5f,
    WHEEL_WIDTH, WHEEL_WIDTH,
    1f, 1f,
    frontWheelBody.getAngle() * MathUtils.radDeg,
    0, 0,
    wheelTex.getWidth(), wheelTex.getHeight(),
    false, false);
... // Repeat a draw() call for each bike component
batch.end();
```

11. Finally, remember to dispose the allocated resources:

```
public void dispose() {
    wheelTex.dispose();
    backDamperTex.dispose();
    frontDamperTex.dispose();
    frameTex.dispose();
    batch.dispose();
    world.dispose();
}
```

12. Execute your code now and the bike from the previous diagram will appear on the screen.

There's more...

This implementation uses an approach consisting of a mixture of `RevoluteJoint` and `PrismaticJoint`, but you could accept the challenge, take another path, and develop it with the `WheelJoint`.

As future work, you could do a search on the Internet for the structure of a car and carry it out yourself. The possibilities are endless.

Reacting to collisions

Box2D takes collision response to an awesome level of realism where bodies act exactly as expected in most cases. However, there are a lot of situations within a game that demand custom collision dealing, such as receiving damage, controlling a ball, or simply pushing enemies.

After reading this recipe, you will easily be able to manage those special circumstances that will surely appear in your game.

Getting ready

The sample code will implement a balloon-breaker mini-game where a shuriken will follow your cursor looking for fragile balloons to destroy before they leave the scene dimensions.

You can find the code within the Box2DCollisionReactionSample.java file. Remember to import sample projects.

How to do it...

In the next lines, you will find the content of the Box2DCollisionReactionSample.java file broken down into nine steps:

1. Initialize Viewport, SpriteBatch, World, Box2DDebugRenderer, and a groundBody for our scene. Feel free to go back to the first recipe of this chapter, *Introduction to Box2D*, if you need to refresh your memory.

2. Create a big shuriken kinematic body using the ChainShape class with the following vertices:

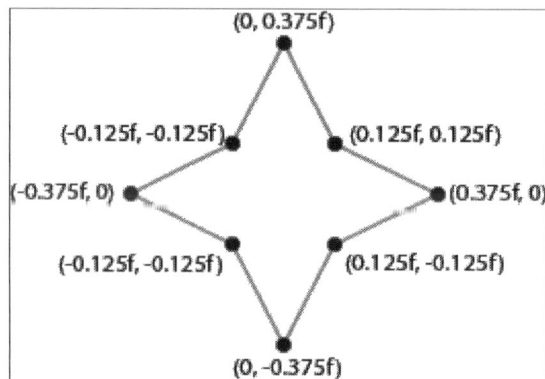

3. Once the body is created, it must follow the cursor. You can take two separate paths to carry out this mission depending on the required degree of precision:

   ❑ **High precision**: In this, we set the shuriken body type to the kinematic body and update its position manually.

   ❑ **Low precision**: In this, we use a `MouseJoint`, updating its target position to the cursor location if necessary and applying a force to reach that point. The shuriken must be implemented through a dynamic body in this case.

The first path is more precise because the position of the body is manually set to a certain point while the second one relies on a force to push the body to the target point.

As we have not used a kinematic body yet, we will take the high precision approach. So make sure you set the proper body type in `FixtureDef`:

```
shurikenBodyDef.type = BodyType.KinematicBody;
```

4. We have to update the shuriken body position within the overridden `mouseMoved(...)` function:

```
public boolean mouseMoved(int screenX, int screenY) {
  // Translate into world coordinates
  viewport.getCamera().unproject(point.set(screenX,
    screenY, 0));
  pointerBody.setTransform(point.x, point.y, pointerBody.
    getAngle() + 5 * MathUtils.degreesToRadians);

  return true;
}
```

Since we have to specify an angle, let's add some visual interaction with a small rotation.

5. Up until now, we have only defined one of the two main actors of this example. Balloons will be instantiated within the screen bounds with the `createBalloon()` function, which will basically create a balloon body that contains a fixture with a precise shape created with the physics editor mentioned in the *Introducing more complex shapes* recipe. Each of these bodies will carry a flag, false by default, to indicate whether it should be deleted as soon as possible. This is due to the need to delete physics elements outside of the simulation process as well should non delete objects that the `World` instance is working with. Otherwise, your game might crash.

The physics properties for balloons will be:

```
float balloonDensity = 0.0099999f;
float balloonFriction = 0.90f;
float balloonRestitution = 0.0f;
```

To simplify this, we will store the flag under the `UserData` field:

```
balloonBody.setUserData(false);
```

6. Every second, we will instantiate a new balloon within the `render()` function thanks to the `time` variable, which is originally set to zero:

```
float delta = Gdx.graphics.getDeltaTime();
if((time += delta) >= 1f) { //Every second
  time-=1f;
  createBalloon();
}
```

7. Right after this piece of code, we will apply a buoyancy force to each and every balloon to make them look more realistic:

```
for(Body balloon : balloons) // Keep balloons flying
  balloon.applyForceToCenter(buoyancyForce, true);
```

In order to calculate `buoyancyForce` (yes, air is physically a fluid), we need to obtain some other variables first because the resulting formula is:

```
Vector2 buoyancyForce = new Vector2(0f, displacedMass * 9.8f);
```

The calculation of `displacedMass` needs the area, but for simplicity's sake, we will consider the balloon as an ellipse (A = PI * semi-major axis * semi-minor axis):

```
private static final float BALLOON_WIDTH = 0.5f;
private static final float BALLOON_HEIGHT = 0.664f;
private static final float BALLOON_AREA = MathUtils.PI *
  BALLOON_WIDTH * 0.5f * BALLOON_HEIGHT * 0.5f;
```

We will set the `airDensity` value to `0.01` and consequently, the `displacedMass` value:

```
float displacedMass = BALLOON_AREA * airDensity;
```

As theoretical explanation about physics is not the goal of this book, I strongly recommend you to go to `http://www.iforce2d.net/b2dtut/buoyancy` if you are interested in a deeper explanation.

8. At this point, we have a scene where the shuriken pushes balloons when colliding. As we want to manually deal with those collisions, our sample class will implement the `ContactListener` interface. We must also inform to the `World` object of this:

```
world.setContactListener(this);
```

This will force us to define some functions. For now, we will focus on `BeginContact(...)` because we need to know exactly when two fixtures start touching. The rest of the functions will be covered in the *How it works...* section. Take into account that we must consider both contact points when checking the two fixtures:

```
public void beginContact(Contact contact) {
  Fixture fixtureA = contact.getFixtureA();
  Fixture fixtureB = contact.getFixtureB();
```

```
Body bodyA = fixtureA.getBody();
Body bodyB = fixtureB.getBody();

if(bodyA == pointerBody && bodyB != groundBody)
    bodyB.setUserData(true);
else if(bodyB == pointerBody && bodyA != groundBody)
    bodyA.setUserData(true);
}
```

What we do here is consult which fixtures have taken part in the contact and if one of them is the shuriken and the other is not the ground, it means that the second is a balloon. All we have to do is mark it as pending to be deleted at the end of the current step of the simulation.

9. The last line of the `render()` function should be responsible for cleaning the house by calling `freeBalloons()`. It will just loop over the balloons container and remove those that are set as broken (`false` flag) or have simply flown away from the screen limits:

```
void freeBalloons() {
    Iterator<Body> i = balloons.iterator();
    while (i.hasNext()) {
        Body balloon = i.next();
        boolean broken = (Boolean) balloon.getUserData();

        if(((balloon.getPosition().y - BALLOON_HEIGHT*0.5f) >
            SCENE_HEIGHT) || // Top limit
            /*Bottom limit*/ ||
            /*Right limit */ ||
            /*Left limit  */ ||
            broken) {
            world.destroyBody(balloon);
            i.remove();
        }
    }
}
```

How it works...

Classes that implement the `ContactListener` interface will be able to listen for overlapping fixtures at every stage of the collision anatomy through these functions:

▶ void beginContact (Contact contact): This function is called once when two fixtures overlap and cannot be called again over the same ones until endContact (...) has finished. You cannot disable the contact here.

- ▶ `void endContact (Contact contact)`: This function is called when two fixtures are no longer touching.

- ▶ `void preSolve (Contact contact, Manifold oldManifold)`: This function gives you the opportunity to manually deal with the contact between two bodies instead of delegating to Box2D, which will just calculate the collision response according to their physics properties. You can disable the contact here.

- ▶ `void postSolve (Contact contact, ContactImpulse impulse)`: This function allows us to get the characteristics of the collision response once it is done.

Whenever the system detects a contact within a simulation step, `BeginContact` is called, and from now on, `PreSolve` and `PostSolve` will be called respectively on each simulation step until `EndContact` is executed.

You can find a deeper explanation together with some examples at `http://www.iforce2d.net/b2dtut/collision-anatomy`.

There's more...

The `Contact` object stores the necessary information to know what fixtures are colliding. But it can also disable the Box2D future response by:

```
contact.setEnabled(false);
```

This is a temporary flag because it will be reset in the next timestep. This is the reason why it only works in `presolve` as it gets called as long as the fixtures are colliding.

You can also modify friction and restitution properties for the contact by calling these functions:

```
contact.setFriction(0.1f);
contact.setRestitution(0.3f);
```

The `Manifold` object stores information about the contact point in local coordinates. Use `WorldManifold` to get it in the world coordinates. You can retrieve such information with:

```
manifold.getPoints();
```

It might be useful to know whether a bullet has impacted the chest, the head, or the leg so you can act as a consequence.

Finally, you can query a `world` object for all the contact points with:

```
world.getContactList();
```

See also

- ▶ The *Sensors and collision filtering* recipe
- ▶ The *Querying the world* recipe

Sensors and collision filtering

Modern games include fixtures that do not react physically to collisions with other fixtures but still have an important mission, just like radars that detect intruders within an area.

Usually, allies do not crash between themselves and others like ghosts will collide only with fire.

All such gameplay variables are easily implemented with Box2D, so you will not have to fill your collision handlers with many lines of code. In addition, filtering collisions will allow you to decrease the CPU load.

In this recipe, you will learn how to use sensors and manage the different ways of filtering your collisions depending on the complexity of the game.

Getting ready

If you have already taken a look at the `Box2DCollisionFiltering.java` file, you will have noticed the two quiet dinosaurs that get really angry whenever any of the friendly cavemen get closer to them. The characters that belong to the same faction will not collide.

How to do it...

The code of this example comes with two inner classes defined with the purpose of making things clearer. Each of them will represent a faction: cavemen and dinosaurs. As their content is mostly not new for us, we will not put them in the spotlight but please feel free to take a look at the source code.

Sensors

Each dinosaur will have a nonvisible sphere around him to detect whether a caveman is within its vicinity, as shown in the following screenshot:

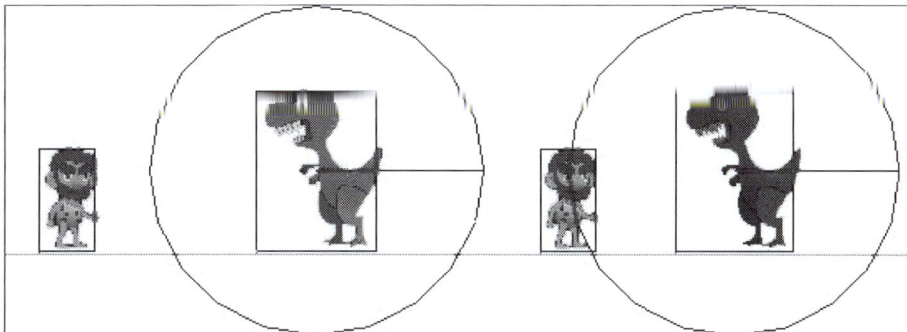

That is what we will call a sensor, and its usage is really simple:

1. Create a second fixture for each enemy body and enable the sensor flag:

```
CircleShape circle = new CircleShape();
circle.setRadius(1f);

FixtureDef sensorFD = new FixtureDef();
sensorFD.isSensor = true;
sensorFD.shape = circle;
enemyBody.createFixture(sensorFD);
```

2. Implement the `ContactListener` interface and within the `beginContact(...)` function, check whether the sensor is overlapped by another fixture:

```
if (fixtureA.isSensor()) {
  Enemy e = (Enemy) bodyA.getUserData();
  e.setAngry(true);
}
```

A reference to the object itself is attached into the `UserData` field of the body within the `Enemy` constructor so that it can be retrieved later. In addition, the `SetAngry` function will just change the tint of the dinosaur to red when the received argument is `true`.

The brightest readers will have realized that we are only checking whether one of the fixtures involved in the contact is a sensor and it is an insufficient condition to determine that a caveman has gone into a dinosaur's territory. However, that simple condition becomes valid because of collision filtering, which directly omits the undesired fixtures.

Group collision filtering

Filtering collisions by groups is the simplest and quickest way to avoid collisions between certain types of bodies. It is intended for games where bodies can collide with anyone except for the ones that belong to its own group.

Configuring our example with groups would be very easy but it will not be flexible enough to deal with all the conditions automatically, so some extra code will be necessary. For educational purposes, the group approach is described here but notice that it is not present in the sample source code:

1. The first thing is to declare the groups as member fields:

```
final short GROUP_CAVEMAN = -1;
final short GROUP_DINOSAUR = -2;
final short GROUP_SCENERY = 3;
```

The common positive value means *always collide* while the same negative value means *never collide*.

2. Next, match the groups with your bodies. Set sensors as GROUP_DINOSAUR so they will not have the chance of colliding with the real dinosaur fixture:

```
FixtureDef sensorFD = new FixtureDef();
sensorFD.isSensor = true;
sensorFD.shape = circle;
sensorFD.filter.groupIndex = GROUP_DINOSAUR;
enemyBody.createFixture(sensorFD);
...
```

Once group collision filtering is explained, it is not hard to find out that sensors will collide as much with cavemen as with the ground, so it would need extra work to distinguish them.

Flexible collision filtering

The long route takes you through a more tedious path but much more powerful too. It consists of categories and masks.

The categories should have one entry for each object type while the masks filters collisions between them. They both are bit fields represented by shorts, which can store up to 16 varieties as they have 16 bits.

1. If you are afraid of this notation, you will soon realize how simple it is to define new categories:

```
final short CATEGORY_PLAYER = 0x0001;
final short CATEGORY_ENEMY = 0x0002;
final short CATEGORY_GROUND = 0x0004;
final short CATEGORY_SENSOR = 0x0008;
```

Some readers will prefer going for another notation that makes use of bit shifting operations while keeping the decimal numerical system. The next code snippet is equivalent to the previous one:

```
final short CATEGORY_PLAYER = 1<<0;
final short CATEGORY_ENEMY = 1<<1;
final short CATEGORY_GROUND = 1<<2;
final short CATEGORY_SENSOR = 1<<3;
```

Feel free to use the notation that you are more comfortable with.

2. With those categories ready to be used, masks are even easier:

```
// Cannot collide with player objects
final short MASK_PLAYER = ~CATEGORY_PLAYER;
// Cannot collide with enemy objects
final short MASK_ENEMY = ~CATEGORY_ENEMY;
// Can collide only with players
final short MASK_SENSOR = CATEGORY_PLAYER;
// Can collide with everything
final short MASK_GROUND = -1;
```

3. All you have to do now is to assign the proper categories and masks to each fixture, as shown in the following example:

```
FixtureDef sensorFD = new FixtureDef();
sensorFD.isSensor = true;
sensorFD.shape = circle;
sensorFD.filter.categoryBits = CATEGORY_SENSOR;
sensorFD.filter.maskBits = MASK_SENSOR;
enemyBody.createFixture(sensorFD);
```

How it works...

All these bits calculation might seem complex but in the next paragraphs, you will find a brief explanation to make it clear.

The way that Box2D determines whether to filter a certain collision or not, is performed with the following code snippet:

```
const b2Filter& filterA = fixtureA->GetFilterData();
const b2Filter& filterB = fixtureB->GetFilterData();

if (filterA.groupIndex == filterB.groupIndex && filterA.groupIndex
  != 0)
{
  return filterA.groupIndex > 0;
}

bool collide = (filterA.maskBits & filterB.categoryBits) != 0 &&
  (filterA.categoryBits & filterB.maskBits) != 0;
```

For group filtering, Box2D makes use of signed integers.

On one hand, two fixtures will collide if they share the same positive `groupIndex`. On the other hand, they will not collide if they belong to the same `groupIndex` and it is negative. For the rest of the cases, colliding delegates to category/mask filtering.

Masks and categories are set through bit fields. The previous code checks that after applying an AND operation to the mask bits of a fixture and the category bits of another, it does not result in 0. An example might shed some light on this:

```
final short CATEGORY_PLAYER = 0x0001;
final short CATEGORY_ALLY = 0x0002;
final short MASK_PLAYER = ~CATEGORY_ALLY;
```

The explanation of why a player cannot collide with an ally is because doing an AND operation between `CATEGORY_ALLY(00000010)` and `MASK_PLAYER(11111101)` results in 0 (`00000000`).

> When defining the mask, you will have come across the ~ symbol. It represents one's complement, which in bit terms means replacing 0s with 1s and vice versa.

Bit fields are stored as short values, which in Java takes 16 bits, ranging from -32768 up to 32767. The next table shows the correspondence between decimal and hexadecimal values:

Hexadecimal	Decimal
0x0000	0
0x0001	1
...	...
0x7FFF	32767
0x8000	-32767
0x8001	-32766
...	...
0xFFFF	-1

As you will have seen, the decimal column is not ordered, which can lead to errors when setting a bit field to a specific value. This is one reason to find hexadecimal notation more frequently within this context.

In addition, values must be powers of two under this scope.

There's more...

Groups, categories, and masks can live together, being aware of the higher precedence of groups. However, my advice here is to keep it as simple as possible.

In addition, you can explicitly find a set of cases in the Box2D manual where they internally make use of collision filtering:

- A fixture on a static body can only collide with a dynamic body.
- A fixture on a kinematic body can only collide with a dynamic body.
- Fixtures on the same body never collide with each other.
- You can optionally enable/disable collision between fixtures on bodies connected by a joint.

See also

▶ The *Querying the world* recipe

▶ The *Implementing a deferred raycaster* recipe

Querying the world

Game worlds can be a fully interactive environment where realism usually plays an important role and actions occur coherently to the player's eye. To achieve these sensations, you will need to query the physics world. A good example is **Line of Sight** (**LOS**) tests for artificial intelligence or even a 3D sound system, which should attenuate the sound received from the vicinity if there is any wall between the audio source and the listener. This check is easy to carry out by casting a ray between the two world points.

Another way of receiving direct feedback from the physics world is area queries, which can help you to detect dynamic obstacles and jump to avoid them. Even less common cases are where lots of people are upon a wooden bridge, so you can calculate their total weight and make them fall if it reaches a certain threshold.

Useful, right?

Getting ready

The code for this example resides in the `Box2DQuerySample.java` source file and covers both of the earlier mentioned ways of querying the world with the help of 10 boxes that will randomly fall from the sky.

In our example, raycasting is performed by clicking/touching and dragging, so a line is drawn representing the query range. At the same time, a fixed **Axis-aligned bounding box** (**AABB**) or simply a virtual box is placed at one end of the scenery, so if any of the other 10 boxes fall into its bounds, a white sphere will appear on its interior to highlight them.

How to do it...

As the proverb says, *divide and rule*, so each type of world query will have its separate explanation in the next lines. However, there is a common old known utility to instantiate in order to draw some visual representation:

```
ShapeRenderer sr = new ShapeRenderer();
```

Raycasting

1. First of all, initialize four Vector2 objects to represent the origin (p1) and the end (p2) of the raycast, as well as its normal in case it gets overlapped by another body:

```
Vector2 p1, p2, collision, normal;
p1 = new Vector2();
...
```

Look at the following figure to get a better understanding of these four concepts:

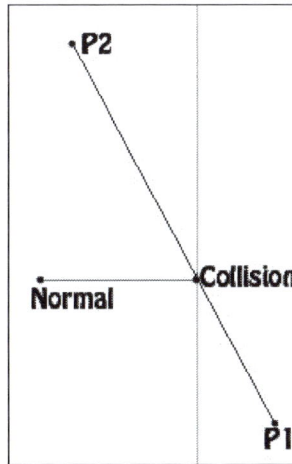

A ray is cast from point p1 to point p2. The collision vector represents the location on the ray of the contact point where the line hits a body. The normal vector represents the normalized perpendicular vector of the surface on that body at the contact point.

2. With each player's click/touch, we will always update p1 and p2 according to the position of the cursor while normal and collision will be reset to zero. At this point, we have all the required information to perform the query:

```
public boolean touchDown (int x, int y, int pointer, int
    button) {
    // Screen coordinates to World coordinates
    viewport.getCamera().unproject(point.set(x, y, 0));

    if (button == Input.Buttons.LEFT) {
        p1.set(point.x, point.y);
        p2.set(point.x, point.y+0.00001f);
        normal.set(Vector2.Zero);
        collision.set(Vector2.Zero);
        // Make the query
        world.rayCast(callback, p1, p2);
```

```
            return true;
        }
        return false;
    }
```

[✎ Be aware that you cannot have a 0 length raycast, that is
    why 0.00001 is added to the y component in the p2 vector.
    Otherwise, it will crash.]

3. You will surely wonder what the `callback` variable is. It is nothing more than an object
    whose type is an anonymous class that implements the Box2D `RayCastCallback`
    interface. It implies that you must override the `reportRayFixture(...)` method to
    obtain the resulting collision data. The following code will make you see things clearer:

```
RayCastCallback callback = new RayCastCallback() {
    public float reportRayFixture(Fixture fixture, Vector2
        point, Vector2 normal, float fraction) {
        collision.set(point);
        Box2DQuerySample.this.normal.set(normal).add(point);

        //Process collision data

        return 1;
    }
};
```

Once a fixture is found in the path of the ray, we update our already declared
`Vector2` points: `collision` and `normal`. After that, do whatever you need, for
instance, print that collision data on the screen. A further explanation on this function
and its return value will be provided in the *How it works...* section.

4. Clicking or touching is not the only way to interact with the former code because if the
    user keeps dragging, `p2` should be updated to its end point if and when it is not the
    same as `p1`:

```
public boolean touchDragged(int x, int y, int pointer) {
    viewport.getCamera().unproject(point.set(x, y, 0));
    if(Gdx.input.isButtonPressed(Buttons.LEFT)) {
        if(p1.x != point.x && p1.y != point.y) {
            p2.set(point.x, point.y);
            world.rayCast(callback, p1, p2);
            return true;
        }
    }
    return false;
}
```

Be aware that we are raycasting every frame (or almost every frame) that we drag.

5. Finally, draw the visual representation of our four `Vector2` points:

```
sr.setProjectionMatrix(viewport.getCamera().combined);
sr.begin(ShapeType.Line);
sr.line(p1, p2);
sr.line(collision, normal);
sr.end();
```

> Remember that `ShapeRenderer` works in screen coordinates by default, so do not forget to update its projection matrix to be the same as the camera's.

Area querying

Adding an area query example will follow the same line as the raycast one: instantiate some visual elements, define a callback, and finally draw the model.

1. The first step is to define an AABB region to query. As it will make easier its later drawing, we will work with a plain old Java array where two subsequent float numbers will represent a pair of x-y coordinates. The first two and last two numbers must be the same in order to close the box:

```
float[] aabb = new float[10];

aabb[0] = 1f;
aabb[1] = 1.5f;
aabb[2] = 4f ;
aabb[3] = 1.5f;
aabb[4] = 4f ;
aabb[5] = 4.5f;
aabb[6] = 1f;
aabb[7] = 4.5f;
aabb[8] = 1f;
aabb[9] = 1.5f;
```

2. Next, we will query the world for the fixtures located within the `aabb` bounds, specifically you will have to provide its maximum and minimum (x,y) coordinates. In the same way as before, a callback object must be passed too:

```
world.QueryAABB(areaCallback, aabb[0], aabb[1], aabb[4],
    aabb[5]);
```

3. The interface to inherit from is not the same for area callbacks. In this case, `QueryCallback` is the one that will provide us with the set of fixtures that match the condition:

```
QueryCallback areaCallback = new QueryCallback() {
    public boolean reportFixture(Fixture fixture) {
```

```
      if(fixture.getBody().getType() != BodyType.StaticBody)
        bodiesWithinArea.add(fixture.getBody());
      return true;
  }
};
```

To carry on with our example, we ensure that we do not mark the ground.

> The last if statement is performed to keep the example as simple as possible, but consider using collision filtering techniques in your games.

4. The final steps are destined to draw the model. The aabb field can be drawn with no effort thanks to the polyline function from ShapeRenderer. You will just have to add it to the previous batch of shapes:

```
sr.begin(ShapeType.Line);
...
sr.polyline(aabb);
...
sr.end();
```

5. Marks are represented with a white sphere over the boxes. You will have to specify how many segments will form those circles. In our case, set it to 20 to get a decent precision:

```
sr.begin(ShapeType.Filled);
for(Body b : bodiesWithinArea)
  sr.circle(b.getPosition().x, b.getPosition().y, 0.2f,
    20);
sr.end();
```

How it works...

The RayCastCallback interface requires you to implement this method:

```
float reportRayFixture(Fixture fixture, Vector2 point, Vector2
  normal, float fraction)
```

Not everybody will know what all those parameters are for. Do not fear, a friendly graphic explanation is waiting for you:

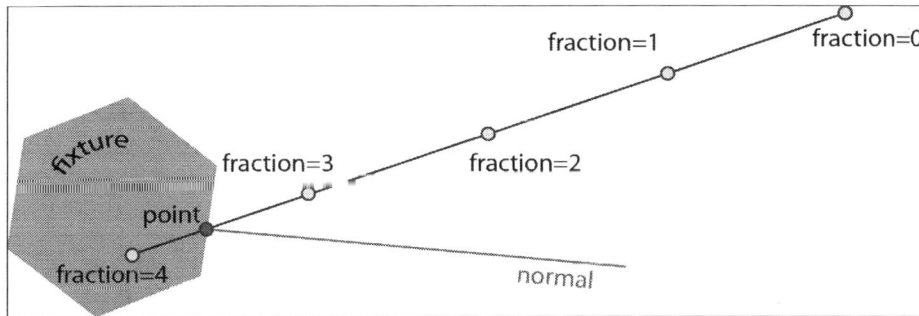

With the diagram, it is easy to see that the **fixture** is the shape, **point** represents the exact place where collision has occurred, and **normal** is a perpendicular vector to the colliding segment from the fixture. The **fraction** is the distance that the ray had to go through in order to find an intersection.

In addition to the parameters, the reason why the function returns a float value is because it accepts the following values:

▸ **-1**: Box2D will just filter the current fixture and carry on with the next

▸ **0**: This will stop the query process

▸ **Fraction**: Raycast will be clipped to the returned value, so you will be raycasting its closest shape

▸ **1**: Box2D will just continue processing as if no hit occurred

Regarding AABB queries and the hidden magic that Box2D appeals to in order to determine intersections, there are still some loose ends that the most curious readers would like to tie up.

Separating Axis Theorem (**SAT**) is the underlying technique to check whether two convex polygons are overlapping. For those who do not know it, a convex polygon is the one with all its interior angles lower than 180 degrees.

SAT consists of checking whether there is a gap between two shapes by projecting every side of one polygon into its perpendicular vector (normal) and checking whether any of the other polygons' projections overlap. This is shown in the following diagram where we project the left-hand side of box **3** into its normal (brought to the bottom of the diagram for clarity reasons):

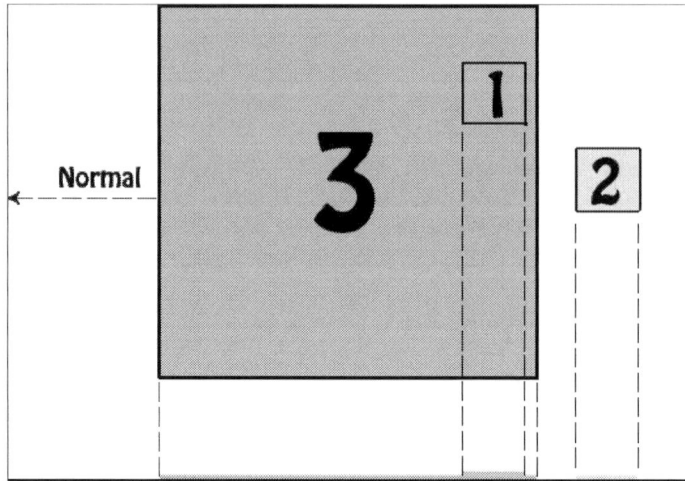

The result of this tiny example says that box **1** and box **3** are colliding as you can see that the first projection collides with the second.

Specifically in the case of circles that the normal vector will be the one that joins the center of the circle with the closest vertex on the polygon.

There's more...

Raycasting and AABB intersection are awesome tools widely used within the industry. Apart from the aforementioned examples, there are a lot of situations where querying could be useful:

- ▶ A line of fire test.
- ▶ Flying objects that need to avoid obstacles.
- ▶ Cover posture detection.
- ▶ Gap detection (jump!).
- ▶ Checking whether a character is not too tall to go through a path.
- ▶ Games such as *The Sims* provide you with a tool to spawn objects in a world. Is there any obstacle that prevents you from placing that pool table in the living room?

There are a lot of possibilities, does any other possibility come to mind?

▶ The *Implementing a deferred raycaster* recipe

Building a physics world from level data

Physics for levels can be hardcoded in the source code with terrible consequences for maintenance purposes, but I am sure that you have already heard about the data-driven approach that suggests a solution.

Most level editors include mechanisms to attach physics data to the final level file and one of them, Tiled, is familiar to you from *Chapter 8, User Interfaces with Scene2D*. It supplies a layers system where you can define geometric shapes and some metadata for their properties.

As all the data is parsed by the map, you can create a generic physics populator for your games so the process of applying them to static bodies becomes almost automatic.

Getting ready

The juice of this recipe is concentrated into two Java source files: `Box2DMapPopulator Sample.java` and `MapBodyManager.java`. At the end, you will have a bunch of your game objects with their physics shapes properly attached on your screen.

How to do it...

Fortunately, you are a master in dealing with 2D maps so we can focus on the real purpose of this recipe: populating a map with physics elements. This example will make use of the tiled output but it is not hard to adapt it to any other program.

However, it will not be enough with 2D maps, you must be a jack-of-all-trades as we will go through some JSON stuff as well as the typical Libgdx Java code.

Defining materials

First things first, we will start with one of the basic pillars of this recipe: the material file. Already known Box2D physics properties will define its structure. We will code it using JSON standard, but, as always, it applies perfectly for anyone:

```
[
    { "name" : "ice", "density" : 0.92, "restitution" : 0.1,
      "friction" : 0.1 },
    { "name" : "sand", "density" : 1.78, "restitution" : 0.0,
      "friction" : 0.8 },
    { "name" : "grass", "density" : 1.1, "restitution" : 0.0,
      "friction" : 0.6 }
]
```

This can be extremely useful to add an extra degree of realism to your game because characters will slide when walking over an icy surface or run slower over dry sand.

Save the file as `materials.json` and keep reading.

Generating the physics metadata

You will have to edit your old tiled map by following these steps:

1. Add a new object layer named `physics`.

2. Within this layer and using the shape tools, create your physics forms. Do not forget to give them a name. Otherwise, it will be a mess when having a lot of them.

3. Right-click on the ones that you want to add physical attributes to. Select **Object Properties** and add a new property called `material` with your desired material name as value from the ones that you defined in `materials.json`, as shown in the following screenshot:

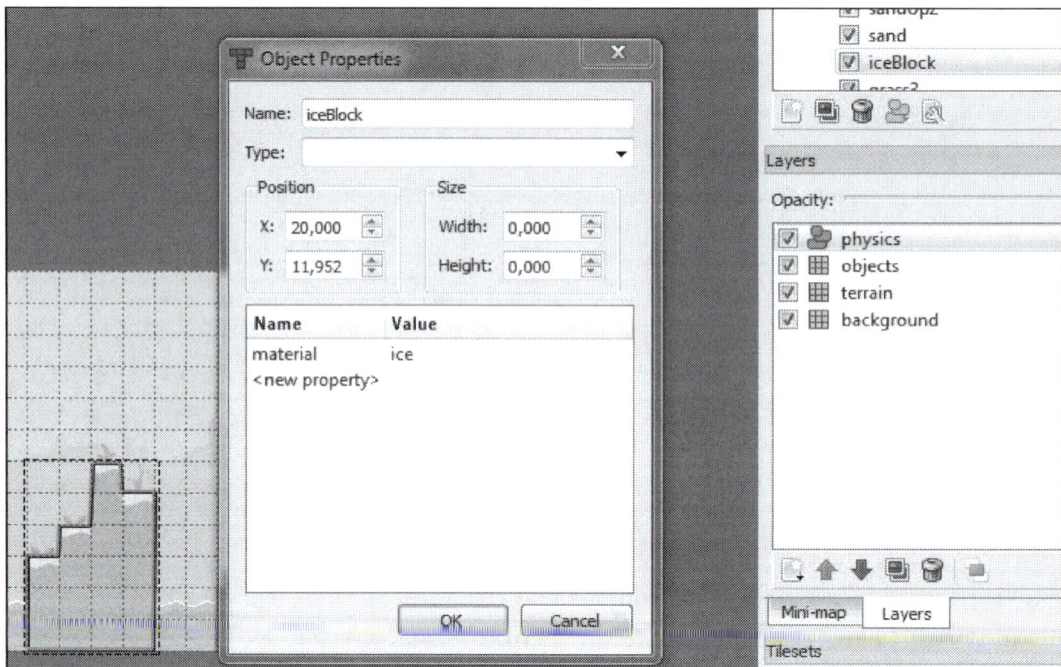

4. Repeat step 3 for each of your desired shapes in order to assign physics properties to them.

Populating your world

Keeping the same structure as the other Box2D examples to complete this recipe should not be too complex:

1. Import the map populator class:

    ```
    import com.cookbook.box2d.MapBodyManager
    ```

2. Add a class field that will define the scale ratio for the maps' textures. Otherwise, they will appear really small as we are working in world units:

    ```
    private static final float SCREEN_TO_WORLD = 30f;
    private static final float WORLD_TO_SCREEN =
      1/SCREEN_TO_WORLD;
    private static final float SCENE_WIDTH = 12.80f ;
    private static final float SCENE_HEIGHT = 7.20f;
    ```

3. Declare a `MapBodyManager` object as well as the typical map fields:

    ```
    MapBodyManager mbm;
    private TiledMap map;
    private TmxMapLoader loader;
    private OrthogonalTiledMapRenderer renderer;
    ```

4. Once those map fields are initialized, taking into account that the renderer must be aware of units translation, do the same with our populator and extract the whole pack of physics shapes and properties:

    ```
    renderer = new OrthogonalTiledMapRenderer(map,
      WORLD_TO_SCREEN);

    mbm = new MapBodyManager(world, SCREEN_TO_WORLD,
      Gdx.files.internal("data/box2D/materials.json"),
      Logger.INFO);
    mbm.createPhysics(map);
    ```

    The `MapBodyManager` constructor requires the physics world, the number of screen units per Box2D units, the already created materials file, and the verbosity of the embedded logger.

5. Render the map as usual and ... mission accomplished!

How it works...

The magic-like usage of the `MapBodyManager` constructor is the most beautiful part of this recipe but you know that, sooner or later, the moment to face the truth will come, which makes this section the essence of this recipe.

The populator will make use of the following fields:

```
private Logger logger;
private World world;
private float units;
private Array<Body> bodies = new Array<Body>();
private ObjectMap<String, FixtureDef> materials = new
   ObjectMap<String, FixtureDef>();
```

It is necessary to highlight that `units` is the conversion ratio from screen units to Box2D ones. To keep track of the potentially generated physics data, there are `bodies` and `materials`. The type of the latter is a Libgdx custom implementation of an unordered map, which works fast at retrieving, consulting, and removing data.

> Remember that you should use Libgdx data types whenever possible for compatibility and performance reasons.

Within the `MapBodyManager` constructor, we will initialize `world`, `units`, and `logger` variables. Moreover, it will end by checking the file existence, and, that being the case, its content will be parsed and loaded into the `materials` object. The next lines of code are destined to show the function in charge of carrying out the last part:

```
private void loadMaterialsFile(FileHandle materialsFile) {
   logger.info("adding default material");

   FixtureDef fixtureDef = new FixtureDef();
   fixtureDef.density = 1.0f;
   fixtureDef.friction = 1.0f;
   fixtureDef.restitution = 0.0f;
   materials.put("default", fixtureDef);

   logger.info("loading materials file");

   try {
     JsonReader reader = new JsonReader();
     JsonValue root = reader.parse(materialsFile);
     JsonIterator materialIt = root.iterator();

     while (materialIt.hasNext()) {
       JsonValue materialValue = materialIt.next();

       if (!materialValue.has("name")) {
         logger.error("material without name");
         continue;
       }
```

```
        String name = materialValue.getString("name");

        fixtureDef = new FixtureDef();
        fixtureDef.density = materialValue.getFloat("density",
          1.0f);
        fixtureDef.friction = materialValue.getFloat("friction",
          1.0f);
        fixtureDef.restitution = materialValue.getFloat
          ("restitution", 0.0f);
        logger.info("adding material " + name);
        materials.put(name, fixtureDef);
      }
    } catch (Exception e) {
      logger.error("error loading " + materialsFile.name() + " " +
        e.getMessage());
    }
  }
}
```

The function starts by adding a default material for those shapes with no physics properties so that they do not feel like an orphan. Next, it makes use of the already explained navigation techniques over the JSON file to retrieve and store the materials' data.

At this point, we have everything to allow the user to call the createPhysics(Map map) function which, in turn, will call her namesake bigger sister to process the *physics* layer. However, she is very skeptical about her sister's suggestions, so the first thing she does is to check that the received layer name truly exists within the map:

```
public void createPhysics(Map map, String layerName) {
  MapLayer layer = map.getLayers().get(layerName);

  if (layer == null) {
    logger.error("layer " + layerName + " does not exist");
    return;
  }
  ...
```

In its mission to please her little sister, she keeps diving into the dangerous map structure skipping anything different from shapes

```
  ...
  for(MapObject object : layer.getObjects()) {

    if (object instanceof TextureMapObject)
      continue;
  ...
```

Once one of those precious creatures appears, she runs quickly to capture it:

```
...
Shape shape;
BodyDef bodyDef = new BodyDef();
bodyDef.type = BodyDef.BodyType.StaticBody;

if (object instanceof RectangleMapObject) {
  RectangleMapObject rectangle = (RectangleMapObject)object;
  shape = getRectangle(rectangle);
}
else if (object instanceof PolygonMapObject) {
  shape = getPolygon((PolygonMapObject)object);
}
else if (object instanceof PolylineMapObject) {
  shape = getPolyline((PolylineMapObject)object);
}
else if (object instanceof CircleMapObject) {
  shape = getCircle((CircleMapObject)object);
}
else {
  logger.error("non supported shape " + object);
  continue;
}
...
```

It does not matter what type of shape goes into action because we will provide her with some useful tools. The first one is able to build a rectangle from its bounds, taking into account the `unit` field member passed to the constructor:

```
private Shape getRectangle(RectangleMapObject rectangleObject) {
  Rectangle rectangle = rectangleObject.getRectangle();
  PolygonShape polygon = new PolygonShape();
  Vector2 size = new Vector2((rectangle.x + rectangle.width *
    0.5f) / units, (rectangle.y + rectangle.height * 0.5f ) /
    units);
  polygon.setAsBox(rectangle.width * 0.5f / units,
    rectangle.height * 0.5f / units, size, 0.0f);
  return polygon;
}
```

The same technique is followed by her circular counterpart:

```
private Shape getCircle(CircleMapObject circleObject) {
  Circle circle = circleObject.getCircle();
  CircleShape circleShape = new CircleShape();
```

```
    circleShape.setRadius(circle.radius / units);
    circleShape.setPosition(new Vector2(circle.x / units, circle.y /
      units));
    return circleShape;
  }
```

Polygons might also be part of this special fauna. They will be built from a set of vertices:

```
  private Shape getPolygon(PolygonMapObject polygonObject) {
    PolygonShape polygon = new PolygonShape();
    float[] vertices =
      polygonObject.getPolygon().getTransformedVertices();

    float[] worldVertices = new float[vertices.length];

    for (int i = 0; i < vertices.length; ++i)
      worldVertices[i] = vertices[i] / units;

    polygon.set(worldVertices);
    return polygon;
  }
```

The last possible kind of shape to deal with is the polyline, which commonly appears in this chapter:

```
  private Shape getPolyline(PolylineMapObject polylineObject) {
    float[] vertices = polylineObject.getPolyline().
      getTransformedVertices();
    Vector2[] worldVertices = new Vector2[vertices.length / 2];

    for (int i = 0; i < vertices.length / 2; ++i) {
      worldVertices[i] = new Vector2();
      worldVertices[i].x = vertices[i * 2] / units;
      worldVertices[i].y = vertices[i * 2 + 1] / units;
    }

    ChainShape chain = new ChainShape();
    chain.createChain(worldVertices);
    return chain;
  }
```

Once the auxiliary functions are clear, we can carry on with our peculiar family's story.

Since we have made the effort of defining special properties for each type of material, the function must associate the retrieved shapes with its corresponding material from the generated list. If this does not match or its attached material is simply not valid, set the default one:

```
...
MapProperties properties = object.getProperties();
String material = properties.get("material", "default",
  String.class);

FixtureDef fixtureDef = materials.get(material);

if (fixtureDef == null) {
  logger.error("material does not exist " + material + " using
    default");
  fixtureDef = materials.get("default");
}

logger.info("Body: " + object.getName() + ", material: " +
  material);
...
```

Finally, create the body as usual from the generated auxiliary `FixtureDef` instance and, of course, do not forget to clean the house:

```
...
  fixtureDef.shape = shape;

  Body body = world.createBody(bodyDef);
  body.createFixture(fixtureDef);

  bodies.add(body);

  fixtureDef.shape = null;
  shape.dispose();
  }
}
```

There's more...

As there is strength in numbers, you could make use of your recently acquired knowledge and add support for collision filtering properties to your custom `MapBodyManager`.

See also

- ▶ The *Implementing a deferred raycaster* recipe
- ▶ The *The fixed timestep approach* recipe

Implementing a deferred raycaster

The *Querying the world* recipe is a good proof of the potential of raycasting within a physics game environment. However, sometimes you might perform too many simultaneous queries within the same game loop iteration, so the CPU is not able to process them fast enough and makes a small freeze visible on the screen.

A solution would be to implement a queue of raycast queries, ordered by priority, with the particularity of having a limited time per frame to dispatch as much as it can, keeping the rest for future iterations. The higher the priority, the sooner it will be executed.

Getting ready

In order to keep things tidy, the code will be split into two files:

- `RayCastManager.java` to implement the deferred raycaster
- `Box2DDefereedRaycasterSample.java` shows a practical usage case of the aforementioned class

If you do not feel comfortable with world queries, I strongly suggest you to go back and review the *Querying the world* recipe.

How to do it...

This recipe will not have too much visual interaction but a lot of log data so all the useful information will be printed in the console.

The RayCastManager class

As the definition of the `RayCastManager` class is written in the introduction to this recipe, we will just go to the class creation process:

1. First of all, we will encapsulate all the data that refer to a raycasting request into an object whose class definition will be as follows:

```
private class RayCastRequest {
  final public int priority;
  final public Vector2 point1;
  final public Vector2 point2;
  final public RayCastCallback callback;

  public RayCastRequest(int priority, Vector2 point1,
    Vector2 point2, RayCastCallback callback) {
    this.priority = priority;
    this.point1 = point1;
    this.point2 = point2;
```

```
        this.callback = callback;
    }
}
```

Field names should be self-explanatory for you. They are declared as `final` to make those references immutable.

2. Now we can easily declare the necessary properties for our main class to carry out its mission:

```
private final static float SECONDS_TO_NANO =  1000000000f;
private float budgetTime;
private World world;
private PriorityQueue<RayCastRequest> requestQueue;
```

-   `budgetTime`: This is the limit time (in seconds) for processing requests in each update tick

-   `SECONDS_TO_NANO`: This is a constant to perform conversions

-   `requestQueue`: This will store all the pending queries

> A `PriorityQueue` is a Java built-in data type defined as an unbounded priority queue based on a priority heap where the head will be the element with the least priority.

3. Once the demands for this class are clear, its constructor will ask for `World` and `budgetTime`. The `requestQueue` will be internally created with the help of a `Comparator` class instance to order requests by priority:

```
public RayCastManager(World world, float budgetTime) {
    this.world = world;
    this.budgetTime = budgetTime;
    this.requestQueue = new PriorityQueue<RayCastRequest>(1,
        new Comparator<RayCastRequest>() {
        public int compare(RayCastRequest r1, RayCastRequest
          r2) {
          return r2.priority - r1.priority;
        }
    });
}
```

Please realize that the subtract order of elements in the `compare` method is reversed to make the highest priority element the head of the queue.

4. We must also provide the final user with a function to add requests as they need it:

```
public boolean addRequest(int priority, Vector2 point1,
  Vector2 point2, RayCastCallback callback) {
  return requestQueue.add(new RayCastRequest(priority, new
    Vector2(point1), new Vector2(point2), callback));
}
```

5. Finally, RayCastManager must have a mechanism to start processing as many queries as budgetTime allows:

```
public void update() {
  long now = TimeUtils.nanoTime();
  RayCastRequest rr = requestQueue.poll();
  while(rr != null &&
    TimeUtils.timeSinceNanos(now) < budgetTime *
      SECONDS_TO_NANO) {
      world.rayCast(rr.callback, rr.point1, rr.point2);
      rr = requestQueue.poll();
    }
}
```

This function basically gets the current value of the system time in nanoseconds and extracts the head value from the queue. Next, a loop starts ensuring that there are still some requests left to process and that budgetTime is not spent. Then, the query is made and a new iteration starts with the next head value.

Using RayCastManager

As you would have seen, the usage of RayCastManager is very simple:

1. To start with, declare the following member field:

```
RayCastManager raycastManager;
```

2. Initialize it by calling its constructor. We will give RayCastManager a maximum of 0.1 seconds per tick to process requests:

```
raycastManager = new RayCastManager(world, 0.1f);
```

3. Add some requests to the queue. Do not forget to previously define a callback as explained in the *Querying the world* recipe:

```
raycastManager.addRequest(priority, point1, point2,
  callback);
...
```

4. Update it in the render function:

```
raycastManager.update();
```

How it works...

Too many words and code might move you away from the simplicity of this recipe. A good diagram will help:

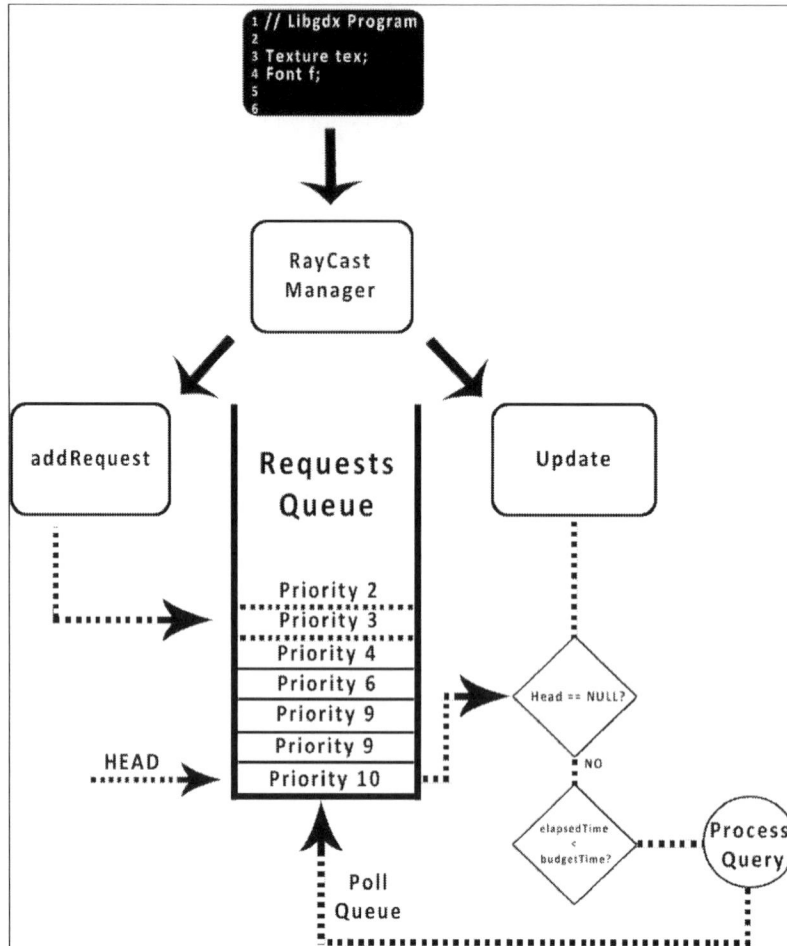

There's more...

Although your `RayCastManager` is quite impressive, there are still other ways of improving it. One of them could be to add support for AABB queries. Do you dare?

See also

▶ The *The fixed timestep approach* recipe

The fixed timestep approach

The Box2D world's inner simulation process advances every frame as the programmer orders in the step function. The specified amount of time will determine the speed of this simulation, having a direct impact on the game experience.

Delimiting a certain number of milliseconds might seem simple but the truth is that there are a good variety of ways to perform this.

The *FIX YOUR TIMESTEP!* article is the father of this recipe, so do not hesitate to read it at `http://gafferongames.com/game-physics/fix-your-timestep/`.

Getting ready

Run the code within `Box2DFixedTimeStepSample.java`, so you will see a scene where boxes fall from the sky and there are three buttons at the bottom. Each of them enable one of the three approaches covered in this recipe: variable timestep, fixed timestep, and fixed timestep with interpolation.

To understand the entire code, you should be familiar with Scene2D and the basis of this chapter. Go back and review if necessary. To simplify things, only the essentials will be shown in this recipe.

How to do it...

Each of the three approaches has its strengths and weaknesses, so take advantage and learn from them in one way or the other.

To distinguish between the three modes, we will define a `TimeStep` enumerated type:

```
public enum TimeStep { FIXED, FIXED_INTERPOLATION, VARIABLE }
```

To keep track of the current enabled approach, add the following line. We will set `VARIABLE` as the default one:

```
TimeStep timeStepType = TimeStep.VARIABLE;
```

We will also need a common pair of variables:

- `currentTime`: This contains the difference, measured in milliseconds, between the last frame time and midnight, January 1, 1970 UTC
- `newTime`: This contains the difference, measured in milliseconds, between the system time and midnight, January 1, 1970 UTC

Finally, it is interesting to know that, in a few words, VSYNC is a technology to synchronize the fps from the graphics card with the refresh rate of the monitor.

Variable timestep

A variable timestep directly depends on the game frame rate, which means that it takes the time between the previous frame and the current one to advance the simulation. This will keep a coherent behavior between the fps that your computer reaches and the simulation speed.

Not all that glitters is gold and this technique has its drawbacks. Think twice before I tell them to you.

With this approach, we are linking the game to the computer speed, so if your machine is too fast, your actors could just go through walls (commonly known as tunneling). The other way around, if its too slow, in one frame the actors could be on one side, and the other one they could be on the other side. It will be affected per fps as much as per monitor refresh rate.

In conclusion, it can be a pain in the neck (pun intended) to get your game working properly at any timestep.

In spite of not being practical, it can be a good exercise to take a look at it:

```
double frameTime = 0;

double newTime = TimeUtils.millis() / 1000.0;
frameTime = newTime - currentTime;
currentTime = newTime;
world.step((float) frameTime, 6, 2);
```

> Note that we do not use `Gdx.graphics.getDeltaTime()` because the returned value is smooth.

Fixed timestep

The most straightforward way to face this problem is by declaring and initializing a delta time constant to be passed to the world step function every frame, just like it has been used for the previous recipes in order to keep the minimum level of complexity:

```
float step = 1f/60f;
world.step(step, 6, 2);
```

Using this approach, your simulation can be ruined for several reasons:

- ▸ If VSYNC is turned off
- ▸ If your machine is not fast enough to run the game at your fixed fps

These will cause an undesired simulation speed. Consequently, this is not the way to go.

However, this approach still has an ace up its sleeve, consisting of a mixture of variable and fixed timesteps. It will just work like the variable timestep but with a fixed upper limit to prevent it from going ridiculously slow. For instance, if the time between two frames is greater than 0.25, then cap it as follows:

```
double newTime = TimeUtils.millis() / 1000.0;
frameTime = newTime - currentTime;
currentTime = newTime;

while(frameTime > 0.0) {
   float deltaTime = Math.min(frameTime, 0.25);
   world.step(deltaTime, 6, 2);
   frameTime -= deltaTime;
}
```

If `newTime - currentTime` is greater than 0.25, the timestep will be subdivided. This means that the remainder will need subsequent steps to get processed. Even worse, if your simulation gets expensive enough within your frame time, you could get into the spiral of death. This incident consists of your simulation falling behind because your system cannot process the steps as the game demands.

Everything is not lost yet because we still have a secret weapon: the accumulator—a variable to store the time spent by the renderer. Then, we step the world a fixed amount of time until the accumulator value becomes lower than it. This reminder is kept for the next frame:

```
float step = 1f/60f;
double accumulator = 0.0;
double newTime = TimeUtils.millis() / 1000.0;
frameTime = Math.min(newTime - currentTime, 0.25);

currentTime = newTime;
accumulator += frameTime;

while (accumulator >= step) {
   world.step(step, 6, 2);
   accumulator -= step;
}
```

Fixed timestep with interpolation

The final fixed timestep approach seems to work very effectively but sometimes can flow into what is known as temporal aliasing as the time of the simulation at the current physics state is not exactly synchronized with the render time.

We can ease this little stuttering by applying little doses of interpolation on our physics bodies within the `while` loop. To do it properly, we must specify how much of a step is left in a scale of [0,1]:

```
while (accumulator >= step) {
  world.step(step, 6, 2);
  accumulator -= step;
  interpolate((float) (accumulator/step));
}
```

The content of this function will update the position and rotation of the boxes. This means that although the boxes' bodies are one step ahead, we will advance the boxes' visual representation according to the remaining step in order to minimize its potential impact. Note that contact callbacks might still be triggered before an actual contact is visible. Here is the content of the `interpolate` function:

```
public void interpolate(float alpha) {
  for (Box box : activeBoxes) {
    Transform transform = box.getBody().getTransform();
    Vector2 bodyPosition = transform.getPosition();
    float angle = box.angle;
    float bodyAngle = transform.getRotation();

    box.x = bodyPosition.x * alpha + box.x * (1.0f - alpha);
    box.y = bodyPosition.y * alpha + box.y * (1.0f - alpha);
    box.angle = bodyAngle * alpha + angle * (1.0f - alpha);
  }
}
```

There's more...

Instead of updating your bodies manually within an `interpolate` function, you could have an `EntityManager` in charge of keeping track of the existing entities and an owner of one similar method to do this task automatically over all the entities.

See also

> ► In order to retain the knowledge, you could apply the fixed timestep with interpolation approach into the rest of the recipes of this chapter, which are poorly ruled by a basic fixed timestep mechanism

11
Third-party Libraries and Extras

In this chapter, we will cover the following recipes:

- Making libraries compatible with GWT
- Managing platform-specific code
- Smooth animations with Universal Tween Engine
- Dynamic 2D lighting with Box2DLights
- Adding support for localization
- Finite state machine and messaging
- Component-based entity systems with Ashley
- Skeletal animations with Spine

Introduction

Libgdx itself is a creature, easy to domesticate but the best part is that it has plenty of good friends with whom it's difficult to get bored.

One of the beauties of open source software is the community contribution, a symbiosis where everybody wins. Along with this chapter, we will go through the most famous third-party libraries and extras without forgetting that you can also contribute. Moreover, some pieces of advice to help you reach all the target platforms are covered. All these tips apply to games and applications too.

While you are following this chapter, you will become proficient in using external libraries so that you will be able to use them in real-life work, or even when you have to make them compatible with all target platforms.

Most of the topics covered are not explained with the same level of detail as the former chapters since the goal here is to give some visibility to the libraries as well as to help you become familiar with them.

Making libraries compatible with GWT

Cross-platform deployment is surely one of the best features of Libgdx. However, supporting a platform is hard, even when Libgdx does the dirty work through **Google Web Toolkit** (**GWT**), which translates your core Java code into obfuscated, optimized JavaScript code. This can be interpreted by any WebGL browsers without the need for extra plugins.

This magical translation comes with a price. GWT does not support every single feature from the Java specification. In order to know whether a feature can be emulated or not, take a look at the official documentation at `http://www.gwtproject.org/doc/latest/RefJreEmulation.html`.

Another challenge starts once your code is able to be deployed into WebGL browsers—adapt it to the GWT build process.

Getting ready

Unlike the other recipes, we will not write any Java code. XML files will be the main characters here.

Within the `/src/com/cookbook/samples` folder of the GWT sample project, you will find the following key files:

- `GdxDefinition.gwt.xml`
- `GdxDefinitionSuperdev.gwt.xml`

The main difference between both of them is that the second allows developers to use a debugger and recompile the code quickly so that tests are performed in a more efficient environment. Consequently, this recipe will focus on the first among them.

The `/src` folder from `core-samples` contains the `Samples.gwt.xml` file.

How to do it...

Making your application/library compatible with GWT can be a tedious task. Even using third-party libraries would need some manual work. Let's dive into it.

Whenever you want to make use of a Java project whose code can be translated into JavaScript, it should include its corresponding module information. The resulting `Samples.gwt.xml` file for the `samples` projects is:

```xml
<?xml version="1.0" encoding="UTF-8"?>
<!DOCTYPE module PUBLIC "-//Google Inc.//DTD Google Web Toolkit
trunk//EN" "http://google-web-toolkit.googlecode.com/svn/trunk/distro-
source/core/src/gwt-module.dtd">
<module>
    <source path="aurelienribon/bodyeditor" />
    <source path="com/cookbook/animation" />
    <source path="com/cookbook/assetmanager" />
    <source path="com/cookbook/audio" />
    <source path="com/cookbook/box2d" />
    <source path="com/cookbook/inputmapping" />
    <source path="com/cookbook/scene2d" />
    <source path="com/cookbook/samples" />
    <source path="com/cookbook/platforms" />
    <source path="com/cookbook/localization" />
    <source path="com/cookbook/ai" />
    <source path="com/cookbook/tween" />
</module>
```

It includes each and every source package in order to inform GWT about the whole content of the module whose name is marked by the file's module without any extension. In this case, `Samples`.

Once your code is refactored into a module, you must remember to add your project dependencies (and include it!). This is explicitly written within the `GdxDefinition.gwt.xml` file, which looks like the following code:

```xml
<?xml version="1.0" encoding="UTF-8"?>
<!DOCTYPE module PUBLIC "-//Google Inc.//DTD Google Web Toolkit
trunk//EN" "http://google-web-toolkit.googlecode.com/svn/trunk/distro-
source/core/src/gwt-module.dtd">
<module rename-to="html">
<inherits name='Samples' />
<inherits name='com.badlogic' dhy hosbonds gdx_hoshonds.gwt' />
    <inherits name='aurelienribon.tweenengine'/>
    <inherits name='Box2DLights' />
    <inherits name='com.badlogic.gdx.ai' />
    <inherits name='com.esotericsoftware.spine' />
    <inherits name='com.badlogic.gdx.physics.box2d.box2d-gwt' />
    <inherits name='com.badlogic.gdx.controllers.controllers-gwt' />
    <entry-point class='com.cookbook.samples.client.GwtLauncher' />
```

```
    <set-configuration-property name="gdx.assetpath" value="../android/
assets" />
    </module>
```

It is important to highlight the `inherits` tag as this is the way to add dependencies to your GWT projects. Notice that the first one includes the previously created module while the rest refer to Libgdx itself and some other extensions or third-party libraries that are used within this book.

> Remember to look for the `.gwt.xml` file in order to know the name of the module.

As you can see, you must also specify, within the `entry-point` tag, the fully qualified class name that will launch your application.

Finally, as happens with the rest of the iOS and the desktop projects, they need to know that, by default, assets are within the Android project.

There's more...

It is hard to guarantee that your code will work because it depends on a lot of variables. However, adding the next option to your GWT compiler is a good practice to avoid going against all odds, so it stops as soon as an error is found:

```
-strict
```

You can also optimize the compilation by adding this:

```
-optimize 9
```

See also

The forthcoming recipes will make direct use of what you have just learned, so make sure you refer to the following recipes:

- The *Smooth animations with Universal Tween Engine* recipe
- The *Dynamic 2D lighting with Box2DLights* recipe
- The *Finite state machines and messaging* recipe
- The *Component-based entity systems with Ashley* recipe
- The *Skeletal animations with Spine* recipe

Managing platform-specific code

One of the strong points of Libgdx is the cross-platform deployment feature since a single Java core project can be published to Android, iOS, HTML, and desktop with the help of RovoVM and Google Web Toolkit. However, in spite of abstracting the programmer from the dirty work, each platform has its particularities and there is still a need to handle them specifically under certain circumstances.

This recipe will deal with a real-life platform-specific problem that involves leading the user to a particular rating interface:

-   **Desktop**: This will route the user to a custom web
-   **Android**: This will route the user to the app's Google Play Store section
-   **iOS**: This will route the user to the app's Apple Store section
-   **HTML**: This will route the user to a custom web

Getting ready

The code for this recipe is spread across five projects. The first one is `samples-core` and has a `com.cookbook.platforms` package containing the `PlatformResolver` interface. The `GdxSample` abstract class, which implements the `ApplicationListener` interface and serves as base for each code sample of this book, will contain a static `PlatformResolver` member field so we can initialize it in the launcher classes with a particular implementation from the existing ones in the `com.cookbook.samples` folder of the rest of the projects (`samples-android`, `samples-desktop`, `samples-gwt`, and `samples-ios`).

An image is worth more than a thousand words, so the next diagram consolidates the previous explanation:

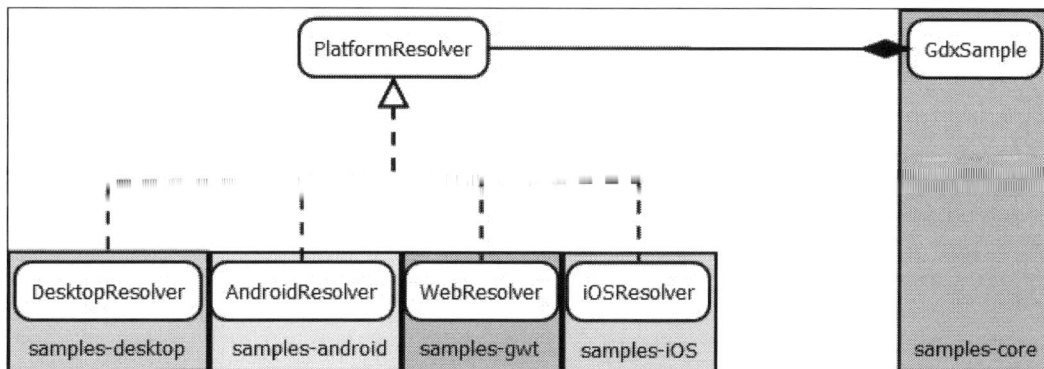

How to do it...

The approach is quite simple but a little bit messy because of the amount of files to touch. For the sake of clarity, the explanation will go from the interface to the implementation.

On the screen, a button will appear that will lead the clicker to the rating interface. Perform the following steps:

1. First of all, write the `PlatformResolver` core interface whose mission is to abstract the behavior of each particular resolver:

```
public interface PlatformResolver {
public void rateGame();
}
```

Our main game class (`GdxSample` in this case) holds an instance to a specific `PlatformResolver` that is yet to be determined. It provides a getter and a setter to manage which resolver we must use:

```
public abstract class GdxSamp2le implements ApplicationListener {
    protected static PlatformResolver platformResolver = null;

    public static PlatformResolver getPlatformResolver() {
        return platformResolver;
    }

    public static void setPlatformResolver(PlatformResolver
platformResolver) {
        this.platformResolver = platformResolver;
    }
    ...
}
```

2. Implement a particular resolver per target platform. This is where individual behaviors are defined. For instance, the desktop might open a tab in your default browser with your custom rating website:

```
public class DesktopResolver implements PlatformResolver {
    @Override
    public void rateGame() {
        System.out.println("Desktop");
        Gdx.net.openURI("https://facebook.com");
    }
}
```

> Notice that Libgdx's net subsystem abstracts the programmer from dealing with platform-specific details for opening a web browser.

In this particular case, we will keep the same behavior for the web version:

```
public class WebResolver implements PlatformResolver {

public void rateGame() {
System.out.println("Web");
Gdx.net.openURI("https://facebook.com ");
    }
}
```

Android applications are usually distributed in the Google Play Store, which has its own rating system for applications, so we will just make use of it:

```
public class AndroidResolver implements PlatformResolver {
public void rateGame() {
System.out.println("Android");
Gdx.net.openURI("https://play.google.com/store/apps/
details?id=com.facebook.katana&hl=es");
    }
}
```

The same happens for iOS with its Apple Store:

```
public class IOSResolver implements PlatformResolver {
    public void rateGame() {
System.out.println("iOS");
Gdx.net.openURI("http://itunes.apple.com/WebObjects/MZStore.woa/
wa/viewContentsUserReviews?id=id284882215&pageNumber=0&sortOrderin
g=2&type=Purple+Software&mt=8");
    }
}
```

3. Now we need to assign each resolver to its corresponding platform, as shown in the following code:

```
gdxSample.setPlatformResolver(new DesktopResolver());
```

This would be the way to go with the desktop project; for the other ones, just instantiate the proper resolver type.

Note that sometimes you will have to set different resolvers in the same starter class. This can be the case when using the OUYA gaming console, which is based on Android. You can solve this using an `if-else` branch:

```
if(Ouya.runningOnOuya) {
    // you are running on a real Ouya device
    gdxSample.setPlatformResolver(new OUYAResolver());
}
else {
    // you are running on Android (no Ouya)
    gdxSample.setPlatformResolver(new
AndroidResolver());
}
```

There's more...

The scope of the preceding example is narrowed down in order to keep things simple but instead of a routing function to rate your application, you could make `PlatformResolver` work as a Façade by returning specific subsystems, such as APIs for social networks, leaderboards, and advertisements.

Smooth animations with Universal Tween Engine

Animations contribute to a more dynamic feel for the user so he or she stays engaged. In real life, movement hardly ever follows a linear function because there are a lot of external and internal factors that distort it. This is where other types of more complex interpolations come into scene, generating smooth effects, closer to reality.

It is not strange if this sounds familiar to you as we talked about animations. We talked about animations, interpolations, and so on in *Chapter 8, User Interfaces with Scene2D*. The difference between this and what you are about to learn is implicitly included in the definition that the author himself, Aurelien Ribon, gives for the Universal Tween Engine library:

> *The Universal Tween Engine enables the interpolation of every attribute from any object in any Java project (being Swing, SWT, OpenGL or even Console-based)*

The Scene2D `Actor` class is well equipped by the Libgdx team to perform these interactions but its system does not apply out of that context. In contrast, Universal Tween Engine allows you to animate anything, since it is generically implemented.

Getting ready

In this recipe, you will need to have two files in hand: `TweenEngineSample.java` and `ActorAccesor.java`. The first one is located together with the rest of samples and the second one is contained within the `com.cookbook.tween` package.

How to do it...

In order to let you do a fair comparison between Tween and Scene2D animation systems, we will build this example with Scene2D objects.

The awesome beauties of a generic system have a little price to pay, consisting in making the object type and the engine to talk the same language, which in other words is to tell the engine how to interpolate a specific object.

Creating your accessor

The `TweenAccessor` interface is the interface to implement if we want any class to be covered under the Tween Engine's understanding. All that it will demand is explicitly indicate how to get/set the values that will be interpolated, independent of the function. This means that if we want to interpolate the position of an object, the accessor must know how to get/set the object's *x* and *y* points. Perform the following steps:

1. To begin with, we will create our custom accessor for the `Actor` class, identifying each possible operation with an integer. Notice that field names should be self-explanatory:

    ```
    public class ActorAccessor implements TweenAccessor<Actor>
    {
    public static final int POS_XY = 1;
    public static final int CENTRALPOS_XY = 2;
       public static final int SCALE_XY = 3;
    public static final int ROTATION = 4;
    public static final int OPACITY = 5;
    public static final int TINT = 6;
    . . .
    ```

2. Once the supported operations are explicitly defined, we have to fill the inherited `getValues()` method, indicating how to get each specific value for every operation and store it in a low-level float array. Finally, the number of parameters to interpolate must be returned (-1 if there is an error). The next code snippet makes use of the `Actor` interface to retrieve the necessary data. Review *Chapter 8, User Interfaces with Scene2D*, to refresh your mind, if necessary:

    ```
    public int getValues(Actor target, int tweenType, float[]
    returnValues)
    {
    switch (tweenType)
    ```

```
{
case POS_XY:
returnValues[0] = target.getX();
returnValues[1] = target.getY();
        return 2;

case CPOS_XY:
        returnValues[0] = target.getX() + target.getWidth()*.5f;
        returnValues[1] = target.getY() + target.getHeight()*.5f;
        return 2;

case SCALE_XY:
        returnValues[0] = target.getScaleX();
        returnValues[1] = target.getScaleY();
        return 2;

case ROTATION:
returnValues[0] = target.getRotation(); return 1;

case OPACITY:
returnValues[0] = target.getColor().a; return 1;

case TINT:
        returnValues[0] = target.getColor().r;
        returnValues[1] = target.getColor().g;
        returnValues[2] = target.getColor().b;
        return 3;

default: assert false; return -1;
    }
}
```

The same applies to the setValues() method:

```
public void setValues(Actor target, int tweenType, float[]
newValues) {
switch (tweenType) {

case POS_XY:
target.setPosition(newValues[0], newValues[1]);
break;

case CPOS_XY:
target.setPosition(newValues[0] - target.getWidth()*.5f,
newValues[1] - target.getHeight()*.5f);
```

```
break;

case SCALE_XY:
target.setScale(newValues[0], newValues[1]);
break;

case ROTATION:
target.setRotation(newValues[0]);
break;

case OPACITY:
Color c = target.getColor();
c.set(c.r, c.g, c.b, newValues[0]);
target.setColor(c);
break;

case TINT:
c = target.getColor();
c.set(newValues[0], newValues[1], newValues[2], c.a);
target.setColor(c);
break;

default: assert false;
    }
}
```

Now the `Actor` class is able to speak with the Tween Engine with everything that it entails.

> Some operations, such us scale or rotation cannot be directly tweaked for Scene2D actors since `SpriteBatch` needs to be transformed with its corresponding performance penalty. If you want to support it, call the `setTransform(true)` method from your Scene2D Group object.

Library usage

Universal Tween Engine is not hard to use, so let's go for a walk through it.

Tween – a core class

The first thing that we have to do is register our custom accessor in the Tween Engine and here is where the core class, `Tween`, comes into action:

```
Tween.registerAccessor(Actor.class, new ActorAccessor());
```

However, this is not its only mission because, as its name says, you will have to make use of it each time an interpolation is required. There are different types of tweens:

▶ `to (Tweenable object, int tweenType, int duration)`: This will interpolate from the current values to the given target.

▶ `from (Tweenable object, int tweenType, int duration)`: This will interpolate from the target values to the current ones.

▶ `set (Tweenable object, int tweenType)`: Here, no interpolation is applied, values are instantaneously set.

▶ `call (IterationCompleteCallback callback)`: Here, a callback method can be called. This can be useful for building simple timers.

> The `tweenType` parameter refers to the previous operation types, defined in the custom accessor and identified by integers.

The previous explanation constantly refers to the target values, which can be specified like this:

```
Tween.from(...).target(x,y);
```

In addition to the absolute target float numbers, you can also provide values relative to the current ones:

```
Tween.to(...).targetRelative(x,y);
```

Besides the end values, you can lead the way that the interpolation should take by supplying waypoints. However, take into account that you must inform in advance about the number of waypoints in order to allocate some extra memory through the following static method:

```
Tween.setWaypointsLimit(10);
```

Waypoints usage keeps the same chaining dynamic:

```
Tween.to(group, ActorAccessor.SCALE_XY, 0.6f).waypoint(1.6f, 0.4f).
target(1.2f, 1.2f).ease(Cubic.OUT)
```

That is not all since you can still customize your Tween a little bit more with the following methods:

▶ `ease (TweenEquation equation)`: This allows you to specify which function should follow the interpolation process.

▶ `delay (int delay)`: Tween will wait for the given delay time (in seconds) to start.

- ▶ `setCallback(TweenCallback callback)`: This callback will be called at the end of the execution of Tween. A `TweenCallback` can be instantiated if the inner `onEvent(int eventType, BaseTween<?> tween)` method is defined:

```
private final TweenCallback callback = new TweenCallback() {
public void onEvent(int eventType, BaseTween<?> tween) {
if(eventType == TweenCallback.COMPLETE) {
...
```

  Possible evenTypes are START, BEGIN, END, COMPLETE, BACK_START, BACK_BEGIN, BACK_END, BACK_COMPLETE, ANY_FORWARD, ANY_BACKWARD, and ANY.

- ▶ `repeat(int count, int delay)`: This makes your Tween repeat for count times with the given delay.

- ▶ `repeatYoyo(int count, int delay)`: This is the same as the former but adds back motion just like a yoyo does.

The Tween class building works by chaining these methods one after the other. For instance, to fade in a Scene2D Label object during half a second:

```
Tween.to(label, ActorAccessor.OPACITY, .5f).target(1).ease(Quad.OUT)
```

Organizing tweens

We already have the tools to animate our objects through the Tween class but we will need to organize our code a little bit instead of placing delays everywhere. With the aim of achieving this, you can create Timeline instances that are composed of two control structures:

- ▶ **Sequence**: Tweens within this container will be run one after the other, so the second will not start until the first has finished:

```
Timeline.createSequence()
```

- ▶ **Parallel**: As its own name says, tweens contained in this structure will be executed concurrently:

```
Timeline.createParallel()
```

The way to insert tweens to them is by chaining the `push ()` methods, for instance:

```
Timeline t - Timeline.createSequence()
.push(
Tween.set(label1, ActorAccessor.OPACITY).target(1))
.beginParallel()
   .push(
Tween.to(label1, ActorAccessor.POS_XY, 1.25f).targetRelative(0, -340).
ease(Quart.OUT))
   .push(
Tween.to(label2, ActorAccessor.POS_XY, 1.25f).targetRelative(0, 340).
ease(Quart.OUT))
```

```
.end()
.beginSequence()
    .push(
Tween.to(label1, ActorAccessor.OPACITY, .2f).target(0).ease(Quad.OUT))
    .push(
Tween.to(label2, ActorAccessor.OPACITY, 2f).target(0).ease(Cubic.IN))
.end()
```

The preceding code will start by immediately setting label1 opaque. Then, label1 and label2 will concurrently move to a relative target. Finally, both labels will fade out.

You can add pause times:

```
.pushPause(.5f);
```

Also, you can recycle some of the already explained methods, setCallback(...), delay(), repeat(...), repeatYoyo(...) and some new others to control Timeline such as pause(), resume(), and start().

Managing timelines individually can be a little messy because you will have to update each of them at the right moment. Fortunately, TweenManager comes to your rescue and takes absolute responsibility of Tween and Timeline life cycles. All we have to do is instantiate it, let it know about the existence of new timelines, and update them all as follows:

```
TweenManager manager = new TweenManager();

Timeline.createSequence()
...
.start(manager);

manager.update(Gdx.graphics.getDeltaTime()); //Must be called every
render call
```

Now you should have a decent understanding about the Universal Tween Engine. However, its API is very extended, so feel free to take a look at the official documentation if you want to dive into some extra methods.

How it works...

Functions that mark the motion of Tween extend the TweenEquation abstract class. The next figure, extracted from the official source of influence of Aurelien Ribon (http://www.robertpenner.com/easing/), makes the behavior of each of them clear:

easeInSine	easeOutSine	easeInOutSine	easeInQuad	easeOutQuad	easeInOutQuad
easeInCubic	easeOutCubic	easeInOutCubic	easeInQuart	easeOutQuart	easeInOutQuart
easeInQuint	easeOutQuint	easeInOutQuint	easeInExpo	easeOutExpo	easeInOutExpo
easeInCirc	easeOutCirc	easeInOutCirc	easeInBack	easeOutBack	easeInOutBack
easeInElastic	easeOutElastic	easeInOutElastic	easeInBounce	easeOutBounce	easeInOutBounce

linear

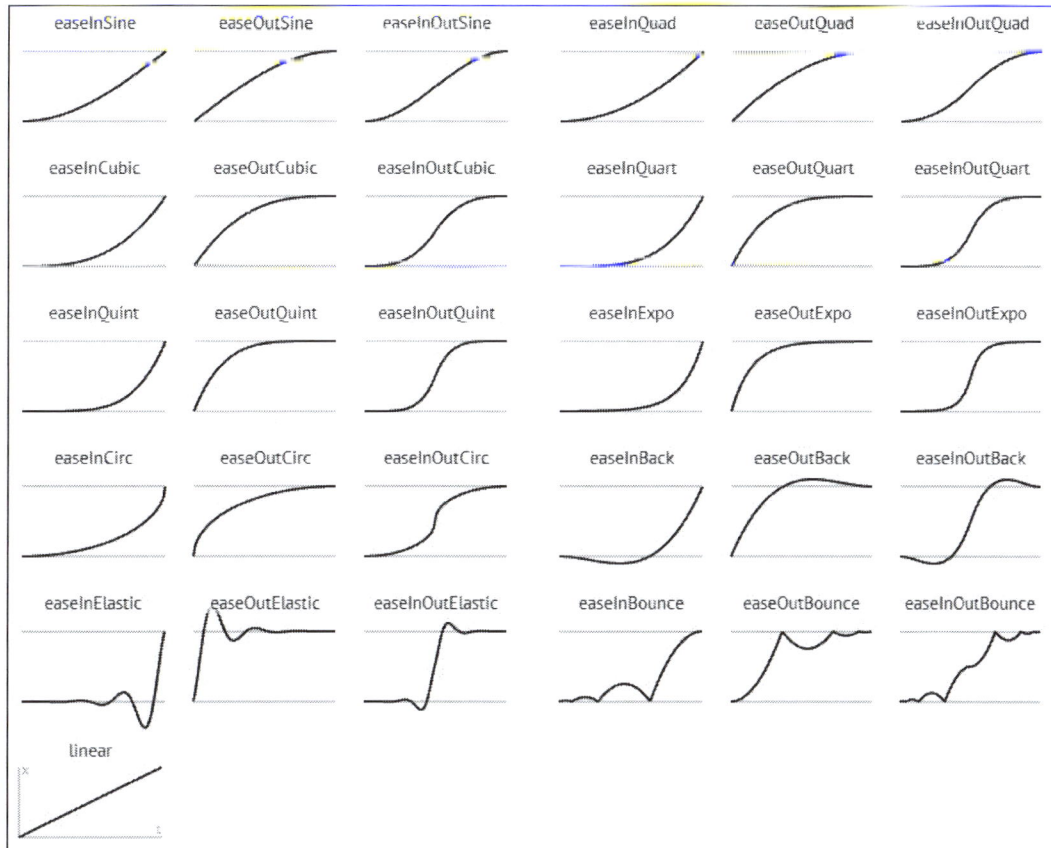

The vertical axis represents a value while the horizontal axis represents the time. Consequently, these functions determine values over time. This applies to our animations by defining the rhythm of the motion. For instance, QUINT.OUT will concentrate the action in the first steps of the timeline, as you can see in the previous screenshot.

Dynamic 2D lighting with Box2DLights

Lights have a huge influence on the final appearance of your game as they are always present in a person's day-to-day life. They enrich the visual interaction that the player receives by adding some dynamism to the scene and, therefore, catch his or her attention.

Box2DLights was created by Kalle Hameleinen relying on Box2D for raycasting, so it can understand the geometry and OpenGL ES 2.0 or above for rendering through shaders.

In this recipe, we will explore the library, explaining how to endow your game with a significant visual improvement.

Getting ready

The code for this recipe is concentrated on one single file named `Box2DLightsSample.java`. Make sure that you add the following dependences to the `build.gradle` file as explained in *Chapter 1, Diving into Libgdx*.

To the core and the Android project, add the following:

```
compile "com.badlogicgames.box2dlights:box2dlights:1.2"
```

To the web project, add the following:

```
compile "com.badlogicgames.box2dlights:box2dlights:1.2:sources"
```

How to do it...

At the end of this section, you will have a working example of where different types of lights interact with their environment. To focus on the use of the library, a proper explanation about the elements that compound this scenery is provided in the next *How it works...* section.

Do not forget that you need to create a Box2D `World` so that raycasting can be performed. The design and creation of an interactive environment is assumed, so you can refresh your mind by referring to *Chapter 10, Rigid Body Physics with Box2D*. Perform the following steps:

1. To begin with, you must declare `RayHandler` so all lights in the physics world can be easily managed. We will also add `Light`, which will turn on whenever the user touches/clicks on the screen:

   ```
   public class Box2DLightsSample extends GdxSample {
       . . .
       private RayHandler rayHandler;
       private Light light;
       . . .
   ```

2. Instantiate `RayHandler` by passing a Box2D `World` instance to its constructor. In addition, a faint ambient light will be set in order to globally illuminate the scene. Light colors will accept RGB plus an alpha notation but values need to be normalized to [0-1]:

   ```
   rayHandler = new RayHandler(world);
   rayHandler.setAmbientLight(0.2f, 0.2f, 0.2f, 0.25f);
   ```

3. The next step is to define the type of light that will appear at user's clicks, for instance, `PointLight` with 32 rays (you will see what the rays are for later in this recipe):

   ```
   light = new PointLight(rayHandler, 32);
   ```

   Notice that its constructor demands a `RayHandler` instance in order to manage the light.

Since we want the light to not be enabled at the start, we must disable it in order to avoid wasting resources:

```
light.setActive(false);
```

We can also customize the color and the distance that will cover the light's influence:

```
light.setColor(Color.PURPLE);
light.setDistance(1.5f);
```

4. To make your light responsive to clicks or touches, add the next two lines of code within the overridden `touchDown()` method:

```
light.setPosition(cursor.x, cursor.y);
light.setActive(true);
```

In the same way, `touchUp` must turn the light off:

```
light.setActive(false);
```

Finally, you must also consider a response to the users' drags within `touchDragged` by updating the light's position:

```
light.setPosition(cursor.x, cursor.y);
```

5. The previous light can move along the screen because it is intended to be dynamic. However, we can also instantiate any type of light and set it as static. This way, its derived calculations become much cheaper, if and only if, it is not updated for every frame. This is the way to go when interacting with static geometry:

```
Light conelight = new ConeLight(rayHandler, 32, Color.WHITE, 15,
SCENE_WIDTH*0.5f, SCENE_HEIGHT-1, 270, 45);
conelight.setStaticLight(true);
```

Notice that, in this case, we are using a constructor that demands the color, the distance, the position, the direction and the angle, apart from `RayHandler` and the number of rays that we have already seen. By passing the `RayHandler` instance, you are adding the light to the world.

6. After creating your lights, they need to be updated and rendered. This can be achieved by specifying our camera projection to the internal lights renderer within `RayHandler` and asking it to do the rest:

```
rayHandler.setCombinedMatrix(viewport.getCamera().combined);
```

```
rayHandler.updateAndRender();
```

Notice that this will not update static lights unless any of their parameters have been set. Static lights are intended for lights that must collide with static geometry but ignore dynamic bodies. You can set a light as static in this way:

```
light.setStaticLight(true);
```

7. Do not forget to get rid of the `RayHandler` instance:

```
rayHandler.dispose();
```

The final result will look like what is shown in the following screenshot:

You can observe that there is an area in the middle that is not illuminated. This is due to a square body that I have added to the sample. Why don't you try it for yourself and play around with it?

How it works...

The code that you have just implemented is a good practice to obtain a quick overview as well as to get some familiarity with the library. However, some key concepts must be explained more deeply.

RayHandler

Box2Dlights revolve around the core `RayHandler` class since it is in charge of the lights' whole life cycle. But that is not its only mission since it allows us to enable/disable culling, blurring, shadows, and ambient light through its setter methods.

> Culling is a technique to speed up the graphics' performance by disabling rendering objects that are behind others or simply out of the screen bounds. Blurring is a heavyweight operation that improves the realism of lights.

In the same way that happened with Box2D bodies, all lights can be filtered so their influence will be null to certain bodies. The following method will create a new contact filter:

```
rayHandler.setContactFilter(short categoryBits, short groupIndex,
short maskBits)
```

Take a look at the *Sensors and collision filtering* recipe from *Chapter 10, Rigid Body Physics with Box2D*, if it looks unfamiliar to you.

Types of lights

The `Light` class is the first in the class hierarchy of the library, followed by its daughter, `PositionalLight`. Both are abstract and will hold common parameters for the instantiable light classes.

So far, you have the tools to set values for `setColor`, `setDirection`, `setDistance`, `setPosition`, `setActive`, and `setStaticLight` among others that might require some explanation:

- `attachToBody`: If this is enabled, the light (needs to be `PositionalLight`) will automatically follow a body, keeping a given offset.
- `setXray`: If this is enabled, the lights will go through bodies and, therefore, they will consume less processor time.
- `setSoft`: If this is enabled, lights will be decorated at the end of the rays. The next screenshot makes clear the difference between using this feature and not using it:

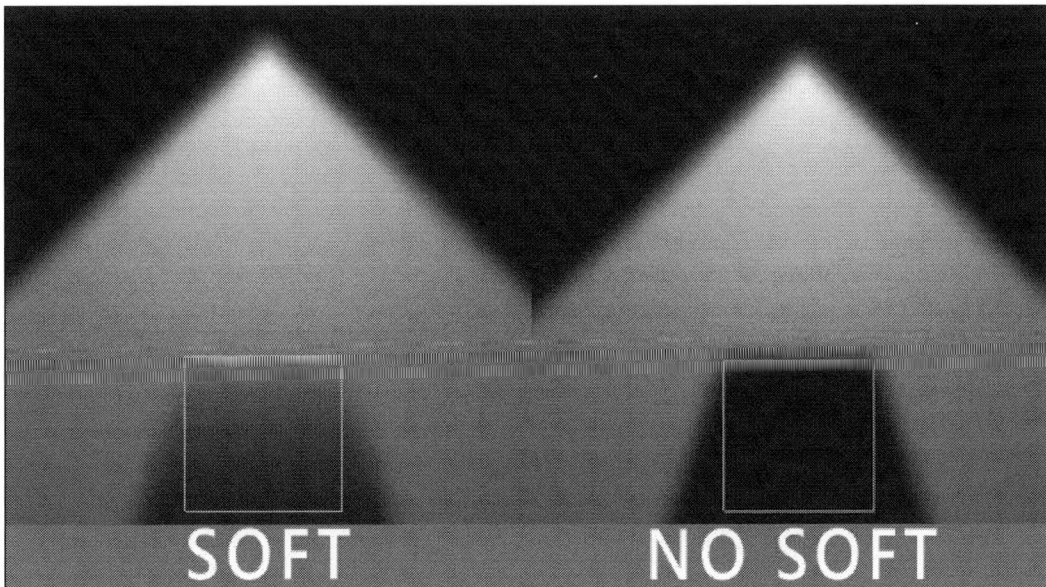

The preceding explanation is purely theoretical as they are not instantiable classes but their properties and behaviors will serve as base for the next light types:

- ▶ **Point light**: This is composed of all the aforementioned attributes and its shape is circular although the number of rays passed will define the circle precision. A good outcome can usually be achieved by setting a value within the range [5,128]. Refer to the following screenshot:

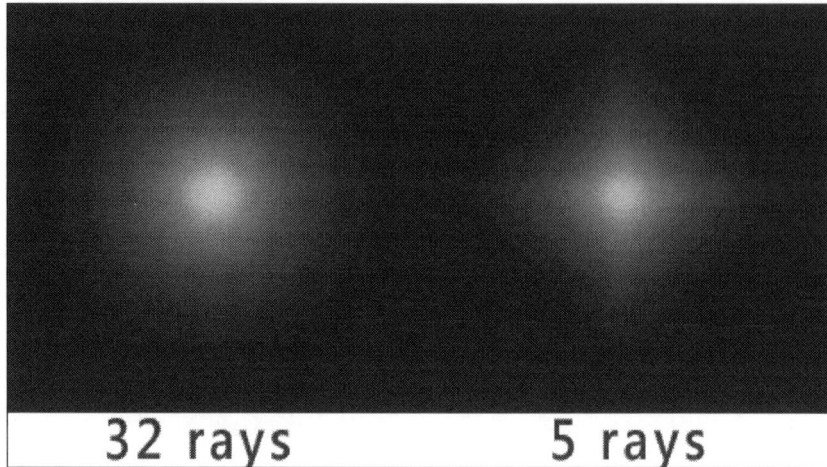

- ▶ **Cone light**: This is very similar to the previous one but with only a part of the full circle. This cut is marked by two additional attributes: direction and cone degree. The first will orientate the heading of the light and the second the angle of influence at each of the sides.

  The previous sample code makes use of this class, setting the direction to 270 and the cone degree to 45; the resulting light is shown in the following screenshot:

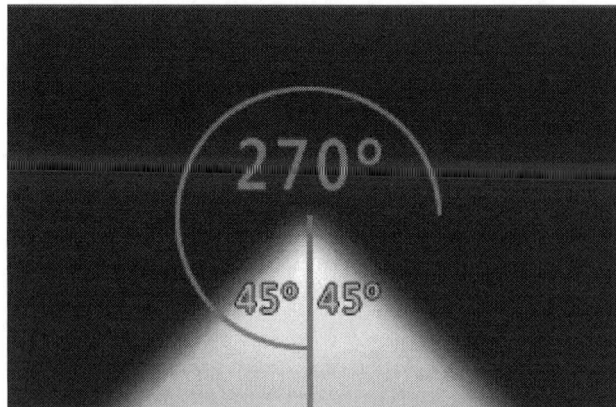

▶ **Directional light**: This simulates the effect of the sun light since direction, which must be provided, and intensity are uniform. It does not extend `PositionalLight` and therefore, does not have a position (nor can it be attached to a body).

There's more...

Without a doubt, Box2DLights is powerful enough to take your game to the next level with awesome effects and light simulations. However, it can take up a lot of resources in the hands of a greedy and incautious programmer. That is why it is strongly recommended that you have several considerations in mind:

▶ Use the minimum number of rays that allow you to get your expected smooth grade.

▶ Make proper use of dynamic and static lights.

▶ Disable unnecessary lights, or even reuse them.

▶ Do not abuse softness; disable it if not needed.

▶ Enable culling.

▶ Set the frame buffer object (`fbo`) size to a small value. This can set through a second `RayHandler` constructor:

```
public RayHandler(World world, int maxRayCount, int fboWidth, int fboHeigth)
```

You can read more about FBO at `http://en.wikipedia.org/wiki/Framebuffer_Object`.

This advice and the optimizations are simple to carry out, but if you plan to squeeze every last drop of lights performance, you should visit the official Box2DLights Libgdx wiki section.

Adding support for localization

The union of the previous recipes of this book provides you with a complete set of tools to develop what could be a successful game except for its narrow audience.

Libgdx comes with an out of the box **internationalization and localization (i18N)** system, which means that you will be able to localize your application according to the user's needs without the hassle of implementing your own or hardcoding. In addition, this will allow you to have one or more language files that will contain all the strings of your application, identified by a name that will abstract you from dealing with each language separately.

This data-driven approach fits perfectly for nonprogrammers, translators, or community projects where everybody can contribute with new translations just by editing a friendly text file.

Getting ready

Firstly, check whether you have imported the sample projects into your Eclipse workspace as described in *Chapter 1, Diving into Libgdx*.

Language files are located in the `i18n` folder within the `assets` directory of the Android project:

- `strings_en_GB.properties`
- `strings_es_ES.properties`

You can guess that Spanish (es) and English (en) are the chosen languages, specifying their variation from Great Britain (GB) and Spain (ES), respectively, in capital letters. Other language variations of the same countries are en_UK (United Kingdom) and es_MX (Mexico).

To keep things tidy, we will have a `LanguageManager.java` class within the `com.cookbook.localization` package, in charge of abstracting the programmer from dealing with each language.

Finally, the nub of the issue can be found in `LocalizationSample.java`, where a practical example of usage is provided.

How to do it...

The process to localize your application is divided into three sections.

Creating language files

One of the main targets of this recipe is to keep the addition of new languages as simple as possible, so we will have a plain text file with the `.properties` extension containing a set of strings together with their identifier. In the following examples, `bookTitle` and `introduction` are keys and the right parts of the equalities are values associated with them:

```
bookTitle =  Libgdx for Cross Platform Game Development Cookbook
introduction = {0} pragmatic recipes to master cross platform 2D game
development using the powerful Libgdx framework.
```

There is an intruder {0} whose value is replaced at runtime, so it works as a parameter. However, this magic is made by `java.text.MessageFormat`, which considers them as patterns that are processed and placed at the appropriate places. Double a left curly bracket in order to escape it so you can write it within your text strings.

The following patterns can be built by specifying at least the first of the following properties:

- ▶ `ArgumentIndex`: This sets which argument will replace the pattern.
- ▶ `FormatType`: This can be used to format the pattern to number, date, time, or choice.
- ▶ `FormatStyle`: This will give extra precision to the format so a number can be an integer, a currency, or a percent. A date or a time can be formatted to short, medium, long, or full. You can add your custom styles too through `DecimalFormat` or `SimpleDateFormat`. A choice will take the style to specify which message must be shown under certain conditions.

Some practical code examples will shed light on its usage:

```
Introduction = It's {0, time} on {0,date}. The world is swarming with
zombies.
Options = Please, select at least {0, choice, 1# option|1<{0,
number,integer} options}
```

> GWT only supports `ArgumentIndex`, throwing an `IllegalArgumentException` if you try to apply `FormatType` and `FormatStyle`. In addition, it will convert every argument into a string without taking into account its locale. In case you want to keep uniform behavior in all your platforms, you should make use of `setSimpleFormat(true)` from the `I18NBundle` class that we will cover later on.

Managing languages

We can have a set of structured files with all the translations data, but we need to make our application able to understand and process them. The next approach is intended for applications that want to support constant language switching. Perform the following steps:

1. Here is where `I18NBundle` comes into action, loading a locale-specific language property file:

   ```
   I18NBundle.createBundle(Gdx.input.Internal("i18n/strings_en
   CR.properties", Locale.UK));
   ```

2. However, having an `I18NBundle` class field for each language is not elegant neither maintainable. Instead, we can create a `LanguageManager` class to gather all loaded languages and keep track of the selected one:

   ```
   public class LanguageManager {
       private ObjectMap<String, I18NBundle> languages;
       private String currentLanguage;
       ...
   ```

3. Its constructor will have the responsibility of initializing those fields:

```
public LanguageManager() {
languages = new ObjectMap<String, I18NBundle>();
currentLanguage = null;
}
```

4. We must also provide an interface to load languages into memory either receiving an `I18NBundle` or creating a new one:

```
public void loadLanguage(String name, I18NBundle bundle) {
if(name!=null && !name.isEmpty() && bundle != null)
languages.put(name.toLowerCase(), bundle);
    }


public void loadLanguage(String name, FileHandle fileHandle,
Locale locale) {
if(name!=null && !name.isEmpty() && fileHandle != null && locale
!= null)
languages.put(name.toLowerCase(), I18NBundle.
createBundle(fileHandle, locale));
}
```

5. A getter and setter for the `currentLanguage` field must be included too, so the user can consult it or modify it at runtime:

```
public String getCurrentLanguage() {
return currentLanguage;
}
public void setCurrentLanguage(String name) {
if(languages.containsKey(name.toLowerCase()))
currentLanguage = name;
}
```

6. Finally, the next method will avoid the user to know or explicitly write the current language every time so he will just deal with a general `I18NBundle`:

```
public I18NBundle getCurrentBundle() {
return languages.get(currentLanguage);
}
```

Usage example

Implementing the preceding approach makes your localization code simpler and cleaner than handling each `I18NBundle` separately. Perform the following steps:

1. Consequently, let's create the `LanguageManager` object and populate with some bundles through the `loadLanguage(...)` method:

```
LanguageManager langManager = new LanguageManager();

FileHandle englishFileHandle = Gdx.files.internal("i18n/strings_
en_GB");
FileHandle spanishFileHandle = Gdx.files.internal("i18n/strings_
es_ES");

lm.loadLanguage("English", englishFileHandle, Locale.UK);
lm.loadLanguage("Spanish", spanishFileHandle, new Locale("es",
"ES"));
```

2. Once it is initialized, we must set a bundle as active:

```
lm.setCurrentLanguage("English");
```

3. Now it is time to add some code for retrieving strings so they can be shown on the screen, independent of which language is currently set:

```
I18NBundle bundle = lm.getCurrentBundle();
String title = bundle.get("bookTitle");
String introduction = bundle.format("introduction", 81);
String body = bundle.get("body");
```

4. Whenever you want to translate the screen text at runtime, just call `setCurrentLanguage("Spanish")` and update the UI text containers as written in the previous code snippet.

There's more...

You can still improve the `LanguageManager` class by automatically detecting, within its constructor, the system default language and using it as the current one for the application:

```
currentLanguage = Locale.getDefault().toString();
```

> Bear in mind that some font types might not fit certain locales because of special characters.

See also

▶ This recipe revolves around text resources so do not hesitate to take a look at *Chapter 6, Font Rendering* and *Chapter 8, User Interfaces with Scene2D*

Finite state machine and messaging

A finite state machine is a computation model consisting in a finite set of states, from which can only be in one at a time. Transitions between them are produced under certain conditions.

Game characters' behavior is usually modelled by a series of states and transitions. A clear example is a spy game where enemies patrol all over the map under apparent calm. Suddenly, one of them hears a noise and turns into track state. Seconds later, the alarm is raised because the spy has been spotted, so all nearby enemies enter into alert state. In conclusion, they are no more than a finite state machine capable of communicating with other agents.

This recipe illustrates a new episode of the caveman and the dinosaur whose interaction will be textually outputted to the console.

Getting ready

As a Libgdx extension, the Artificial Intelligence library must be added as a dependency to the `build.gradle` file. Go back to *Chapter 1, Diving into Libgdx*, if you need to learn how to carry out it.

The code resides in several files:

▶ `Caveman.java`: This file contains the caveman's attributes, states, and methods

▶ `Dinosaur.java`: This file contains the dinosaur's attributes, states, and methods

▶ `MessageType.java`: This file contains all the possible messages between two agents in the game

▶ `ArtificialIntelligenceSample.java`: This file makes use of the former files leaving the dinosaur and the caveman interact within the render loop

Notice that the first three files are located within the `com.cookbook.ai` package.

How to do it...

State machines provide a high degree of freedom in order to create an unreadable monster, so if you plan to have a lot of transitions between states, you should consider not using this approach (an alternative is provided in the *There's more...* section of this recipe).

As it might be tedious and repetitive for you, only a few states from the caveman will be shown. You can find the rest in the source files. The real goal is to understand the whole set of tools provided by the Libgdx AI extension.

The hardest part in this recipe is to create the agents that will interact between them because once this is done, their use is pretty straightforward.

Creating the agents

Every entity in your game that is capable of sending/receiving a message to/from another entity must implement the `Agent` interface, so we already have where to begin with. Perform the following steps:

1. Define the `Caveman` class by implementing the `Agent` interface and make it contain a finite state machine and several properties:

```
public class Caveman implements Agent {

private StateMachine<Caveman> fsm;
    private float hungry; // [0-100]
    private float energy; // [0-100]
    private boolean threatened;
    ...
```

   The `StateMachine` interface offers a complete API to navigate through all the states at any order. The method names are self-explanatory:

   - `void changeState(State<E> newState)`
   - `void revertToPreviousState()`
   - `void setInitialState(State<E> state)`
   - `State<E> getCurrentState()`
   - `State<E> getPreviousState()`
   - `boolean isInState(State<E> state)`

2. Create an `enum` to define some states that the caveman can come into. Every state will implement the `State` interface, and consequently, it must override four methods:

   - `enter(...)`: This is implicitly called when the agent enters into State
   - `update(...)`: This will contain the logic of `State` and will be called explicitly by the programmer
   - `exit(...)`: This is implicitly called when the agent leaves `State`
   - `onMessage(...)`: This is called to deal with messages while running `State`, so you can give a specific response

The sequential call order for an `Agent` to change from state A to state B would be:

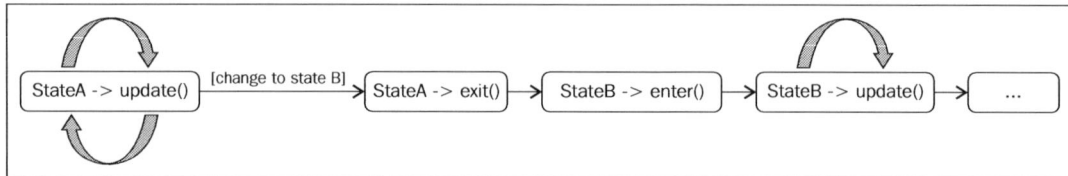

The resulting code would be something like this:

```
public enum CavemanState implements State<Caveman> {
SLEEP() {
public void enter(Caveman caveman) {
      caveman.say("Good night!");
}

public void update(Caveman caveman) {
caveman.increaseEnergy(.08f);
caveman.increaseHungry(.01f);

if(caveman.energy==100) {
caveman.say("(yaaaaawn) I'm a new man");
caveman.getFSM().changeState(IDLE);
      }
}

public void exit(Caveman caveman) {}

public boolean onMessage(Telegram telegram) {
   return false;
}
},
... //Next state
}
```

3. The `StateMachine` interface can also have a global state that will be executed every time `update` is called:

```
GLOBAL_STATE() {
   public void enter(Caveman caveman) {}

public void update(Caveman caveman) {
// 1 in 1000
if (MathUtils.randomBoolean(0.001f) &&
   !caveman.getFSM().isInState(PAINTING)) {
caveman.say("OH! Gotta pee");
caveman.getFSM().changeState(PAINTING);
}
```

```
        }

    public void exit(Caveman caveman) {}

    public boolean onMessage(Telegram telegram) {
    return false;
    }
    },
    ... // other states
```

In addition, StateMachine can handle messages in a general way through its boolean handleMessage(Telegram telegram) method. False is returned if the telegram has not been successfully handled, so it is routed to the current state handler and if the same happens, it arrives to the global state handler.

4. Once all the states are defined, just focus on Caveman itself by writing your custom methods. A possible constructor might be:

```
public Caveman() {
fsm = new DefaultStateMachine<Caveman> (this, CavemanState.IDLE);

hungry = MathUtils.random(0, 100);
energy = MathUtils.random(0, 100);
threatened = false;

fsm.setGlobalState(CavemanState.GLOBAL_STATE);
}
```

As you can observe, IDLE would be the initial CavemanState.

5. The caveman likes eating a lot so he needs to go hunting very often. However, an unfriendly dinosaur might stand in his way and growl loudly. Consequently, we should prepare our caveman to act fast and run home:

```
HUNTING() {
...
@Override
public boolean onMessage(Telegram telegram) {
if (telegram.message == MessageType.GRRRRRRR! {
    Caveman caveman = (Caveman)(telegram.receiver);
caveman.threatened = true;
    caveman.getFSM().changeState(RUN_TO_HOME);

    return true;
}
return false;
    }
}
```

Notice that we have introduced a new element, `MessageType.GRRRRRRRR`. It is one of the possible messages defined in the `MessageType.java` file, which would look as follows:

```
public class MessageType {
public static final int GRRRRRRRR = 0;
}
```

Then, the dinosaur would just have to call this code:

```
MessageDispatcher.getInstance().dispatchMessage (
0.0f, // no delay
dinosaur, dinosaur.caveman, MessageType.GRRRRRRRR, null);
```

The `MessageDispatcher` class is just a singleton class in charge of sending telegrams from an `Agent` to another in a specific delay time. The last parameter is expected to be an `Object` and allows some extra information to be included.

Usage example

After some tedious work of designing your finite state machines, it is time to make use of them. Perform the following steps:

1. First of all, declare the dinosaur and the caveman as agents:

    ```
    public class ArtificialIntelligenceSample extends GdxSample {
        . . .
    private Agent caveman, dinosaur;
    ```

2. Initialize them:

    ```
    public void create () {
    super.create();
        . . .
        caveman = new Caveman();
    dinosaur = new Dinosaur((Caveman) caveman);
    }
    ```

3. Update the agents and, therefore, both the state machines:

    ```
    public void render () {
        . . .
        float delta = Gdx.graphics.getDeltaTime();
    caveman.update(delta);
    dinosaur.update(delta);
    }
    ```

How it works...

Although for the sake of simplicity, the whole example has not been encompassed, the next diagram illustrates all the possible transitions between states except for the aforementioned case where the GRRRRRRRR message goes into action. It is only sent if the caveman is in a HUNTING state while the dinosaur is in a GO_FOR_A_WALK state and also a luck component (only happens 1/1000 times).

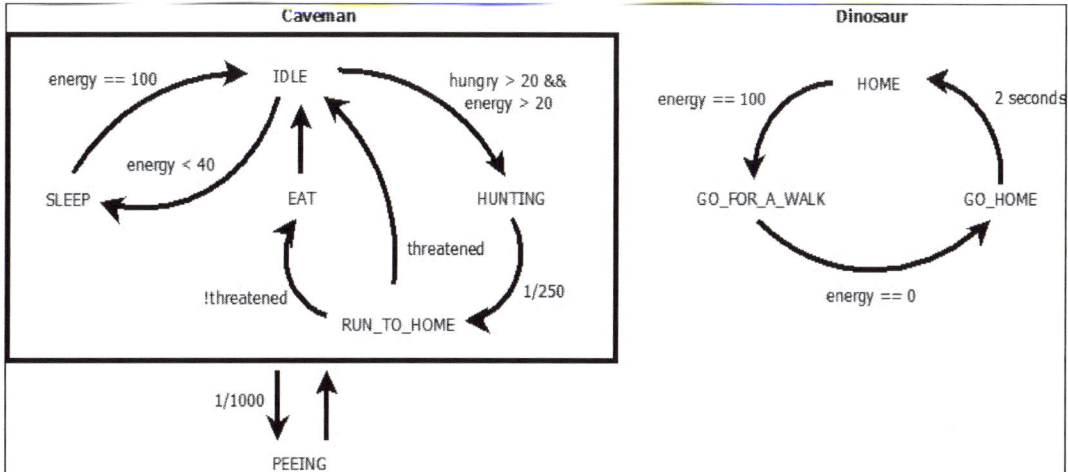

```
Caveman                                              Dinosaur

energy == 100        IDLE      hungry > 20 &&                 HOME      2 seconds
                                energy > 20    energy == 100

    energy < 40

SLEEP         EAT        HUNTING        GO_FOR_A_WALK              GO_HOME

                  threatened

!threatened          1/250                     energy == 0

        RUN_TO_HOME

1/1000

        PEEING
```

There's more...

It is not necessary to be a genius to realize the potential mess of state machines as they proliferate. Adding the concept of substate would be a step forward in this aspect, so we get to the commonly known as hierarchical finite state machines. However, this might not be enough and changing the approach to behavior trees would fit our needs.

This is a more restrictive idea but, at the same time, more structured as it includes control nodes all along its directed acyclic graph organization keeping the natural hierarchical order from trees. This contributes to reusability and good memory management.

Explaining behavior trees is not the goal of this recipe but if it piqued your curiosity, do not hesitate to search for it on the Internet because there are a lot of good resources such as this series of posts by Bjoern Knafla at http://www.altdev.co/2011/02/24/introduction-to-behavior-trees/.

Component-based entity systems with Ashley

Making games is an art and as such, it has a high degree of creative freedom, which means that there is no one single way to reach your goal.

On one hand, traditional hierarchy-based games development is quite intuitive as you can see in the next diagram:

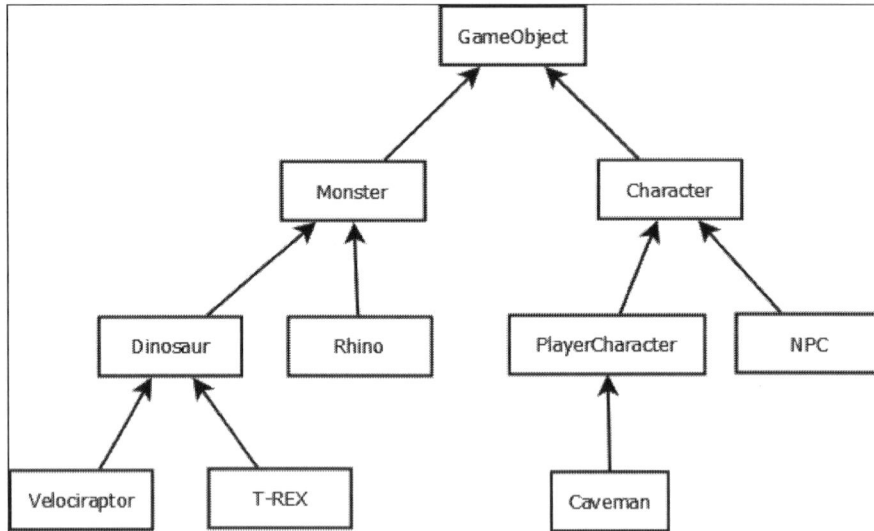

However, as the game grows, the class hierarchies become more annoying and hardly reusable.

On the other hand, a viable alternative to destroy that pyramid from hell is component-based development. In this way, we would have, for instance, our T-Rex class working as a container for a series of behaviors called components. The advantage of this is that those components are highly reusable for the rest of the entities in that game or any other one.

Ashley is a tiny high-performance entity framework integrated into the Libgdx family with a clear and easy to use API. You can learn more about it by visiting https://github.com/libgdx/ashley.

Understanding this new approach will take some time and you will need to practice first.

Getting ready

The code for this recipe is spread across different files within the `samples-core` project. As usual, you will find the one that works as the main file called `AshelySample.java` and the rest lives under the `com.cookbook.ashley` package.

However, you must add the Ashley dependency to the different projects through the gdx-setup tool for new projects (by ticking the Ashley checkbox) or updating your `gradle.build` file:

- ▶ Add compile `com.badlogicgames.ashley:Ashley:1.1.0` to the dependency container of the core and Android project
- ▶ Add compile `com.badlogicgames.ashely:Ashely:1.1.0:sources` to the gwt project

At the end of this recipe, you will see the brave caveman following the user's clicks/taps, carried out through an underlying component-based implementation.

How to do it...

First of all, it is important that the main roles of this play remain fully explained:

- ▶ **Entities**: They are no more than bags to be filled up of components.
- ▶ **Components**: They work as data containers. Their base class definition is empty.
- ▶ **Systems**: They will perform all logic operations required to process game entities.
- ▶ **Families**: They group entities that satisfy certain conditions about containing all, one, or none of the specified components.

Once you have in mind a general idea of what we are about to do, it is time to get down to business. Perform the following steps:

1. Everything begins in the `AshelySample.java` file by initializing the Ashley engine in charge of updating all entity systems:

   ```
   Engine ashelyEngine = new Engine();
   ```

2. We cannot go any further without defining some components along with their corresponding systems. We will start by giving some improvement in the entities through the most basic components:

   - ❑ `TransformComponent`: This stores the position, rotation, and scale of any entity and is implemented as follows:

     ```
     public class TransformComponent extends Component {
     public final Vector2 pos = new Vector2();
     public final Vector2 scale = new Vector2(1.0f, 1.0f);
     public float rotation = 0.0f;
     }
     ```

As you would have seen, the components' fields will be directly accessed as they are public.

❑ `MovementComponent`: This will add the velocity feature to the entity:

```
public class MovementComponent extends Component {
    public final Vector2 velocity = new Vector2();
}
```

❑ `MovementSystem`: Now that we have the basis, we are ready to deal with our first entity system. In general terms, it will just take all entities that are composed of `TransformComponent` as well as `MovementComponent` and will add their current velocity to their position according to the elapsed time. However, we must first instantiate `ComponentMapper` for each of the component types to retrieve the ones belonging to the entity class in question:

```
public class MovementSystem extends IteratingSystem {
    private ComponentMapper<TransformComponent> tm =
ComponentMapper.getFor(TransformComponent.class);
    private ComponentMapper<MovementComponent> mm =
ComponentMapper.getFor(MovementComponent.class);
```

Its constructor needs to know which entities must be processed every update. Ashley makes it easy and provides you with the `Family` class that gathers all the entities that contain a certain set of components. In order to provide movement, we just need both the components that we have just implemented:

```
public MovementSystem() {
    super(Family.getFor(TransformComponent.class,
MovementComponent.class));
}
```

The action takes place within the overridden `processEntity()` method responsible for the logic. Pay special attention on the way the components are retrieved for each individual entity making use of the previously defined `ComponentMapper`:

```
public void processEntity(Entity entity, float deltaTime) {
    TransformComponent transform = tm.get(entity);
    MovementComponent movement = mm.get(entity);

    transform.pos.x += movement.velocity.x * deltaTime;
    transform.pos.y += movement.velocity.y * deltaTime;
}
```

- TextureComponent: We have provided support for moving entities but it means nothing if we do not show some screenshots to represent them. Consequently, the next step is creating a TextureComponent that works as a container:

```
public class TextureComponent extends Component {
    public TextureRegion region = null;
}
```

- SizeComponent: At this point, we have everything to properly render our entities except for their size. This attribute allows us to make entities' size independent from the image file, so it will perfectly fit into the scene dimensions. The code looks as follows:

```
public class SizeComponent extends Component {
    public float width;
    public float height;
}
```

3. Now, we definitely have all the required information to render our entities. However, we can carry out this with a component-based approach too:

- RenderSystem: In order to show an entity with accuracy on the screen, we need its position, rotation, scale, width, height, and image. The RenderSystem class will keep track of all the entities whose components cover those attributes with the purpose of rendering them according to the camera settings every update tick.

This functionality is translated as the following class fields:

```
public class RenderSystem extends EntitySystem {
    private ImmutableArray<Entity> entities;

    private SpriteBatch batch;
    private OrthographicCamera camera;

    private ComponentMapper<TransformComponent> tm =
ComponentMapper.getFor(TransformComponent.class);
    private ComponentMapper<TextureComponent> vm =
ComponentMapper.getFor(TextureComponent.class);
    private ComponentMapper<SizeComponent> sm =
ComponentMapper.getFor(SizeComponent.class);
```

Its constructor will just deal with the initialization of the Spritebatch instance and store a reference to the camera.

The `entities` field from which the system will take the instances to draw is filled up through the following method:

```
public void addedToEngine(Engine engine) {
entities = engine.getEntitiesFor(Family.
getFor(TransformComponent.class, TextureComponent.class,
SizeComponent.class));
}
```

Finally, the `update()` function assumes the responsibility for looping over the `entities` array and retrieve the necessary components to render each entity of the game using the long version of the draw method from the previously defined `SpriteBatch`. Having said this, the code remains easy to understand:

```
public void update(float deltaTime) {
camera.update();

batch.begin();
batch.setProjectionMatrix(camera.combined);

for (int i = 0; i < entities.size(); ++i) {

Entity e = entities.get(i);

        TransformComponent transform = tm.get(e);
        TextureComponent visual = vm.get(e);
        SizeComponent size = sm.get(e);

        batch.draw(visual.region,
            transform.pos.x, transform.pos.y,
            size.width*.5f, size.height*.5f,
            size.width, size.height,
            transform.scale.x, transform.scale.y,
            transform.rotation);
    }

    batch.end();
}
```

4. After this `Component` and `EntitySystem` parenthesis that we made once the Ashley engine was initialized, we can carry on and put them into practice.

    First of all, we must instantiate the systems with the required arguments:

    ```
    MovementSystem movementSystem = new MovementSystem();
    RenderSystem renderSystem = new RenderSystem(camera);
    ```

    The next step is adding them to the engine:

    ```
    ashleyEngine.addSystem(movementSystem);
    ashleyEngine.addSystem(renderSystem);
    ```

It is now when our first `Entity` instance can be created. As usual, the caveman will be the protagonist:

```
Entity caveman = new Entity();
```

However, this is no more than an empty container. Let's fill it up with some components:

```
TextureComponent texture = new TextureComponent();
TransformComponent transform = new TransformComponent();
SizeComponent size = new SizeComponent();
MovementComponent movement = new MovementComponent();
```

As entities, components are empty and need data to be meaningful. Here is where the image, dimensions, position, scale, and/or rotation are set:

```
texture.region = new TextureRegion(new Texture(Gdx.files.
internal("data/caveman.png")));
size.width = 1f;
size.height = 1.5f;
transform.pos.set(SCENE_WIDTH*.5f - size.width*.5f, SCENE_
HEIGHT*.5f - size.height*.5f);
```

Once these components are ready, add them to the `caveman Entity`:

```
caveman.add(texture);
caveman.add(transform);
caveman.add(size);
caveman.add(movement);
```

The next diagram illustrates what is really happening:

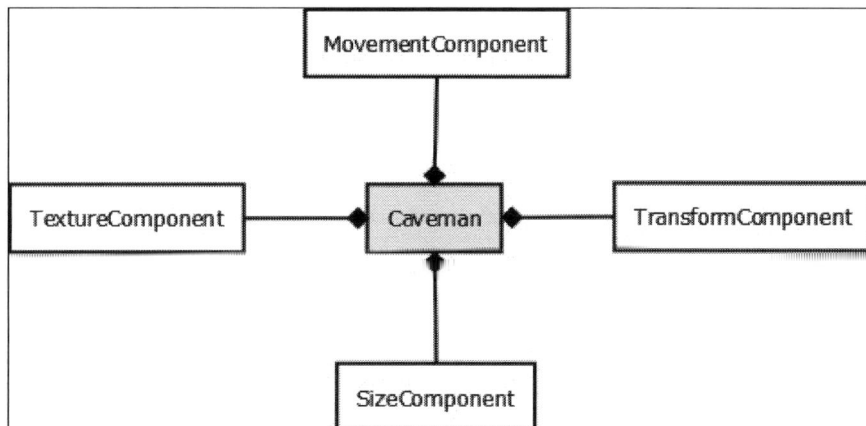

Finally, add the `caveman` `Entity` to the engine and let the `RenderingSystem` class know what to draw:

```
ashleyEngine.addEntity(caveman);
renderSystem.addedToEngine(ashleyEngine);
```

5. The logic is internally managed by the different systems, so all we have to do is update the Ashley engine every frame through the `update()` method:

```
ashleyEngine.update(Gdx.graphics.getDeltaTime());
```

If we run the sample, the versatile caveman will now appear on the screen.

6. Take this introduction as a starting point to think about the possible components and systems to implement. One more option is making the caveman move following the users' clicks or taps. All that you would have to do is define an empty `UserControlledComponent` and its corresponding `UserControlledSystem`. The mission of the last one would be dealing with each individual entity inside of the `processEntity` function so that a velocity is applied in the direction of the user's click/tap. All this making use of the `TransformComponent` and the `MovementComponent` classes.

It is worth putting this recipe into practice but if you still need some extra help, do not hesitate to take a look at the `UserControlledSystem.java` file within the `samples-core` project.

How it works...

Although the idea of the component-based approach and a practical use case is given, there are still some gaps about the internal behavior of Ashley.

First of all, it is a good idea to show an overview diagram about Ashley's architecture:

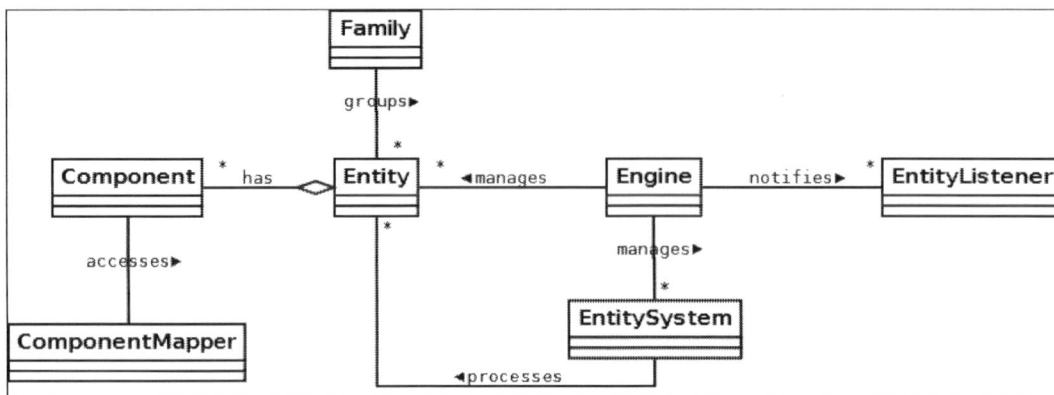

In the preceding diagram, we can find some unexplained classes such as `EntityListener`, `EntitySystem`, or its specific class, `IteratingSystem`. The first of them is an additional feature that is explained in the *There's more...* section, whereas the other two highly contribute to understand the underlying behavior of the Ashley framework.

The `EntitySystem` class is an abstract class to add the functionality of processing sets of entities. Its `update()` method is called every tick, so you can manually set what those entities will do. This implementation is the chosen one for `RenderSystem` to avoid calling the `begin()` and `end()` `SpriteBatch` functions for each entity processing.

The `IteratingSystem` class is the simplest way of repeating a set of actions with each entity from a family of entities as it will execute the content of `processEntity` every update tick.

There's more...

Ashley also gives you the chance of being notified every time an entity is added or removed from the engine. All you have to do is create your own listener that implements `EntityListener` so that `entityAdded` and `entityRemoved` are overridden:

```
public class MyListener implements EntityListener {
    @Override
    public void entityAdded(Entity entity) {
        // Do whatever
    }
    @Override
    public void entityRemoved(Entity entity) {
        // Do whatever
    }
}
```

Finally, add/remove your custom listener to/from the engine:

```
MyListener mylistener = new MyListener();
ashleyEngine.addEntityListener(mylistener);
ashleyEngine.removeEntityListener(mylistener);
```

See also

▶ Component-based development is a vast topic that you can explore. Some famous games using this approach are *Dungeon Siege*, *Resistance 1* and *2*, *Tony Hawk Pro Skater 3*, *Thief: The Dark Project*, and many more!

Skeletal animations with Spine

Animation is not a new concept within our Libgdx set of cookbooks. *Chapter 2, Working with 2D Graphics*, guides you on how to manage sprite sheet-based animations, which is definitely the most common choice in general terms. However, it is not the only alternative, since there is commercial software that takes us through a more streamlined animation process, covering topics that range from the creation of animations to using them within your games.

This is the case of **Spine**, a popular skeletal animation editor created using Libgdx and offers runtimes for most of the programming languages in the market, adapting a lot of their variants to specific game engines/frameworks, where Libgdx is included too.

In Spine, you can create a hierarchy of bones you can animate using key frames and create interpolations between them. Textures can be attached to bones, resulting in smoothly animated characters. Spine also has a free license but doesn't allow exporting to .json or binary.

In this recipe, we will make an awesome hero come to life.

Getting ready

The code for this recipe is in the SpineSample.java file. It is important to have the following assets located:

- data/spine/hero.json: This contains all the skeleton-related information, including bones, slots, skins, and animations
- data/spine/hero-1.png: This contains the graphics for the hero's default skin
- data/spine/hero.atlas: This splits the former file into atomic graphic elements such as arms, legs, and head

Do not forget to import the sample projects in order to run the Spine sample.

How to do it...

Before getting your hands dirty with code, we have to create our skeleton with the Spine editor. It includes a lot of options and, therefore, this single recipe would not be enough to provide a decent level of understanding over the tool. Fortunately, the official documentation at http://esotericsoftware.com/spine-documentation is rich and fulfills its duty beyond expectations.

It is divided into two big sections: editor and runtimes. The first one will teach you how to use the tool with text and videos. The second one shows you how to include your creations within your game.

The following screenshot gives a face to our hero. Observe the supported animations on the right-hand side, and the ones worth being highlighted are idle, run, or punch as they will be mentioned later on.

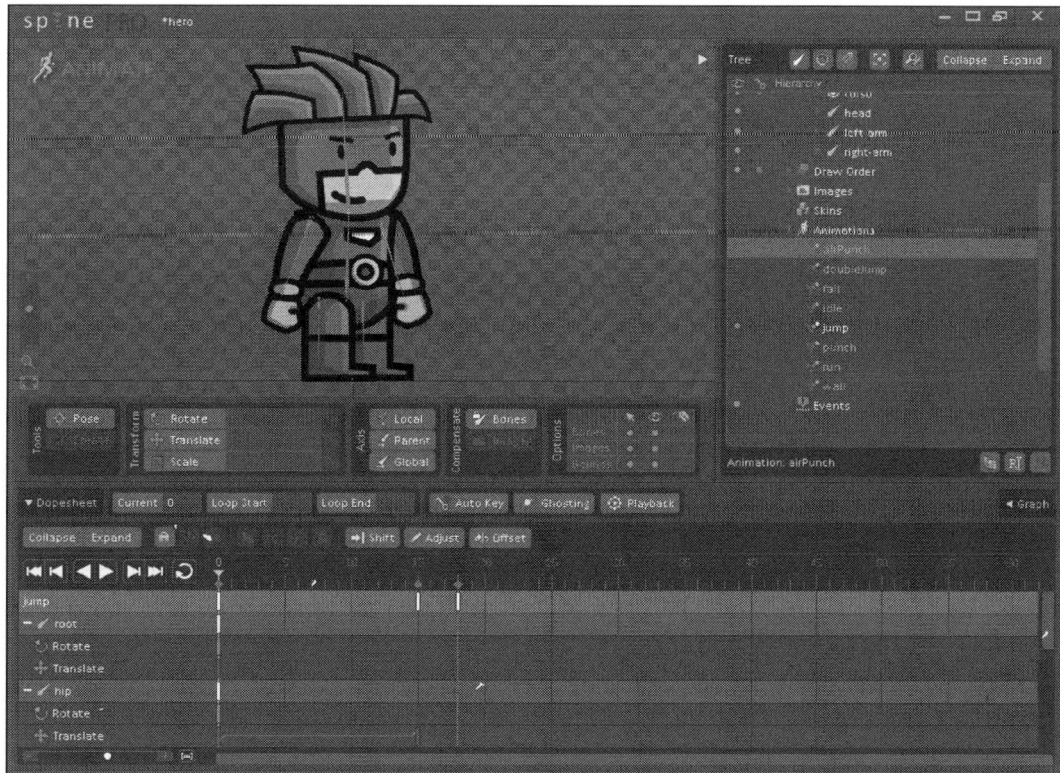

Perform the following steps:

1. Once our artist's soul is reflected into several files, you can load your skeleton from a `.json` or a binary file. We will work with the first of them because it is readable. This file will contain all the information related to bones, slots, skins, and animations.

2. Besides the `.json` file, we will need an `.atlas` (explained in *Chapter 2, Working with Sprite Animations*). So this is what we will begin with:

```
void loadSkeleton (FileHandle skeletonFile) {
String atlasFileName = skeletonFile.nameWithoutExtension();
FileHandle atlasFile = skeletonFile.sibling(atlasFileName +
".atlas");
TextureAtlasData data = new TextureAtlasData(atlasFile, atlasFile.
parent(), false);
```

```
TextureAtlas atlas = new TextureAtlas(data) {
...
}
   SkeletonJson json = new SkeletonJson(atlas);
```

The `SkeletonJson` class will allow us to scale all the parts of our hero uniformly with the following method:

```
json.setScale(.5f);
```

Then, the skeleton data is parsed from the `.json` file:

```
SkeletonData skeletonData = json.readSkeletonData(skeletonFile);
```

3. At this point, we have all input files under control, so we must feed other classes with them. First of all, let's create a `Skeleton` instance:

```
Skeleton skeleton = new Skeleton(skeletonData);
```

Next, we can place it in a x, y position elsewhere in the screen, taking into account that we must project to screen coordinates just in case we are working with our own custom unit:

```
viewport.getCamera().project(point.set(SCENE_WIDTH * .5f, 0, 0));
skeleton.setX(point.x);
skeleton.setY(point.y);
```

After that, make sure to update the skeleton's transform component, which, in this step, refers only to its position:

```
skeleton.updateWorldTransform();
```

4. To get a better idea about the current progress, let's just render it. First of all, declare and create an instance of `SkeletonRenderer`:

```
SkeletonRenderer renderer = new SkeletonRenderer();
```

Then, set one of the skins that you have previously created on the editor. For instance, the first one is as follows:

```
skeleton.setSkin(skeletonData.getSkins().first());
```

Finally, just draw it:

```
public void render() {
...
batch.begin();
renderer.draw(batch, skeleton);
batch.end();
```

The static hero will pose like this:

5. The `skeleton` instance will internally hold animations that can be easily retrieved as follows:

```
Animation idleAnimation = skeletonData.findAnimation("idle");
Animation runAnimation = skeletonData.findAnimation("run");
```

6. However, handling animations individually is generally not the best approach. That is why an `AnimationState` instance should be created:

```
AnimationStateData stateData = = new AnimationStateData(skeletonDa
ta);
AnimationState state = new AnimationState(stateData);
```

The `AnimationState` class covers the concept of tracks, so animations are applied on top of each other according to its position.

In this way, setting a specific animation becomes really simple; we just have to supply the number of the track, the animation name, and whether it should loop or not:

```
state.setAnimation(0, "idle", true);
```

This will require a string lookup. If you want to save it, just pass one of the previously created `Animation` instances, faster than a string lookup:

```
state.setAnimation(0, idleAnimation, true);
```

In addition, animations can be queued so that they start when the end of the current one is reached:

```
state.addAnimation(0, "run", true);
```

It is necessary to update each `AnimationState` every frame so it can keep track of the time:

```
state.update(Gdx.graphics.getDeltaTime());
```

Then, apply such state to the skeleton and let it know that he should update its world transform since the scale, rotation, or translation of its bones might have changed:

```
state.apply(skeleton);
skeleton.updateWorldTransform();
```

7. Spine also provides us with a powerful API to blend animations in order to get smooth transitions. All we have to do is specify how long it will take (in seconds) to finish the mixing between two animations:

```
stateData.setMix("run", "idle", 5f);
```

Then, just set one after another and the transition will be magically made:

```
state.setAnimation(0, "run", true);
state.setAnimation(0, "idle", true);
```

8. Be aware that sometimes you might want to clear all the tracks if you switch from a multiple-track action to a single-track one:

```
state.clearTracks();
```

In addition, you should bear in mind that whenever `Animation` is set, bones' scale, rotation, or translation might change so the next one will start from that situation. If you want to reset the hero's position just write this:

```
skeleton.setToSetupPose();
```

9. Similar to Box2D library, you can visually highlight the bowels of Spine in your scene so that the debug process becomes quite easier. All you have to do is instantiate a debug renderer:

```
SkeletonRendererDebug debugRenderer = new SkeletonRendererDebug();
```

10. Customize the visual information you want to receive:

```
debugRenderer.setBones(true);
debugRenderer.setRegionAttachments(true);
debugRenderer.setBoundingBoxes(true);
debugRenderer.setMeshHull(true);
debugRenderer.setMeshTriangles(true);
```

11. Finally, draw it:

```
debugRenderer.draw(skeleton);
```

The resulting image will include all the debug information distinguished by different colors:

How it works...

An overall explanation on how skeletal animations work is already given but analyzing the `.json` output of the Spine project can be of great help to get an in-depth idea.

As you would have expected, we will break down the `hero.json` file whose structure is divided into four big groups: `bones`, `slots`, `skins`, and `animations`.

The first of them looks like this:

```
{
"bones": [
    { "name": "root" },
    { "name": "hip", "parent": "root", "x": -14.77, "y": 219.55 },
    { "name": "torso", "parent": "hip", "length": 175.35, "x": 0.17,
"y": 18.6, "scaleX": 1.228, "scaleY": 1.228, "rotation": 88.66 },
    ]
```

A quick look is enough to discover the importance of choosing a good self-explanatory name for each bone. In addition, some of them have a reference to another bone within its parent property. This means that any transformation performed over a bone will be inherited to its children, producing, in this way, a realistic response. In addition, some adjusts and constraints, such us rotation, length, scale or offset, are usually necessary so that the skeleton fits the target sprite perfectly.

The next section consists of slots and is basically in charge of linking a bone with a region from the atlas (attachment within this context). For instance, an arm or the torso:

```
"slots": [
    { "name": "left-arm", "bone": "left-arm", "attachment": "parts/
left-arm" },
    { "name": "torso", "bone": "torso", "attachment": "parts/torso" },
    ...
```

The third group defines sets of visual appearance that fit the skeleton mechanics:

```
"skins": {
  "default": {
    "left-arm": {
       "parts/left-arm": { "x": 102.47, "y": 4.05, "scaleX": 0.813,
       "scaleY": 0.813, "rotation": 77.1, "width": 165, "height": 318 }
    },
    "torso": {
       "parts/torso": { "x": 49.59, "y": 5.11, "scaleX": 0.813, "scaleY":
       0.813, "rotation": -88.66, "width": 276, "height": 333 }
       }
```

The name of the skin is `default`, and each inner entry refers to a previously defined slot. In this way, regions can take up the expected bone surrounding area.

Last but not least, a set of bone transformations composes the `animations` section:

```
"animations": {
  "run": {
    "bones": {
       "torso": {
         "rotate": [
           { "time": 0, "angle": -14.91 },
           { "time": 0.1333, "angle": -10.61 },
           { "time": 0.2666, "angle": -14.91 },
           { "time": 0.4, "angle": -10.61 },
           { "time": 0.5333, "angle": -14.91 }
       ],
         "translate": [
           { "time": 0, "x": -0.67, "y": -3.81, "curve": "stepped" },
           { "time": 0.2666, "x": -0.67, "y": -3.81, "curve": "stepped" },
           { "time": 0.5333, "x": -0.67, "y": -3.81 }
           ]
         }
    ...
```

As you can see, Spine stores bone transformations (rotations, translations, and scale) over time in order to join a group of them and create an animation

The big advantage over traditional sprite sheet-based animations is that we are only storing a single image source file containing the graphics instead of the repetitive and massive amount of images to produce an animation.

The dirty work is made into a readable .json file with the necessary information to organize the former graphics into different animations.

There's more...

We can even blend two animations so that the hero punches while running. This can be achieved by setting each animation to a different track number:

```
state.setAnimation(0, "run", true);
state.setAnimation(1, "punch", true);
```

This last feature can also be carried out by creating two AnimationState instances, setting each one to a different animation and applying them to the same Skeleton.

12
Performance and Optimizations

In this chapter, we will cover the following recipes:

- ► Profiling your application with VisualVM
- ► Using Libgdx features to avoid garbage collection
- ► Avoiding unnecessary render calls with frustum culling

Introduction

Developing games is not just dealing with images and the way they interact with the user and their environment. There are a lot of considerations to take into account in order to publish a professional game.

This chapter covers some basic tips to improve your application's performance and, in this way, reach a homogeneous user experience on all target platforms.

Profiling your application with VisualVM

Computer resources are the gasoline for running applications and, therefore, they should be one of the main worries of a game programmer. Most software come with a system requirements list that draws the line between a computer that runs it properly and another one that doesn't. Testing your application on a wide range of target systems is a good practice but it is not the only one.

VisualVM is a free tool to view real-time detailed information about Java programs through an intuitive interface. It brings with it monitoring charts, threads breakdown, and some other utilities to profile your application.

It can help you to optimize slow games, improving the game experience, or even widen your target audience.

Getting ready

You will need to have a Java project on hand to fit the requirements of this recipe. For example, `sample-desktop` can be a good candidate to import into your Eclipse workspace.

In addition, once you have JDK 7 running on your system, a VisualVM distribution must be downloaded from its official website at the following link:

`http://visualvm.java.net/download.html`

In order to integrate VisualVM with Eclipse, download its plugin from the following link:

`http://visualvm.java.net/eclipse-launcher.html`

Do not forget to unzip both of them before going any further.

How to do it...

The process of installation and integration of VisualVM within your development environment is not fully automatic. Several manual steps must be performed prior to monitoring and profiling your application.

Installing VisualVM

Starting from locating the aforementioned folders, follow the upcoming indications to integrate VisualVM into your Eclipse IDE. Perform the following steps:

1. Go to **Help | Install New Software**. Click on **Add | Local** and select the extracted plugin folder. Give it a name and click on **OK**.

2. Enable the **VisualVM Launcher Feature** checkbox. Click on **Next** twice, accept the license, and click on **Finish**.

   This will add a new configuration tab that can be accessed through the following:

3. Go to **Window | Preferences**. Enter **Run/Debug | Launching | VisualVM Configuration** and set **VisualVM Executable** to the `visualvm.exe` file placed within the `bin` folder of your VisualVM directory.

4. You must also enter the JDK 7 directory.

Changing the launcher

Once VisualVM is properly linked to your IDE, we must find a way to specify whether the default or the VisualVM launcher will take the responsibility of starting the application. Perform the following steps:

1. Go to **Run | Run Configurations** and click on the new launch configuration button while having selected the **Java Application** item from the list on the left-hand side.

New launch configuration button

2. Give it a name and set the `sample-desktop` project together with its `main` class. Remember to change its working directory to `android-sample/assets`.

3. Now that the configuration is set up, you should see the following message in the lower part of the present dialog:

4. Click on **Select one...**, make sure to check the **Use configuration specific settings** option and then select **VisualVM Launcher**. Click on **OK** to save this change.

5. Finally, you are ready to click on the **Run** button in order to launch your application parallel to its own tab within the VisualVM interface, as shown in the following screenshot:

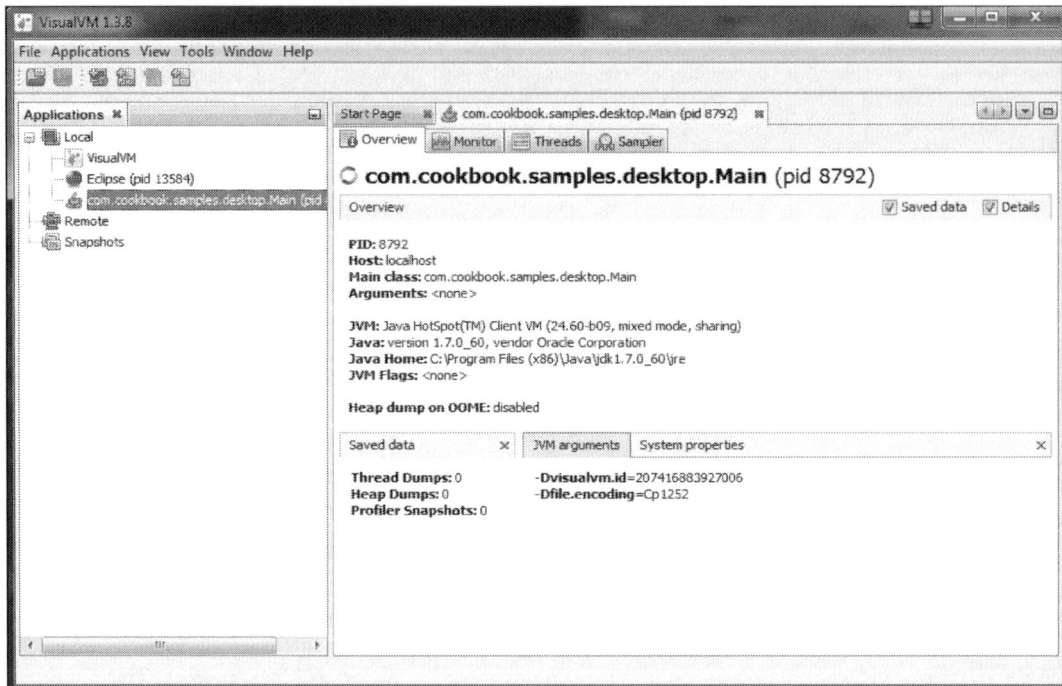

Monitoring and profiling

The VisualVM interface is not too bloated so you can focus on what is truly important. As you can observe in the previous screenshot, inside of the **Applications** tab, you can double-click on the cookbook application that is running. This will have an immediate effect on the main frame, showing real-time information split into the following sections that can be accessed through the tabs at the top of the aforementioned frame:

1. **Monitor**: A general overview of your application resources consumption is displayed through four fancy charts:

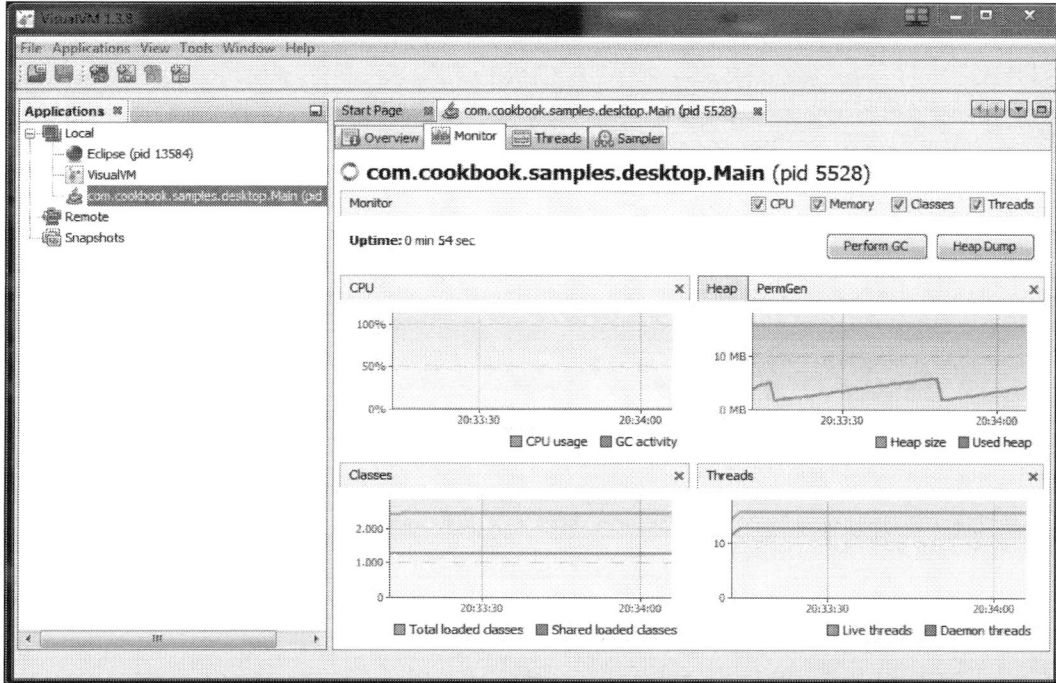

A quick look allows you to find out the ratio CPU usage or the **garbage collector** (**GC**) activity which must be minimized as much as possible since, otherwise, they can produce short freezes in your game. The following screenshot illustrates high GC activity:

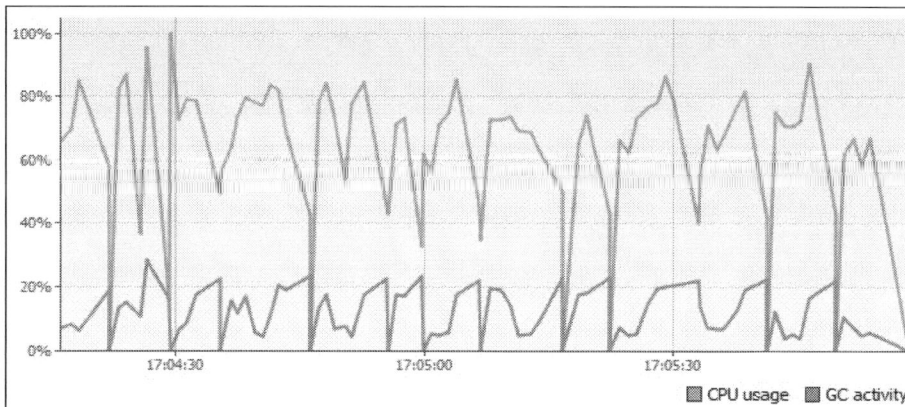

It also displays the number of loaded classes, the number of threads in use, and the allocated memory. This last indicator has two graphs because of the different JavaVM memory spaces:

- **Heap**: This is responsible for allocating class instances created within your application.

- **PermGen**: This memory area is reserved for all the classes that have been loaded by your application. In addition, it contains optimization information.

> Bear in mind that this memory distribution is no longer valid for Java 8. Search for *metaspace* if you want to find out more about it.

This chart with condensed memory information makes it easier to find leaks. You will easily identify them since they usually have a tooth-like appearance, shown in the following screenshot:

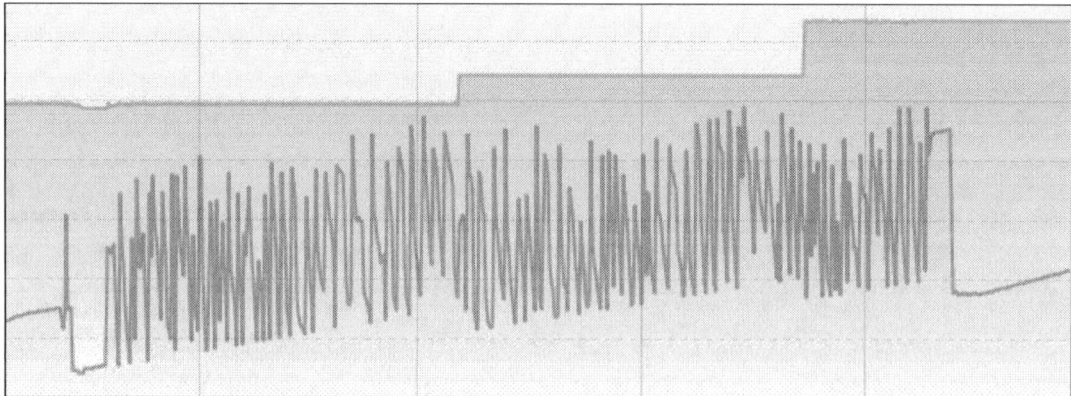

- **Threads**: A timeline with the threads life cycle is shown, tinting each of them with a color according to its state (green, purple, yellow, and orange for running, sleeping, wait, and monitor states, respectively), as shown in the following screenshot:

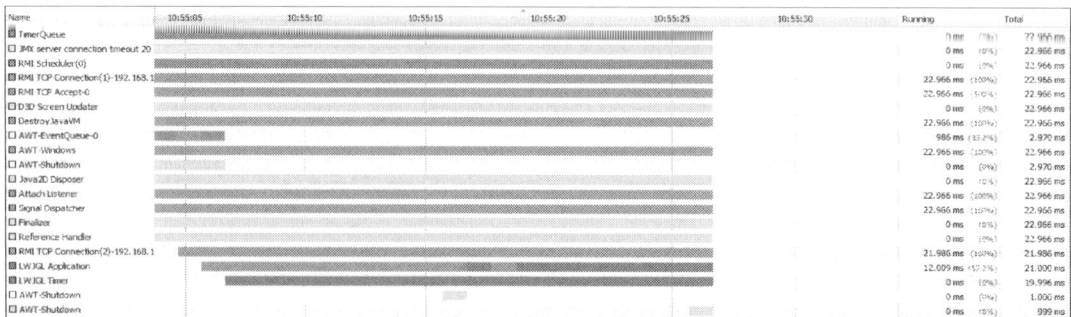

More information about the states can be found in the official Java documentation at `http://docs.oracle.com/javase/7/docs/api/java/lang/Thread.State.html`.

If you play around with the VisualVM interface, you will realize that it lists the number of normal and daemon threads. The main difference between them is that the last ones are abandoned when JVM terminates, which means that they are good candidates for doing housekeeping tasks.

➤ **Sampler/Profiler**: This option allows you to obtain more specific information related to either the CPU or the memory. Sampling means analyzing stack traces, while profiling is instrumenting your code so classes and methods broadcast whenever they are executed. Intuitively, the first one is faster but less accurate than the second one.

The Startup Profiler plugin must be installed by navigating to **Tools** |**Plugins**| **Available Plugins** | **Startup Profiler** | **Install**. After this, you must restart for the **Profiler** tab to become available. Moreover, you will have to calibrate the profiler before using it for the first time.

Next, we'll cover a more specific description about the two different sample types:

❑ **CPU samples**: This shows the detailed performance data on method or thread level. CPU samples are shown in the following screenshot:

CPU samples	Thread CPU Time					
Snapshot						Thread Dump
Hot Spots - Method	Self Time [%] ▼	Self Time	Self Time (CPU)	Total Time	Total Time (CPU)	
org.lwjgl.opengl.Sync.**sync** ()		703.076 ms (62.9%)	99,3 ms	704.962 ms	1.985 ms	
org.netbeans.lib.profiler.server.Monitors$SurvGenAndThreadsMonitor.**run** ()		193.008 ms (17.3%)	0,000 ms	196.406 ms	3.397 ms	
org.netbeans.lib.profiler.wireprotocol.WireIO.**receiveCommandOrResponse** ()		171.091 ms (15.3%)	171.091 ms	171.091 ms	171.091 ms	
org.lwjgl.opengl.WindowsContextImplementation.**nSwapBuffers[native]** ()		44.179 ms (4%)	44.179 ms	44.179 ms	44.179 ms	
org.lwjgl.WindowsSysImplementation.**nGetTime[native]** ()		1.886 ms (0.2%)	1.886 ms	1.886 ms	1.886 ms	
org.netbeans.lib.profiler.server.system.Threads.**getAllThreads[native]** ()		1.297 ms (0.1%)	1.297 ms	1.297 ms	1.297 ms	
org.netbeans.lib.profiler.server.system.Threads.**getThreadsStatus[native]** ()		1.202 ms (0.1%)	1.202 ms	1.202 ms	1.202 ms	
org.netbeans.lib.profiler.server.system.GC.**getCurrentGCEpoch[native]** ()		299 ms (0%)	299 ms	299 ms	299 ms	
org.netbeans.lib.profiler.server.system.GC.**getGCStartFinishTimes[native]** ()		299 ms (0%)	299 ms	299 ms	299 ms	
org.netbeans.lib.profiler.server.ThreadInfo.**releaseDeadThreads** ()		299 ms (0%)	299 ms	299 ms	299 ms	
org.lwjgl.opengl.GL11.**nglDrawElements[native]** ()		100 ms (0%)	100 ms	100 ms	100 ms	

It can be quite interesting to detect bottlenecks. A clear example is shown in the following screenshot where a method call takes most of the execution time:

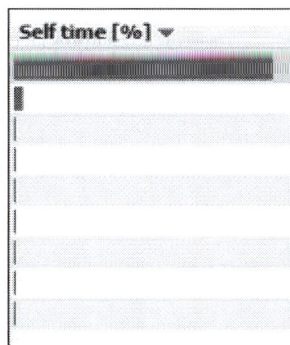

- ❑ **Memory samples**: All the classes that have allocated objects are listed together with their amount of bytes taken and the number of instances, as shown in the following screenshot:

Sometimes, you might want your application to freeze in an exact moment of execution so that the specific context can be calmly analyzed. To this effect, you can take a snapshot of your application, heap dumps, and thread dumps, which can be saved and loaded at any time.

Heap dumps are particularly interesting because if you double-click on a class, the interface will show you a rich source of valuable information about all the instances of the classes, as shown in the following screenshot:

How it works...

Profiling is achieved through an underlying process consisting in adding byte-codes to methods in order to gather data without modifying the behavior of your application. Some of this information is the space (memory), the time, the usage of particular instructions, the frequency, and duration of function calls.

More information is given within the official Java Instrumentation interface at the following link:

```
http://docs.oracle.com/javase/7/docs/api/java/lang/instrument/
Instrumentation.html
```

There's more...

VisualVM is not only useful for local applications but you can monitor and profile remote ones.

The process is quite similar except for the connection steps. Perform the following steps:

1. Go to **File | Add Remote Host**.
2. Enter the IP address or name of your remote host.
3. Give it a name and click on **OK**.

All Java applications running on the given system will appear within the **Remote** section of the **Applications** menu.

Using Libgdx features to avoid garbage collection

On one hand, unmanaged languages leave the responsibility of allocating and deallocating memory to the programmer, which allows them to choose the most convenient moment to make use of the required system resources and thus avoiding stuttering.

On the other hand, Java has a double-edged feature that handles the process of deallocating memory automatically whenever an object is no longer in use. This is commonly known as garbage collection. Every now and then, the GC kicks in and checks whether there are unreferenced objects to free up, but this takes time (and can occur in a nonsuitable moment within the game execution).

Sometimes Java programmers rely on its effectiveness and tend to forget about memory stuff when developing for desktop. However, it will not take a lot to realize about the need to manually deal with it when publishing for mobile platforms as their games experience slowdowns from time to time.

Once more, it is important to highlight the critical nature of videogames as a particular type of simulation that directly interacts with the user. This means that one of our highest priorities must be to give the best and smoothest user experience possible. Consequently, we need to have under control the CPU workload at every stage and therefore the garbage collector.

Getting ready

This recipe contains a set of tips along with small code snippets, so a separate code file will not be necessary.

How to do it...

Libgdx is aware of the potential garbage collector malice; hence, it includes some features to minimize its impact. In the next lines, you will also find some general tips that apply to any Java game.

Before diving into particular considerations, the golden rule to avoid garbage collection is *not to allocate temporary memory*, putting special emphasis within the game loop considering that mistakes are maximized under this context. Instead, cache the information as member variables so as the garbage collector will perform its laborious work very rarely.

Collections

In addition to putting a great deal of effort into having multiplatform support with high performance, Libgdx collections concern about creating garbage. Proof of this is that they are more memory efficient than `java.utils.collections`.

Apart from that, the `Array` class always returns the same instance when calling its `iterator()` method, which implies that it must not be used in nested loops. This pursues the goal of keeping GC from running frequently.

> The `ArrayIterator` constructor allows you to instance new iterators for the `Array` class.

Caching

Following the maxim of not creating new objects, paying special attention to critical sections such as loops, it is interesting to consider using one of the most powerful optimization techniques: **caching**. A clear example is a typical `for` loop over an `ArrayList` just like the following code:

```
ArrayList<Foo> array;
...
for(int i = 0; i < array.size(); i++)
```

```
{
...
}
```

With the sufficient array length, it is possible to measure that accessing a class field is more expensive than using a local variable. One of the reasons is the `size()` method, which creates a short-lived `int` on every loop iteration. In fact, every read-only method (returns an object that must not be modified, consequently makes use of the `new` keyword) in Java will create a new object. In addition, function calls might have an extra cost too. Do not panic, the previous code can be easily optimized for the scenarios where the length stays immutable within the loop by caching the array length value:

```
ArrayList<Foo> array;
...
final int length = array.size();

for(int i = 0; i < length; i++)
{
...
}
```

Object pooling

To minimize the garbage collector workload, we can reuse objects whose mission has finished. In order to understand the real potential of this subject, think of a shooter game where bullets appear and disappear from the screen continuously. Creating new instances every frame can be disastrous for the garbage collector overhead and that is why object pooling will just reuse the unused instances by resetting and reactivating them.

Fortunately, Libgdx comes with an out-of-the-box pooling mechanism that applies to any class defined by the programmer, for instance, Bullet. Perform the following steps:

1. The first step is to make it implement the `Poolable` interface. This will request for the `reset()` method to be overridden, so it gets called whenever the object is freed in order to leave it ready to be reused. It means that this is the place where fields must be set to default values and object references to null:

```
public class Bullet implements Poolable {
    private Vector2 position;
    private boolean visible;
...
    public void reset() {
position.set(0,0);
visible = false;
}
}
```

2. Now, we need to create a `Pool` instance to store the references to our `Bullet` objects. As you can see in the next code snippet, it is necessary to specify the way to construct a new object, so we will just make use of its constructor:

```
private final Pool<Bullet> bulletPool = new Pool<Bullet>() {
protected Bullet newObject() {
return new Bullet();
}
};
```

The way to interact with the `Pool` class comes defined by five methods:

▶   `obtain()`: This returns a new or freed object

▶   `free(T object)`: This puts the object back in the pool if not full (containing the same number of instances than the value set to its max public field)

▶   `freeAll(Array<T> objects)`: This puts all the instances contained in objects back in the pull if not full, ignoring the null ones

▶   `clear()`: This gets rid of all objects within the pool

▶   `getFree()`: This returns the number of available instances within the pool

It is good to know the basis of object pooling but there is a shortcut class called `Pools`, that you might want to explore in order to dynamically create a specific pool instance so the process is summarized in a single line of code making use of reflection:

```
Pool<Bullet> bulletPool = Pools.get(Bullet.class);
```

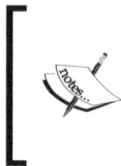

> Java has its own Reflection API which is able to examine and make modifications to the code itself at runtime by using introspection. For more information refer to `http://docs.oracle.com/javase/7/docs/api/java/lang/reflect/package-summary.html`.

Note that the garbage collector problem is mainly an Android (Dalvik Virtual Machine) issue. For other platforms, it might actually be counter-productive, as pooling increases the number of references, which makes garbage collecting more expensive on other platforms than it would be when creating a new object each time. However, if your memory needs are great, pooling would save you from having a lot of garbage collection which can be worth the hassle on all platforms. In conclusion, the best way always is to profile so you can draw true conclusions.

There's more...

You are perfectly capable of minimizing garbage collector usage by following the previous bunch of tips.

The other way to reduce the generated garbage is by using `StringBuffer` instead of the ı concatenation operator. So instead of doing it this way:

```
"Libgdx Cross Platform" + "Game Development" + "Cookbook"
```

You can do it as follows and save some valuable resources:

```
StringBuffer sb = new StringBuffer();
Sb.append("Libgdx Cross Platform").append("Game Development").
append("Cookbook");
```

However, if you want to dive a little bit more into the topic, do not hesitate to take a look at the *Google I/O 2009* conference about *Writing Real-Time Games for Android* by Chris Pruett at the following link:

```
https://www.youtube.com/watch?v=U4Bk5rmIpic
```

Avoiding unnecessary render calls with frustum culling

Rendering is the most essential operation within a video game. However, it is not a cheap process, as it requires sending data from memory to the GPU as well as a sequence of steps within your GPU to transform the input data into the final 2D image.

This input data consists of vertices that are no more than points with extra attached information, such as texture coordinates. They will serve as a base for constructing basic shapes.

The following is a summarized and simplified screenshot about this process:

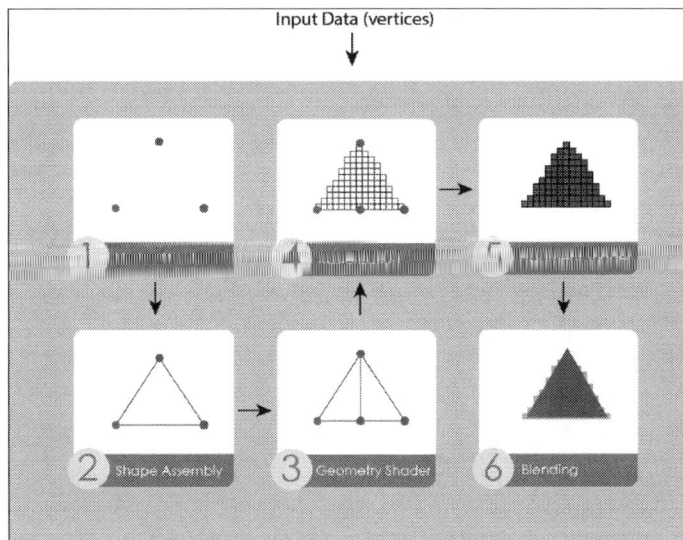

Here is a brief but concise explanation:

- **Vertex shader**: The main goal of this option is processing the aforementioned vertices. Additionally, it works as a walkway for later steps to receive important attributes such as color and texture coordinates.

- **Shape assembly**: This option joins those vertices in order to form primitive shapes.

- **Geometry shader**: This option evaluates the primitives passed from the previous step, and modifies them if necessary.

- **Rasterization**: This option is in charge of translating the visible parts of the former shapes into pixel-sized fragments that still contain interpolated values of the attached attributes.

- **Fragment shader**: This option allows each fragment to receive a color that can be determined by textures, lights, shadows, special effects, or simply a plain color.

- **Tests and blending**: This option produces the final output by blending all fragments and accepting/discarding some of them.

Some game scenes can be crowded with game entities that swallow the precious system resources. Rendering time is an important portion of this cake and reducing it to the minimum is the goal of this recipe.

As usual, we will focus on 2D graphics but it is easily adaptable to 3D.

Getting ready

The code for this recipe lives in the `FrustumCullingSample.java` file within the `samples-core` project that comes together with this book.

Right after running this sample, 20 game entities will be instantiated on the screen in front of a black background that can be freely explored by the user's taps/clicks. As the camera moves and loses the track of an entity, a text label, placed on the top of the window, will display the updated number of entities that are being rendered.

> It might be a good idea to read the *How it works...* section prior to the *How to do it section...* to lay the foundations of this recipe

How to do it...

In order to determine whether an entity is within the camera range and thus render it, it is necessary to know its position, dimensions, and scale. Additionally, the `Entity` class will contain `TextureRegion` to draw as well as a rotation:

```
public class Entity {
public Vector2 position;
public Vector2 dimensions;
public Vector2 scale;
public float rotation;
public TextureRegion region;
    . . .
```

The `Entity` constructor will initialize those fields, whereas two separate functions will be in charge of checking whether the entity must be visible or not and render it. As this functionality might vary from one entity type to another, there will be abstract methods pending to be implemented by the extender class:

```
public Entity(TextureRegion region, float x, float y, float width,
float height, float rotation, Vector2 scale) {
    this.dimensions = new Vector2(width, height);
    this.position = new Vector2(x + (width*.5f), y + (height*.5f));
    this.region = region;
    this.rotation = rotation;
    this.scale = new Vector2(scale);
}
```

We will store the central position as the entity's position. It is calculated from the original bottom-left position plus half of each dimension.

The nub of the issue comes with a method to determine whether the entity is visible or not. This is where Libgdx helps us with a single rescuer function. However, a camera must be passed in order to know the exact space that is under its range. We will adapt the 2D entity's position to 3D through two cached `com.badlogic.gdx.math.Vector3` called `point1` and `point2`:

```
public boolean isVisible(Camera cam) {
return cam.frustum.boundsInFrustum(point1.set(position, 0), point2.
set(dimensions,0));
}
```

The bounds of the entity are calculated thanks to the `position` and `dimensions` fields that we stored previously. Nevertheless, we might have some other entities allowed to rotate. This feature would ruin our former strategy because the calculated bounds would not fit the rotated object. Manually rotating coordinates is a laborious option. A simple and effective approach would be thinking of it as a sphere because it covers all the possible rotations, just as shown in the following screenshot:

Consequently, the `Caveman` class must store an extra variable called `diagonal`. The next screenshot shows what it consists of and how to calculate it:

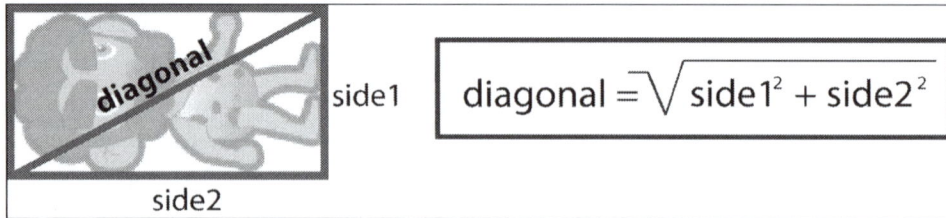

$$diagonal = \sqrt{side1^2 + side2^2}$$

In code terms, this would be translated to the following:

```
this.diagonal = (float) Math.sqrt(Math.pow(width*scale.x, 2f) + Math.
pow(height*scale.y, 2f));
```

The `isVisible()` method will change slightly. In this case, we must apply the half diagonal of the entity rectangle as the sphere radius:

```
public boolean isVisible(Camera cam) {
return cam.frustum.sphereInFrustum(point1.set(position, 0), diagonal *
5f);
}
```

Finally, the `render()` function will just draw the `TextureRegion` on the screen according to the other stored attributes:

```
public void render(final SpriteBatch batch) {
batch.draw(
region,
position.x-dimensions.x*.5f, position.y-dimensions.y*.5f,
position.x, position.y,
dimensions.x, dimensions.y,
scale.x, scale.y,
rotation);
    }
```

Once the `Entity` class is implemented, we will create a good amount of instances by calling its constructor repeatedly. We will store all instances within `Array<Entity>` called `entities` in order to have them all localized, just as follows:

```
Vector2 scale = new Vector2(1f,1f);
entities.add(new Entity(cavemanTextureRegion, point2.set(x, y), 0.4f,
0.75f, 0f, scale));
```

With the same goal as `point3`, `point2` is a cached `Vector2`.

When rendering your scene, your code will be really simple:

```
for(Entity entity : entities) {
if(entity.isVisible(camera)) {
entity.render(batch);
renderCount++;
    }
}
```

The `renderCount` variable will store the updated number of entities that are within the camera's frustum.

How it works...

The way that Libgdx determines whether an entity is within the camera's viewport might seem magic but you should already have a vague idea after reading *Chapter 2, Working with 2D Graphics*. The answer is included in the title of this recipe: **frustum**.

A frustum is the pyramid of vision of a camera and, as its shape determines, it is formed of six planes. Once more, our brave caveman friend will try to make things clear, as shown in the following screenshot:

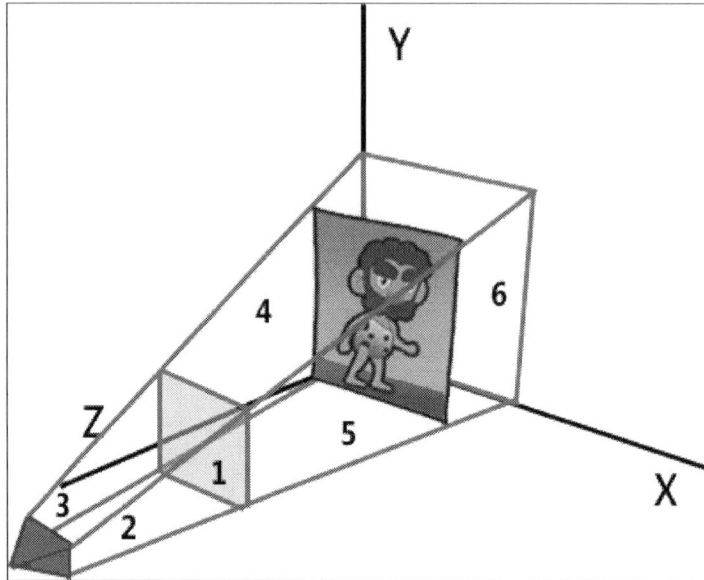

The top (**4**), left (**3**), bottom (**2**), and right (**5**) planes define the bounds of the pyramid whereas near (**1**) and far (**6**) planes cut the frustum perpendicular to the viewing direction so the shape becomes closed.

In this way, Libgdx's functions just check whether the received sphere/bounds are within the frustum.

There's more...

Some games organize their entities in a hierarchical way, so the visibility testing is performed recursively. This can save you a lot of time but requires more dedication to construct the scene tree.

In addition to frustum culling, you can save some milliseconds not rendering entities that are occluded by others. This is known as **occlusion culling** and it is very common in 3D games.

To avoid rendering some entities of your game can save precious time but what if you could get rid of unnecessary frames? Of course, it does not apply to all kind of games. However, card, sudokus, or riddle games can probably benefit from this optimization.

Libgdx comes with the feature of disabling continuous rendering. All you have to do is write this line of code within the `create()` method of your `ApplicationListener`:

```
Gdx.graphics.setContinousRendering(false);
```

From now, in advance, you will have to request for rendering manually through the following method:

```
Gdx.graphics.requestRendering();
```

> iOS is currently not compatible with the noncontinuous rendering feature, so it will keep rendering in spite of receiving those code instructions.

Apart from the previous case, `render()` will also go into scene if an input event is triggered or `Gdx.app.postRunnable()` is called.

13
Giving Back

In this chapter, we will cover:

- ▶ Releasing your Libgdx game on desktop
- ▶ Releasing your Libgdx game on Android
- ▶ Releasing your Libgdx game on iOS
- ▶ Releasing your Libgdx game on browsers
- ▶ Working from sources
- ▶ Creating a new test for your fresh feature
- ▶ Sending a pull request on GitHub

Introduction

I have not the slightest doubt that toil describes the process to get here. However, the remaining work is a bed of roses compared to what you have already done.

Within this chapter, you will learn how to transform your, up until now useless, Eclipse projects to each possible platform and how to contribute back to the community, especially the Libgdx one.

Even though this is the last chapter, this is not a goodbye as we expect to see you in the market.

Releasing your Libgdx game on desktop

Fantastic! You have just finished your awesome Libgdx game and want to release it to Windows, GNU/Linux, and Mac users.

You could pack your project into a JAR file and distribute it, although it is far from optimal. First of all, your users will need to have a JRE; otherwise, they will not be able to run the game. Moreover, if their JRE is not compatible with the game's JAR archive, it may crash or cause all sorts of problems. Finally, you might not want your users to know that you are using Java.

The best way to go about distributing Libgdx games on desktop platforms is by packing your game with a JRE of your choice into a platform-specific binary. That way you will make sure it works without any surprises.

In this recipe, you will learn how to make a platform-specific binary of your Libgdx game.

Getting ready

We will be using **Packr**, an open source tool that does exactly what we need. Packr was created by Mario Zechner (author of Libgdx) and is maintained by the community. Go to its GitHub repository at `https://github.com/libgdx/packr` and follow the **Download Packr** link.

How to do it...

To pack your game with a JRE into a platform-specific binary package, follow these steps:

1. Generate a JAR package for your desktop project. From Eclipse, you can right-click on the project and select **Export | Java | Runnable JAR file**. Click on **Next** and make sure you select the **Package required libraries into generated JAR file** option. Finally, select a destination and click on **Finish**. Alternatively, you can run the `:jar` task with Gradle.

2. Download the OpenJDK ZIP file that matches your desired Java version and platform from `https://github.com/alexkasko/openjdk-unofficial-builds`. Please note that you can choose between 64- and 32-bit builds.

> Packr lets you generate Windows, GNU/Linux, and Mac packages independently of your operating system.

3. Run Packr from the command line:

```
java -jar packr.jar \
    -platform windows \
    -jdk "openjdk-1.7.0-u60-unofficial-windows-i586-
      image.zip" \
    -executable mygame \
    -appjar mygame.jar \
    -mainclass "com/my/game/MainClass" \
```

```
        -vmargs "-Xmx1G" \
        -minimizejre "soft" \
        -outdir out
```

Here is a description of all the parameters:

- ▶ `-platform`: This is either `windows`, `linux32`, `linux64`, or `mac`.
- ▶ `-jdk`: This is the path to the zipped build of a compatible OpenJDK.
- ▶ `-executable`: This is the name of your executable file.
- ▶ `-appjar`: This is the path to your game's JAR package.
- ▶ `-mainClass`: This is the fully qualified path of the main class of your desktop project using forward slashes to separate package names.
- ▶ `-vmargs`: This is the list of arguments for the Java virtual machine separated by `;`. For example, `-Xmx1G` gives a 1 GB RAM allowance for your game to run.
- ▶ `-outdir`: This is the directory name where the generated files will be placed.
- ▶ `-resources`: These are the additional resources, separated by `;`, you want packed besides your JAR file.
- ▶ `-minimizejre`: This removes the unnecessary files from the JRE, you can either select `"soft"` or `"hard"`.

Done! Now your application is completely self-contained; you will not have to worry about the JRE your users have.

There's more...

Packr can be used programmatically to automatically package your projects. First of all, you will need to add the following dependency to your Gradle file:

```
compile "com.badlogicgames.packr:packr:1.2.0"
```

Create a `Config` object, set the appropriate parameters, and instantiate Packr. Finally, call the `pack()` method with the previously created `config` object:

```
Config config = new Config();
config.platform = Platform.windows;
config.jdk = "d:/user/Build/Development/OpenJDK-1.7.0-u60-
   unofficial-windows-i586-image.zip";
config.executable = "mygame";
config.jar = "mygame.jar";
config.mainClass = "com/my/game/MainClass";
config.vmArgs = Arrays.asList("-Xmx1G");
config.minimizeJre = new String[] {};
config.outDir = "out";

new Packr().pack(config)
```

See also

▶ **Launch4J**: This only generates Windows binaries, available from
`http://launch4j.sourceforge.net`

▶ **GCC for Java**: This compiles Java code into Linux binaries and is avalaible from
`http://gcc.gnu.org/java`

Releasing your Libgdx game on Android

It has been a long way till here. You are now about to generate an **Android Application PacKage** (**apk**) file for your own game. Fortunately, the hardest part is done and creating it is quite easy.

You will also discover some features to explore that Google provides to enrich your game experience as much to players as to developers.

Getting ready

All you need to go further on this recipe is a Libgdx Android project, for instance, `samples-android` along with the core one, such as `samples-core`. Make sure you have the **Android Development Tools** (**ADT**) plugin installed in your Eclipse IDE. It is available at `http://developer.android.com/sdk/installing/installing-adt.html`.

How to do it...

Once the environment is properly set up, the process is quite simple:

1. Right-click on your Android project. Then, click on **Export**. Go to **Android | Export Android Application**. Then, click on **Next**.

2. In the current window, just check that the selected project is compatible with Android. Click on **Next**.

3. This step depends on whether you already have a **keystore** or you need to create one. It is necessary to sign applications so they can be uploaded to the Google Play store. It is a binary file in charge of storing a oot of private keys

   Enter a system path to store it along with a filename and a password. Click on **Next**.

   In order to create a private **key** for our keystore, enter an alias (it will just be useful to identify that key), password, validity (in years), and some personal data (first and last name or organization is enough). Click on **Next**.

4. Finally, select a destination location for your final `.apk` file and click on **Finish**.

Your file is now ready to be uploaded to Google Play. All you have to do is link your Google account to your developer console. You can get access to such a console from `https://play.google.com/apps/publish/`.

It has cost of $25 that you just have to pay once.

Once inside, you will have a control panel to manage your app's life cycle: uploading, updating, maintaining, and removing.

Note that you can also distribute your application out of the market by enabling **Unknown sources** (**Settings | Security**) installations in the device.

> It is important to point out that Libgdx 1.0.0 and above can officially export to Android 2.2 or higher because it removes the support for OpenGL ES 1.x while preliminarily adding it for OpenGL ES, 3.0 although it is not stable yet. If you are interested in deploying for earlier Android versions, please use Libgdx 0.9.9. Be aware that incompatible features with the final device will just do nothing.

There's more...

Google Play Developer Console also provides you with a **Game services** option. You can find it within the touchpad tab:

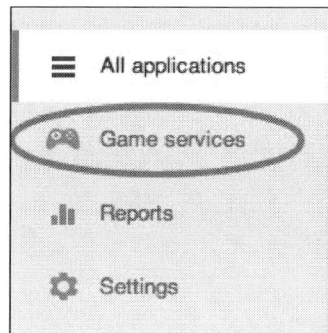

After accepting different Google Terms of Service, you will be allowed to add new games to your space. In this way, you will enable support for leaderboards, saved games, quests, rewards, and multiplayer. You can learn more about that at `https://developers.google.com/games/services/`.

The first step to integrate the service with your code is by installing Google Play Games Services within your Android SDK. Then, import as a library a copy of the project placed at `<android-sdk>/extras/google/google_play_services/libgproject/google-play-services-lib/`. Then, make your project depend on it and add the following lines to your manifest:

```
<meta-data android:name="com.google.android.gms.version"
  android:value="@integer/google_play_services_version" />
```

Finally, import the `BaseGameUtils` project that you can find within the Google Play Game Services GitHub space at `https://github.com/playgameservices/android-basic-samples/tree/master/BasicSamples/libraries/BaseGameUtils`.

Releasing your Libgdx game on iOS

On one hand, Libgdx is widely prevalent in the Android market according to AppBrain, which claims that 1.53 percent of the apps (August 13, 2014) are made with this framework. If you have already taken a look at the *Releasing your Libgdx game on Android* recipe, you will quickly realize that it is quite easy to target that platform.

On the other hand, iOS has the most restrictive deployment process but it is still worth the hassle because of its huge market, which really offers you an opportunity to promote your game.

With this recipe, you will find the way to finally publish your Libgdx game on the Apple App store.

Getting ready

The first wall that you will hit within this recipe is the need of having an OS X machine with Xcode installed on it. The next requirement is an active iOS developer subscription, and you can read more about it at `https://developer.apple.com/programs/ios/`.

You must also have a distribution certificate from Apple in order to sign your applications and upload them to the store.

Finally, the RoboVM Eclipse plugin needs to be installed. Typing `RoboVM` within the Eclipse marketplace (**Help | Eclipse Marketplace**) search bar is the easiest way of carrying it out.

How to do it...

The deployment process takes place in two different IDEs: Xcode and Eclipse. The first one is required to sign the application, whereas the second one is for the deployment itself. The next steps describe both stages:

1. Launch Xcode, click on its menu with the same name, and go to **Preferences**. Then, enter **Accounts** and log in.

2. Click on the **View Details** button in the bottom-right corner of the window and do likewise with the **Recycle** button. After that, all the certificates are accessible for the RoboVM Eclipse plugin.

3. Switch to Eclipse, and right-click on your iOS project, for instance, `samples-ios`, then go to **RoboVM tools | Package for App-Store/Adhoc Distribution**.

4. Select a destination folder for the compressed **iOS App Storage Package (ipa)** file that you are about to generate.

5. Choose the identity that you want to sign with and the Apple provisioning profile.

6. Finally, you have the `.ipa` file that contains your game. Now, you just have to upload it to the Apple Store. Check out `https://developer.apple.com/library/ios/documentation/LanguagesUtilities/Conceptual/iTunesConnect_Guide/Chapters/SubmittingTheApp.html` if you need some help with how to do it.

There's more...

Before submitting your game to the Apple Store, it is usually a good idea to test it with some reliable players that can help you to significantly raise the game's quality. Some good options to distribute it are `www.testflightapp.com` or `www.hockeykit.net`.

Releasing your Libgdx game on browsers

There still is a good pool of casual gamers on the web. Traditional ways of deploying games for this platform required an extra plugin to be installed, but now, thanks to GWT and Libgdx, you can export your games directly to Javascript/HTML code.

GWT supports any of these browsers: Firefox, Internet Explorer (versions 8, 9, 10, and 11), Safari (versions 5 and 6), Chromium, Chrome, and Opera (latest version).

Getting ready

In order to go further in this recipe, it is necessary to install the Google plugin on your Eclipse. All you have to do is go to **Help | Eclipse Marketplace**. Then, search for `Google Plugin` and install the proper one according to your Eclipse version.

Finally, restart Eclipse and you will be ready to deploy to the browsers.

As can be expected, the `samples-gwt` project can be used to try the deployment process.

How to do it...

As happens with the other deployment processes, you will not have to invest a lot of effort. Basically, the project is exported into a directory that must be copied into your server, just as described here:

1. Right-click on your GWT project by navigating to **Google | GWT Compile**. The following window will appear:

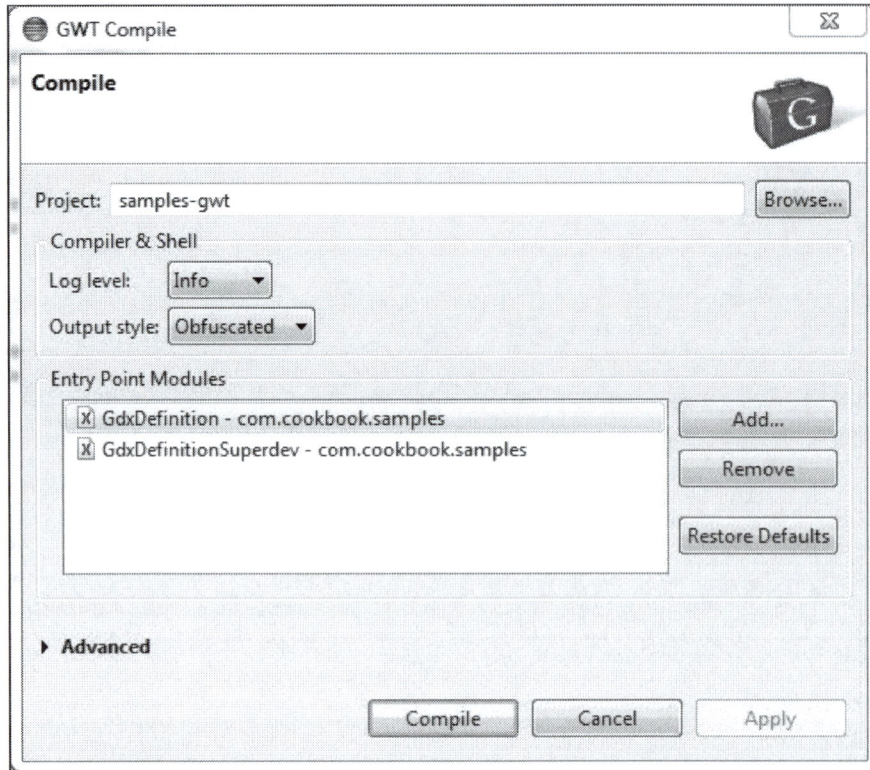

GdxDefinition is intended for debug purposes, whereas **GdxDefinitionSuperDev** is the way to go when releasing your game. Select one of them and click on **Compile**.

2. Select a directory to store your web application files. Then, the cross-compilation process to Javascript will start. It can take a little bit of time to complete due to the permutations needed to reach different browsers and localizations.

3. Once it has successfully finished, copy the generated folder (for instance, `samples-gwt`) into the `webapps` directory of your web server. After that, you will be able to access your application at `http://yourserverurl/samples-gwt/`.

There's more...

The test page does not exactly stand out for its decoration but that has an easy solution. You can modify the `index.html` file that you have just generated and apply it some **CSS** styles.

Working from sources

Libgdx is truly awesome and it will probably suit your needs perfectly. However, some people might need extra behavior or a slightly different API.

The first thing you should try is to add the desired functionality on top of an official stable Libgdx release. Were that to prove impossible, you would have to modify Libgdx itself to make it behave the way you want.

Throughout this recipe, you will learn how to grab Libgdx's repository, make changes to it, and use it for your game.

Getting ready

You will need a Git client to clone the Libgdx repository. We discussed that topic in the *Using source control on a Libgdx project with Git* recipe of *Chapter 1, Diving into Libgdx*.

Libgdx uses **Apache Ant**, which is an open source Java-based build system, very much like Gradle. You can grab the latest binary distribution from `http://ant.apache.org/bindownload.cgi`.

Download the latest one, unzip it in the folder of your choice, and add the `bin` subfolder to your `PATH` environment variable.

The Libgdx project itself still uses Eclipse projects; it is recommended you have that IDE installed on your machine. Refer to the *Setting up a cross-platform development environment* recipe in *Chapter 1, Diving into Libgdx*, for more details.

How to do it...

Everything should be ready now. Follow these steps in order to work from Libgdx sources.

1. Clone the Libgdx repository using `git@github.com:libgdx/libgdx.git`. You can either use SourceTree, the Git client of your choice, or plain old Git.
2. Open a command-line window in the Libgdx folder.

3. Libgdx depends on a few binaries that are not in the GitHub repository for space reasons. However, you can easily retrieve those dependencies with Apache Ant as follows:

```
ant -f fetch.xml
```

4. Now you can build Libgdx using Ant:

```
ant
```

5. Once the process has finished, proceed to import the projects in an Eclipse workspace. Right-click on the **Package Explorer** window, select **Import | General | Existing Projects into Workspace**. Hit **Next** and click on **Browse** to find the clone directory. Check all the projects and select **Finish**.

6. Now you are free to make any changes you want to the code.

7. In order to use your changes, you will have to make your projects depend on the Libgdx sources as described in the following list. Note that this cannot be used in combination with the Gradle setup as explained in *Chapter 1, Diving into Libgdx*.

   - The core project has to depend on `gdx`
   - The desktop project has to include `gdx-backend-lwjgl`
   - The Android project will have to use `gdx` and `gdx-backend-android`
   - The HTML project has to depend on `gdx-backend-gwt`
   - The iOS project will have to use `gdx-backend-robovm`

How it works...

By making your game depend on Libgdx sources, you can make changes to the core and see them reflected on the game right away. Additionally, you can still keep pulling changes from the main repository to stay up to date. Naturally, this has the downsides of requiring you to be extra careful and a bit more cumbersome.

See also

- The *Using source control on a Libgdx project with Git* recipe of *Chapter 1, Diving into Libgdx*

Creating a new test for your fresh feature

Plenty of ideas related to Libgdx would have been raised in your head as you read this book. Now is the time to let your creativity loose and contribute, but first, you must check that your fresh idea really works.

Libgdx comes with its own testing environment that gives you several facilities to get your feature running sooner.

Getting ready

In this recipe, we will suppose that you want to add a new feature to the official Libgdx project, so it needs to be imported into your Eclipse workspace. If you do not know how to do it, please take a look at the *Using source control on a Libgdx project with Git* recipe of *Chapter 1, Diving into Libgdx*.

How to do it...

All the tests are gathered from the directory at `https://github.com/libgdx/libgdx/tree/master/tests/gdx-tests/src/com/badlogic/gdx/tests`.

If you play around with some of them, it will not take too much to realize that the common factor is to extend `GdxTest`, which is placed within the `utils` folder. Basically, it is an abstract class that implements `ApplicationListener` and extends `InputAdapter`, so you can create and manipulate graphics as well as listen for events.

The `GdxTest` class includes the `create`, `resume`, `render`, `resize`, `pause`, and `dispose` methods for you to implement in your custom tests.

Creating tests is very important for you to understand how Libgdx works and for the community to rely on your fresh new feature. So, please try to cover a wide range of potential use cases.

Sending a pull request on GitHub

Now that you have mastered the Libgdx framework, a great opportunity to give back to the community has opened. Improving, adding, or fixing code are good challenges to test your knowledge. However, the Libgdx core team must approve your contributions first.

This process is performed through the official Libgdx GitHub repository.

Getting ready

Everything starts by clicking on the **Fork** button within the Libgdx forge while being logged in with your GitHub user account:

libgdx / libgdx		👁 Watch ▾	743	★ Star	4,335	⑂ Fork	3,154

After that, import it into your Eclipse workspace through any of the offered methods according to the instructions provided in the *Using source control on a Libgdx project with Git* recipe of *Chapter 1, Diving into Libgdx*. You can get the repository URL from a box like this:

Then, open a ticket within the issue tracker of the GitHub repository, so the community can give their opinion about your potential contribution. If an agreement is reached about the need of accepting your request, move on to the real deal.

> Note that opening a ticket is a common practice in software development communities, but it is optional; you can take a shortcut and go directly to the next section.

How to do it...

Once you have the Libgdx project imported into Eclipse, you are ready to start tweaking the code. Before getting into any explanation, the next screenshot gives an overview of the whole process:

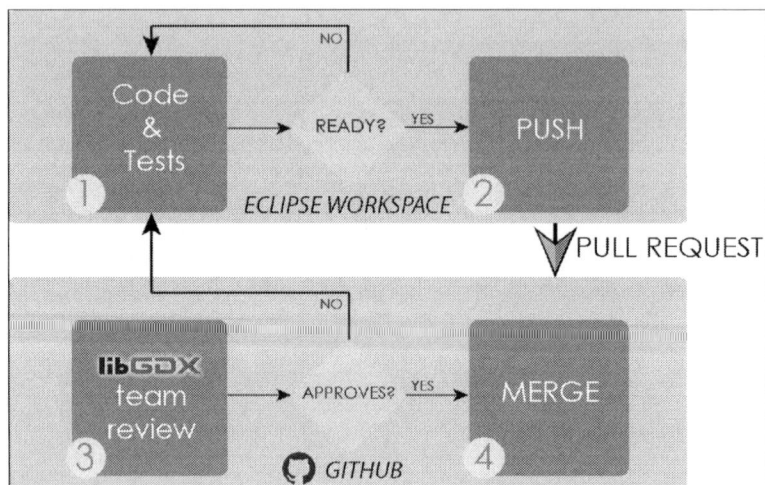

This is how we start:

1. The first step is to add, modify, or remove code. Bear in mind that attaching new tests or modifying existing ones is a recommended practice to demonstrate the strength of your contribution.

2. Whenever you feel happy with your work and all tests have passed, commit and push it to the master branch. However, there is a set of common sense practices that help with the creation and maintenance of pull requests within the community. The first thing is to add the ticket number of the issue to its title so that it becomes more visible and places the reader in context. Then, a little more information is required, which can be organized in multiple ways. A template might consist of the description, dependencies (optional), screenshots (optional), and the test process. In the end, the result should be something like this:

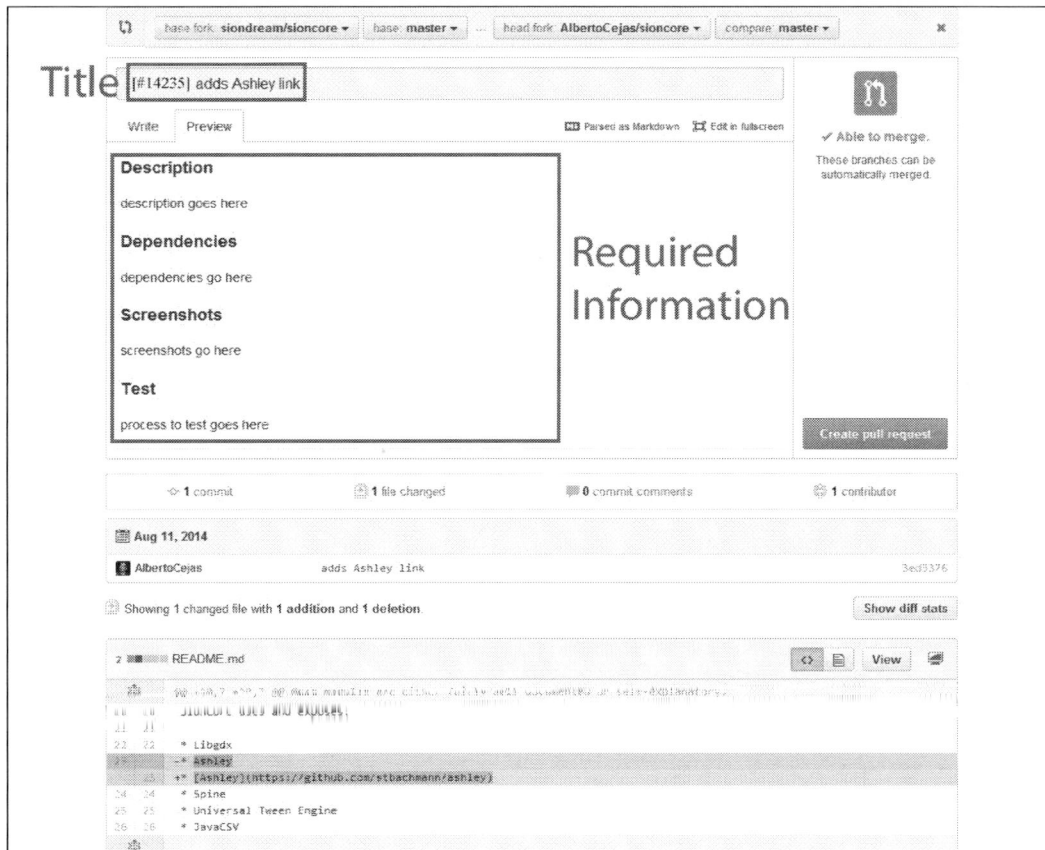

This structure will allow nonfamiliar developers to quickly understand the pull request and even test it.

Moreover, you can directly close an open issue ticket by writing `fixes #issuenumber` within the description.

Click on the **Create pull request** button when all the fields are properly filled up.

3. Up until here, it was your effort. Now, someone from the Ligbdx core team will evaluate your request and give you some feedback. If it is not positive, just make the convenient modifications and try again. Do not get disappointed if it is not accepted at the first try; the advice, tips, or demands given will make you a better programmer.

4. Finally, whenever your pull request is ready, the Libgdx team will merge it with the master branch.

There's more...

Libgdx is not the only project that you can lend a hand to. Ashley, Universal Tween Engine, Box2DLights, and others are auxiliary open source libraries that we have mentioned in this book, and they are willing to receive contributions.

See also

▸   The *Creating a new test for your fresh feature* recipe

Index

L

label widget 285
language files
  creating 426
Launch4J
  URL 476
level data
  physics world, building from 389
Libgdx
  distance field fonts, rendering in 243, 244
  JSON shape data, loading into 354
  map metadata, querying from 335-337
  URL 58, 232, 238, 241
  used, for rendering bitmap font files 234, 235
  used, for rendering particle effects 116-119
Libgdx collections 462
Libgdx extensions
  adding 38
  additional file dependencies, adding 42
  Artificial Intelligence (AI) 41
  Box2D 40
  bullet 38
  Controllers 40
  external repositories, adding 42
  FreeTypeFont 39
  GWT dependencies, managing 42
  Tools 41
Libgdx features
  used, for avoiding garbage
      collection 461-464
Libgdx filesystem
  directory listings, filtering 218
  files, copying 217
  files, deleting 217
  files, handling 214
  files, reading 216
  files, streaming 219
  files, writing 216
  information, retrieving from files 215
  temporary files, creating 218
  tree structures, traversing 216
Libgdx game
  releasing, on Android 476-478
  releasing, on browsers 479-481
  releasing, on desktop 474-476
  releasing, on iOS 478, 479

Libgdx loaders
  URL 341
Libgdx official demos
  Cuboc 56
  importing 56-58
  Invaders 56
  Metagun 56
  Pax Britannica 56
  running 56-58
  Super Jumper 56
  The Plane That Couldn't Fly Good 56
  Vector Pinball 56
  Very Angry Robots 57
Libgdx sources
  working from 481, 482
Libgdx sprites
  bounds, using for collision detection 80, 81
  using 77-79
  working 80
Libgdx window
  embedding, into Java desktop
      application 152-155
Line of Sight (LOS) 382
lines
  rendering 99
Listener class 206
list widget 291
load() method 180
local files 218
localization support
  adding 425, 426
  language files, creating 426
  languages, managing 427, 428
  usage example 429
logging
  using 24
LWJGL (Light Weight Java Game Library) 17

M

Mac users
  Android SDK, installing for 11
  Java Development Kit, installing for 9
MapBodyManager constructor
  working 391-396
Map class 331

Thank you for buying
Libgdx Cross-platform Game Development Cookbook

About Packt Publishing

Packt, pronounced 'packed', published its first book "*Mastering phpMyAdmin for Effective MySQL Management*" in April 2004 and subsequently continued to specialize in publishing highly focused books on specific technologies and solutions.

Our books and publications share the experiences of your fellow IT professionals in adapting and customizing today's systems, applications, and frameworks. Our solution based books give you the knowledge and power to customize the software and technologies you're using to get the job done. Packt books are more specific and less general than the IT books you have seen in the past. Our unique business model allows us to bring you more focused information, giving you more of what you need to know, and less of what you don't.

Packt is a modern, yet unique publishing company, which focuses on producing quality, cutting-edge books for communities of developers, administrators, and newbies alike. For more information, please visit our website: www.packtpub.com.

About Packt Open Source

In 2010, Packt launched two new brands, Packt Open Source and Packt Enterprise, in order to continue its focus on specialization. This book is part of the Packt Open Source brand, home to books published on software built around Open Source licenses, and offering information to anybody from advanced developers to budding web designers. The Open Source brand also runs Packt's Open Source Royalty Scheme, by which Packt gives a royalty to each Open Source project about whose software a book is sold.

Writing for Packt

We welcome all inquiries from people who are interested in authoring. Book proposals should be sent to author@packtpub.com. If your book idea is still at an early stage and you would like to discuss it first before writing a formal book proposal, contact us; one of our commissioning editors will get in touch with you.

We're not just looking for published authors; if you have strong technical skills but no writing experience, our experienced editors can help you develop a writing career, or simply get some additional reward for your expertise.

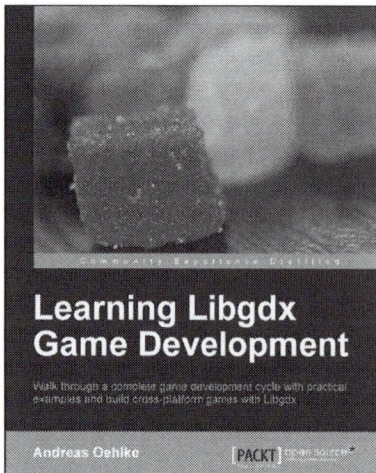

Learning Libgdx Game Development

ISBN: 978-1-78216-604-7   Paperback: 388 pages

Walk through a complete game development cycle with practical examples and build cross-platform games with Libgdx

1. Create a libGDX multi-platform game from start to finish.

2. Learn about the key features of libGDX that will ease and speed up your development cycles.

3. Write your game code once and run it on a multitude of platforms using libGDX.

4. An easy-to-follow guide that will help you develop games in libGDX successfully.

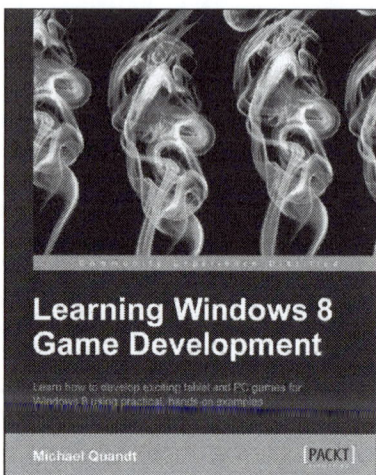

Learning Windows 8 Game Development

ISBN: 978-1-84969-744-6   Paperback: 244 pages

Learn how to develop exciting tablet and PC games for Windows 8 using practical, hands-on examples

1. Use cutting-edge technologies like DirectX to make awesome games.

2. Discover tools that will make game development easier.

3. Bring your game to the latest touch-enabled PCs and tablets.

Please check **www.PacktPub.com** for information on our titles

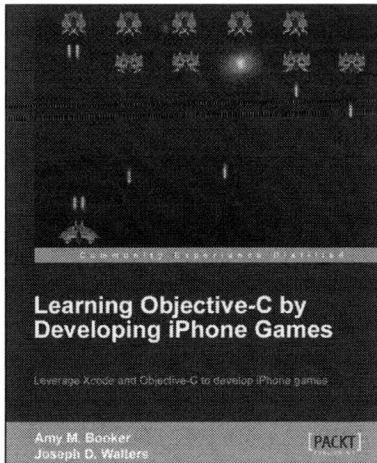

Learning Objective-C by Developing iPhone Games

ISBN: 978-1-84969 610 4   Paperback. 284 pages

Leverage Xcode and Objective-C to develop iPhone games

1. Get started with the Xcode development environment.

2. Dive deep into programming with Objective-C.

3. A practical and engaging tutorial to create vintage games such as Space Invaders and Galaga.

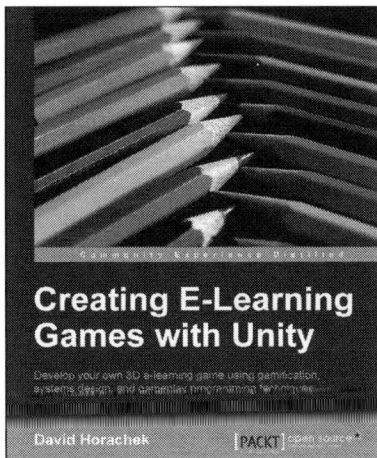

Creating E-Learning Games with Unity

ISBN: 978-1-84969-342-4   Paperback: 246 pages

Develop your own 3D e-learning game using gamification, systems design, and gameplay programming techniques

1. Develop a game framework for a 3D e-learning game.

2. Program dynamic interactive actors and objects to populate your game world.

3. An easy-to-follow guide along with an extensive source code to support and guide readers through the concepts in the book.

Please check **www.PacktPub.com** for information on our titles

Printed in Great Britain
by Amazon.co.uk, Ltd.,
Marston Gate.